Developing Cross-Cultural Competence

WITHDRAWN

DEVELOPING CROSS-CULTURAL COMPETENCE

A GUIDE FOR WORKING WITH YOUNG CHILDREN AND THEIR FAMILIES

edited by

Eleanor W. Lynch, Ph.D.
Department of Special Education
San Diego State University

and

Marci J. Hanson, Ph.D.
Department of Special Education
San Francisco State University

·P A U L·H·
BROOKES
PUBLISHING C⁰

Baltimore • London • Toronto • Sydney

Paul H. Brookes Publishing Co.
P.O. Box 10624
Baltimore, Maryland 21285-0624

Typeset by Brushwood Graphics, Inc., Baltimore, Maryland.
Manufactured in the United States of America by
The Maple Press Company, York, Pennsylvania.

Permission to reprint the following quotation is gratefully acknowledged: Pages 89–
90: Quotation from Henry Old Coyote and Allen Quetone, in Morey, S.M.L., &
Gilliam, O.L. (Eds.). (1974). *Respect for life: Traditional upbringing of American
Indian children,* pp. 181 and 193. Garden City, NY: Waldorf Press. Reprinted by
permission.

This book is printed on recycled paper. ♻

Library of Congress Cataloging-in-Publication Data
Developing cross-cultural competence : a guide for working with young children and
    their families / edited by Eleanor W. Lynch and Marci J. Hanson
        p.   cm.
    Includes bibliographical references and index.
    ISBN 1-55766-086-7
    1. Social work with handicapped children—United States—Cross-cultural studies.
    2. Family services—United States—Cross-cultural studies.   3. Minorities—
    United States.   I. Lynch, Eleanor W.   II. Hanson, Marci J.
HV888.5.D48   1992
362.7'08'693—dc20   91-45397
                                                                           CIP

CONTENTS

Contributors xiii
Preface xvii
Acknowledgments xxi

PART I   INTRODUCTION 1
Chapter 1   **Ethnic, Cultural, and Language Diversity
            in Intervention Settings**
                 Marci J. Hanson 3
            Cultural Considerations for the Interventionist 4
            Importance of Cross-Cultural Effectiveness 5
                 Changing Demographics 7
                 PL 99-457 8
            Nature of Intervention in the Early Years 9
                 Why Intervention Is Done—Attitudes
                      Regarding Intervention 9
                 What Methods Are Used and Where Services
                      Are Located 10
                 Who Does Early Intervention 13
                 How Services Are Provided—Styles of
                      Interaction and Communication 13
            Concept of Cultural Identity 14
                 Factors that Mitigate the Influence of Cultural
                      Identity 14
                 Continuum of Cultural Identification 15
            Summary 17
            References 17
Chapter 2   **From Culture Shock to Cultural Learning**
                 Eleanor W. Lynch 19
            Concept of Culture Shock 22
                 Defining Culture Shock 23
                 Navigating the Stages of Culture Shock 25
            Ameliorating Culture Shock for the Family 27
                 New Immigrants 28
                 Long-Term Residents 31
            Sensitizing the Interventionist to the Impact of
                 Culture Shock 31
            Summary 33
            References 33
Chapter 3   **Developing Cross-Cultural Competence**
                 Eleanor W. Lynch 35
            Self-Awareness 36

Culture-Specific Awareness and Understanding 39
  Gathering Culture-Specific Information 39
  Culture-Specific Issues and Intervention 41
  Cautions 44
Cross-Cultural Communication 44
  General Principles of Effective Cross-Cultural
    Communication 44
  Acknowledging and Respecting Cultural
    Differences Rather than Minimizing Them 50
  Communicating Attitudes Through Words 50
  General Characteristics of Effective
    Cross-Cultural Communicators 51
  Working with Interpreters and Translators 52
Summary 56
References 57
Appendix A: A Cultural Journey 60

PART II CULTURAL PERSPECTIVES 63
Chapter 4   Families with Anglo-European Roots
             Marci J. Hanson 65
Background 66
  Geographic and Historical Origins 66
  Religious Origins 68
  Language Origins 69
Contemporary Life 69
  Equal Rights 70
  Family Patterns 70
  Immigration Patterns 70
Values 71
  Individualism and Privacy 71
  Equality 72
  Informality 72
  The Future, Change, and Progress 73
  Goodness of Humanity 73
  Time 74
  Achievement, Action, Work, and Materialism 74
  Directness and Assertiveness 74
  Family Life 74
  Religion 75
Beliefs 76
  Childrearing 76
  Medical and Health Care 78
  Causation 79
  Disability 79
Summary and Recommendations 80
  Summary 80
  Recommendations for Interventionists 81

References 83
Appendix A: Contrasting Beliefs, Values,
and Practices.................................. 84
Appendix B: Cultural Courtesies and Customs 85
Appendix C: Significant Cultural Events/
Holidays/Practices 86

Chapter 5   Families with Native American Roots
Jennie R. Joe and Randi Suzanne Malach 89
Background 91
Historical Origins 91
Religious Origins 97
Language Origins 97
Contemporary Life 98
Values 99
Harmony with Nature 100
Time Orientation 101
Family Roles and Relationships 101
Group Orientation 103
Acceptance 103
Self-Reliance and Autonomy 104
Beliefs 104
Wellness and Unwellness, Causation
and Disability............................... 105
Childrearing 106
Issues of Language 108
Language and Education 108
Language and Communication Issues 109
Summary and Recommendations 110
Summary 110
Recommendations for Interventionists 111
References 114
Appendix A: Contrasting Beliefs, Values,
and Practices 116
Appendix B: Cultural Courtesies
and Customs................................ 117
Appendix C: Significant Cultural Events/
Holidays/Practices........................... 119

Chapter 6   Families with African American Roots
Winnie Willis 121
Background 121
Geographic Origins 121
Historical Origins 122
Religious Origins 126
Language/Linguistic Origins 127
Contemporary Life 128
Values 131
Family 131

Religion 136
Beliefs 137
   Childrearing 137
   Medical Care 139
   Causation 142
   Disability 142
Issues of Language 143
Summary and Recommendations 144
   Summary 144
   Recommendations for Interventionists 144
References 145
Appendix A: Contrasting Beliefs, Values,
   and Practices............................... 147
Appendix B: Cultural Courtesies
   and Customs................................ 148
Appendix C: Significant Cultural Events/Holidays 149
Appendix D: Language 150

Chapter 7   **Families with Latino Roots**
   Maria E. Zuniga 151
Background 151
   Geographic and Historical Origins 152
   Religious Origins 155
   Language/Linguistic Origins 156
Contemporary Life 157
   Acculturation Process 158
   Social Supports 158
Values 161
Beliefs 164
   Childrearing 164
   Medical Care 166
   Causation and Disability 168
Issues of Language 169
Summary and Recommendations 171
   Summary 171
   Recommendations for Interventionists 172
References 173
Appendix A: Contrasting Beliefs, Values,
   and Practices............................... 176
Appendix B: Cultural Courtesies and Customs 177
Appendix C: Significant Cultural Events/Holidays 178
Appendix D: Vocabulary 179

Chapter 8   **Families with Asian Roots**
   Sam Chan 181
Chinese Americans 183
   Geographic and Historical Origins 183
   Religious Origins 186
   Language/Linguistic Origins 190

Contemporary Life 191
Korean Americans 192
   Geographic and Historical Origins 192
   Religious Origins 195
   Language/Linguistic Origins 196
   Contemporary Life 197
Southeast Asian Americans 198
   Geographic and Historical Origins 199
   Religious Origins 205
   Language/Linguistic Origins 207
   Contemporary Life 208
Values 211
   Family 211
   Harmony 213
   Education 213
   Selected Virtues 213
Beliefs 214
   Childrearing 214
   Medical Care 221
   Disability 225
Issues of Language 231
Summary and Recommendations 235
   Summary 235
   Recommendations for Interventionists 238
Alternative Service Delivery and Training
   Models 243
References 244
Appendix A: Contrasting Beliefs, Values,
   and Practices.................................. 251
Appendix B: Cultural Courtesies and Customs 253
Appendix C: Significant Cultural Events/
   Holidays/Practices............................. 255
Appendix D: Vocabulary 257

Chapter 9   **Families with Pilipino Roots**
   Sam Chan 259
Background 260
   Geographic and Historical Origins 260
   Religious Origins 266
   Language/Linguistic Origins 267
Contemporary Life 269
Values 271
   Family 271
   Authority 272
   Harmony 273
   Alternative Concepts and Other Values 274
Beliefs 277
   Childrearing 277

Medical Care 282
Disability 285
Issues of Language 287
Summary and Recommendations 288
Summary 288
Recommendations for Interventionists 290
References 292
Appendix A: Contrasting Beliefs, Values,
and Practices 295
Appendix B: Cultural Courtesies and Customs 296
Appendix C: Significant Cultural Events/
Holidays/Practices 299
Appendix D: Vocabulary 300

Chapter 10   **Families with Native Hawaiian and Pacific Island Roots**

Noreen Mokuau and Pemerika Tauili'ili 301
Background 302
Geographic Origins 302
Historical Origins 302
Religious Origins 303
Language Origins 304
Contemporary Life 304
Values 305
Native Hawaiian Values 306
Samoan Values 307
Beliefs 308
Native Hawaiian Beliefs 308
Samoan Beliefs 310
Issues of Language 312
Summary and Recommendations 312
Summary 312
Recommendations for Interventionists 313
References 314
Appendix A: Contrasting Beliefs, Values,
and Practices 315
Appendix B: Cultural Courtesies and Customs 316
Appendix C: Significant Cultural Holidays/
Events/Practices 317
Appendix D: Vocabulary 318

Chapter 11   **Families with Middle Eastern Roots**

Virginia-Shirin Sharifzadeh 319
Background 320
Geographic Origins 320
Historical Origins 320
Religious Origins 321
Language Origins 323
Contemporary Life 324

Immigration to the United States 324
Political Events and Recent Immigration
    Patterns 325
Values and Beliefs 326
    Role of the Family 327
    Family Size 329
Beliefs 330
    Pregnancy and Childbirth 330
    Feeding and Health Care 331
    Proximity and Physical Contact 332
    Attachment versus Individuation 333
The Child in the Context of the Family 334
    Entertainment 335
    Young Children and Guests 335
    Children's Responsibilities and Work 336
    Role of the Father 337
    Discipline 338
    Intellectual Development 340
    Attitudes Toward Disability 340
Issues of Language 343
Summary and Recommendations 345
    Summary 345
    Recommendations for Interventionists 346
References 347
Appendix A: Contrasting Beliefs, Values,
    and Practices 348
Appendix B: Cultural Courtesies and Customs 349
Appendix C: Significant Cultural Holidays/
    Events/Practices 350
Appendix D: Vocabulary 351

PART III SUMMARY AND IMPLICATIONS 353
Chapter 12 **Steps in the Right Direction: Implications
            for Interventionists**
            Eleanor W. Lynch and Marci J. Hanson 355
Reviewing the Themes 356
    Cross-Cultural Competence: What It Is and
        What It Is Not 356
    Transactional and Situational Nature of
        Cultural Identity 356
    Mitigating Factors in Cultural Identification 358
    Personal Growth and Change 359
Creating a Culturally Appropriate Intervention
    Process 361
    Establishing Family–Professional
        Collaboration and Assessment Planning 361
    Data Gathering and Assessment 362

Developing the Intervention Plan 365
Implementation 366
Monitoring and Evaluating 368
In Conclusion 369
References 370

Suggested Readings 371
Anglo-European American 371
Native American 372
African American 373
Latino 374
Asian 375
Pilipino 376
Native Hawaiian and Pacific Island 376
Middle Eastern 376
Miscellaneous 377

Author Index 379
Subject Index 385

CONTRIBUTORS

THE EDITORS

Eleanor W. Lynch, Ph.D., Department of Special Education, San Diego State University, San Diego, California 92182

Eleanor W. Lynch is Professor of Special Education at San Diego State University (SDSU). She received her doctorate in exceptional children with minors in developmental and school psychology from Ohio State University. Before joining the faculty at SDSU, she served on the faculty at Miami University (Ohio) and the University of Michigan. For the past 18 years, she has been involved in teaching, research, and community service that focus on improving services to young children who are at risk or disabled and their families, with emphasis on the importance of parent–professional partnerships, interdisciplinary teaming, interagency collaboration, and cross-cultural issues. She has directed a model early intervention program and currently coordinates the Early Childhood Special Education Graduate Training Program and is a faculty member in the Interdisciplinary Graduate Certificate Program in Early Intervention at SDSU. Dr. Lynch has lived and worked in special education in Indonesia, taught in American Samoa, given invited presentations in Australia and Taiwan, and lived in India while her husband served on a U.S. Agency for International Development (U.S.-A.I.D.) project. She is the author of numerous articles and chapters, and editor and author of two other books in special education: *Early Intervention: Implementing Child and Family Services for Infants and Toddlers Who Are At-Risk or Disabled,* with Dr. Marci Hanson; and *Exceptional Children and Adults: An Introduction to Special Education,* with Dr. Rena Lewis.

Marci J. Hanson, Ph.D., Department of Special Education, San Francisco State University, 1600 Holloway Avenue, San Francisco, California 94132

Marci J. Hanson is Professor of Special Education and Coordinator of Early Childhood Special Education, Department of Special Education, San Francisco State University (SFSU). Dr. Hanson received her doctorate in special education in 1974 from the University of Oregon with a minor in developmental psychology. Prior to joining the faculty at SFSU, she worked as a research scientist in charge of the Early Intervention Unit of the Institute for the Study of Exceptional Children, Educational Testing Service, Princeton, New Jersey. Currently, Dr. Hanson coordinates a graduate personnel preparation program in early childhood special education that emphasizes a family-focused, interdisciplinary, and cross-cultural approach to service delivery. She also directs an interdisciplinary early intervention program, San Francisco Special Infant Services, that provides services to children from birth through 3 years who are at risk or disabled and their families. Both the graduate training program and the early intervention program reflect the cultural diversity of the Bay Area. Dr. Hanson has lived in Austria and consulted widely in the United States and in Italy and Egypt. She is the author of numerous articles and chapters and she has edited, co-authored, or authored the following books: *Teaching the Infant with Down Syndrome: A Guide for Parents and Professionals; Atypical Infant Development; Teaching the Young Child with Motor Delays: A Guide for Parents and Professionals,* with Dr. Susan Harris; and *Early Intervention: Implementing Child and Family Services for Infants and Toddlers Who Are At-Risk or Disabled,* with Dr. Eleanor Lynch.

THE AUTHORS

Jennie R. Joe, Ph.D., Native American Research and Training Center, University of Arizona, 1642 East Helen Street, Tucson, Arizona 85719

Jennie R. Joe is a medical anthropologist and member of the Navajo tribe. Presently she directs research and training projects at the Native American Research and Training Center, University of Arizona, that assist agencies and/or workers providing services to Native Americans with disabilities.

Randi Suzanne Malach, M.Cl.Sc., CCC-SP, Southwest Communication Resources, Inc., P.O. Box 788, Bernalillo, New Mexico 87004

Randi Suzanne Malach is a speech-language pathologist with 10 years experience providing services on the Indian reservations in New Mexico. Presently, she directs a home-based early intervention program and a national demonstration project with Southwest Communication Resources, Incorporated, training non-Indian service providers to work more effectively with Indian families.

Winnie Willis, R.N., Sc.D., Maternal and Child Health, Graduate School of Public Health, San Diego State University, San Diego, California 92182

Winnie Willis is Associate Professor of Public Health at San Diego State University's Graduate School of Public Health. She is an African American who has spent her professional career as an advocate for better health and social services for poor women, children, and families. Her work with multiethnic families and high-risk infants has encompassed clinical services, program planning and administration, policy development, research, and education.

Maria E. Zuniga, Ph.D., School of Social Work, San Diego State University, San Diego, California 92182

Maria E. Zuniga is a professor of Social Work at San Diego State University. She has trained graduate social work students for the past 16 years to work with culturally diverse clients in schools and in health, mental health, and social service agencies. She was raised as a Mexican American and has used that socialization to support her commitment to working with Latino families, with particular concern for the obstacles they encounter as immigrants. She has been attracted to multidisciplinary settings and continues to work as a consultant to national, state, and local agencies to increase service access for those who are underserved.

Sam Chan, Ph.D., California School of Professional Psychology, 1000 Fremont Avenue, Alhambra, California 91803

Sam Chan is the Director of the Psychological Services Center at the California School of Professional Psychology in Los Angeles. Sam received his doctorate from the University of California–Los Angeles (UCLA) in clinical psychology with minors in developmental psychology and community mental health. His father is Chinese and Mongolian, and his mother is Anglo-European. Dr. Chan identifies with the Hawaiian–Japanese term *hapa haoli* meaning half white, but as his father's first-born son, he is proudly carrying forward many of the traditional Asian values to the next generation of his family. For the past 20 years, Dr. Chan has focused his work on early intervention with infants and young children with special needs. He has developed parent education, advocacy, and leadership programs for predominantly Asian and Latino immigrant populations as well as models for promoting multicultural competence among students and professionals in the education and human services fields.

Noreen Mokuau, D.S.W., School of Social Work, Hawaii Hall, 2500 Campus Road, University of Hawaii at Manoa, Honolulu, Hawaii 96822

Noreen Mokuau is Associate Professor and chair of the undergraduate social work program at the School of Social Work at the University of Hawaii at Manoa. She is a native Hawaiian interested in multicultural issues in social work practice and is specifically concerned about Pacific Islander populations. Author of several journal articles and book chapters, she has edited a book titled the *Handbook of Social Services for Asian and Pacific Islanders*, released by Greenwood Publishing Group in late 1991.

Pemerika Tauili'ili, M.A., Director, Land Grants, American Samoa Community College, Pago Pago, Samoa 96799

Pemerika Tauili'ili is Dean and Director of the American Samoa Community College Agriculture Department. He was the former director of the American Samoa Department of Agriculture and holds two *Matai* (high chief) titles: *Tauili'ili* and *Leiataua*. As the head of two extended families, he is actively involved in Samoan village cultural activities and as a deacon and lay preacher in the Methodist church. He is also involved in a wide range of civic activities including membership on the Goodwill Industries Board of Directors.

Virginia-Shirin Sharifzadeh, M.A., San Diego State University–Claremont Joint Doctoral Program, College of Education, San Diego State University, San Diego, California 92182

Virginia-Shirin Sharifzadeh has an undergraduate degree in psychology and a master's degree in special education. She is currently completing her doctorate in the San Diego State University–Claremont Joint Doctoral Program in Education with an emphasis on special and multicultural education. Born in the United States of Iranian parents, she was brought up in Iran and considers herself an Iranian by culture. Her years of work at the John F. Kennedy Center for Handicapped Children in Tehran, which was founded by her mother Shanaz Shahnavaz, brought her into contact with families of children with disabilities in Iran. In Lebanon, where she received her undergraduate degree, she came into contact with other cultures of the Middle East and gained insight into family relations, childrearing practices, and issues in special education.

PREFACE

Since the early 1980s, the population of the United States has changed dramatically. Diversity in culture, ethnicity, and language has become a hallmark of America's large cities as well as a growing presence in smaller communities throughout the country. A kaleidoscope of color, customs, and language has added new energy and new concerns. The concerns have been especially evident in agencies, programs, and services designed to serve families of children who are disabled or at risk for disabilities—because as the definition of "best practices" in service delivery has changed, so too have the families.

Best practices in service delivery to families of children who are disabled or at risk for disabilities have moved toward a much more family focused or family centered approach. This approach emphasizes the importance of parent–professional partnerships and shared decision making in assessment, intervention, and evaluation. It also underscores the belief that services for young children must be offered in the context of the family and views the entire family system as the partner and client, not just the child. However, at the same time that services have become more family focused, the families served by many intervention programs have become increasingly diverse. Many families are characterized by attitudes, beliefs, values, customs, languages, and behaviors that are unfamiliar to interventionists. It is not uncommon for interventionists in our cities to work with families from as many as 10 different cultures, and many work with more. In a large local school district, for instance, over 50 languages may be spoken. Although the urban areas of California where we, the editors, live and work undoubtedly represent a more heterogeneous mix of cultures than found in other parts of the United States, the population is becoming more diverse everywhere in this country.

OUR REASONS FOR WRITING THIS BOOK

As professors in personnel preparation programs, directors of early intervention programs and projects, consultants, and active members of the early intervention community, we often have been asked questions regarding the provision of services to families from a range of cultural backgrounds. In researching and pursuing this knowledge ourselves, we encountered both the void of published information and also the excitement of learning more about the customs of many of the individuals and families with whom we work. Conversations with friends, students, and colleagues from different cultures have provided understanding and insight on many occasions. A number of excellent handbooks have helped us learn, as has participation in specific cross-cultural experiences and training programs—but no single source combined a strong conceptual framework with the specific information that we felt we and our students needed to know. This book is designed to combine those features. It is based upon literature that describes best practices in early intervention, the literature on intercultural effectiveness, and information and insights from contributing authors who are bicultural and often bilingual.

The book is designed to be of use to the range of professionals providing educational, health care, and social services (e.g., educators, nurses, speech and language specialists, audiologists, occupational and physical therapists, physicians, social workers, psychologists) to families who have young children who are disabled or at risk for disabilities. Regardless of the agency, program, service, setting, or one's professional discipline, having the attitudes and skills that facilitate effective cross-cultural interactions is a must in today's society.

Although the focus of this book is on families of young children who are disabled or at risk for disabilities, it could also be valuable to individuals in many other programs and settings. Much of the information that is included is equally applicable to teachers, day-care providers, and volunteers who work with families from diverse cultures who do not have children with disabilities.

PHILOSOPHY

This book has an underlying philosophy that is based upon three primary emphases. It is our intent that the following perspectives are clear throughout.

1. A prerequisite to any successful intervention is an understanding of our own cultural, ethnic, and language background and the values and beliefs that we hold about individuals who are different from ourselves.
2. All families/children/clients/patients are unique. Although they are influenced by their ethnic, cultural, and language backgrounds, they are not fully defined by them. Therefore, differences in these areas should be used to enhance our interactions rather than to stereotype or to serve as the sole determiner of our approach to intervention.
3. Our role as interventionists is twofold. It is our obligation to work with families to develop interventions that are culturally sensitive. It is also our obligation to interpret the new (or mainstream) culture to families and help them find ways to negotiate it.

ORGANIZATION AND CONTENT OVERVIEW

This book is organized into three sections. Part I provides the reader with an introduction to issues surrounding working with families from diverse cultural, ethnic, and language groups. Best practices in early intervention as well as best practices in training in intercultural effectiveness underpin Chapters 1 through 3; and suggestions are provided to help interventionists work more effectively with families whose culture, language, or ethnicity is different from their own.

Part II, the core of the book, introduces the reader to a number of the major cultural and ethnic groups that make up the population of the United States. Each group is described in terms of its history, values, and beliefs, with particular emphasis on issues related to the family, childrearing, and disability. The cultural groups represented in this volume are not exhaustive or inclusive of the wide range of cultural and ethnic groups in this country. Rather, groups were chosen because they represent a large segment of the population and/or because they reflect new immigration patterns. The contributing authors who describe these groups were carefully selected for their dual expertise and knowledge of the culture, and their experience in working with families of children who are at risk or disabled. They come from many different professional disciplines including education, nursing, psychology, medical anthropology, and social work.

The final section of this book, Part III, synthesizes the information presented in Parts I and II and provides recommendations for interventionists working in service delivery systems. It is the intent of these recommendations to enhance the sensitivity and awareness of service providers to issues of variability across families in childrearing, health care, and communication. It is also the intent of the recommendations to increase the skills of interventionists in their interactions with families from diverse cultures.

TERMINOLOGY

With respect to the terminology used in this volume, several decisions must be explained. The terms that were chosen to describe each of the cultural groups represented in the book were selected by the chapter authors in keeping with accepted terminology at the time of the writing. Because many of the terms were selected to reflect what is accepted nationally, readers in various regions of the country may be more familiar with variations that are less inclusive (e.g., Hispanic versus Latino). Throughout Part II, various terms have been chosen to refer to Anglo-European Americans who make up the dominant culture in the United States. The inconsistency in terms is another example of differing cultural perspectives and was intentionally preserved in the text. Readers should keep in mind that the terms selected may change and that the goal is to be aware of and use the terms that people within the group prefer.

Whenever possible, native spellings and pronunciations are provided; however, in cases where readability was compromised, this practice was not followed. Throughout the book, non-English words are set in italics.

The term "interventionist" is used throughout the book to refer to a person who provides educational, health, or social services to children and families. The use of this term is not meant to imply that these individuals act upon or change the family. Rather, these are service delivery personnel whose role is that of consulting with and providing information to families, supporting families, and providing direct services to children and families within the sphere of their disciplinary expertise.

IN CLOSING

Ideally, families in need of services for their children receive assistance from professionals who are knowledgeable and competent in their discipline, who speak the same language as family members, and have the ability to establish rapport and work in partnership with family members to implement interventions for the child and family. However, the current match between many professionals and the families whom they serve is not perfect. This does not mean, however, that families cannot receive high-quality services. It simply means that interventionists must increase their cross-cultural competence and learn to respond in sensitive and appropriate ways. It is our hope that this book will help interventionists in these efforts.

ACKNOWLEDGMENTS

The editors would like to acknowledge Melissa A. Behm for her enthusiastic support of the project, Susan Hughes Gray for her editorial expertise, Roslyn A. Udris for her ability to bring the project to completion, and all of the other Brookes staff members who provided time, talent, and teamwork throughout the process. We would also like to express our appreciation to the many families who allowed their photographs to be used to bring life to the pages that follow, with special thanks to the San Francisco Special Infant Services Program and the San Diego Southeast Asian Developmental Disabilities Prevention Project.

Finally, we would like to acknowledge the contributing authors for the significant roles that they each played in the creation of this book. Their wisdom, sensitivity, and willingness to serve as our cultural guides have resulted in a book that is rare in its content and readability, and a process that was, for us, a personal and professional joy. Although we may never reach the destination, we thank you for accompanying us as we begin the journey.

To Leo and Virginia Whiteside and Max and Maxine Hanson,
who gave us roots and wings

and to

Patrick Harrison, who understands and values both,
EWL

and

Laura and Jillian, that I might do the same for them
MJH

DEVELOPING CROSS-CULTURAL COMPETENCE

PART I

INTRODUCTION

The opening section of this text provides the reader with an introduction to issues surrounding working with families from diverse cultural, ethnic, and language groups. Interventionists are challenged to examine and understand their own cultural background and the values and beliefs they hold. With an awareness of their own backgrounds, they are led to examine considerations in communication and service delivery to families from a wide range of backgrounds. Chapters 1–3, thus, focus on the development of intercultural effectiveness. Suggestions are provided to help interventionists work more effectively with families whose culture, language, or ethnicity may differ from their own.

chapter 1 _____

ETHNIC, CULTURAL, AND LANGUAGE DIVERSITY IN INTERVENTION SETTINGS

Marci J. Hanson
_____

Culture is the sum of all the forms of art, of love and of thought, which,
in the course of centuries, have enabled man to be less enslaved.
—André Malraux

A walk through a garden reveals a panoply of lovely plants—all varied in form, blossoms, and size. All share such basic needs as soil, water, and sunlight; yet each plant may have different needs as to the type of soil, amount of water, and degree of sunlight required for life and growth. Each type of plant is of interest to the observer and offers its own beauty and special characteristics. However, seen together, as a whole, the plants form a wondrous garden to behold. Like the garden, communities are made up of individuals—all of whom contribute their own unique characteristics to the sense of place in which they live. However, communities also are highly interactive, dynamic enterprises where individuals are constantly interacting and responding to one another and where the characteristics of those individuals are being modified through those interactions. Although communities are not static and not planned, societies do have cultural mores and practices that guide human behavior and provide a socialization framework that shapes interactions.

Culture is this framework that guides and bounds life practices. According to Anderson and Fenichel (1989), the "cultural framework must be viewed as a set of tendencies of possibilities from which to choose" (p. 8). Thus, culture is not a rigidly prescribed set of behaviors or characteristics, but rather a framework through which actions are filtered or checked as individuals go about daily life. These cultural frameworks are constantly evolving and being reworked (Anderson & Fenichel, 1989). Further, although persons of the same cultural background may share tendencies, not all members of a group who share a common cultural background/history will behave in the same manner. Rather, behavior is governed by many factors—socioeconomic status, sex, age, length of residence in a locale, education—each of which will have an impact on cultural practices as well. Finally, individuals may differ by the degree to which

3

they choose to adhere to a set of cultural patterns. Some individuals identify strongly with a particular group; others combine practices from several cultural groups.

Cultural practices, as well as the individual characteristics of the person or family, may influence the interactions between service providers or interventionists and the families receiving services. Like the plants in the garden, the individuals within a community all share basic needs—but they will differ as to their specific needs and the types of environment that support growth. The interventionist or service provider, like the gardener, must individualize interventions for each family in order to address families' concerns and priorities and tailor the treatments to families' needs. Being sensitive, knowledgeable, and understanding of the families' cultural practices enhances this process and relationship.

CULTURAL CONSIDERATIONS FOR THE INTERVENTIONIST

The train traveler crossing the European continent is struck by the range of cultural practices encountered in a single day or two. While sitting in the same berth, this passenger may experience vast differences with each border crossing. These differences are noted not only in language, but also by the dress of the conductors, by the degree of formality or informality of communication, by the style or maintenance of trains and buildings, and by the scheduling—to name only a few.

Service providers/interventionists work with a variety of families through the provision of a range of education, health, and social services. In this process, they may travel, like the train passenger, through many cultures in a given day; the differences among these families from various cultural groups often are much more pronounced than those found by the traveler crossing the European continent.

Many interventionists also travel into the homes of the families with whom they work. Such travel brings them into close, and potentially more intrusive, contact with family members. Further, this contact often occurs at a sensitive period in the child's and family members' lives. The child is young and the family may still be adjusting to the inclusion of a new family member. Additionally, the presence of a disability, illness, or other at-risk condition may necessitate that the family interact with professionals and persons outside of the family. Thus, the interventionist comes to the family because someone perceives a need for services related to the child's developmental and/or health status. This referral for services may be sought or welcomed by the family, or the family may hold significant reservations about the need and desirability of such services. Coming at a time that is often emotionally charged, this close contact can be difficult for families and stressful for interventionists. When the interventionist and family are from different cultures, routines and recommendations may be misunderstood by either party. The potential for "cultural clashes" emerges.

This book has been designed to assist interventionists who are working with families from various cultural groups. Given the diversity of the population of the United States, it is likely that interventionists will work with families from cultural, ethnic, and linguistic groups that differ from their own. The information provided here will help interventionists not only become more sensitive to cultural differences, but also develop effective skills for working with families from diverse backgrounds and identities.

Each chapter in Part II of this book provides information about most of the major cultural groups that make up the population of the United States. The purpose of this information is not to serve as a comprehensive cultural guide to or "cookbook" about different groups. Indeed, interventionists are cautioned against overgeneralizing or characterizing all members of a cultural or ethnic group as alike. As Anderson and Fenichel (1989) related:

> Cultural sensitivity cannot mean knowing everything there is to know about every culture that is represented in a population to be served. At its most basic level, cultural sensitivity implies, rather, knowledge that cultural differences as well as similarities exist. . . . For those involved in early intervention, cultural sensitivity further means being aware of the cultures represented in one's state or region, learning about some of the general parameters of those cultures, and realizing that cultural diversity will affect families' participation in intervention programs. Cultural knowledge helps a professional to be aware of possibilities and to be ready to respond appropriately. (pp. 8–9)

An appreciation and respect for cultural variations, as well as group and individual differences, is crucial for the interventionist. It is hoped that the information garnered from these pages will enable the interventionist to work more effectively with families.

IMPORTANCE OF CROSS-CULTURAL EFFECTIVENESS

As our society has become more heterogeneous, cross-cultural effectiveness has emerged as an essential skill for all interventionists who work with young children who are disabled or at risk for developmental disabilities and who interact with their families. The need to be cross-culturally competent is just as critical for neonatal intensive care nurses, social workers, or physicians in health care settings as it is for child-care providers, educators, psychologists, physical therapists, occupational therapists, speech-language therapists, and aides in educational settings. For instance, the health care provider must be aware of the meaning that families assign to the use of surgery and drugs for medical treatments, just as educators must be knowledgeable as to family beliefs about childrearing and developmental expectations. All interventionists must be sensitive to differences across families in communication style, deci-

sion making, and the need or willingness to seek assistance from members outside the family.

Because of the age of the children, the issues on which families and professionals focus in providing services for infants, toddlers, and preschoolers are closely related to the family's values, beliefs, and traditions. The most basic issues—health care, sleeping, eating, regulating body states, building relationships, and exploring the environment—are central concerns for those who work with young children. These issues are also the ones that families control, and in which there is typically no "outside" interference unless there has been some evidence of gross mistreatment. When a child has a disability, however, many outsiders may become involved with the child and family. The potential for conflict related to childrearing practices thus emerges. Developing a respect for the values base of other cultures can help diminish these possible clashes.

Two powerful changes, one in society and one in service delivery, have increased professional awareness of the importance of cross-cultural sensitivity. The first is the change in the demographics of the United States. The second is the implementation of PL 99-457 (Education of the Handicapped Act Amendments of 1986). This law emphasizes the partnership between families and professionals in the provision of early intervention services to children from birth through 3 years of age who have a disability or are at risk for one.

Changing Demographics

The cultural composition of the United States is changing. In 1987, the population of the United States had reached 243,381,000 (The World Bank, 1988). Of that number, 17% were individuals of non-European ancestry (Research and Policy Committee of the Committee for Economic Development, 1987). This contrasts with 1970 census figures in which approximately 12% of the population was nonwhite (Bureau of the Census, 1973). In 1984, 36% of the babies born in the United States were born to nonwhite, non-Anglo families (Research and Policy Committee of the Committee for Economic Development, 1987). Again, this contrasts to figures from the previous decade in which approximately 16% of the population under age 5 was from "all races other than white" (Bureau of the Census, 1973). Estimates suggest that by the year 2000, 38% of all U.S. children under 18 will be nonwhite, non-Anglo (Research and Policy Committee of the Committee for Economic Development, 1987). According to figures released by the Children's Defense Fund (1989), in the year 2000, there will be "2.4 million more Hispanic children; 1.7 million more African-American children; 483,000 more children of other races; and 66,000 more white, non-Hispanic children" than there were in 1985 (p. 116).

Although the number of children as a percentage of the overall population in the United States is on the decline (Counting the Children, 1989), the above-cited increases in the number of children from families of non-European ancestry are expected to continue. The Children's Defense Fund predictions for the year 2030 are even more dramatic: "There will be 5.5 million more Hispanic children; 2.6 million more African-American children; 1.5 million more children of other races; and 6.2 million fewer white, non-Hispanic children" (1989, p. 116). In the 45 years between 1985 and 2030, the proportion of children from nonwhite, non-Anglo groups will rise from 28% to 41%, and the total number of children in these groups will have increased by 53%. These increases can be accounted for by the higher birth rate among nonwhite, non-Anglo women, the greater numbers of women of childbearing age within these groups, and the increased immigration of non-Europeans (Hanson, Lynch, & Wayman, 1990).

As of July 1988, 18.5 million of the nearly 64 million children in the United States were under age 5 (Children's Defense Fund, 1990; Counting the Children, 1989). Using a very conservative estimate of 3%, 555,000 of the 18.5 million children between birth and age 5 would have identified disabilities. This figure is a conservative estimate because of an increasing number of children born at risk due to conditions such as maternal use of alcohol, cocaine, or other drugs during pregnancy, and human immunodeficiency virus (HIV) infection.

Although the number of nonwhite, non-Anglo children and their families who require services is increasing, existing training programs for professionals who are most likely to work with children with disabilities and their families still have relatively few students who represent cultures with non-European roots (for data from California personnel preparation programs, see Hanson, 1990). Thus, in the year 2000, early intervention programs will include an increasing number of nonwhite, non-Anglo children, yet they will continue to be predominantly staffed by whites. Averting the potential problems in this cultural mismatch between families and service providers needs to become a priority both through the recruitment of students from groups not represented previously and the expansion of training curricula to reflect cross-cultural competency. Interventionists and the families with whom they work may not be matched culturally in all cases, and the cultures to which each adhere will not be changed—but the ways in which professionals work with families *can* be altered.

PL 99-457

PL 99-457, passed in 1986, with full implementation scheduled in the early 1990s, is the second force that has brought cross-cultural competence to the forefront in early intervention programs. Since their inception, early intervention programs for infants, toddlers, and preschoolers with disabilities or for those who are at risk for developmental disabilities have worked to develop services and supports that address the needs and desires of the child's family (Hanson & Lynch, 1989). Part H of the 1986 amendments to Title 1 of the Education of the Handicapped Act (retitled in 1990 as the Individuals with Disabilities Education Act [IDEA], PL 101-476), carried this emphasis further by encouraging states to develop a comprehensive system of service delivery for infants and toddlers who have a disability or who are at risk for developmental delay. One of the underpinnings of the law is the focus on enhancing family *capabilities* by helping families gain access to resources and acquire skills that will help them to meet the needs of their children (Title 1, Part H, Section 671[a] [4]. Services are to be delivered based upon an Individualized Family Service Plan (IFSP), and according to the implementing regulations of PL 99-457, the plan is to be developed collaboratively by families and professionals involved in assessment and service delivery (Lynch, Mendoza, & English, 1990). The IFSP process includes developing goals and services for children and families (as they are related to meeting the needs of the children) and identifying child and family strengths and resources, as well as needs.

While Part H of PL 99-457 establishes services from birth through age 3 for children and families, Part B addresses services for the 3- to 5-year age range. Although the legislative mandate for a family-focused approach to services for children with disabilities from 3 through 5 years of age is not as strong in Part B, the logic is just as compelling. Young children can only be viewed as part of a larger family system, and the importance of working closely with parents and other designated family members is essential to success. This renewed focus on the family—their concerns, priorities, needs, strengths, and resources—in the delivery of early intervention services underscores the need for early interventionists to work effectively with family members. To work closely with a family requires respect, knowledge, and awareness of the family's cultural, ethnic, and linguistic heritage.

NATURE OF INTERVENTION IN THE EARLY YEARS

The term "early intervention" implies the imposition or availability of a set of services provided in the early years of a child's life. The goal of intervention is change and the assumption is made that change is both possible and valued. Thus, even as families begin contact with service professionals in the helping sciences, they encounter mainstream American cultural values regarding the benefits of action and change. In some cultures, change may not be deemed so necessary or desirable; a fatalistic or "wait-and-see" approach to the issue of a disability or illness may predominate.

Even the concept of intervention may be foreign to some families. As professionals in the helping disciplines charge ahead on their steeds of hope and good will, they may leave many families in the dust. Even initial inquiries to families regarding the availability of services and the need for their participation may prove an undesirable and upsetting intervention to their family dynamics and beliefs. Understanding the cultural beliefs and practices to which families adhere may help prevent unfortunate misunderstandings.

The following discussion highlights several notions about early intervention that may produce confusion or differences between interventionists' practices and family members' beliefs. These notions are organized around the following categories: why intervention is done, what methods are used and where services are located, who does early intervention, and how services are provided (styles of interaction and communication).

Why Intervention Is Done—Attitudes Regarding Intervention

Different cultures attach very different meanings to the presence of disabling or at-risk conditions. Views related to disability and its causation range from those that emphasize the role of fate to those that place responsibility on the person or his or her family (Hanson et al., 1990). Persons who ascribe to the fatalistic view of disability see little recourse or remedy. For example, Green (1982) noted that in the Vietnamese culture, individuals may see that they have little power to escape from their fate and, thus, seek mainly to achieve harmony in this life.

In some cultures, blame may be attached to the parents for the child's disorder. Some may see the disability as a punishment for sins; others may view it as resulting from some action the mother or father took while the mother was pregnant. Still other groups may attribute causation to mind–body imbalances or the presence of evil spirits in the child's body (Hanson et al., 1990).

Causative factors for various disabilities have long been debated in American culture. Causation may be assigned to a variety of factors such as disease, brain injury, genetic disorders, chemical imbalances, or environmental factors (e.g., child abuse). For some types of disabilities, multiple factors may account for difficulties, while for others no single factor or specific cluster of factors can be found responsible. However, regardless of causation, in mainstream American culture, typically some sort of intervention is viewed as possible and desirable. The key is finding the appropriate methods.

Certainly, the views held by families about causation and disability will influence their need or willingness to seek help or intervention. Further, these views will affect the degree to which the family elects to participate and the type of participation. If families who ascribe to a less direct and action-oriented path to change than that found in the mainstream American culture do elect to seek or participate in services, their level of comfort during the process of help seeking and intervention may be compromised.

What Methods Are Used and Where Services Are Located

Mainstream American cultural values regarding educational and therapeutic practices in the children's early years have focused on planned and active interventions for children with the involvement of their families (Lynch, 1987). Historically, early intervention practices have moved from little parental involvement, to parents as teachers of their youngsters, to a broader view of parents as partners in the intervention process (Hanson & Lynch, 1989).

Service delivery systems for young children typically bridge several professions, agencies, and places of service delivery. Interventions may be carried out in hospitals, clinics, or the child's home. This results in some adaptations that are not required of families who do not have a child with a disability. For example, frequent visits to hospitals or clinics where the family's behavior is made public may be disconcerting to those whose childrearing practices differ from those of the dominant culture. Conversely, many early intervention programs provide services in the family's home. The degree of intrusion that this represents and the forced intimacy may produce discomfort for both the family and the interventionist. The discussion that follows illustrates these points.

Children with disabilities or those who are at risk for disabilities may have serious medical problems that require intervention. Because medical practices are linked to cultural traditions, interventionists and family members may find that there is conflict about the course of action being recommended. For example, the mainstream American culture places a high value on prevention of disease and the use of high technology in medical practice. The latest diagnostic techniques and the most aggressive approaches to managing illness are viewed as important advancements by the majority of Americans. Surgery and prescription drugs are typical treatments (Lynch, 1987).

In the United States, there is an assumption that good health is a basic right and that medical science should be able to cure everything. These beliefs are far from universal. Among some Native American Indian tribes, the medicine man or shaman and tribal community are considered essential to the healing process. As described in Lynch (1987),

> the family discusses the illness with the medicine man, determines the cause of the sickness (for example, contact with a ghost), and organizes a community sing which attempts to eliminate the cause and the disease. It is not uncommon for Navajos to use both Western medical practices and indigenous treatments to heal members of the community (R.B. Lewis & J. Lewis, personal communication, Dec. 16, 1985). (p. 85)

The nurse, physician, and hospital social worker who are advocating for surgery, drug treatments, or other medical procedures need to be aware of the family's beliefs and practices and also the value and significance of these rituals to the family and the community.

Once a young child is medically stable, he or she is often referred to a developmentally or educationally oriented intervention program. These interventions may also produce cultural conflicts. The earliest learning experiences of the young children are centered on their own senses and perceptions and are mediated by the reactions of their primary caregivers. Because early learning focuses on such basics as eating, sleeping, communicating, establishing relationships, and regulating emotional responses, learning in this period is inex-

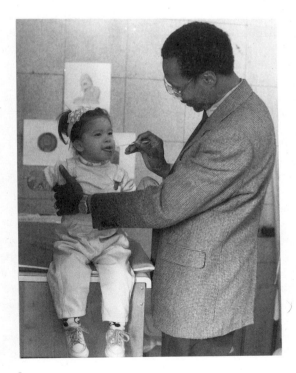

tricably bound to cultural values, beliefs, and traditions. As a result, some of the interventions that may seem innocuous to one interventionist or family may seem strange and unusual to others with different childrearing practices. The following examples illustrate.

Independence and privacy are highly valued in mainstream American culture, and children typically are encouraged to become independent almost from birth. Families strive to have separate rooms for each child; infants sleep alone, often in rooms by themselves. However, to many families, for example, those from Mexico, Central and South America, and Asia, the isolation of young children in a dark room in a crib or single bed is considered to be inappropriate. Infants typically sleep in the same bed with the parents and are not left alone during sleep.

Feeding practices for young children may also be quite varied. For some families, mealtimes are highly structured; for others, there is much less definition. The meal may be prepared and kept out for family members, with each person taking whatever he or she wants whenever it is desired. When there is neither a formal mealtime nor specific preparations for it, suggesting that a family work on language skills for a child when the family sits down to dinner is not an intervention that can be incorporated into that family's normal routine. For interventions to be effective, they must respect and, to the extent possible, incorporate the practices of the family.

Professionals and assistants who work with families from cultures different from their own are in a unique position to bridge the two cultures. For families who have recently immigrated to the United States, interventionists may assist as the family learns to function in a new environment by: 1) interpreting the mainstream culture; 2) learning about the family's practices related to childrearing, health care, and socialization; and 3) helping to design interventions that match the family's preferences. Interpreting the mainstream culture may be the most difficult role, for interventionists may be called upon to explain why some cultural practices are discouraged in the United States. For example, some healing techniques, such as *bat gio* (pinching) or *cao gio* (coining, the striking or scratching of the skin to rid the body of disorders like headaches and colds), most common among the Mien, Vietnamese, and ethnic Chinese in Southeast Asia, are not acceptable practices in the United States because of their perceived potential to cause harm to the child (Schreiner, 1981). It may be the interventionist's role to provide information about the new culture that will help the family adapt to new demands and beliefs, while helping the family maintain the elements of their traditional culture of origin that they wish to preserve. This is not an easy task, and the difficulties encountered by both the family and the interventionist are made more challenging by these differences that exist across cultures.

In other instances, it will be the interventionists' task to accept the practices of families as valid and important although they may be different from those practiced by the interventionists or by the dominant culture in that geographical area. For example, in the United States, toilet training between the child's second and third birthday is a fairly common practice and is in fact highly valued by many families. However, this practice may be viewed by many other cultural groups as unnecessary and too early. Expectations for children concerning feeding, sleeping, and speaking, as well as the use of discipline, to mention only a few, may vary widely across cultural groups.

Who Does Early Intervention

Best practices in early intervention services in the United States typically define the providers as a team of professionals from a wide variety of disciplines who work collaboratively with one another and in partnerships with family members (Hanson & Lynch, 1989). The professional disciplines that mostly commonly provide early intervention services and that are identified in PL 99-457 include: education, medicine, nursing, nutrition/dietetics, occupational therapy, physical therapy, psychology, social work, and speech-language pathology and audiology. Individuals from many of these professional backgrounds may in fact specialize in serving young children and their families.

The mainstream cultural notions of interventionists may differ widely from those held by other cultural groups. Members of other cultural groups may turn to elders, other family members, friends, or folk healers for assistance in child health and behavior issues. To illustrate differences across cultural groups, Randall-David (1989, p. 26) provided the following list of therapeutic agents or people whose help is sought for psychosocial disorders:

Mainstream White American	*Mexican American*
Counselors	Curanderos
Psychiatrists	
Psychologists	*Puerto Rican*
Social workers	Espiritistas
Ministers	Santerios
African-American	*Cuban*
Ministers	Santerios
Root workers	
Voodoo priests	*Southeast Asian American*
	Herbalists
Haitian	Family/friends
Voodoo priests	Diviners
Native American	
Medicine men	
"Singers"	

How Services Are Provided—
Styles of Interaction and Communication

The styles whereby individuals exchange information and converse may differ widely for various cultural groups. Particularly when dealing with sensitive issues such as the disability or illness of a family member, communication style may play a key role in establishing effective interactions with families. The dominant communication style in mainstream American culture is often characterized as direct and fairly informal. In early intervention services, family input and participation is typically highly valued; indeed, PL 99-457 stipulates the importance of family involvement in defining goals and participating throughout the intervention process. For some families, direct confrontation and questioning may bring shame. Inquiries and informal questions surrounding these personal issues may be deemed highly inappropriate. Other families may seek opportunities to discuss their children's conditions with professionals.

Preferences and practices with regard to method of greeting (formal versus informal), type of dress (highly professional versus informal), degree of eye contact when interacting, person to whom inquiries are directed (mother, father, elder), method through which information is gathered (orally versus written, structured questions versus open-ended) may differ dramatically from culture to culture. The interventionist's first interactions with families may determine whether or not an effective working relationship will be established. "Getting off on the right foot" by understanding and recognizing the communication styles practiced by various families will facilitate the process.

CONCEPT OF CULTURAL IDENTITY

Although the purpose of this book is to help the reader become more sensitive to cultural differences and more knowledgeable about variations in cultural practices, a person's cultural identification cannot be viewed as the exclusive determinant of one's actions. Rather, many other factors also influence an individual's actions. In addition, individuals vary as to the degree to which they identify with a cultural group. Such factors limit the role that culture may play in influencing behavior. Some of these factors are discussed briefly below.

Factors that Mitigate the Influence of Cultural Identity

Regional labels ("northerner," "southerner," "easterner," "westerner," "midwesterner") may connote a set of characteristics noted in an area's inhabitants. While some persons may hold strong chauvinistic regard for their geographical region, most resist being labeled and stereotyped on the basis of their place of residence. Likewise, generalizations cannot be made about the characteristics and behaviors of any given cultural group. Although members of the groups may hold some beliefs and life practices in common, many other factors will influence their behavior and how they define themselves as individuals. In fact, some of these factors may play a more significant role in determining a person's behavior at any given moment than does her or his cultural identity. For example, if a family is homeless, the absence of consistent shelter and food is likely to have a stronger influence on the day-to-day practices of a family than is their cultural origin.

Other influences or factors that may mitigate the influence of an individual's cultural identity include: socioeconomic status; length of residence in the United States or in a particular region of the country; the type of region (e.g., urban, suburban, rural); the person's age and sex; the amount and type of education; the number and type of resources or family support systems; and, in the case of immigrants, the reason for the immigration and/or the "wave" of immigration with which the person was associated. Any of these factors may exercise a powerful effect upon the individual's lifeways and, in many cases, may play a more dominant role than does the cultural framework in which the individual was socialized.

Continuum of Cultural Identification

Assumptions about an individual's behavior based upon a cultural label or stereotype may result in inaccurate, inappropriate, or harmful generalizations. Although individuals may identify with a given cultural group by way of birthplace, skin color, language, or religious practices, to name a few factors, these factors will not determine the *degree* to which individuals see themselves as members of a group.

In *American Ways: A Guide for Foreigners in the United States,* Althen (1988) stated: "The predominant ideas, values, and behaviors of 'Americans' are those of the white, middle class. People in that category have long held the large majority of the country's most influential positions" (p. xiii). Further, he reviewed some general notions about American "culture"—notions that are derived both from how many Americans see themselves and also from how foreigners see Americans. Predominant American values and assumptions, according to Althen (1988), include emphases on: 1) individualism and privacy; 2) equality; 3) informality; 4) the future, change and progress; 5) goodness of humanity; 6) time; 7) achievement, action, work, and materialism; and 8) directness and assertiveness (see discussion in chapter 4, this volume). Many long-term residents of the United States ascribe to these values; some do not. Likewise, many new immigrants will adopt all or some of these "mainstream" values, while others will choose to retain the major values of their first culture—particularly when those values differ radically from those of the mainstream or dominant society.

Sanday (cited in Green, 1982) discussed four categories of cultural integration that reflect the degree to which members of a cultural group have integrated their values with those of the dominant or mainstream culture in the place in which they live. She labeled these groups as: 1) mainstreamers, 2) bicultural individuals, 3) culturally different individuals, and 4) individuals who are culturally marginal. Mainstreamers are identified as those individuals who have assimilated or adopted the standard values accepted by the dominant or mainstream culture. Bicultural individuals may participate dually in both the dominant culture and in a nondominant culture (their culture of origin). These individuals may have a commitment to both cultures. It should also be noted that some individuals may comfortably negotiate and maintain commitments to more than two cultures. Culturally different individuals are those persons who have been exposed to the dominant or mainstream culture but choose to remain apart in their enclave of cultural origin. These persons may interact on occasion with institutions of the dominant culture (e.g., health care services) but maintain most of their activity within their contained or isolated group. Persons identifying as members of enclaves such as "Chinatowns" and "Little Italys" may fall into this category. English may or may not be spoken in these cultural enclaves and, if spoken, may not be used in daily practice in the homes. Members of these groups may be recent immigrants or they may be long-term residents of the United States. Finally, culturally marginal individuals are identified as those individuals who essentially follow their own way and hold no attachment to any particular cultural group.

While this paradigm may be helpful in understanding differences in the degree of identification among individuals, a more interactional or transactional approach to cultural identification is needed from the standpoint of the interventionist. Green (1982) explained that the degree to which persons are acculturated is "situational rather than absolute and can be modified to suit the needs of different kinds of cross-cultural encounters" (p. 13). For example, a family may adhere to most practices and proponents of the dominant culture (e.g., work lifeways, housing standards, recreational practices), but differ radically on one dimension, such as health care. Recent cases, involving parents who as Christian Scientists elected to use prayer rather than surgery to treat their child's bowel obstruction and a Chinese mother who elected to use Chinese medicine rather than Western practices (drugs and surgery) to treat her child's juvenile rheumatoid arthritis ("Does Doctor," 1990), exemplify situational cultural identification. Family members may adopt some aspects of the dominant culture(s) in which they reside but not all. Further, these beliefs may shift over time. Families may opt at one point, for instance, to send their children to a "mainstream" school that represents the ways of the dominant culture, but later decide to educate their children in a "native" school operated by and for members of their particular cultural group. Sanchez-Hucles (1990) discussed the potential difficulties experienced by persons with bicultural identification. These difficulties include the pressure felt by individuals to "select the 'right' response from their repertoire of two cultures" (Sanchez-Hucles, 1990, p. 13) and to minimize their ethnicity and act like members of the dominant culture.

Historically (as reviewed by Marsella, 1990), ethnocultural identity was viewed from the degree of "assimilation" or "acculturation" to the dominant culture. In the United States, as the population has become increasingly diverse in terms of cultural heritage, a more pluralistic view has been adopted. This view acknowledges the contributions of the many cultures that make up this society, but it fails to describe the dynamic and interactional perspective of cultural identity.

In summary, while our culture or ethnicity plays a role in defining who we are as people and how we conduct our lives, multiple dimensions form that identity. The degree to which we identify with a particular group(s), under what circumstances, or in what aspects, and the other social and demographic factors that may influence our identity all play a role as well. Cultural/ethnic identification is but one facet, albeit a very instrumental facet, in shaping our behavior. The interventionist who is able to value and respect these cultural differences among families will find his or her job more understandable and infinitely more rewarding.

SUMMARY

For years, the United States was characterized proudly as a great melting pot where persons from various lands and cultures met to forge a new and homogeneous society. That characterization has been replaced by a pluralistic view. No longer is our society viewed as a melting pot. Today, individuals maintain their separate identities while contributing to the whole composition. However, Green (1982) cautioned that neither the melting pot nor pluralistic categorical approaches to understanding ethnicity are particularly useful. Rather, he argued for a more transactional approach that examines the relations between individuals who identify with various ethnic or cultural groups and the larger society. Cultural modifications and mixing will occur as groups recognize value in each other's practices.

For interventionists, a transactional and situational approach is particularly applicable. The lesson learned throughout the years is to view each child as an individual with unique characteristics, strengths, and needs. Like the individual, families also have unique concerns, priorities, and resources—these are not static, but rather are constantly shifting and changing.

Our cultural and ethnic identities help to shape our beliefs and practices, and who we are as individuals and as family members. These identities are not the script for our behavior, but they do provide a texture and a richness—and they can both bind us together in groups and separate us from one another. Knowledge and understanding, sensitivity, and respect for these cultural differences can significantly enhance the effectiveness of service providers in the helping professions.

REFERENCES

Althen, G. (1988). *American ways: A guide for foreigners in the United States.* Yarmouth, ME: Intercultural Press.

Anderson, P.P., & Fenichel, E.S. (1989). *Serving culturally diverse families of infants and toddlers with disabilities.* Washington, DC: National Center for Clinical Infant Programs.

Bureau of the Census. (1973). *Characteristics of the population: Vol. 1.* Washington, DC: United States Department of Commerce.

Children's Defense Fund. (1989). *A vision for America's future.* Washington, DC: Author.

Children's Defense Fund. (1990). *S.O.S. America! A children's defense budget.* Washington, DC: Author.

Counting the children. (1989, May). *Education Week,* p. 3.

Does doctor know best? (1990, September). *Newsweek,* p. 84.

Green, J.W. (1982). *Cultural awareness in the human services.* Englewood Cliffs, NJ: Prentice-Hall.

Hanson, M.J. (1990). *Final report: California Early Intervention Personnel Study Project.* San Francisco: San Francisco State University, Department of Special Education. (Available from Early Intervention Programs, Department of Developmental Services, 1600 9th Street, Sacramento, CA 95814)

Hanson, M.J., & Lynch, E.W. (1989). *Early intervention: Implementing child and family services for infants and toddlers who are at-risk or disabled.* Austin, TX: PRO-ED.

Hanson, M.J., Lynch, E.W., & Wayman, K.I. (1990). Honoring the cultural diversity of families when gathering data. *Topics in Early Childhood Special Education, 10*(1), 112–131.

Lynch, E.W. (1987). Families from different cultures. In M. Bristol & C. Kasari (Eds.), *The Family Support Network series: Monograph one* (pp. 80–88). Moscow: University of Idaho, Family Support Network Project.

Lynch, E.W., Mendoza, J. M., & English, K. (1990). *Implementing individualized family service plans in California: Final report.* (Available from Early Intervention Programs, Department of Developmental Services, 1600 9th Street, Sacramento, CA 95814)

Marsella, A.J. (1990). Ethnocultural identity: The "new" independent variable in cross-cultural research. *Focus* (American Psychological Association), *4*(2), 14–15.

PL 99-457, Education of the Handicapped Act Amendments of 1986.

PL 101-476, Individuals with Disabilities Education Act of 1990.

Randall-David, E. (1989). *Strategies for working with culturally diverse communities and clients.* Washington, DC: Association for the Care of Children's Health.

Research and Policy Committee of the Committee for Economic Development. (1987). *Children in need—Investment strategies for the educationally disadvantaged.* New York: Author.

Sanchez-Hucles, J.V. (1990). Biculturalism in American ethnic minorities: A direction for a society that values diversity. *Focus* (American Psychological Association), *4*(2), 13–14.

Schreiner, D. (1981). *Southeast Asian healing practices/child abuse?* (Available from Peck Health Center, 2415 S.E. 43rd Street, Portland, OR 97206)

The World Bank. (1988). *The World Bank atlas 1988* (21st ed.). Washington, DC: Author.

chapter 2 _____

FROM CULTURE SHOCK TO CULTURAL LEARNING

Eleanor W. Lynch

_____

We do everything by custom, even believe by it; our very axioms, let us boast of free-thinking as we may, are oftenest simply such beliefs as we have never heard questioned.
                                                              —*Thomas Carlyle*

All of us are products of one or more cultural, language, and ethnic groups. For some, cultural, language, and ethnic origins continue to be a major part of their overt identity. The foods that are served, how major holidays and life events are celebrated, and the values held regarding family, childrearing, time, ambition, authority, responsibility, and spirituality reflect their cultural and ethnic heritage. Their roots are very near the surface, and day-to-day life tends to be shaped by their global place of origin, its culture and its language.

For others, roots are deeply buried; layers of adjustment and adaptation have blunted awareness of their origins. They may think of themselves as products of the American culture with little reference or connection to an ethnic, cultural, or global heritage. However, regardless of how long ago or how recently our ancestors came to the United States, our roots—in subtle and not-so-subtle ways—influence our attitudes and behaviors.

The influence of culture, language, and ethnicity is always easier to see in other people than in ourselves. Culture, like a second skin, is something that we have grown so accustomed to that we have ceased to notice that it exists; but it is not surprising that culture has such a profound influence on our behavior. Guthrie (no date, cited in Draine & Hall, 1986) described five reasons for the difficulties that people experience when they try to understand or function in a culture other than their own:

1. *Cultural understanding in one's first culture occurs early and is typically established by age 5.* Culture, like language, is acquired very early in life (Brown & Lenneberg, 1965). Every interaction, sound, touch, odor, and experience has a cultural component that is absorbed even when it is not directly taught. Lessons learned at such early ages become an integral part of thinking and behavior. Table manners, the proper behavior when inter-

acting with adults, and the rules of acceptable emotional response are an-chored in culture. There are many behaviors and beliefs learned at an early age that persist into adulthood. Perhaps there were rules about how to dress in different settings, for example, a place of worship versus school. Learning to eat may have involved using a knife, fork, and spoon; chop-sticks; or one's right hand. There may have been rules related to speaking to adults: As children, some people may have been allowed to initiate a conversation with an adult; some may have been required to use titles of respect; some may have been taught to look at the adult while speaking and some may have been taught to look down.

2. *Children learn new cultural patterns more easily than adults.* As in lan-guage learning, children are more adept at acquiring new cultural skills than are adults. Whether it is because they have the ability to be more flexible, because their patterns of behavior are less established, or because they have less information to manage, children tend to cross cultures more easily than adults. When children of varying ethnic groups play together, in most instances, they find constructive ways to adapt to new rules, differ-ent languages, and different behaviors. They may act out what is supposed to happen, negotiate a resolution verbally and nonverbally, ignore behavior that they do not understand, or confront the other child about the behavior. Although it does not always go smoothly, children are typically able to make cross-cultural interactions work.

3. *Values are determined by one's first culture and may have to be revised to be effective in a second culture.* Values are responsible for many of our built-in biases. The importance that individuals ascribe to cooperation versus competition, action versus passivity, intelligence versus physical prowess, family versus friends, or individuality versus team spirit reflects cultural values. The concept of competition is a good example. In the mainstream American culture, children are encouraged from an early age to excel in whatever they do—to be better than anyone else. There are contests for everything from spelling to pie eating to hog calling. The free enterprise economy is built upon entrepreneurial competition. Newspapers are filled with the latest records set in high and low temperatures, sports, and the stock market. In the United States, competition is highly prized. However, the reverse is true in many Native American Indian, Hispanic/ Latino, Asian, Pacific Island, and Southeast Asian cultures. Competition is viewed as self-serving; and the emphasis is upon cooperation and team-work. To be viewed as competitive rather than cooperative would bring shame rather than pride, because competition is a negative trait.

4. *Understanding of one's first culture introduces errors in interpreting the second culture.* Individuals interpret situations based upon their past expe-rience, and these interpretations are never culture free. For example, the rules for touching differ from culture to culture. In the United States, it is

quite common to see members of the opposite sex holding hands, walking with their arms around one another, or kissing in public. In many other parts of the world such public displays of affection between men and women are not tolerated; however, it would be commonplace to see members of the same sex walking hand-in-hand or with their arms around one another. In the United States, such behavior is a signal of sexual preference; in other countries, it is more likely to be a demonstration of friendship.

5. *Long-standing behavior patterns are typically used to express one's deepest values.* Old habits are not easily changed. Everyone has his or her own story of reverting to old behaviors out of habit or in times of high emotion or stress. From the caller who realizes she is saying thank you to a computer voice to the American in England who discovers himself looking for the steering wheel on the left side of the car, individuals discover that behaviors they have practiced for years are difficult to modify. We behave as we have been culturally programmed to behave, and sometimes our cultural program conflicts with someone else's. For example, careful time management and punctuality are values that are held by many in the dominant, U.S. culture. Everyday conversations are replete with comments about time—if I just had more time; when I have time; what a time waster that was; I can't, I'll be late; check your calendar. However, this preoccupation with time as a commodity to be bought, sold, or apportioned is not typical in much of the rest of the world. In Central and South America, parts of Asia, Southeast Asia, the Middle East, Africa, the Mediterranean, the Pacific Islands, and among many ethnic groups within the United States, time is generously shared. People are more important than clocks; and individuals operate on their sense of priority rather than on predetermined times. This difference is particularly problematic when the two cultures attempt to work together. The interventionist is infuriated when families are late for their appointments, and the family does not imagine that clock time would take precedence over everything else.

Because cultural influences are such an integral part of lives, they are often elusive. However, when we are out of touch with our own culture and its influence on us, it is impossible to work effectively with people whose cultures differ from our own. Only when we examine the values, beliefs, and patterns of behavior that are a part of our own cultural identity can we distinguish truth from tradition. Such an examination is not easy: It requires a consideration of all of the things that we have learned from childhood and an acknowledgment that those beliefs and behaviors represent only one perspective—a perspective that is *not* inherently "right." (The reader should complete the Cultural Journey Exercise in Appendix A in Chapter 3 to examine his or her own cultural values and beliefs.) Culture, language, and ethnicity are not the only determiners of

one's values, beliefs, and behaviors. Socioeconomic status, educational level, occupation, personal experience, and personality all exert a powerful influence over how individuals view themselves and how families function. Although this chapter focuses on culture, it should be understood that culture is only one element that families use to define themselves.

CONCEPT OF CULTURE SHOCK

Anyone who has traveled outside his or her own hometown has probably experienced some form of culture shock. Whether it is the Bostonian trying to adjust to the language and lifestyle of southern California, the Texas rancher negotiating the New York subway, or the West Virginian in Las Vegas, each is confronted with sounds, sights, odors, and behaviors that are unfamiliar. The unfamiliarity that each of these travelers experiences may produce interest, excitement, fear, anger, frustration, confusion, or disgust; but regardless of the emotion that it evokes, it is certain to have an impact. The farther that individuals travel from their home, the greater the likelihood that they will be confronted with the unfamiliar. Thus, an American in Paris, a Japanese in Fiji, a Native American Indian in New Delhi, or an Italian in Beijing is more likely to experience confusion, frustration, or anger with the unfamiliar than the Bostonian in southern California, the Texan in New York, or the West Virginian in Las Vegas. It is these confrontations with the unfamiliar that create culture shock.

In the academic literatures of anthropology, sociology, psychology, and communications, the concept of culture shock and its stages and characteristics continue to be debated (Brislin, 1981). Some of the early work that described the stages of culture shock (Gullahorn & Gullahorn, 1963) has not been successfully replicated in more recent studies (Klineberg & Hull, 1979). However, individuals who have worked, studied, or traveled extensively in cultures different from their own are usually able to describe their experience on this curve of cultural adjustment and learning. Those preparing others to work cross-culturally also use the concept of culture shock as a framework for helping individuals understand what they are experiencing emotionally and physically. Thus, culture shock has been included in this book as a paradigm that can assist interventionists as they work with families who are newly arrived and experiencing culture shock as well as a framework for examining the interventionist's own feelings when faced with unfamiliar values, beliefs, and practices.

Culture shock was first described by Oberg (1958, 1960). Although many investigators have elaborated on Oberg's work and used other words to describe the phenomenon and explain its cause and manifestations (e.g., Ball-Rokeach, 1973; Byrnes, 1966; Guthrie, 1975; Smalley, 1963), in this chapter the term culture shock is used to describe a normal and universal response to the unfamiliar. Culture shock is most often discussed and studied when businesspersons, students, project staff members, or government officials are being prepared to live and work or study outside of their own country. However, the concept of culture shock may also "be experienced by individuals who have face-to-face contact with out-group members within their own country" (Brislin, 1981, p.155). Thus, culture shock may occur in the encounters that families and interventionists from different backgrounds have when they work together. Understanding the concept of culture shock and its characteristics and stages provides a framework that enables individuals to recognize their feelings, analyze the cause, alter their approach, consciously manage their own behavior, and regain emotional equilibrium.

The sections that follow examine the concept of culture shock and apply its stages and principles to the transactions between interventionists and families when the interventionist and family do not share the same ethnic or cultural heritage. Culture shock is conceptualized as a two-way street—one that both families and interventionists travel as they work together.

Defining Culture Shock

Culture shock is the result of a series of disorienting encounters that occur when an individual's basic values, beliefs, and patterns of behavior are challenged by a different set of values, beliefs, and behaviors. Although values are typically unacknowledged until challenged, they are the cornerstones of our being and behavior (Bohm, 1980).

> Since values are the products of basic human and societal needs, the number of human values is small, and they focus on similar important concepts the world over. Values reflect a culture's view toward such central issues as politics, economics, religion, aesthetics, interpersonal relationships, morality and the environment. Cultural differences and conflicts arise from the fact that individuals and societies order these values in differing hierarchies. (Brislin, Cushner, Cherrie, & Yong, 1986, p. 299)

Culture shock occurs when the strategies that the individual uses to solve problems, make decisions, and interact positively are not effective, and when the individual feels an overwhelming sense of discomfort in the environment (Draine & Hall, 1986). The discomfort may manifest itself in emotional or physical ways such as frustration, anger, depression, withdrawal, lethargy, aggression, or illness; in any of these states, it is difficult for the individual to take constructive action.

Families who have recently arrived in the United States typically experience culture shock as they attempt to negotiate a new culture, language, and set of behaviors. What was accepted behavior in their homeland may be misunderstood, disdained, laughed at, or even illegal in their new country. For example, in many countries outside the United States, spitting or blowing nasal mucus onto the ground is commonplace. Capturing saliva or mucus in a tissue or handkerchief that would then be put back into a pocket or purse is considered to be a filthy habit. No one would carry something like that with them! In the United States, expectorating on the ground would be viewed with disgust; in some cities, it would even be a misdemeanor. Although both cultures have placed a value on personal hygiene, its interpretation is drastically different.

Behaviors that were appreciated and valued in a family's country of origin may be confusing to individuals in the United States. As a result of different behaviors and interpretations of those behaviors based upon culture, ethnicity, or language, families and interventionists may become confused in their interactions with one another. Confusion leads to discomfort and may cause both parties to withdraw. A typical transaction in the United States when an infant or toddler attracts the attention of a stranger in a supermarket, office, or other public place is an example. The adult usually engages in a game of peek-a-boo with, makes faces at, or talks in a sing-song fashion to the baby. When the adult or the child tires of the game, the adult usually turns to the child's parents/caregivers and comments on how attractive, alert, or delightful the child is. The parents/caregivers express pleasure at the compliment and are pleased that the stranger has recognized the superiority of their child. In many other cultures, however, this would be a very disquieting interaction for the parents. In some Mexican and Central American, Islamic, and Native American Indian cultures, calling attention to the child's positive traits can alert evil spirits to the child; the evil spirits may then cause harm.

Different values and differing interpretations of behaviors introduce confusion and discomfort into cross-cultural interactions. The discomfort is often heightened by limited ability to verbalize the conflict. Families who are not conversant in English and interventionists who speak nothing else may quickly encounter barriers that are difficult to overcome.

Navigating the Stages of Culture Shock

Gullahorn and Gullahorn (1963) described a predictable set of stages of adjustment that long-term, overseas sojourners experienced. The ups and downs of their experience can be depicted in a W-shaped curve. At the beginning of the experience, spirits and expectations are high and individuals feel extremely satisfied with the experience. During the middle phase of the experience, individuals become dissatisfied. By this time, they have discovered that their problem-solving strategies are ineffective in the foreign environment; their expectations are not being met; and they often become angry and lash out. This period of anger and frustration is followed by an improvement in outlook and a general upswing in mood and effectiveness that peaks near the end of the experience. The return to being highly satisfied with the experience is a period during which the individuals begin to function comfortably in the environment.

Interestingly, many long-term sojourners experience reverse culture shock when they return to their home country and go through a shorter series of readjustments or relearning that mirror those they experienced in the overseas experience. As an example, the author of this chapter had a difficult readjustment following a 5-month assignment in Indonesia. In the first few weeks back in the United States, on several occasions, trips to the grocery store were abandoned because other shoppers seemed so large, so loud, and so aggressive—opposites of the Indonesian people.

The time that it takes any individual to pass through the hypothesized stages of culture shock is not predictable. Each person brings different needs and different resources to the situation and finds ways to cope that slow or hasten the passage. Like the grief cycle that is used so frequently to describe parents' reactions to the birth of child with a disability (Solnit & Stark, 1961), culture shock is an experience without temporal norms.

The Family's Viewpoint

Imagine the stages of culture shock as they might apply to a family with a young child with a disability who has recently arrived in the United States. The family has chosen to emigrate to the United States and has high expectations for its success here. Although they recognize that the streets are not paved with gold, they are imagining a land of opportunity that will incorporate them and the many skills that they bring. The feelings of enthusiasm and great expectation that they have are slowly eroded by everyday experiences. For example, only the father speaks English and his skills in the language were learned from a textbook rather than through conversations with native speakers. Every interaction is a struggle that leaves him very tired at the end of the day. Because he is the family's only communicator with the new environment, he is constantly in a position of trying to make himself understood as well as explain what is going on to other members of the family. In addition to the problems of spoken English, there are the problems of written English. It seems that every interaction results in the need to complete a stack of forms, and comprehending and completing the forms is even more difficult than speaking.

In their homeland, the family arose with the sun, rested in the heat of the day, and returned to work late in the afternoon. In their new community, all activity seems to be governed by the clock instead of by any natural rhythm; so even though they have conquered jetlag, they have not yet adjusted to these new patterns. Getting things done is also very different and often results in no results or very unpleasant exchanges. For example, several people have spoken to them very rudely at the post office and in the bank about not standing in line; but in their own country, everyone crowded around the windows to get stamps or money. Similar things have happened in the car. On several occasions, people have yelled and gestured angrily just because they did not come to a full stop or caused a pedestrian to jump back onto the sidewalk. They were driving just as they had learned to drive in their homeland where they had never had an accident, but the reactions to their style in the United States were very disconcerting. It is also difficult to be expected to do things here that servants did at home—washing, cleaning, caring for the children, shopping. How can anyone of their family background be expected to do these menial tasks for themselves? Another thing that has caused real frustration is related to their child with the disability. Everyone keeps suggesting programs and services for this baby, but she is only 4 years old. Why should a 4-year-old go to school? And why do all of these well-educated people keep asking the family's opinion, wanting them to participate, to set goals? That is a job for them, not a job for the family. How presumptuous it would be to tell those professionals what they should do to help; they are the experts.

At this point, the family has probably reached the low point on the W-shaped curve of culture shock. Their expectations are not being met. Patterns of behavior that have worked for them for years in their home country do not produce the expected results here, and everything about this new place seems almost too demanding to endure. If the family members persevere, continue to interact and learn about the new culture, in several months or a year they will become more positive about their experiences. They will learn what is expected in the many situations that they encounter, and each day their lives will become easier. This does not mean that they abandon their own culture's values, beliefs, and practices, but it does mean that they learn new behaviors and strategies that can be used to meet the demands of the new culture.

The Interventionist's Viewpoint

Now imagine the same scenario from the interventionist's point of view. The nurse on the team was assigned to the family because of the child's medical problems. After many attempts to make contact, the family reluctantly allowed her to make a home visit. Everyone in the family was there, but only the father did any talking. He knew almost nothing about the child's eating and sleeping patterns and the care that she had had in their home country, but he was the only one who spoke. He also kept referring to her as the baby even though she is already 4 years old. Imagine a 4-year-old and no intervention; what would have happened if they had just tried to enroll her in kindergarten next year! The whole family seemed to turn to stone when the interventionist asked what their goals were and how they would like to be involved in their daughter's education—really uninvolved. The other thing that was really upsetting was a sense of hostility that seemed to be a palpable presence in the home. Everyone was polite, but they seemed angry. If they're going to be that hard to work with, why bother? After all, there are lots of other families who appreciate what interventionists do and want to be part of their child's program.

Assume that you are one of the interventionists who meets the family when they are unhappy and confused by their experiences in the United States—when they are at the lowest point in the culture shock curve. They may appear angry, uncooperative, uncommunicative, resistant, or withdrawn; many of the verbal and nonverbal cues may be inconsistent with your expectations of involved and caring families. The whole situation may be tense and uncomfortable, and it may be very tempting to give up. However, this is a time when helping families understand and negotiate the new culture is most needed. Acknowledging the difficulties that they are encountering and finding ways to reduce those problems through translators; professionals or paraprofessionals who share the same background; or watching, listening, and making small gestures may be the key to serving both the child and the family at all. It will certainly be the key to serving both effectively.

AMELIORATING CULTURE SHOCK FOR THE FAMILY

Culture shock requires adjustment—adjustment of families who are unfamiliar or inexperienced in the ways of the service systems that they encounter, and adjustment of the interventionists who are unfamiliar and inexperienced in the ways of the families whom they meet. Culture shock is most pronounced when individuals initially discover that there are dramatic differences between their beliefs and values and those of the people around them. Thus, families who have recently arrived in the United States may be most affected by culture shock. However, some families who have spent many generations in the United States may still find the predominant culture unfriendly and frustrating. Likewise, interventionists may experience greater degrees of culture shock when they are working with families who are newly arrived; but they may also experience some degree of culture shock when they work with families who have been in the United States for many years but have beliefs, values, and practices that are foreign to the interventionist's. This section focuses on culture shock from the perspective of families who are new immigrants and from those who have spent many generations in the United States apart from the mainstream.

New Immigrants

Families who have recently arrived in the United States are most affected by culture shock. Even those immigrants who are financially secure and skilled in English typically experience a period of adjustment that may resemble a ride on a rollercoaster. For those who have limited resources, are unfamiliar with English, and have experienced considerable trauma leaving their country of origin, the shock of a new culture is magnified. Although culture shock is very personalized, several issues may interfere with effective interventions during this period of time: language barriers, systems barriers, differing perceptions of professional roles, family priorities, and the family's belief system. Each is briefly elaborated in the paragraphs that follow.

Language is the primary means of access to understanding, relationships, and services. It is also "one of the most significant markers of ethnic diversity" (Green, 1982, p. 68). Whenever someone is operating in a second language, they are putting more effort into the communication. Thus, families may be frustrated by difficulties in communication. Even if they speak and understand English, the language of interventionists is often highly technical. When family members do not speak the language of the interventionist, they must rely on interpreters who may or may not provide accurate information. That "something got lost in the translation" is an understatement in many situations. Because few programs are able to call upon interpreters who have both the language and the intervention skills, translations are often imperfect. Many times younger or extended family members are asked to interpret, and their own concerns may shape the information being transmitted. In other instances adequate translations do not exist for the concepts that are being shared. Just as English speakers are unable to express the fine distinctions among the kinds of snow that Alaskan Eskimos describe easily, so too is it difficult to explain the nuances of behavior management to someone who has never felt that it was necessary to change a young child's behavior.

Focusing so much attention on a situation that tradition tells them is to be handled in another way may be a part of the culture shock that some families experience when they encounter interventionists. In a world in which an estimated 17 million children from developing countries die each year from a combination of poor nutrition, diarrhea, malaria, pneumonia, measles, whooping cough, and tetanus, the luxury of early intervention programs can be overwhelming (Chandler, 1986). Many families, particularly those who have been in refugee camps, have come from situations in which basic sanitation, nutrition, and health care were nonexistent. To arrive in a country in which specialized services exist for young children with disabilities is almost unbelievable; it may take time for them to accept the services. In addition, systems are not typically organized to be responsive to cultural differences. Translating agency brochures into Farsi, Spanish, Vietnamese, Tagalog, or other languages and leaving them in the racks at the agency does not respond to family needs. Strategies for reaching out to groups using the structures that are part of the culture—such as sharing information about services with elders, religious leaders, healers, political leaders, cultural advocacy groups, patriarchs, or matriarchs—may be the most effective way to infuse information into the entire cultural community (Lynch, 1987).

Family–professional partnerships in treatment and education are now being emphasized across service delivery systems in the United States (Dunst, Trivette, & Deal, 1988; Hanson, Lynch, & Wayman, 1990; Johnson, McGonigel, & Kaufmann, 1986; Kjerland, 1986; Lynch, Mendoza, & English, 1990; Turnbull & Turnbull, 1990). This focus on including parents and other family members as full participants on the intervention team has not been the typical perspective of many agencies; such participatory decision making is uncommon in many other countries and cultures. Among people from the majority of world cultures, professionals are held in high esteem—particularly teachers and healers. Thus, expecting families from many cultural groups to be assertive, talkative participants in developing and evaluating services for their children is unrealistic. In fact, the implied definition of active participant typically varies from one culture to another (Lynch & Stein, 1987). Asking parents to state their concerns and priorities to the interventionist in a formal meeting may be an extremely upsetting and embarrassing request that adds to the family's confusion and culture shock. However, this does not mean that their concerns, priorities, and resources should be ignored. Rather, a slower approach, more informal strategies, and careful observation of what each family prefers will probably be more effective than direct approaches.

Family priorities should guide all interventions with young children with disabilities, but they are especially important when working with families from cultures that are different from the interventionist's. Culture shock may emerge as families who have recently arrived in the United States encounter priorities that differ dramatically from their own. For example, many mainstream United States families regard toilet training as a crucial milestone that should occur as soon as possible; they regard independent feeding as an important step in development; and they are eager to enroll their children in toddler and preschool programs that emphasize educational activities and experiences. Members of other cultures do not always feel the same way. In other cultures, there is typically less pressure around toilet training. In many Asian, Southeast Asian, and Pacific Island cultures, young children are not diapered. Adults expect young

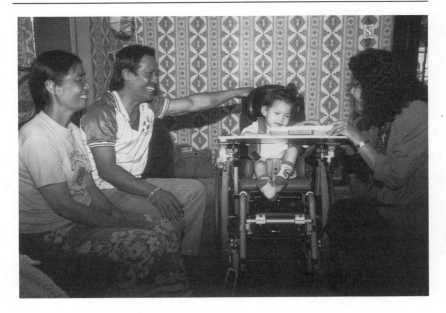

children to relieve themselves freely, and both the child and the adult are simply washed as needed. Breastfeeding may continue much longer among other cultural groups and then be followed by an extended period of adults or older children feeding the youngest child. Because *interdependence* rather than *independence* is more often the value, caring for a younger child or one who is disabled is not viewed as burdensome. Additionally, home and family are viewed as the appropriate place for young children to be. Educational programs for children under age six or seven are not commonplace, and families prefer not to send their children away from home at such an early age. Any intervention that is designed will have a much greater likelihood of success if family priorities form the foundation of the plan.

Finally, the family's belief system will affect the degree of culture shock that family members experience. If a family believes that all that happens is attributable to fate or is in the hands of God, seeking to control any situation will seem contradictory, if not blasphemous. If a family believes that women should be shielded from all outside influences, the interventionist's desire to make home visits or to have both parents participate in program activities may cause conflict or confusion. If a family believes that a traditional shaman has the power to exorcise the evil spirits that cause illness, they may not see the need for sophisticated medical, diagnostic tests. The recommendations that interventionists make so readily may seem extremely strange to the family and may increase culture shock.

Long-Term Residents

In many areas of the country, interventionists work with families from diverse cultures who have been in the United States for many years; many times, the parents have even been born here. But these families have not adopted the beliefs, values, and language of the dominant culture. In many barrios, Spanish is the primary language, and customs are an amalgamation of those from the residents' original culture and the mainstream U.S. culture. Many large cities have Chinatowns or Japantowns that have existed for decades with few changes. Although the concept of culture shock does not make sense when describing the reactions of families who have maintained such close ties to their original culture and language, there are explanations for their reluctance to get involved with the new culture and the system. Lack of trust of the system, different priorities, and decisions about the degree of acculturation that they desire may interfere with effective relationships with intervention programs.

When many of these families first came to the United States, there was considerably less attention being paid to cultural pluralism. Immigrants were expected to assimilate, and little was done to assist them. As a result of this policy, many families were extremely successful in joining the American mainstream; others were not. Those who were not may have had negative experiences with various systems that have caused them to remain isolated and enculturated. Other families may believe that systems are not the appropriate vehicle for taking care of their needs. In many cultures, families are responsible for providing for any family member who cannot provide for him- or herself, and using the services of "outsiders" would represent a loss of face in the cultural community. Finally, some families may have consciously chosen to isolate themselves from the mainstream culture. There is considerable evidence that "sizeable numbers of people prefer a single set of values and behaviors" (Brislin, 1981, p. 290). Maintaining the values, beliefs, language, and practices that are understood and comfortable is more attractive to some families than risking loss of some of those aspects of their lives through exposure to another culture.

SENSITIZING THE INTERVENTIONIST TO THE IMPACT OF CULTURE SHOCK

Throughout this chapter, the concept of culture shock has been viewed as a two-way street. Just as families from different cultures may be confused, frustrated, or upset by their encounters with the mainstream culture, interventionists may also be uncomfortable with their encounters with practices that differ from their own. Interventionists may discover that they disapprove of practices that they encounter, or they may find that some families are engaging in behaviors that are generally unacceptable in the United States. In addition to the culture shock that they may experience, interventionists may also have concerns about their lack of cross-cultural training and the lack of time to assist families to the extent that they would like.

For example, in the United States, the majority of interventionists are women. They are accustomed to lives in which they are free to make decisions, earn money, and speak openly on any subject. In many other countries, women do not have the same rights; even within the United States, groups may differ radically in their views of women's roles and rights. Wives may defer to husbands or to their mother-in-law. Although it is their responsibility to carry out whatever is decided, they may have little or no role in decision making. For interventionists, these situations may be very difficult; however, advocating for the rights of the mother would be a direct affront to the cultural tradition, and that may be upsetting to her and to the rest of the family.

In rare instances, interventionists may encounter practices that they find difficult to accept. Unfamiliar foods such as snake, squid, sweetbreads, or Rocky Mountain oysters; healing practices such as coining; or purification rituals that keep mother and newborn separate for several weeks following delivery are often difficult for the mainstream interventionist to understand and accept. Consequently, the interventionist may experience some of the same emotional turmoil in working with the family that the family is feeling toward the new culture. Anger, frustration, and a desire to pull away are normal. There is nothing wrong, or even unusual, about these sensations; however, they do signal a need for the interventionist to assess his or her feelings, seek consultation from colleagues, and decide whether they can continue to be effective with the family. In most instances, a short time-out and a discussion with a colleague who is knowledgeable about the culture are all that is needed to regain one's equilibrium. Now and then, another interventionist may need to be assigned to the family.

Separate from the issues of culture shock are the concerns that many interventionists express about their lack of cross-cultural training and the time demands of effective intercultural interactions. Although professionals are typically well trained in their own disciplines, few have been trained to work with families from cultures different from their own. Even those who come from the same culture or speak the same language may represent different socioeconomic strata or educational levels and find it difficult to relate to families with complete comfort. One of the goals of this book is to assist interventionists in the field as they develop cross-cultural skills; another is to provide a book that can be used in university classes so that students in training in the 1990s will enter their professions with the skills and knowledge that will be needed as we move into the next century.

The issue of the time that it takes to learn cross-cultural skills and to work with families from diverse cultures is less easily solved. Interventionists are currently overburdened by growing caseloads and new demands; the range and extent of many families' needs strain the capability of the service delivery system. However, the time spent working respectfully and sensitively with families from different cultures is a sound investment, for it may ensure that needed intervention occurs.

SUMMARY

Working effectively with families from cultures that differ from one's own requires an understanding of one's own beliefs and values as well as a recognition that one's language, culture, and ethnicity influence interactions. As the demographics of the United States change to include growing numbers of people from Mexico, Central and South America, Asia, Southeast Asia, Africa, central Europe, and the Middle East, the need to work cross-culturally will increase. This brings new opportunities as well as new demands. Families and interventionists may experience confusion, alienation, and general discomfort as they struggle to understand and appreciate each other's perspectives. This discomfort, sometimes referred to as culture shock, typically occurs in predictable phases. After initial excitement and enthusiasm about the new culture, people may become overwhelmed and disenchanted. Positive feelings may turn negative; enjoyment of the new challenges may be replaced by withdrawal, anger, and frustration. Although neither families nor interventionists can be effective when they are experiencing the negative aspects of culture shock, the disillusionment can be overcome. Time, understanding, continued exposure, and a sensitive mediator can be crucial to success for everyone involved.

REFERENCES

Ball-Rokeach, S.J. (1973). From pervasive ambiguity to a definition of the situation. *Sociometry, 36*, 3–13.

Bohm, D. (1980). On insight and its significance for science, education, and values. In D. Sloan (Ed.), *Education and values* (pp. 7–22). New York: Teachers College Press.

Brislin, R.W. (1981). *Cross-cultural encounters: Face-to-face interaction.* New York: Pergamon Press.

Brislin, R.W., Cushner, K., Cherrie, C., & Yong, M. (1986). *Intercultural interactions: A practical guide.* Beverly Hills: Sage Publications.

Brown, R., & Lenneberg, E. (1965). Studies in linguistic relativity. In H. Proshansky & B. Seidenberg (Eds.), *Basic studies in social psychology* (pp. 244–252). New York: Holt, Rinehart and Winston.

Byrnes, F.C. (1966). Role shock: An occupational hazard of American technical assistants abroad. *Annals of the American Academy of Political and Social Science, 368,* 95–108.

Chandler, W.U. (1986). Investing in children. In L. Brown, W.U. Chandler, C. Flavin, C. Pollock, S. Postel, L. Starke, & E.C. Wolfe (Eds.), *State of the world 1986* (pp. 159–176). New York: W.W. Norton.

Draine, C., & Hall, B. (1986). *Culture shock! Indonesia.* Singapore: Times Books International.

Dunst, C.J., Trivette, C.M., & Deal, A.G. (1988). *Enabling and empowering families: Principles and guidelines for practice.* Cambridge, MA: Brookline Books.

Green, J.W. (1982). *Cultural awareness in the human services.* Englewood Cliffs, NJ: Prentice Hall.

Gullahorn, J., & Gullahorn, J. (1963). An extension of the U-curve hypothesis. *Journal of Social Issues, 19*(3), 33–47.

Guthrie, G.M. (1975). A behavioral analysis of culture learning. In R.W. Brislin & W.J. Lonner (Eds.), *Cross-cultural perspectives on learning* (pp. 95–115). New York: John Wiley & Sons.

Hanson, M.J., Lynch, E.W., & Wayman, K.I. (1990). Honoring the cultural diversity of families when gathering data. *Topics in Early Childhood Special Education, 10*(1), 112–131.

Johnson, B.H., McGonigel, M.J., & Kaufmann, R.K. (Eds.). (1989). *Guidelines and recommended practices for the individualized family service plan.* (Available from Association for the Care of Children's Health, 3615 Wisconsin Ave., N.W., Washington, DC 20016)

Kjerland, L. (1986). *Early intervention tailor made.* Eagan, MN: Project Dakota.

Klineberg, O., & Hull, F. (1979). *At a foreign university.* New York: Praeger.

Lynch, E.W. (1987). Families from different cultures. In M. Bristol & C. Kasari (Eds.), *The Family Support Network series: Monograph one* (pp. 80–88). Moscow: Family Support Network Project, University of Idaho.

Lynch, E.W., Mendoza, J. M., & English, K. (1990). *Implementing individualized family service plans in California: Final report.* (Available from Early Intervention Programs, Department of Developmental Services, 1600 9th St., Sacramento, CA 95814)

Lynch, E.W., & Stein, R.C. (1987). Parent participation by ethnicity: A comparison of Hispanic, Black, and Anglo families. *Exceptional Children, 54,* 105–111.

Oberg, K. (1958). *Culture shock and the problem of adjustment to new cultural environments.* Washington, DC: Department of State, Foreign Service Institute.

Oberg, K. (1960). Cultural shock: Adjustment to new cultural environments. *Practical Anthropology, 7,* 177–82.

Smalley, W. (1963). Culture shock, language shock, and the shock of self-discovery. *Practical Anthropology, 10,* 49–56.

Solnit, A., & Stark, M. (1961). Mourning the birth of a defective child. *The Psychoanalytic Study of the Child, 16,* 523–527.

Turnbull, A.P., & Turnbull, H.R. (1990). *Families, professionals, and exceptionality: A special partnership* (2nd ed.). Columbus, OH: Charles E. Merrill.

chapter 3 ─────────────

DEVELOPING CROSS-CULTURAL COMPETENCE

Eleanor W. Lynch

Everything man is and does is modified by learning and is therefore malleable.
— *Edward T. Hall, Beyond Culture (1976, p. 42)*

Culture is the widening of the mind and of the spirit.
— *Jawaharal Nehru*

Culture is akin to being the observer through the one-way mirror; everything we see is from our own perspective. It is only when we join the observed on the other side that it is possible to see ourselves and others clearly—but getting to the other side of the glass presents many challenges. Achieving cross-cultural competence requires that we lower our defenses, take risks, and practice behaviors that may feel unfamiliar and uncomfortable. It requires a flexible mind, an open heart, and a willingness to accept alternative perspectives. It may mean setting aside some beliefs that are cherished to make room for others whose value is unknown; and it may mean changing what we think, what we say, and how we behave. But there are rewards—the reward of assisting families who need someone who can help them bridge two disparate cultures as well as the reward of knowing more about ourselves and becoming more effective interpersonally.

This chapter focuses on the knowledge and skills that interventionists can use to help build bridges between themselves and families who come from cultures different from their own. It is organized into three major areas: 1) self-awareness; 2) culture-specific awareness and understanding; and 3) communication issues, including working with interpreters and translators. The material presented suggests specific strategies that can be used to assist interventionists to improve their ability to work sensitively and effectively with families from cultures different from their own. It is designed to be used by those who are just beginning to develop cross-cultural competence as well as to provide a refresher for those who are skilled in cross-cultural interactions. Although built

───────────

The section of the chapter titled "Working with Interpreters and Translators" was contributed by Samuel Q. Chan, Ph.D.

upon openness and a willingness to try new ways of interacting, the strategies are not just an experiential splash in unknown waters; they are, instead, the beginning steps in a long journey toward discovering new ways of knowing oneself and others. They require action, practice, review, feedback, and evaluation. As Storti (1989, p. 51) so aptly stated in *The Art of Crossing Cultures:* "The old proverb notwithstanding, we cannot put ourselves in someone else's shoes; or, rather, we can, but it's still our own feet we will feel." Although it may be impossible to feel or experience what someone else is feeling, becoming more culturally competent can help interventionists understand, appreciate, and support families more effectively.

The elements of cross-cultural competence for interventionists have been described by Cross, as cited by Chan (1990). Chan listed three critical elements in building cross-cultural competence: 1) self-awareness, 2) knowledge of information specific to each culture, and 3) skills that enable the individual to engage in successful interactions. Hanson, Lynch, and Wayman (1990) discussed four slightly different but related elements: 1) clarification of the interventionist's own values and assumptions, 2) collection and analysis of ethnographic information related to the community in which the family resides, 3) determination of the degree to which the family operates transculturally, and 4) examination of the family's orientation to specific childrearing issues. Researchers and theorists in intercultural communication continue to work toward unified theories of cross-cultural competence and communication, particularly in relation to effective functioning in overseas assignments (e.g., Abe & Wiseman, 1983; Hammer, 1989; Kealey & Ruben, 1983; Ruben, 1989; Spitzberg, 1989; Spitzberg & Cupach, 1984). This chapter does not presume to provide answers to questions that these theorists are posing nor does it deal with successful interactions overseas. Instead, it focuses on strategies that have been demonstrated to be effective through research and clinical experience working with families in the United States whose cultural, racial, ethnic, or language background is different from that of the interventionist. According to Brislin, Cushner, Cherrie, and Yong (1986) the goals of cross-cultural competence are threefold. When applied to service providers who work with families from diverse cultures, the goals are to assist interventionists to: 1) feel comfortable and effective in their interactions and relationships with families whose cultures differ from their own, 2) interact in ways that enable families from different cultures to feel positive about the interactions and the interventionists, and 3) accomplish the goals that each family and interventionist establish.

SELF-AWARENESS

Everyone has a culture, but often individuals are not aware of the behaviors, habits, and customs that are culturally based (Althen, 1988). According to Hall (1976):

> There is not one aspect of human life that is not touched and altered by culture. This means personality, how people express themselves (including shows of emotion), the way they think, how they move, how problems are solved, how their cities are planned and laid out, how transportation systems function and are organized, as well as how economic and government systems are put together and function. (pp. 16–17)

Although this is true for all people, Anglo-Europeans who are part of the dominant or mainstream United States culture may have the least awareness of the ways in which their culture influences their behavior and interactions. This is true because Anglo-Europeans have predominated in the United States, and their culture, customs, and habits have shaped the society more than any other single group. In addition, the "melting pot" to which America aspired during the early waves of immigration also took its toll on the diversity among Anglo-European groups; the diminishing of these early immigrants' roots has resulted in some mainstream Americans feeling that they do not have a culture, that they are "cultureless."

To understand and appreciate fully the diversity that exists among the families that interventionists serve, interventionists must first understand and appreciate their own culture. Self-awareness (Chan, 1990; Tiedt & Tiedt, 1990) is the first step on the journey toward cross-cultural competence. But how does cultural self awareness begin? What are the steps? And how does cultural self-awareness lead to improved understanding of other cultures? This section of the chapter addresses those questions.

Cultural self-awareness begins with an exploration of one's own heritage. Issues such as place of origin, time of immigration, reasons for immigration, language(s) spoken, and the place of the family's first settlement in the United States all help to define one's own cultural heritage. The political leanings, jobs, status, beliefs, and values of the first immigrants help to paint a cultural picture of one's family as do the economic, social, and vocational changes that subsequent generations have undergone. Perhaps the most enriching way to gather this information is through the recollections of the oldest family members as they tell stories of their early lives and the lives of their grandparents and great-grandparents. Although oral history is often neglected among mainstream Americans, it can provide a wonderful bridge between generations. In some families, oral traditions may be supplemented by photographs, journals, family albums, or notes of important events in family Bibles. When none of the above is available, a document search in county court houses can reveal clues to the family's past through marriage records; records of births and deaths; and titles to lands bought, sold, or occupied. In some areas of the country, church or parish records provide a wealth of information about family history. Some public libraries also contain extensive collections specifically for those interested in genealogy; more recently, computer-based search strategies have become available through electronic genealogy forums and bulletin boards.

Learning about one's own roots is the first step in determining how one's values, beliefs, customs, and behaviors have been shaped by culture. This new knowledge helps individuals separate the ways of thinking, believing, and behaving that have been assumed to be universal from those that are based upon cultural beliefs and biases. When one has explored one's own cultural heritage, the second step of discovery can begin.

The second step is to examine some of the values, behaviors, beliefs, and customs that are identified with one's own cultural heritage. Although educational level, socioeconomic status, and degree of identification and affiliation with one's culture are potent forces in shaping one's value system and behavior, there are certain salient characteristics for which cultures are known. (For a more in-depth description of the values and beliefs of the cultural groups addressed in this book, see Part II, Chapters 4–11.) For example, Althen (1988) identified eight values and assumptions that characterize dominant American culture:

1. Importance of individualism and privacy
2. Belief in the equality of all individuals
3. Informality in interactions with others
4. Emphasis on the future, change, and progress
5. Belief in the general goodness of humanity
6. Emphasis on the importance of time and punctuality
7. High regard for achievement, action, work, and materialism
8. Pride in interactional styles that are direct and assertive

Robertiello and Hoguet (1987), in discussing the culture of white Anglo-Saxon Protestants (WASPs) in the United States, listed 39 values that underpin WASP behavior. Among these are stoicism in adversity, honesty, courage, frugality, resourcefulness, optimism, fairness, wit and sense of humor, physical attractiveness, being cheerful, and having good taste.

Interventionists who are members of the Anglo-European American culture, or are strongly influenced by it, may want to examine these values to determine their degree of identification with each and the extent to which these values affect their practice. For example, interventionists who value punctuality and careful scheduling may need to examine their frustration with families who place less emphasis on clock and calendar time. Interventionists who value optimism and humor may discover that they are uncomfortable with clients who are depressed or those whom they see as complainers. Interventionists who value frugality may have trouble understanding why a family with very limited resources has just purchased a video cassette recorder (VCR). Interventionists who pride themselves in sensitive but direct communications may have difficulty with families who do not look them in the eye or those who nod "yes" when the answer is "no"; those who value privacy may have difficulty understanding why a preschooler is still sleeping in the parents' bedroom.

Likewise, interventionists who do not come from the mainstream culture of the United States and are not highly identified with it must examine their values and beliefs in relation to the families that they serve. Cultures that value interdependence over independence, cooperation above competition, authoritative rather than permissive childrearing, and interaction more than efficiency may need to examine how these values affect their practice. For example, families who are striving to toilet train their child at a very young age, are encouraging self-feeding, and are leaving the child with nonfamily babysitters from infancy on may be puzzling to interventionists who place a higher value on interdependence than independence. Or, when a young child talks back or interrupts adult conversations, many Anglo-European American parents view the child's behavior as his or her right to personal expression. Native American, Asian, Latino, and African American parents and interventionists may see the same behavior as disrespectful and obnoxious.

The examples in the previous paragraphs illustrate the ways in which cultural beliefs may affect practice. All cultures have built-in biases, and there are no right or wrong cultural beliefs. However, there are differences that must be acknowledged. Cultural self-awareness is the bridge to learning about other cultures. It is not possible to be truly sensitive to someone else's culture until one is sensitive to one's own and the impact that cultural customs, values, beliefs, and behaviors have on practice. For a further examination of one's personal cultural heritage, the reader is encouraged to review the activity "A Cultural Journey," at the end of this chapter.

CULTURE-SPECIFIC AWARENESS AND UNDERSTANDING

After interventionists become familiar with their own culture and its effects on the ways in which they think and behave, the foundation for learning about other cultures has been laid. The next step is to learn about other cultures through readings, interactions, and involvement. As Storti (1989, p. 92) stated: "The success of any interaction, in or outside our own culture, rests primarily on our ability to anticipate the behavior of others, including their reactions to our behavior. If we cannot do this, . . . then even the possibility of successful interaction is largely precluded." Culture-specific information helps explain the cultural values, beliefs, and behaviors that are encountered in cross-cultural interactions. Because Part II of this book provides a wealth of culture-specific information, this section offers only a brief introduction to the topic.

Gathering Culture-Specific Information

There are many ways to learn about other cultures. Perhaps the four most effective ways are: 1) learning through studying and reading about the culture, 2) talking and working with individuals from the culture who can act as cultural guides or mediators, 3) participating in the daily life of another culture, and

4) learning the language of the other culture. Although reading is not sufficient, it may be the best place to start when gathering information about other cultures. Readings may range from history and geography to poetry, biography, and fiction. Authors may be from the culture or writing about the culture, but a key to developing a new understanding is to view the culture from its members' point of view. Therefore, books by authors from the culture provide critical insights and perspectives that are not available through other sources. It has been said that biography and fiction are often more telling than history; a list of books that focus on cross-cultural interactions from many points of view is provided in Suggested Readings, at the end of this volume. Some of these books focus on encountering mainstream culture in the United States; others focus on encounters with other cultures. In some, culture is the major theme; in others it is the backdrop. Although the list is neither exhaustive nor complete, it does give the reader an opportunity to explore cultural encounters and other world views through literature.

A second way to learn about other cultures is through open discussion and interpersonal sharing with members of another culture. These cultural mediators or guides can highlight feelings, beliefs, and practices that may be unfamiliar. From their own experiences of living bi- or transculturally, they can describe the world in a way that allows monocultural people to reframe their perceptions. Friends, colleagues, and neighbors can all serve as cultural guides; the important prerequisites are trust and respect of each other and each others' culture. It is also important to recognize that both parties will filter their information through a personal lens that has been affected by all of their life experiences; thus, no individual can accurately portray the range of his or her own culture's beliefs, values, and practices.

Participating in the life of the community of diverse cultures is a third way to increase cross-cultural understanding. Celebrating holidays, joining in wor-

ship, and getting involved in community projects are all ways in which individuals can increase their understanding and appreciation of different cultures. This involvement is different from entering as a helping professional, an observer, or an academic voyeur (Green, 1982). It is entering the community as a guest of friends or colleagues from the culture with the express purpose of increasing one's own participation, awareness, and understanding.

Finally, learning the language of another culture is one of the strongest commitments to learning about and understanding that culture. Because so much of what is described as culture is reflected in language, a hallmark of cross-cultural competence is language learning. In addition to gaining knowledge about the culture through language, being bi- or multilingual opens many doors to additional opportunities to learn and provides immediate access to families and colleagues with other-language backgrounds.

Culture-Specific Issues and Intervention

General information about cultures that differ from one's own is essential to overall awareness and understanding of cultural differences; however, it may also be helpful for interventionists to have very specific information related to cultural views of children and childrearing practices, family roles and structure, views of disability and its causes, health and healing practices, and views of change and intervention (Hanson et al., 1990). These issues are so intertwined with culture and so critical in working with families who have a child with a disability that they merit special attention. Although each is addressed in the chapters included in Part II of this book, the following paragraphs provide a conceptual framework for determining what questions to ask.

Wayman, Lynch, and Hanson (1990) suggested a set of "Guidelines for the Home Visitor" that can be used to learn more about the family's cultural values and preferences within the context of a family systems approach to intervention. Designed for use in early childhood settings, these guidelines could easily be modified to fit families whose children are older (see Table 3.1). Although the guidelines are not to be used as a checklist or interview protocol, they do include questions about family attitudes, beliefs, and practices that could influence the services and the approach to providing services. They can be used to help interventionists determine the kinds of questions and issues that are often mediated by culture and to assist in matching the interventions to the family's way of life.

A cardinal rule in working with all families is to make no assumptions about their concerns, priorities, and resources. This is even more critical when the family's cultural background and identification are different from the interventionist's. However, becoming familiar with culture-specific information and determining its relevance to individual families and family members can reduce the potential tension between interventionists and families from different cultural backgrounds.

Table 3.1. Guidelines for the home visitor

Part I—Family structure and childrearing practices

- Family structure

  - Family composition
    - Who are the members of the family system?
    - Who are the key decision makers?
    - Is decision making related to specific situations?
    - Is decision making individual or group oriented?
    - Do family members all live in the same household?
    - What is the relationship of friends to the family system?
    - What is the hierarchy within the family? Is status related to gender or age?

  - Primary caregiver(s)
    - Who is the primary caregiver?
    - Who else participates in the caregiving?
    - What is the amount of care given by mother versus others?
    - How much time does the infant spend away from the primary caregiver?
    - Is there conflict between caregivers regarding appropriate practices?
    - What ecological/environmental issues impinge upon general caregiving (i.e., housing, jobs, etc.)?

- Childrearing practices
  - Family feeding practices
  - What are the family feeding practices?
  - What are the mealtime rules?
  - What types of foods are eaten?
  - What are the beliefs regarding breastfeeding and weaning?
  - What are the beliefs regarding bottle feeding?
  - What are the family practices regarding transitioning to solid food?
  - Which family members prepare food?
  - Is food purchased or homemade?
  - Are there any taboos related to food preparation or handling?
  - Which family members feed the child?
  - What is the configuration of the family mealtime?
  - What are the family's views on independent feeding?
  - Is there a discrepancy among family members regarding the beliefs and practices related to feeding an infant/toddler?

  - Family sleeping patterns
    - Does the infant sleep in the same room/bed as the parents?
    - At what age is the infant moved away from close proximity to the mother?
    - Is there an established bedtime?
    - What is the family response to an infant when he or she awakes at night?
    - What practices surround daytime napping?

  - Family's response to disobedience and aggression
    - What are the parameters of acceptable child behavior?
    - What form does the discipline take?
    - Who metes out the disciplinary action?

  - Family's response to a crying infant
    - Temporal qualities—How long before the caregiver picks up a crying infant?
    - How does the caregiver calm an upset infant?

(continued)

Table 3.1. (continued)

Part II—Family perceptions and attitudes

- Family perception of child's disability
  - Are there cultural or religious factors that would shape family perceptions?
  - To what/where/whom does the family assign responsibility for their child's disability?
  - How does the family view the role of fate in their lives?
  - How does the family view their role in intervening with their child? Do they feel they can make a difference or do they consider it hopeless?
- Family's perception of health and healing
  - What is the family's approach to medical needs?
    - Do they rely solely on Western medical services?
    - Do they rely solely on holistic approaches?
    - Do they utilize a combination of these approaches?
  - Who is the primary medical provider or conveyer of medical information?
    - Family members? Elders? Friends? Folk healers? Family doctor? Medical specialists?
  - Do all members of the family agree on approaches to medical needs?
- Family's perception of help-seeking and intervention
  - From whom does the family seek help—family members or outside agencies/individuals?
  - Does the family seek help directly or indirectly?
  - What are the general feelings of the family when seeking assistance—ashamed, angry, demand as a right, view as unnecessary?
  - With which community systems does the family interact (educational/medical/social)?
  - How are these interactions completed (face-to-face, telephone, letter)?
  - Which family member interacts with other systems?
  - Does that family member feel comfortable when interacting with other systems?

Part III—Language and communication styles

- Language
  - To what degree:
    - Is the home visitor proficient in the family's native language?
    - Is the family proficient in English?
  - If an interpreter is used:
    - With which culture is the interpreter primarily affiliated?
    - Is the interpreter familiar with the colloquialisms of the family members' country or region of origin?
    - Is the family member comfortable with the interpreter? Would the family member feel more comfortable with an interpreter of the same sex?
  - If written materials are used, are they in the family's native language?
- Interaction styles
  - Does the family communicate with each other in a direct or indirect style?
  - Does the family tend to interact in a quiet manner or a loud manner?
  - Do family members share feelings when discussing emotional issues?
  - Does the family ask you direct questions?
  - Does the family value a lengthy social time at each home visit unrelated to the early childhood services program goals?
  - Is it important for the family to know about the home visitor's extended family? Is the home visitor comfortable sharing that information?

From Wayman, K.I., Lynch, E.W., & Hanson, M.J. (1990). Home-based early childhood services: Cultural sensitivity in a family systems approach. Topics in Early Childhood Special Education, 10, 65–66. Copyright © 1990 by PRO-ED, Inc. Reprinted by permission.

Cautions

Throughout this book, several caveats are emphasized, and they are especially relevant to gathering and using culture-specific information. Culture is only one of the characteristics that determine individuals' and families' attitudes, values, beliefs, and ways of behaving. Socioeconomic status, educational level, degree of affiliation and identification with their roots, the language(s) spoken, the length of time that they have been in the United States, and their reasons for emigrating are all important variables that shape who they are and what they believe and desire. Assuming that culture-specific information gathered from books, cultural mediators, or language learning applies to all individuals from the cultural group is not only inaccurate but also dangerous—it can lead to stereotyping that diminishes rather than enhances cross-cultural competence. When applying culture-specific information to an individual or family, it is wise to proceed with caution.

CROSS-CULTURAL COMMUNICATION

Communication, both verbal and nonverbal, is critical to cross-cultural competence. Both sending messages and understanding messages that are being received are prerequisites to effective interpersonal interactions. Because language and culture are so inextricably bound, communicating with those from different cultural backgrounds is very complex. When the language of the family and that of the interventionist are different, it is clear that communication will be severely compromised; however, speaking the same language does not guarantee communication. This section of the chapter focuses on general principles of effective cross-cultural communication, nonverbal communication, and working with interpreters and translators.

General Principles of Effective Cross-Cultural Communication

Communication in High-Context and Low-Context Cultures

Cultures differ in the amount of information that is explicitly transmitted through words versus the amount of information that is transmitted through the context of the situation, the relationship, and physical cues (Hall, 1976, 1984). High-context cultures rely less on verbal communication than on understanding through shared experience, history, and implicit messages (Hecht, Andersen, & Ribeau, 1989). Fewer words are spoken and less emphasis is placed upon verbal interactions. As might be expected, high-context cultures are more attuned to nonverbal cues and messages. Asian, Native American, Arab, Latino, and African American are examples of high-context cultures in which meaning does not have to be communicated through words. Hecht et al. described high-context communication by stating, "thus facial expressions, tensions, movements, speed of interaction, location of the interaction, and other subtle 'vibes' are likely to be perceived by and have more meaning for people from high-context cultures" (p. 177). High-context culture is best understood by considering examples in one's own life in which high-context communication is used. For instance, couples who have lived together for many years, families, twins, and long-term colleagues often use abbreviated forms of communication that are very meaningful to them but nearly uninterpretable by outsiders. A look, a word, or a gesture may convey the equivalent of paragraphs of spoken words.

Individuals from low-context cultures, such as Anglo-European American, Swiss, German, and Scandinavian, typically focus on precise, direct, logical, verbal communication and are often impatient with communicators and communications that do not get to the point quickly (Hecht et al., 1989). Members of low-context cultures may not process gestures, environmental clues, and unarticulated moods that are central to effective communication in high-context cultures. Thus, communication between high- and low-context cultures often leads to misunderstanding and dissatisfaction for both parties.

High-context cultures tend to be more formal, more reliant on hierarchies, and more deeply rooted in the past (Hall, 1976). In contrast, low-context cultures are more informal, allow more equality in interaction, and have less knowledge about and reverence for the past. As a result, high-context cultures may change more slowly but provide a healthy stability for group members. Low-context cultures may be more responsive to and comfortable with change but lack a sense of continuity and connection with the past.

When families and interventionists differ in the level of context that they use in communication, there may be misunderstandings. On the one hand, lots of talking, clearly specified verbal directions, and detailed demonstrations may seem insensitive and mechanistic to individuals from high-context cultures. They may feel that the talking is proof that the other individual does not truly understand them and cannot, therefore, be of help. On the other hand, members of low-context cultures may be uncomfortable with long pauses and silences, cryptic sentences, and indirect modes of communication such as storytelling. They may feel that these things are time wasters or signs of resistance.

To help bridge this gap, it is the interventionist's responsibility to become aware of the level of context that families use in their communication with outsiders and to adapt to the style that is comfortable for the family. It may often mean that interventionists must slow down, listen more than they talk, observe family communication patterns, and consult with cultural guides or mediators to begin to pace their interactions to the family's communication style.

Nonverbal Communication

Nonverbal behavior often speaks louder than words, and the same nonverbal behaviors often have very different meanings from one culture to another. A gesture or facial expression that is accepted as positive or complimentary in one culture may be viewed as negative or even obscene in another. Although no one can be knowledgeable about the cultural and regional interpretations of all non-verbal behavior, some of the basic issues warrant discussion. The following paragraphs highlight differences that interventionists may encounter, but the discussion is in no way exhaustive. To learn more about the meaning and use of nonverbal behavior across cultures, interventionists may consult members of the culture, read the chapters in Part II of this book, and consult guidebooks describing cultural "do's" and "don'ts."

Eye Contact and Facial Expressions In Anglo-European American culture, eye contact is valued in interpersonal interactions. When one is speaking or being spoken to, one is expected to make eye contact with brief glances in another direction throughout the exchange. Among Anglo-European Americans, trustworthiness, sincerity, and directness are communicated through this accepted form of eye contact (Asante & Davis, 1989). However, eye contact has different interpretations among other cultural groups. Johnson (1971) stated that among African Americans, making eye contact with someone in authority is viewed as disrespectful. Among Asian groups, eye contact between strangers may be considered shameful; and prolonged eye contact may be interpreted as disrespectful in Latino cultures (Randall-David, 1989).

Facial expressions are also subject to various interpretations across cultures. Smiling or laughing is often used to mask other emotions in Asian cultures (Althen, 1988; Randall-David, 1989). Although it may seem incongruous to an interventionist from another culture, it is not unlikely that an Asian family member may smile or laugh softly when describing something that is confusing, embarrassing, or even sad—an event that the interventionist regards as "serious." In the author's experience in Indonesia, laughter was often used to cover embarrassment or as a response when a request was made that could not be fulfilled.

Many Anglo-European Americans show emotion through facial expressions. Smiling typically shows happiness or amusement, a set jaw and an intense stare may show anger, and rolling eyes may show disdain. Members of other groups such as Native Americans and Asians may not communicate emotion to the observer through facial expressions unless the observer has a deep understanding of the person and the cultural norm (Althen, 1988).

Proximity and Touching Cultures differ in the amount of social distance with which they are comfortable. Anglo-European Americans tend to maintain a distance of about 3 feet, or an arm's length, between themselves and others during conversations unless they are very familiar with the other person. Many Latinos, southern Europeans, Middle Easterners, and African Americans are comfortable with closer conversational distances, whereas many Asians prefer more space between the speaker and listener (Althen, 1988; Randall-David, 1989). The social distance that is preferred is usually easy to gauge by observing people's movement patterns in an interaction. When people back up, the other person is usually too close for comfort. When they move toward the other person, they are attempting to get closer and reduce the social distance.

The amount and type of physical contact permissible is highly influenced by culture, but generalizations about touching are particularly dangerous because differences across cultures are confounded by differences in gender, age, religion, and personal preference. Although these same issues affect other forms of communication, one is far less likely to get into trouble for an inappropriate word or gesture than an inappropriate touch. Given that this is an area in which a cultural mediator or guide is of special importance, some examples of different interpretations of touch are highlighted.

Among many Chinese and other Asian groups, hugging, back slapping, and handshaking are not typical and should be avoided by the interventionist. In those cultures in which handshaking is used upon a first introduction, the handshake is often not so hearty as that used in the United States. Variations on handshaking such as the *wai* greeting (bringing the palms of the hand together and raising them to the chest or tip of the nose while lowering the head) practiced by East Indians, people from Thailand, and other Asian groups or the elaborated handshaking seen among African Americans are greetings that may or may not be appropriate for an interventionist to use. For example, the *wai* is a general form of greeting that is a signal of respect, whereas the elaborated handshake used by some in the African American community may be a sign of in-group membership that would be inappropriate to use until invited.

Among Muslims and some non-Muslim Middle Easterners, use of the left hand to touch another person, to reach for something, or to take or to pass food is inappropriate (Devine & Braganti, 1986). Because the left hand is associated with more personal bodily functions, it is not used in other ways. Although interventionists who are left handed need not give up writing in this situation, they may choose to limit the use of their left hand for other functions when they are with a traditional family who holds this belief. Shoes and the soles of one's feet are also considered to be unclean. As a result, stretching out one's legs causing the feet to point at someone or touching someone with your feet is not appropriate.

Many Americans show affection for children by patting them on the head. This is not an acceptable form of touch among many Asians who believe that the head is the residence of the soul or among East Indians who may believe that the head is so fragile that it should not be touched (Devine & Braganti, 1986).

As with the other aspects of nonverbal communication, no one can be expected to learn, know, or always behave in ways that are considered to be culturally appropriate for everyone in the situation. It is, however, a sign of respect to learn the patterns of proximity and touch that prevail among those in one's own community and attempt to behave in ways that are not offensive.

Body Language Positions and postures that are taken for granted by those who have been socialized in the United States may have different meanings for those from other countries or other cultures. Standing with one's hands on one's hips can be viewed as extremely hostile by some Asians. Sitting on the top of a desk or perching on the arm of a chair is seen as rude by many Muslims; sitting so that one's head is higher than the elders or chiefs in the room is interpreted as an affront by Samoans. Although there are a number of popular press books available about body language, interventionists must remember that they are typically written from a Western perspective and will not accurately reflect how the same postures will be regarded by individuals from other cultures.

Gestures   Gestures can be used to supplement verbal communication or as symbols that substitute for verbal expression. Research on the cross-cultural interpretation of gestures suggests that members of different cultures claim recognition of 70%–100% of the gestures from other groups, but that their rate of correct interpretation of these gestures was as low as 30% (Schneller, 1989). As a result, gestural language often contributed more to misunderstanding than to more effective communication. This is a critical piece of information when one considers the extent to which individuals rely on gestures when they do not understand one another's language.

Different cultures use body movements to a different extent when communicating. Anglo-European Americans tend to use "moderate" gesturing to accompany their talk (Althen, 1988, p. 141). Although hand and arm movements are used for emphasis, Anglo-European Americans typically do not allow their elbows to go above their shoulders with the exception of waving in greetings or goodbyes, raising a hand in a class, or voting by a show of hands (Althen, 1988). More expansive gestures are construed as too emotional and are carefully avoided by most Anglo-European Americans. Members of other cultures have different norms related to gestures: Some Latinos, Middle Easterners, and southern Europeans use large gestures with considerable arm waving when they communicate (Althen, 1988); Indonesians respect calmness and control in verbal communication and are often uncomfortable with the arm movement that is the norm for Anglo-European Americans. In addition to speaking with those who know the cultural community and its regional variations, it is perhaps most helpful to observe interactions among community members and to try to bring one's own communicative style into synchrony.

Nodding the head up and down is taken as a sign of understanding and agreement in mainstream culture in the United States. This same gesture is interpreted quite differently in many other cultures. Among Asian, Native American, Middle Eastern, and Pacific Island groups, it often means, "I hear you speaking." It does not signal that the listener understands the message nor does it suggest that he or she agrees. However, because disagreeing would be impolite, head nodding is used. Individuals from India signal that they have heard what has been said by moving their head in a figure-eight pattern (Althen, 1988).

Americans tend to beckon to people by pointing the index finger palm up and curling it toward the body. People from other cultures (e.g., Middle Eastern, Asian, East Indian) use this gesture only when summoning animals (Devine & Braganti, 1986). It is never used with children or adults in such cultures.

Finally, gestures that are common in the United States, such as bringing the thumb and index finger together to form a circle and holding it in the air to signify a job well done or the thumbs up sign to signal readiness or praise are obscene gestures among some Latino cultures. Because gestural language is so easily misunderstood, specific to regions of the country, and sometimes specific to one or more generations, it is important for interventionists to periodically consult with others to determine what is and is not appropriate.

Listening to the Family's Perspective

A long-standing difficulty in communication between people who do not share a common language and world view has been the tendency of the dominant group to describe the nondominant group in pejorative terms (Green, 1982). In an attempt to correct these faulty perceptions, anthropologists led by Franz Boas (1943) introduced another perspective. This new perspective suggested that the way to understand the thoughts of another group is to attempt to understand and analyze their experience in terms of their concepts rather then one's own. Perhaps the first element in developing effective communication is to try to see the world from the family's point of view. For example, most interventionists believe strongly in the concept of change. The very choice of title, "interventionist," suggests that there is a belief that by entering into the situation with information, activities, or special expertise positive change will occur. Thus, the interventionist views an early intervention program for an infant with Down syndrome very positively—almost as a necessity. However, not all cultures share the concept that they can influence change or even that change is a good thing. Instead, they accept what is and place value on living harmoniously with what they have been given. They may not want to enroll their infant in an early intervention program, have a physical malformation surgically corrected, or join a support group for families of children with disabilities. Using the interventionist's concepts to analyze the situation, it might be said that the family is noncompliant or refusing treatment. Using the family's concepts, it would be said that intervention is not useful and, in fact, it may interfere with achieving harmony in the situation.

Seeing the world from the family's point of view is not easy nor is it always reinforcing. It is difficult to consider that the approach that the interventionist's culture values so highly is not valued by others. In interventionists' attempts to prove that intervention is "the right thing to do," families may feel harassed and so may distance themselves from the program. Likewise, when a family chooses not to participate or to follow the recommendations of professionals, interventionists feel that they have failed. Cross-cultural understanding and competence can help defuse the situation. If the family feels that the interventionist is truly listening, honoring their right to make decisions, and respecting the decisions that they make, they will not need to pull away and be "lost to follow-up." If interventionists are able to see the situation from the family's point of view, they need not feel that they have failed. Only in those situations in which abuse or neglect are suspected and the situation must be reported should the interventionist's role be unilateral. Given information about all of the options and assistance in problem solving, the majority of families make decisions that are best for the child and the family. Although their decisions may be different from what the interventionist had hoped for and may not correspond to the interventionist's timeline, if the family "owns" a decision, it will be a decision they are likely to implement.

Acknowledging and Respecting Cultural Differences Rather than Minimizing Them

The United States as a melting pot was popularized in a play written by Israel Zangwill in 1909. Zangwill's conception of the country at that time was a fiery crucible in which people of all cultures would be thrown and in which their differences would be melted away resulting in a fusion of strength and the coming of a "new superman" (cited in Tiedt & Tiedt, 1990).

Today, cultural differences are viewed as strengths rather than weaknesses, and the melting pot is no longer an accurate metaphor for the United States. Rather than melting away differences, the emphasis is on celebrating diversity and strengthening society through contact with other attitudes, values, beliefs, and ways of behaving. As a result, cultural differences are not ignored or swept under the rug, but acknowledged, discussed, and valued.

People in the United States speak openly and publicly about many ideas and issues. Rules related to sexual intimacy are now portrayed on billboards, products for personal hygiene are advertised on prime time television, and there are support groups for almost every real or imagined problem. However, discussions of cultural, racial, ethnic, and language diversity between members of different groups are rarely heard. According to Sam Chan (personal communication, May 10, 1991), a person's color is the first thing that we see and the last thing that we talk about. Effective cross-cultural communication includes the willingness to engage in cross-cultural interactions that explore differences openly and respectfully, interactions that dispel myths and open doors to understanding.

Communicating Attitudes Through Words

Attitudes about different groups of people and the ways in which they live and behave are communicated by the words that one uses to describe the people and their practices. Throughout history, in-groups have used pejorative terms to describe out-groups; and many groups, such as Native Americans, were named by others, not by members of their own group (Helms, 1990). To overcome the negative connotations that have come to be associated with certain words and to increase the sense of group identity, the names of many cultural groups have changed over the years.

Perhaps the most obvious changes in name have been associated with African Americans as self-identity has recast vocabulary. As Neal and Allgood-Hill (1990) noted, "negro" was the word used by the Portuguese to describe the slaves that were brought to the United States, a term probably chosen because it meant "black" in Portuguese. Although early slaves had a preference for the term African, negro was the name used by the slave traders and owners. As the ties to and memories of Africa were lessened by time, many slaves chose to be called "colored"—a common appellation until the mid-1960s. With the birth of the black pride movement of the 1960s, "black" became the preferred term. In the 1990s, a number of prominent black Americans published a statement calling for "African-American" to become the descriptor (Neal & Allgood-Hill, 1990).

These changes in the words used to describe a group are not unique to African Americans. Asian has replaced Oriental (Tong, 1990); there is growing emphasis on using the more specific tribal affiliation of Native Americans (LaDue, 1990); and Latino, in some parts of the country, has replaced Hispanic. Although the debate about names has not been settled, each of the changes represents increasing group identity and empowerment. As interventionists, it is important to keep up with these changes and, as stated by Tiedt and Tiedt (1990, p. 12), "demonstrate our awareness of how thinking has changed by our own use of appropriate terms."

General Characteristics of Effective Cross-Cultural Communicators

In addition to the specific communicative behaviors that have been discussed for increasing one's competence in cross-cultural interactions, there is an extensive literature on the characteristics found to be common among those who are successful in cross-cultural settings (Giles & Franklyn-Stokes, 1989). This literature is extremely complex, driven by a multiplicity of sometimes contradictory theories, and complicated by a stronger interest in sojourners' effectiveness overseas than their effectiveness in intercultural interactions at home. However, even though different researchers and different studies have chosen varying theories, definitions, methodologies, and subjects, there are several characteristics that seem to be shared by people who are effective cross-cultural communicators that are intuitively clear. Communication effectiveness is significantly improved when the interventionist:

- Respects individuals from other cultures
- Makes continued and sincere attempts to understand the world from others' points of view

- Is open to new learning
- Is flexible
- Has a sense of humor
- Tolerates ambiguity well
- Approaches others with a desire to learn

Working with Interpreters and Translators

Ideally, there would be enough bilingual-bicultural interventionists to pair families with interventionists who speak their language and understand their culture; however, most service systems are far from reaching that ideal. Until more interventionists with these skills are available, interpreters and translators will be important resources in human services settings. The following paragraphs suggest strategies for using interpreters and translators more effectively and ways of interacting when a third party (the interpreter or translator) is included in the intervention team.

Characteristics of Effective Interpreters

Ideally, an interpreter should be someone who is: 1) proficient in the language (including specific dialect) of the family as well as that of the interventionist, 2) trained and experienced in cross-cultural communication and the principles (and dynamics) of serving as an interpreter, 3) trained in the appropriate professional field relevant to the specific family–interventionist interaction, and 4) able to understand and appreciate the respective cultures of both parties and to convey the more subtle nuances of each with tact and sensitivity. "These interpreters are ideal because they not only translate the interaction but also bridge the culture gap" (Randall-David, 1989, p. 31). Aside from such ideal competencies, the interpreter should minimally have a basic understanding of the specific nature and purpose of the family interaction, the corresponding content areas to be addressed, and their relative significance. They should be able to translate information *accurately,* including important technical terms as well as the client's own words and true meaning, without omitting, adding, paraphrasing, or otherwise changing the intent or substance of the message through personal interpretation. In other words, they should not gloss over details; present their own abbreviated summaries; spontaneously respond to the family's questions or comments (particularly those requiring technical knowledge); "soften" or edit information that they feel may be difficult for family members to accept; or offer their own opinions, interpretations, and advice.

Accurate translation further entails understanding the difference between literal "word-for-word" translation and context translation that correctly conveys the intent of the communication, particularly when selected English words or terms do not have suitable equivalents (Tinloy, Tan, & Leung, 1986). Interpreters also should know how to "guide" the interventionist respectfully and assertively with regard to pacing, responding appropriately to family cues

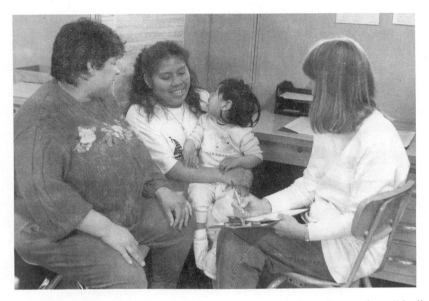

and significant verbal and nonverbal responses, and observing various "dos" and "don'ts." Finally, interpreters should exhibit professionalism in their appearance, sensitivity, and demeanor; their understanding of the importance of honoring family confidentiality; and their obligation to maintain neutrality in their designated role. In other words, they must refrain from pushing the interventionist's and/or their own agenda onto the family and from manipulating the interventionist or the service agency to respond to the family's perceived needs or expectations in ways that are clinically inappropriate.

Using Family Members as Interpreters: Cautions and Concerns

Given the lack of fully qualified interpreters, intermediaries who are friends or other family members are often used to assist interventionists in their interactions with families from different cultural and language backgrounds. Given the qualities described in the preceding paragraphs, the problems that may arise with continued reliance upon intermediaries become more obvious. Even if the individuals are fully bilingual and proficient in the family's native language or specific dialect, communication difficulties and role conflicts may be exacerbated by their personal relationships with the family, by their lack of direct training as an interpreter, and by their limited knowledge of the content of the material and issues that will be addressed in the translation.

The use of immediate family members and relatives as interpreters is particularly problematic. Parents, primary caregivers, or other significant family members are often reluctant and embarrassed to discuss intimate matters with members of the opposite sex or with younger or older family members. As interpreters, family members, in turn, may wish to censor what is disclosed either to shield the family or to keep information within the family, thus minimizing public shame or stigma. The tendency for recent immigrant parents to rely on older siblings as their interpreters often creates significant psychological burdens for these children when involved in clinical interactions or formal meetings with professionals who are serving the family and child with special needs. The role reversals, mutual resentments, and complex family dynamics that can emerge from this process should discourage interventionists from using children, regardless of how mature they seem to be, as interpreters or translators.

Using Non–Family Members as Interpreters: Cautions and Concerns

When utilizing non–family members (whether interpreters from other agencies or bilingual staff), interventionists must be particularly sensitive to the family's right to privacy and their choice of who should serve as an interpreter. There can be major concerns about confidentiality and resistance to working with an interpreter who is unacquainted with the family but from their same community. Problems may also arise when the interpreter has a different ethnic background; country or region of origin; immigration history (e.g., first-wave versus second wave immigrant/refugee); and/or is of a different age, generation, social class, educational level, or gender. Apart from these characteristics, interpreters, like interventionists, also present with varying levels of interpersonal skills, sensitivity, reliability, and overall competence and credibility— all of which have a major impact on the establishment of successful family– interventionist relationships.

Interpreters and Stress

Unfortunately, the exceptionally "good" bilingual staff or experienced interpreters who are well trained; knowledgeable in various aspects of intervention; skilled; sensitive; reliable; and highly regarded by families, colleagues, and their respective ethnic communities are few in number and also extremely vulnerable to burnout. In their work with immigrant/refugee families who have often experienced trauma, profound loss, hardship, culture shock, and continuing struggles for survival in addition to coping with a child with special needs, interpreters may suffer from related stress, fatigue, and possible over identification with the family. This is especially true if they share similar personal experiences. Interpreters must also deal with frequent client "transference" as well as potential "countertransference." This phenomenon occurs when the family focuses their feelings on the interpreter and develops a primary relationship or alliance with him or her in addition to, or instead of, the interventionist. The interpreter, in turn, may fulfill his or her needs and wishes by reinforcing the family's dependency and experiencing reciprocal feelings and attachments. He or she also may feel compelled to establish a more personal, protective relationship with the family as an advocate and extended ethnic "family" member who is expected to attend to the welfare of "one of their own people" in need of special assistance. There is often an accompanying sense of guilt associated with the prospect of ultimately "abandoning" their clients and community since very few, if any, bilingual individuals may be available to "replace" them.

Beyond client-related stresses and obligations, interpreters often face the added pressures and conflicts of working with various interventionists who may be overwhelmed, demanding, difficult, impatient, frustrated, culturally insensitive (if not hostile), and generally unwilling or unable to develop closer relationships with non–English speaking families. Such interventionists may expect the interpreter to be available on very short notice and with little or no preparation for specific types of encounters with families. Interpreters may also be expected to provide their services without compensation, on a voluntary basis, or on their agency's time (Benhamida, 1988). High demand for their unique skills and pressing needs of the families for whom they interpret challenge the interpreters' existing work obligations and career advancement opportunities that require additional time, continuing education, and professional training—all of which must compete with the seemingly "obligatory" provision of hands-on services to families. Thus, while attending to families' needs and their own professional development and responsibilities, interventionists must nurture mutually respectful relationships with interpreters and bilingual staff members.

Interpreter Preparation

Prior to any interaction with a family that requires interpretation, time should be set aside for the preparation of the interpreter. This time should include a briefing in which the interventionist identifies: 1) the major goals and purposes of the contact or session with the family, 2) the important points to be made as well as potentially sensitive areas that will be discussed, 3) specific terms that will be used (the interpreter might review and share corresponding word/phrase equivalents or variations in the family's language), and 4) written documents that will be shown or referred to. The interpreter also may be invited to meet directly with the family before the session to exchange basic background information and establish rapport.

Guidelines for Working with an Interpreter

A number of guidelines for interventionists to follow when working with an interpreter have been suggested (Hagen, 1989; Randall-David, 1989; Schilling & Brannon, 1986):

- Learn proper protocols and forms of address (including a few greetings and social phrases) in the family's primary language, the name they wish to be called, and the correct pronunciation.

- Introduce yourself and the interpreter, describe your respective roles, and clarify mutual expectations and the purpose of the encounter.
- Learn basic words and sentences in the family's language and become familiar with special terminology they may use so you can selectively attend to them during interpreter–family exchanges.
- During the interaction, address your remarks and questions directly to the family (not the interpreter); look at and listen to family members as they speak and observe their nonverbal communication.
- Avoid body language or gestures that may be offensive or misunderstood.
- Use a positive tone of voice and facial expressions that sincerely convey respect and your interest in the family; and address them in a calm, unhurried manner.
- Speak clearly and somewhat more slowly, but not more loudly.
- Limit your remarks and questions to a few sentences between translations and avoid giving too much information or long complex discussions of several topics in a single session.
- Avoid technical jargon, colloquialisms, idioms, slang, and abstractions.
- Avoid oversimplification and condensing important explanations.
- Give instructions in a clear, logical sequence; emphasize key words or points; and offer reasons for specific recommendations.
- Periodically check on the family's understanding and the accuracy of the translation by asking the family to repeat instructions or whatever has been communicated in their own words, with the interpreter facilitating, but avoid literally asking, "Do you understand?"
- When possible, reinforce verbal information with materials written in the family's language and visual aids or behavioral modeling if appropriate. Before introducing written materials, tactfully determine the client's literacy level through the interpreter.
- Be patient and prepared for the additional time that will inevitably be required for careful interpretation.

Good interpreters are invaluable resources for human services agencies in which many of the interventionists do not share the clients' language and cultural background. Developing and maintaining positive relationships with individuals who can help bridge the gap between families and interventionists is critically important for effective cross-cultural communication.

SUMMARY

This chapter has focused on cross-cultural competence, with particular emphasis on learning about one's own culture, learning culture-specific information about the families in the interventionist's community, and strategies to improve cross-cultural communication. This structure is based on a training approach that has been used successfully to prepare individuals for cross-cultural interactions. Although self-awareness is a beginning point, learning culture-specific information and practicing new communication strategies can be worked on simultaneously. Interventionists can work individually to enhance their knowledge and skill; however, people-oriented skills are better learned within a group. Having cross-cultural friends and colleagues who are willing to answer questions, with whom one can practice, and who are able to provide feedback can only improve the learning experience.

Working with families through interpreters and translators requires a special set of skills, described in the final section of the chapter. In addition to some philosophical issues and concerns that programs must address, interventionists must learn and make time to practice the strategies that facilitate communication through a third person.

It would be wonderful if, with the wave of a magic wand, we could all possess the skills and attitudes that it takes to be cross-culturally effective. But unfortunately, there are no short cuts and there is no magic wand. Acquiring the skills is a lifelong process; however, desire, willingness to learn, and the potential outcomes for families and interventionists alike make it a rewarding pursuit. More fully knowing oneself and the world opens doors that can never again be closed. For as Varawa (1989) said, "Culture is the garment that clothes the soul. We may never be able, or even want, to exchange our cloaks, but what matters is the perception of each other's realities . . ." (p. 227–228).

REFERENCES

Abe, H., & Wiseman, R.L. (1983). A cross-cultural confirmation of the dimensions of intercultural effectiveness. *International Journal of Intercultural Relations, 7*, 53–67.

Althen, G. (1988). *American ways—A guide for foreigners in the United States.* Yarmouth, ME: Intercultural Press.

Asante, M.K., & Davis, A. (1989). Encounters in the interracial workplace. In M.K. Asante & W.B. Gudykunst (Eds.), *Handbook of international and intercultural communication* (pp. 374–391). Newbury Park, CA: Sage Publications.

Benhamida, L. (1988) *Interpreting in mental health settings for refugees and others: A guide for the professional interpreter.* Minneapolis: University of Minnesota Refugee Assistance Program, Mental Health Technical Assistance Center.

Boas, F. (1943). Recent anthropology. *Science, 98*, 411–314.

Brislin, R.W., Cushner, K., Cherrie, C., & Yong, M. (1986). *Intercultural interactions: A practical guide.* Beverly Hills: Sage Publications.

Chan, S.Q. (1990). Early intervention with culturally diverse families of infants and toddlers with disabilities. *Infants and Young Children, 3*(2), 78–87.

Devine, E., & Braganti, N.L. (1986). *The travelers' guide to Asian customs and manners.* New York: St. Martin's Press.

Giles, H., & Franklyn-Stokes, A. (1989). Communicator characteristics. In M.K. Asante & W.B. Gudykunst (Eds.), *Handbook of international and intercultural communication* (pp. 117–144). Newbury Park, CA: Sage Publications.

Green, J.W. (1982). *Cultural awareness in the human services.* Englewood Cliffs, NJ: Prentice Hall.

Hagen, E. (1989). *Communicating effectively with Southeast Asian patients.* Los Angeles: Immaculate Heart College Center.

Hall, E.T. (1976). *Beyond culture.* Garden City, NY: Anchor Books.

Hall, E.T. (1984). *The dance of life: The other dimension of time.* Garden City, NY: Anchor Books.

Hammer, M.R. (1989). Intercultural communication competence. In M.K. Asante & W.B. Gudykunst (Eds.), *Handbook of international and intercultural communication* (pp. 247–260). Newbury Park, CA: Sage Publications.

Hanson, M.J., Lynch, E.W., & Wayman, K.I. (1990). Honoring the cultural diversity of families when gathering data. *Topics in Early Childhood Special Education, 10*(1), 112–131.

Hecht, M.L., Andersen, P.A., & Ribeau, S.A. (1989). The cultural dimensions of nonverbal communication. In M.K. Asante & W.B. Gudykunst (Eds.), *Handbook of international and intercultural communication* (pp. 163–185). Newbury Park, CA: Sage Publications.

Helms, J.E. (1990). What's in a name change? *Focus, 4*(2), 1–2.

Johnson, D. (1971). Black kinesics: Some non-verbal communication patterns in black culture. *Florida FL Reporter, 9,* 1–2.

Kealey, D.J., & Ruben, B.D. (1983). Cross-cultural personnel selection criteria, issues, and methods. In D. Landis & R. Brislin (Eds.), *Handbook of intercultural training* (Vol.1, pp. 155–175). New York: Pergamon Press.

LaDue, R. (1990). An Indian by any other name or don't "kemo sabe" me, Tonto. *Focus, 4*(2), 10–11.

Neal, A., & Allgood-Hill, B.A. (1990). The labeling game. *Focus, 4*(2), 7–8.

Randall-David, E. (1989). *Strategies for working with culturally diverse communities and clients.* Washington, DC: Association for the Care of Children's Health.

Robertiello, R.C., & Hoguet, D. (1987). *The WASP mystique.* New York: Donald I. Fine.

Ruben, B.D. (1989). The study of cross-cultural competence: Traditions and contemporary issues. *International Journal of Intercultural Relations, 13,* 229–240.

Schilling, B., & Brannon, E. (1986). *Cross-cultural counseling: A guide for nutrition and health counselors.* Washington, DC: United States Department of Agriculture/Department of Health and Human Services.

Schneller, R. (1989). Intercultural and intrapersonal processes and factors of misunderstanding: Implications for multicultural training. *International Journal of Intercultural Relations, 13,* 465–483.

Spitzberg, B.H. (1989). Issues in the development of a theory of interpersonal competence in the intercultural context. *International Journal of Intercultural Relations, 13,* 241–268.

Spitzberg, B.H., & Cupach, W.R. (1984). *Interpersonal communication competence.* Beverly Hills, CA: Sage Publications.

Storti, C. (1989). *The art of crossing cultures.* Yarmouth, ME: Intercultural Press.

Tiedt, P.L., & Tiedt, I.M. (1990). *Multicultural teaching—A handbook of activities, information, and resources* (3rd ed.). Boston: Allyn & Bacon.

Tinloy, M.T., Tan, A., & Leung, B. (1986). *Assessment of Chinese speaking limited English proficient students with special needs.* Sacramento: Special Education Resource Network, Resource Service Center.

Tong, B.R. (1990). "Ornamental Orientals" and others: Ethnic labels in review. *Focus, 4*(2), 8–9.

Varawa, J.M. (1989). *Changes in latitude—An uncommon anthropology.* New York: Harper & Row.
Wayman, K.I., Lynch, E.W., & Hanson, M.J. (1990). Home-based early childhood services: Cultural sensitivity in a family systems approach. *Topics in Early Childhood Special Education, 10*(4), 56–75.

APPENDIX A
A CULTURAL JOURNEY

Culture is not just something that someone else has. All of us have a cultural, ethnic, and linguistic heritage that influences our current beliefs, values, and behaviors. To learn a little more about your own heritage, take this simple cultural journey.

ORIGINS

1. When you think about your roots, what country(ies) other than the United States do you identify as a place of origin for you or your family?

2. Have you ever heard any stories about how your family or your ancestors came to the United States? Briefly, what was the story?

3. Are there any foods that you or someone else prepares that are traditional for your country(ies) of origin? What are they?

4. Are there any celebrations, ceremonies, rituals, holidays that your family continues to celebrate that reflect your country(ies) of origin? What are they? How are they celebrated?

5. Do you or anyone in your family speak a language other than English because of your origins? If so, what language?

6. Can you think of one piece of advice that has been handed down through your family that reflects the values held by your ancestors in the country(ies) of origin? What is it?

BELIEFS, BIASES, AND BEHAVIORS

1. Have you ever heard anyone make a negative comment about people from your country(ies) of origin? If so, what was it?

2. As you were growing up, do you remember discovering that your family did anything differently from other families that you were exposed to because of your culture, religion, or ethnicity? Name something that you remember that was different.

3. Have you ever been with someone in a work situation who did something because of his or her culture, religion, or ethnicity that seemed unusual to you? What was it?

   Why did it seem unusual?

4. Have you ever felt shocked, upset, or appalled by something that you saw when you were traveling in another part of the world? If so, what was it?

   How did it make you feel? Pick some descriptive words to explain your feelings.

   How did you react?

   In retrospect, how do you wish you would have reacted?

5. Have you ever done anything that you think was culturally inappropriate when you have been in another country or with someone from a different culture? In other words, have you ever done something that you think might have been upsetting or embarassing to another person? What was it?

What did you do to try to improve the situation?

IMAGINE

1. If you could be from another culture or ethnic group, what culture would it be?

Why?

2. What is one value from that culture or ethnic group that attracts you to it?

3. Is there anything about that culture or ethnic group that concerns or frightens you? What is it?

4. Name one concrete way in which you think your life would be different if you were from that culture or ethnic group.

PART II

CULTURAL PERSPECTIVES

Part II, the core of the book, introduces the reader to a number of the major cultural and ethnic groups that make up the population of the United States. Each group is described in terms of its history, values, and beliefs—with particular emphasis on issues related to the family, childrearing, and disability. Appendices are provided at the end of each chapter that contrast the primary beliefs, values, and practices of each group with those of the dominant culture; describe significant holidays or events; outline major cultural courtesies and customs; and provide some basic vocabulary words that may be useful for the interventionist.

Some differences in style and content may be noted from chapter to chapter. Although all authors held to a standard outline, it was necessary to highlight different sections for different groups. The topics most pertinent to intervention with each cultural group are presented.

The cultural groups represented in this volume are neither exhaustive nor inclusive of the wide range of cultural and ethnic groups in this country. Rather, groups were chosen because they represent a large segment of the population and/or because they reflect new immigration patterns. The contributing authors who describe these groups were carefully selected for their dual expertise and knowledge of the culture, and their experience in working with families of children who are at risk or disabled. They come from many different professional disciplines including education, medical anthropology, nursing, psychology, and social work.

chapter 4 _____

FAMILIES WITH ANGLO-EUROPEAN ROOTS

Marci J. Hanson

All men are created equal.

Where there's a will, there's a way.

A penny saved is a penny earned.

Do unto others as you would want done unto yourself.

Time is money.

If at first you don't succeed, try, try again.

Tomorrow is a new day.

The early bird catches the worm.

Great migrations are noted throughout history and most were undertaken for the purpose of invasion or as a crusade. One of the greatest migrations, The Great Atlantic Migration, brought the movement of over 36 million Europeans to the United States between 1820 and 1970 (National Geographic Society, 1975). These immigrants came to this new land for a variety of reasons, including the need to escape devastating economic conditions and/or religious persecution in their land of origin, but most came with the idea of finding new opportunity in a land rich with resources and promise. These immigrants brought "the accumulated cultures of Western Europe, the inheritance of Arabic learning, the traditions and literatures of the classical world, the institutions, theologies, and philosophies of Judaism and Christianity, and the experience of a passage across a perilous ocean" (National Geographic Society, 1975, p. 24).

When the earliest settlers arrived in what was to become the United States, they found a land relatively sparsely populated. The native people, American Indians whose great ancestors had crossed the Bering Strait from Asia centuries before, numbered perhaps 2–3 million in population (National Geographic Society, 1975). These natives were spread across the vast land base and their practices and lifestyle did not change the land. To the early Anglo-European settlers, the land probably represented an unlimited and relatively uninhabited resource. As they sought to settle and shape the land, the fate of the Native American Indians was to be pushed aside.

In addition to the background and practices of western Europe, the vastness of the land, the seeming limitless natural resources, and the heterogeneity of the landscape contributed to shaping the values and culture of this immigrant population. Americans have long revered the values of independence, courage, fortitude, ambition, self-help, and hard work—all functional and needed values for the task they saw of taming the wilderness and forging a new society from a vast, largely uninhabited, and unsettled land.

The society to which these early efforts gave birth became known as a "melting pot"—in other words, a society that absorbed persons from many different cultures and lands into the common but constantly changing whole of the society. Despite the overwhelming natural barriers of distance, mountains, and waterways, a common language was maintained. This feat was made easier due to tremendous technological advances and the pursuit of information transfer (e.g., systems of transportation such as steamboats and railroads; printed publications; and communication systems such as the telegraph and telephone). A united federation of states was established, a remarkable achievement in light of the diverse characteristics of the land. The country's continental mass alone (excluding Alaska and Hawaii) crosses nearly 25 degrees of latitude and nearly 58 degrees of longitude and reaches from several hundred feet below sea level to almost 15,000 feet above sea level. It includes grasslands, farmlands, mountains, everglades, swamps, prairies, deserts, tundra, and rain forests (National Geographic Society, 1975). Regardless of the regional uniqueness and differences, the states bound together to form a united federation, the United States. Although this unification of states, often with different goals and regional interests, has created tensions and even resulted in a devastating civil war, the states have remained unified and an even more centralized government has evolved.

While the United States remains a firm entity with a definable national language, culture, and traditions, the complexion and goals of the society continue to be challenged, questioned, and changed as a result of the influx of newcomers into this society—newcomers who, particularly in recent decades, come from non-Anglo-European roots. The notion of a "melting pot" society is being replaced by one more closely identified with cultural pluralism. Yet, it is in the Anglo-European roots that the "dominant" culture of the United States, as it is currently defined, is to be found.

BACKGROUND

Geographic and Historical Origins

Reports of a New World, a new land rich in resources such as gold and spices, coupled with the post-medieval interest in explorations, brought the first explorers to the Americas. Governments and individuals eager to open new trading markets and expand and claim the new land, as well as the quest for a passage from Europe to Asia, fanned the flames of adventurism. For example, England, Spain, Portugal, France, New Netherlands, and Italy all sent adventurers. The early reports from voyages, such as that launched by Sir Francis Drake in 1577, led England to attempt to colonize the New World.

For the most part, by early accounts, the new colonists found what they had sought: a land rich in natural resources and the freedom to pursue dreams. They acquired land for themselves, which was difficult or impossible to do in the British Isles and Europe, and they acquired the freedom to pursue the political or religious practices of their choosing. Only one group, slaves brought in ships from Africa, were denied access to the riches of the land.

Because the early settlers were able to acquire and own land, they expected to participate in its governance. They soon established forms of self-government from the proprietor lords and fought disease, famine, drought, and endured clashes with Native American Indians to build and maintain their settlements.

The early settlers learned to hunt and to farm and eventually established some central, sustaining crops such as corn and tobacco. Trade with nations of origin also flourished for certain products, and Americans began to engage in some manufacturing.

England, as the protector and administrator of the colonies, also was the primary source for materials. The taxation of the colonies for materials and goods became a central force in the colonists' move to self-governance. Americans refused to submit to England's taxation and wanted their own assemblies and local governments. This move resulted in the establishment of the Continental Congress and ultimately the Revolutionary War of Independence.

The breaking of old political and economic ties brought the formation of a new nation. The "Founding Fathers," in the Declaration of Independence from England, articulated principles of government for the new country that were designed to guarantee freedoms to its citizens (at least white male citizens). These statements of freedom laid the foundations for the dominant American culture and governmental structure that has endured to the present day.

Following this political revolution, the Americans were forced to increase their manufactured goods in order to supply their people. In this atmosphere, the American Industrial Revolution began in the late 1700s. With plans for a spinning machine to make cloth smuggled out of Britain, the spinning mills of America were established, and the American fascination with "the machine" has not abated.

The country continued to grow both through new births of resident citizens and also through a continued migration of persons from other countries, primarily Europeans. Of particular note is the large influx of Europeans to the United States in the 19th and early 20th centuries who came largely through the northeastern portion of the United States, particularly through New York. This influx can be represented in waves (Freedgood, 1970). The first wave included largely settlers from England, Ireland, and Germany. This was followed by the second wave in the 1860s–1890s that brought many Scandinavians. The third major wave of Europeans after the 1890s consisted of immigrants largely from Italy, Russia, and the Austrian-Hungarian empire—immigrants with Mediterranean and Slavic roots. Over 13 million from this group arrived between 1900 and 1914 and many of these newcomers were non–English speaking and unskilled, unlike many of the immigrants in the previous waves. These latter waves of immigrants produced tensions for the largely Anglo-Saxon population, by creating a more heterogeneous society. As a result, immigration restrictions were passed, bringing to an end the flood of immigrants. The Immigration Act of 1924 not only slowed immigration but also imposed severe restrictions or quotas on groups such as eastern Europeans and those from Mediterranean areas. The act was designed to ensure that the cultural composition of the United States remained the same. This influence of this Act essentially remained until the passage of the Immigration Act of 1965, which liberalized the quota system. Such quotas were subsequently abolished in 1968.

As the population of the United States grew, so too grew the desire to expand westward. The large transcontinental land mass allowed the population to continue its expansion across the continent. As settlers pushed westward, there were more clashes with the Native American Indians who continued to move farther west to escape the settlements and pursue their own established way of life. Discoveries in the West—gold, silver, oil, rich farmland, new waterways—provided further incentives for massive migrations and settlements across the American continent. A new group of immigrants, the Chinese, also were brought to the United States to aid in the westward expansion. Although their labor was essential to miners and they also built many of the railroads that linked the Atlantic to the Pacific, they were refused admittance to the mainstream of American society.

The many groups of immigrants to the United States over the years both adopted "American" ways and added their own unique contributions to the cultural practices of the nation. For example, in certain cities, groups such as the Irish and the Italians became active and highly influential in political life. All groups have influenced and enriched the cuisine, arts, music, literature, and folkways of the United States.

Religious Origins

A primary force in shaping the decisions of the early settlers to set out on the long and often treacherous journey to the New Land was the hope for religious freedom. Persecution in their lands of origin stirred many to seek life in a new land. In the early settlements, the doctrine of Puritanism, or Reformed Protestantism, predominated. The influence of this religious force on the developing community was profound. Less distinction was made between church and state at that time, and religion permeated the structure of the original settlements.

For example, this doctrine strongly influenced the education of the young. The Puritans' belief that children were born without the fear of God and with original sin led to the need for children to undergo intense religious training through prayers, scripture reading, and instruction in the religious faith. The larger communal society, as well as each family, was viewed as responsible for educating the young.

Over the years, as new immigrants came to what was to become the United States, many different religious sects (albeit primarily from Western religions) were introduced and flourished. As the nation was formed, religious freedom was guaranteed as a primary right. While no national religion prevails and the government separates church and state, the influence of Western religion over the American culture has been great; indeed, the nation was founded "under God" and currencies bear the inscription "In God We Trust."

Today, a wide range of religions are practiced in the United States. A recent newpaper article ("Religion coats U.S.," 1991) reported data from a survey commissioned by the Graduate School of the City University of New York regarding religious affliations in the United States. The study was conducted from April 1989 to April 1990, and found that more than 9 out of every 10 Americans identify with a religion (representing a wide range of denominations). The survey reported that 86.5% of Americans (214 million) are Christians from a number of different groups. The largest portion of these, 26%, are Roman Catholics, followed by Baptists (19%), Methodists (8%), and Lutherans (5%). Jews make up almost 2% of the population and Muslims represent .5%. Further, the survey found that most Asian Americans and Arab Americans are Christians rather than Buddhist, Hindu, or Muslim as might be expected; the explanation given was that Asians and Arabs who are Christians may be more likely to immigrate to the United States than are other religious groups.

In summary, most Americans report adhering to some religious belief. However, the religious practices are diverse and represent a wide range of denominations and belief systems.

Language Origins

The Anglo-Saxon origins of this country established English as the primary language. Although the United States has absorbed a large number of immigrants throughout its history, English has remained the national language. Accents differ from region to region and many local dialects have emerged, but the use of Standard American English is the norm throughout the country.

CONTEMPORARY LIFE

Three aspects of contemporary life are briefly examined in this chapter: 1) refinements in the definition of equal rights in the United States, 2) shifts in family patterns, and 3) changes in immigration patterns.

Equal Rights

Although citizens of the United States have always expressed pride in their guarantees of freedom of choice and opportunity, these freedoms have always been more readily available to white, male citizens than to other groups. Major challenges to a male dominated society date back at least to the Civil War. Although the Emancipation Proclamation freed the African American slaves, full rights of citizenship, such as the right to vote and the right to own land, were not granted to African Americans even as free men and women. Women, too, did not share in the freedoms guaranteed in the Constitution. Not until 1920 did women throughout the United States gain the right to vote when the 19th Amendment to the Constitution became law (World Book Encyclopedia, 1966).

The next major push for equality began in the 1950s, with protests and court cases demanding equal access to education and freedom to participate equally in public life for African Americans. This civil rights movement helped to reshape and redefine the meaning of freedom and equality in this country. The tumultuous civil rights movement of the 1960s aided the birth of other movements, such as the disability rights movement and the women's rights movement, which further resulted in a reexamination and redefinition of equal access for all citizens.

Family Patterns

For many years the term "family" in the United States was synonomous with a mother, father, and several children. Today, a much broader definition of family applies. For example, one fifth of children are born to single parents (National Center for Clinical Infant Programs, 1986). Family patterns reflect a variety of constellations including nonmarried adults, large extended family groups, as well as the traditional two-parent family. Further, today over 50% of children under age 3 are from households where both parents work outside the home (National Center for Clinical Infant Programs, 1986). Approximately 10.5 million children under age 6 have mothers who work outside the home, and over 72% of mothers with children between the ages of 6 and 13 years were in the labor force in 1988 (Bureau of Labor Statistics, 1988). These factors have created new challenges for American families, among them the need for affordable, quality child-care options.

Immigration Patterns

The original great waves of immigrant groups entered the United States primarily from the Atlantic Coast, and with the general population began to scatter and move westward. However, immigrants in the recent decades have settled predominantly in the West and have entered from the Pacific and from the South. Further, these immigrants represent large numbers of persons from areas not found previously in large immigrant waves, chiefly Asia, Southeast Asia, Mexico, and Central and South America.

VALUES

The cultural backgrounds and practices of immigrants from the British Isles and western Europe, as well as the conditions and opportunities encountered in the new land, shaped the major cultural values and practices of the American people. Some of these values and attributes include a focus on independence, freedom, assertiveness, equality, self-help, and self-directedness. Althen (1988), in his guide for foreigners in the United States, identified the following American values and assumptions: 1) individualism and privacy; 2) equality; 3) informality; 4) the future, change, and progress; 5) goodness of humanity; 6) time; 7) achievement, action, work, and materialism; and 8) directness and assertiveness. Each is discussed briefly as related by Althen. The discussion of these eight values is followed by a brief description of values related to family life and religion in the Anglo-European American culture of the United States.

Individualism and Privacy

Americans traveling abroad may encounter someone who states that Americans have no culture; many Americans may share this view. Because the focus in American society is so strongly on the individual, it is often difficult to see the common or shared practices. Americans are taught to think for themselves and taught that "you made your own bed, so you must lie in it." Self-determination and self-reliance are highly valued. Some of the American folk heroes are persons who overcame adversities and "pulled themselves up by their bootstraps." For example, politicians today still strive to point to humble roots and their climb to a higher status, much like heroes such as Abraham Lincoln. As Althen (1988) related, Americans revere those who do things the biggest, the best, or first. Hence, the fascination with sports legends such as Jesse Owens, Jackie Robinson, and Babe Ruth, and aviator heroes such as Charles Lindbergh, Amelia Earhart, and, more recently, the astronauts.

From an early age, Americans are taught to make decisions and to be self-reliant. Young children often have their own rooms; separation from their parents for short periods of time is acceptable even for the very young; and early self-help skills, such as independent feeding, are encouraged. Children are often given opportunities to make choices and decisions at an early age, and those decisions are respected.

Althen (1988) stated that the concept of privacy is closely related to the quest for individualism. Americans value time for themselves, private thoughts, and boundaries such as their own possessions. This value is reflected in family living practices where children often have their own rooms and also in topics of conversation. Typically, Americans tend to avoid personal topics with others unless they are close friends, family, or professionals (e.g., lawyers, psychologists, physicians) who are governed by rules regarding the divulging of information.

Equality

The United States was founded on the principle that "all men are created equal." Clearly, not all citizens have had equal rights throughout the course of the country's history, but Americans value this notion highly and strive toward this ideal. As such, signs of status may be less apparent than they are in some countries. Although the status of a person is often a factor in an interaction and may influence the way one dresses, is addressed, how and with whom one speaks or sits, the signs of status or influence may be somewhat subtle. An underlying assumption is that no matter what the person's background, he or she has the potential for achievement and deserves respect.

Informality

The informal style practiced by Americans may be seen by others as disrespectful and "uncultured." Americans often greet others in an informal manner and may use first names even when addressing strangers. Casual dress, such as jeans and T-shirts, is common in most parts of the country for many occasions. Further, many Americans use slang in discussions and in greetings, and their style is often friendly, informal, and open, even to strangers.

The Future, Change, and Progress

The United States, relative to most other world powers, has a short history. Perhaps this is a factor in why Americans place so little emphasis on their history but tremendous emphasis on the future. Change, newness, and progress are all highly valued. Americans believe that individuals, as well as people working together, can "make a difference" and that change is positive. Related to these notions is the assumption that social and physical environments are under human control or domination. This is contrasted to a more "fatalistic" belief structure found in many other cultures. This assumption has been borne out throughout American history, as early settlers cleared and reshaped the land in its "settlement."

The belief that individuals and groups are in control of their destinies is a powerful influence on the lives of most dominant-culture Americans, and it is a notion that has proved to be a double-edged sword. On the positive side, it has given people self-confidence and made them feel that they could meet any challenge. On the negative side, it has made many mainstream Americans less tolerant of individuals and groups who have been less successful. It also has fostered a use of force in interactions with the environment and other people that is evident in phrases such as "taming the wilderness," "winning the West," and "conquering space."

Goodness of Humanity

In general, Americans hold the belief that people are essentially good and that they are capable of self-improvement. This belief is consistent with the notion that change is possible and with a futuristic outlook. An emphasis on education—both formal and informal—throughout one's life is apparent and many Americans strive toward self-improvement. Seminars and workshops aimed at self-help, self-reliance, and new skills are common and sought after. "How to" guides and self-help/support groups are in demand. Americans also generally believe that providing more knowledge can help turn people's lives around. Campaigns to provide more or more accurate information in order to remedy society's ills (e.g., smoking, drinking, drugs) are used frequently. Rehabilitation is seen as both positive and possible. Providing persons with the opportunity to improve their situations is valued and those who do so are highly regarded.

Finally, Althen (1988) described Americans' support of volunteerism. Coupled with the belief in the ability of an individual or a collective group to change the situation, many Americans belong to service, charitable, or advocacy organizations designed to improve a societal concern. This focus on change and one's personal responsibility to the common good was underscored in John F. Kennedy's Presidential Inaugural Address (January 20, 1961): "My fellow Americans, ask not what your country can do for you—ask what you can do for your country."

Time

Americans' concept of time can be understood by the phrase "time is money." Efficiency and organization are valued in American life and time is seen as something that is used and must be saved. A primary demonstration of this assumption is the proliferation of fast-food eating establishments in the United States. In these establishments, taste, presentation, and the experience of eating are secondary to the "best value" and the ease and speed with which the food is prepared and delivered. This focus on efficiency and the management of time goes hand-in-hand with the futuristic, change-oriented outlook.

Achievement, Action, Work, and Materialism

Americans can be characterized as achievement, action, and work oriented. Achieving, "getting the job done," and working hard are valued. The outgrowth or product of this work orientation often is the acquisition of material possessions, which has led to the view of Americans as materialistic. Americans are often seen as "on the go," even in their recreational activities. Attention is given to what a person "does"—what the person's job is. The person's income and/or status is often related to the type of job; monetary incentives are provided in many jobs for working longer, harder, or more efficiently.

Directness and Assertiveness

Americans often speak in a forthright manner, even about matters of grave concern. Typically, they are characterized as open, frank, and direct. Masking one's emotions is not a cultural norm; rather, Americans typically convey their feelings as well as express their thoughts on an issue. Certain topics, however, are usually not discussed so openly; these include topics that are considered personal, such as those dealing with body odors or sexual practices. Further, less openness may be displayed when interacting with persons with whom the speaker is not acquainted or persons with whom one does not want to risk an offense or confrontation. For example, a student may be less frank or open with a professor than with a peer, and a business person may be less open with a new business contact than with an established colleague. In such cases, a more indirect communication style may be used.

Family Life

The concept of "family" in the Anglo-European American United States typically refers to immediate family members such as the mother, father, and children. Other extended family members may or may not live close by, and may or may not participate actively in the "nuclear family." Other members are usually termed "relatives" as opposed to "family." Although traditionally families often were characterized by a male head of the household, with male-dominated decision making, this pattern is less likely to be found in homes today. Parents are more often equal partners in decision making and many households are

Case Example #1

Every Tuesday and Thursday after school, Michael, age 7, attends a special tutorial session where he works on reading skills and computer use. Michael's teachers recommended the extra work to remediate his learning difficulties. Michael's attention span is relatively short and he has difficulty reading. However, he is motivated by the computer and likes it best when his "lessons" are in the form of a game on the computer. Nancy, his mother, is highly supportive of the extra teaching sessions, even though it is financially difficult for her to pay for them. Nancy is an administrative assistant at a small local business and is a single parent. Michael's birth was difficult and necessitated prolonged hospitalization. For these reasons, Nancy has worked closely with Michael's pediatrician and with his preschool and public school teachers to monitor his development. The teachers feel that Michael may be learning disabled and they are tracking his school performance carefully. The tutorial sessions were designed to overcome these early difficulties. Nancy is relieved that she is receiving help and she welcomes the extra learning opportunities for Michael because they provide both extra practice and also a quality activity for him while she is at work.

headed by women. Further, the culture is very "child centered" and children have a great deal of say in events and in the practices of the family.

As was previously stated, Anglo-European American families are diverse and represent many different constellations. Several characteristics that do differ from many other cultures are the age at which children leave the home and the care provided for elderly family members. After high school (or college), most young adults leave the primary home and establish their own residences. It is uncommon for persons to return to the home permanently. With respect to elders, typically they do not move into the homes of their children for care in their later years; rather, most elder members of the population maintain their own homes or live in homes for the elderly. This choice often is made by both parties—adult children experience difficulties with the elders moving into their home and the elders feel awkward living with the children and value their own independence.

Religion

As was noted earlier, the laws of the United States protect the individual's right to practice or not practice the religion of her or his choice. No one state religion is supported. Further, the government is characterized by a separation of church and state. Although this doctrine has been debated throughout the history of the country and continues to be questioned by some, this separation essentially remains. Questions such as whether or not prayer should be allowed in public schools and the content of textbooks regarding creation and evolution have produced disagreements. Generally, though, religion is considered a private matter. Americans typically do not discuss their religious preferences or practices outside of their immediate circle of friends and families.

While many different religions are practiced in this country, the United States was founded under a Judeo-Christian belief system and Christianity continues to be the religion practiced by the majority of persons. This focus is seen in the primary religious holidays that are celebrated, such as Christmas and Easter. Although religious references are found in national holidays and practices such as inscriptions on national coins, "being religious" in America typically means going to church and practicing religious activities in the home.

BELIEFS

The values just discussed above translate into belief systems that are reflected in the culture's philosophies regarding childrearing, medical or health care practices, and the causation and treatment of disabilities, to name a few. Each of these variables is discussed as it pertains to practices in the Anglo-European American culture.

Childrearing

Traditionally, households were characterized as male dominated and family roles were apportioned accordingly. Male members, husbands and fathers, were generally the breadwinners and responsible for things outside the home, such as the car and the yard; females, mothers and wives, typically held responsibility for things inside the home, including child care and childrearing, cooking, cleaning, and other aspects of household management. Today, over half of the mothers of young children are employed in the labor force outside the home (National Center for Clinical Infant Programs, 1986), as well as holding responsibility for household tasks. While the traditional male–female family roles are still reflected in many homes, these distinctions are beginning to break down. Adult family members are more likely to share decision-making and family-related tasks. Further, children participate actively. Today's parents typically try to provide their children with a "good life" and children often participate in goal setting for the family or influence the family's allocation of resources. The "child-centeredness" of families often translates into active schedules for children who are involved in school, after school activities, additional learning experiences, and an active social life of their own.

Stemming from the Anglo-European emphases on individuality, achievement, and progress, developmental expectations for self-help and self-reliance are often high for children. Typically, babies are placed in their own beds from birth and may have their own rooms early on. Self-feeding and toileting are encouraged actively in the early years and parents often separate from their children for short periods of time. Given that many mothers are employed out-

side the home in the labor force, many children are placed in child care and spend their days with caregivers other than their parents. Children are often involved in decision making early on. For instance, in a visit to a store or a restaurant, the observer may see parents asking their children (even very young children) which toy or clothing they want or which food they wish to order. Many children also are expected to do their own jobs around the house, such as keeping their room cleaned and setting the table. Later, in their teenage years, many hold part-time jobs. As children reach adolescence they also are expected to rebel and to discover their own identities. At the age of 18 or soon thereafter, it is accepted that they generally leave the family home and establish their own living situations.

Education is highly regarded. Children today often are involved in early education activities, and "preschool" experiences generally are valued. Beyond that, extra lessons for children may be sought, such as in music, dance, sports, or art. Education is compulsory in the elementary years and schools are publicly funded and available to all students. Education is seen as a key determinant of equality and as the mechanism to provide equal access or opportunity in the society.

Case Example #2

Jonathan was born prematurely at 26 weeks gestational age to Susan and Roy. Susan's pregnancy was normal but for unexplained reasons she went into premature labor and was rushed to a hospital. When Jonathan was born, he was placed on oxygen and rushed to the neonatal intensive care unit. There he lived in an incubator for nearly 3 months. His parents feared getting attached to him because they had been told that he only had a 50–50 chance of survival. Yet, they did everything they could to get to know their baby and to ensure that he got the best medical treatment available. They were thankful to the many physicians and nurses who saved their baby's life and thankful for the highly technical equipment and treatments that allowed Jonathan to live and grow. Susan expressed milk from her breasts daily and took it to her baby so that he could get the very best nutrition. When Jonathan finally stabilized and was released home to his parents' care, the parents were loaned a baby monitor designed to alert the parents if he stopped breathing. They also were visited regularly by a nurse specializing in the development of babies born prematurely.

At 9 months, Jonathan was demonstrating some delays in development and his parents were referred to a local early intervention program where he was assessed. In conjunction with the parents, the professional team at the early intervention program determined that Jonathan could benefit from receiving physical therapy services, consultations to the parents on specialized feeding techniques, early learning activities, and developmental monitoring.

Medical and Health Care

Americans' fascination with high technology is reflected in the medical and health care practices. Typically, medical treatments are focused on interventions through prescriptive drugs, surgery, and testing or diagnostic procedures using highly technical equipment (Hanson, Lynch, & Wayman, 1990). Preventive measures are emphasized, with information distributed through educational campaigns. Concern for good health focuses on prolonging life, and health care practices are normally based upon current scientific information on the subject. For example, foods are often selected on the basis of nutritional value or rejected on the basis of the food's association with carcinogenic effects as identified through scientific experimentation. Sources of health care and medical information typically are physicians and other health care providers trained in technical medical regimens.

In recent years, more naturalistic and holistic approaches to medicine are gaining recognition. However, Western medicine, as practiced in the United States, has traditionally separated disorders of the mind and body and relied upon scientific and technical information for diagnosis and treatment.

Causation

The emphasis on education and the futuristic, change-oriented outlook held by many Anglo-European Americans has led to the view of individuals as "masters of their own fate." Typically, adversity is seen as something that can be overcome with enough work, resources, and/or ingenuity. As was related earlier, many American folk heroes are individuals like Helen Keller, who succeeded in life despite great restrictions or initial setbacks. There is a strong belief in the ability of individuals to better their circumstances through change or adaptation, rather than succumb to a preordained fate.

Disability

No single causation is ascribed to disabilities; rather, a variety of reasons based on scientific causes exist, including genetic disorders, environmental agents (e.g., accidents, injuries, toxins), disease (e.g., viruses, severe bacterial infections), and prenatal and perinatal trauma. Some of these factors could be prevented with better diagnostic care, health treatments, or improved living conditions, and some are likely due to random events. While social factors, such as the mother's caregiving style, have been blamed for some types of disabilities over the years, the more complete knowledge of disabilities has eliminated the claims for such causative factors in most cases.

Case Example #3

Harriet and John are the parents of 3-year-old Caitlin. Caitlin was diagnosed at birth as having Down syndrome. The attending physician in the hospital informed Harriet and John of the diagnosis shortly after Caitlin's birth and the parents were referred to the hospital social worker for support and assistance. The social worker met with the family and told them about a local parent group for families of children with Down syndrome and also about an early intervention program in their community. Harriet and John elected to participate in both services. Caitlin has been enrolled in early intervention since she was 3 months old. In the program she has received home- and center-based services from a transdisciplinary team of professionals. Her parents have been active participants in her educational activities.

At age 3, Caitlin is now "graduating" to a preschool in the public school system. Her parents are concerned that she be properly assessed and placed in a preschool program with typically developing youngsters. They are seeking an educator or psychologist with special expertise in Down syndrome to conduct the assessment and they are visiting preschool sites in the community to determine placement options. Their goals are for Caitlin to have friends, enjoy her life, be a productive citizen, and live as independently as possible.

Services related to care of individuals with disabilities have focused increasingly over the years upon appropriate and available educational opportunities from birth and greater access to opportunities in American society, such as employment and independent living. Treatment is aimed at habilitation or rehabilitation or on environmental adaptations to accommodate the needs of the individual. The principles of normalization (Wolfensberger, 1972) and least restrictive environment (PL 94-142, the Education for All Handicapped Children Act of 1975; and the Individuals with Disabilities Education Act [IDEA]) have defined the goals of integrating persons with disabilities into the society in a culturally normative way and with access to educational services with typically developing peers. The disability rights movements of the last several decades have led to legal protections and equal access for persons with disabilities—including a large body of federal legislation culminating in the 1990 Americans with Disabilities Act.

SUMMARY AND RECOMMENDATIONS

Summary

The history of the United States is a short one relative to other countries—a mere 200 years. In those two centuries, a federation or united government of states has been established and the rights of its citizens defined and expanded to include citizens, such as women and African Americans, who were initially denied equal participation. Further, the vast land mass of the continental United States has been explored and changed by new settlers on the land and the country has been expanded beyond the unified land mass to include the states of Alaska and Hawaii.

The United States was founded to establish a new order, a new type of government. Although this new nation attracted settlers from many distant shores, the predominant customs, beliefs, language, and practices in the United States undeniably have their roots in the Anglo-European heritage.

Many American values and assumptions have been forged from this Anglo-European background. These values include: 1) high regard for individualism and privacy; 2) the belief in equality of all individuals; 3) a tendency toward informality; 4) an orientation toward the future, change, and progress; 5) a belief in the goodness of humanity; 6) an emphasis on the importance of time; 7) a focus on achievement, action, work, and materialism; and 8) a directness and assertiveness in approach (Althen, 1988).

These values and assumptions have been translated into belief systems that reflect the culture's philosophies regarding childrearing, medical or health care practices, and the causation and treatment of disabilities, among other issues. Typically, Americans have high expectations for their children's development and they foster early self-help and self-reliance skills in their youngsters. Education is highly valued and sought. The extended family networks found in the early years of the country are not as common today and the primary focus in the American family typically is on nuclear family members. With respect to medical and health care practices, the American fascination with high technology is evident. Medical treatments typically focus on drugs, surgery, and sophisticated, technical, diagnostic procedures. Education and treatment for persons with disabilities have received a large amount of public attention, particularly in recent years. This has led to legal mandates ensuring appropriate public education for children with disabilities and legal protections for all persons with disabilities.

The complexion and goals of the United States continue to be challenged and defined. The growing number of immigrants to this country with non-Anglo-European roots will influence and shape these customs and practices, as have the contributions of immigrants throughout the nation's history.

Recommendations for Interventionists

Language and Communication Style

Most Americans of Anglo-European roots speak directly and honestly and expect service providers to interact with them similarly. In the case of diagnosis of disability or issues surrounding treatments, most expect interventionists to provide honest and factual answers to their questions and professional advice and/or information regarding appropriate treatment practices.

With respect to style of communication, Anglo-European Americans look one another in the eye when speaking and prefer direct, face-to-face interactions. Professional greetings often involve shaking hands, particularly between males. Conversation is characterized by turn taking wherein each person talks for a short while and allows time for others to respond. Personal topics and personal self-disclosure are typically avoided, as are arguments or conflict-producing topics. Both professional and personal conversations typically are conducted in moderated tones of voice with a give-and-take exchange of information. This verbal exchange is encouraged as most Anglo-European Americans rely more heavily upon verbal rather than nonverbal messages.

Different dialects and colloquial expressions are used in different regions of the country. Terms and vocabulary also may differ across different ethnic, religious, and professional discipline groups. However, Standard English is spoken and understood by most. Interventionists are well advised, however, to avoid professional jargon when interacting with families.

View of Family Involvement

Parent/family involvement in children's education has long been a tradition in Anglo-American families. Most parents expect to work as a partner with teachers and other professionals in establishing goals for their children and ensuring that appropriate educational or treatment services are rendered. Parents want to be informed and also want to have a say in the process. Many parents of children with special needs have taken roles as active advocates for their children in the community, as policymakers and as teachers of their children. PL 99-457 (Amendments to the Education of the Handicapped Act which has been retitled the Individuals with Disabilities Education Act), stipulates parent involvement in the education of young children with disabilities. Part H of this law goes further and regulates development of an Individualized Family Service Plan (IFSP) for children and their families participating in early intervention programs for children from birth through age 2 in states participating in services under this law. Current "best practices" in early intervention services for young children who are at risk or disabled reflect a family-focused or family-centered approach to delivering services; parents are viewed as equal partners and decision makers in the intervention process.

Interactions with Family Members

There is no one person or role in the family that is considered the contact or dominant decision maker with respect to services for children. While it is much more common for mothers to be the primary caregiver, other family members (e.g., fathers, siblings, grandparents) may play active, pivotal roles as well. Typically, family members will specify the major contact(s) when asked and also will indicate the other major "players" in the child's life.

Organization and Scheduling

Most families expect appointments to be scheduled and meetings to begin punctually. Many have active and complex lifestyle patterns that necessitate careful scheduling. In today's world where so many parents work outside of the home, flexible meeting times, places, and plans also must be considered, such as evening meetings with parents or meetings with the child's day care provider as part of the intervention effort.

Respect for Individual Differences

Even within the cultural group with Anglo-European roots, many different subcultures are apparent. Individuals, for example, may strongly identify with being Irish, Italian, or Jewish, or they may strongly relate to their geographical area (westerners, southerners, and so on). Likewise, rural, urban, and suburban lifestyle differences hold a strong influence over families' life patterns. The family's social and economic situation may dramatically affect their ability or desire to participate in intervention activities regardless of their ethnic identification. Thus, early interventionists must be respectful and sensitive to the wide range of families with whom they will work. This does not mean trying to become like the family or mimicking their practices, but rather recognizing, allowing, and respecting the individual differences among families as well as within families across the various family members.

REFERENCES

Althen, G. (1988). *American ways: A guide for foreigners in the United States.* Yarmouth, ME: Intercultural Press.

Bureau of Labor Statistics. (1988). [Marital and family characteristics of the labor force: March 1988]. Unpublished data. United States Department of Labor, Washington, DC.

Freedgood, S. (1970). *The gateway states: New Jersey, New York.* New York: Time-Life Books.

Hanson, M.J., Lynch, E.W., & Wayman, K. I. (1990). Honoring the cultural diversity of families when gathering data. *Topics in Early Childhood Special Education, 10*(1), 112–131.

Kennedy, J.F. 1961, January 20 [Inaugural address].

National Center for Clinical Infant Programs. (1986). *Infants can't wait: The numbers.* Washington, DC: Author.

National Geographic Society. (1975). *We Americans.* Washington, DC: Author.

Religion coats U.S. with many colors. (1991, April 10). *San Jose Mercury News,* pp. 1, 12.

United States Department of Agriculture & United States Department of Health and Human Services. (1986). *Cross-cultural counseling: A guide for nutrition and health counselors.* Washington, DC: Author, Nutrition Education Committee for Maternal and Child Nutrition Publications.

Wolfensberger, W. (1972). *Normalization: The principle of normalization in human services.* Toronto: National Institute on Mental Retardation.

World Book Encyclopedia. (1966). *Woman suffrage: Winning the vote.* Chicago: Field Enterprises Educational Corp.

APPENDIX A
CONTRASTING BELIEFS, VALUES, AND PRACTICES

Some Other Cultures' Values	Anglo-American Values
Fate	Personal control over the environment
Tradition	Change
Human interaction dominates	Time dominates
Hierarchy/rank/status	Human equality
Group welfare	Individualism/privacy
Birthright inheritance	Self-help
Cooperation	Competition
Past orientation	Future orientation
"Being" orientation	Action/goal/work orientation
Formality	Informality
Indirectness/ritual/"face"	Directness/openness/honesty
Idealism/theory	Practicality/efficiency
Spiritualism/detachment	Materialism

From United States Department of Agriculture & United States Department of Health and Human Services. (1986). *Cross-cultural counseling: A guide for nutrition and health counselors* (p. 3). Washington, DC: Author.

APPENDIX B
CULTURAL COURTESIES AND CUSTOMS

The following practices represent some major characteristics of interactions.

The notion that all people are more or less equal.

It is customary to treat females and males with equal respect and to treat people providing daily services courteously (e.g., cab drivers, waitresses, secretaries, sales clerks).

People freely express their opinions.

Freedom of speech is a major characteristic of American life. Some topics are typically not openly discussed, however, particularly with strangers. These include topics related to sex, politics, religion, and personal characteristics such as body odors.

Persons are greeted openly, directly, and warmly.

Not a lot of rituals are found in greetings. Typically, persons greet one another openly and directly and get to the point of the interaction. Often persons will shake hands with strangers (particularly males). Eye contact is maintained throughout the interaction and it is considered impolite not to look at the persons to whom you are talking.

A social distance of about an arm's length is typically maintained in interactions.

Most social interactions are conducted about an arm's length from the other person. People (males, in particular) do not expect to be touched except for greetings such as shaking hands. When people walk down the street together they typically do not hold hands or put their arms around one another unless they are involved in a more intimate relationship.

Punctuality and responsibility in keeping appointments are valued.

Time is valued and most people expect punctuality. It is also considered rude to accept an invitation to someone's home and not show up or make an appointment with someone and not keep it.

Appendix C
Significant Cultural Events/Holidays/Practices

New Year's Day*—January 1st

Martin Luther King's Birthday*—January 15th

Valentine's Day—February 14th (a commercialized holiday to honor one's sweetheart and others whom one holds dear)

President's Day*—celebrated in mid-February (to commemorate George Washington's and Abraham Lincoln's birthdays)

St. Patrick's Day—March 17th (a holiday held in honor of the Catholic Saint Patrick, originally celebrated primarily by Irish Americans and now popularized and celebrated by many Americans—the holiday is marked by parades and by wearing green)

Passover—typically in March or April (Jewish holiday commemorating the exodus of the Jews from Egypt)

Palm Sunday—the Sunday before Easter (Christian holiday commemorating Jesus' entry into Jerusalem)

Good Friday—the Friday before Easter (Christian commemoration of Jesus' crucifixion)

Easter—first Sunday after the date of the first full moon that occurs on or after March 21st (Christian holiday commemorating the resurrection of Jesus)

Mother's Day—second Sunday in May (to honor mothers)

Memorial Day*—usually around May 30th (to honor dead members of the armed forces)

Father's Day—third Sunday in June (to honor fathers)

Independence Day*—July 4th (anniversary of the adoption of the Declaration of Independence)

Labor Day*—first Monday in September (in honor of labor)

Rosh Hashanah—first weeks of September (Jewish New Year)

Yom Kippur—usually in early September (Jewish holiday, day of fasting, the Day of Atonement)

Columbus Day*—October 12th (commemorating the discovery of America by Columbus in 1492)

Halloween—October 31st ("the eve of All Saints Day," an originally pagan celebration that has been popularized and is celebrated by children dressing in costumes and going to neighbors' houses to ask for candy & saying "trick or treat")

---

*A legal holiday in most parts of the country and government businesses are normally closed. Some of these federal holidays are celebrated on alternative dates, usually Mondays (e.g., Martin Luther King's birthday, Memorial Day, Columbus Day).

Veteran's Day*—November 11th (to honor veterans of the armed forces)

Thanksgiving Day*—fourth Thursday of November (begun by the Pilgrims to give thanks to God for their survival)

Chanukah—usually in December (8-day Jewish holiday commemorating the victory of the Maccabees over the Syrians in 165 B.C. and the rededication of the Temple in Jerusalem)

Christmas*—December 25th (Christian holiday commemorating the birth of Jesus Christ)

chapter 5 ─────────────────────

FAMILIES WITH NATIVE AMERICAN ROOTS

Jennie R. Joe and Randi Suzanne Malach

Henry Old Coyote: We Indians are taught to take into consideration the less fortunate members of our tribe. We believe that if you help a pauper who does not have means, you will get reward, not from him but from some other source. . . . Getting kind thoughts from people who express their wishes for your well-being means more than material things. . . .

My wife, for example, might go down the street and see a man with both legs gone, holding a cup with some pencils. She will give him something, but she won't take the pencils. She would rather hear that man say "Thank you." As he says it, she might think, "This good thought is for my little granddaughter."

Allen Quetone: Generosity is probably one of the strongest feelings or values Indian people have. It is always there among our people. Many in the dominant culture, especially the local non-Indian communities, view this trait in Indian people with low regard. It conflicts with the acquisitive nature of the non-Indian cultures.

We are always willing to share. We have a pool, a source at home, and it's called "traditionalism." Within each of our tribes there are certain people who are traditionalists. These are the people who hold onto and perpetuate our customs and traditions. They provide those of us who are on the outside, who are in the Bureau of Indian Affairs and other places across the country, with an opportunity to come back and participate. In other words, any time I want to charge my battery, I can go back and enjoy many of these Indian ways; I can participate in

them, I can regain a feeling for our traditional values; and
I might say that it is the greatest feeling there is.[1]

When Christopher Columbus landed in the Bahamas in 1492 and mistook the island for India and called its inhabitants Indians, the North American continent was home to 5 million Native Americans (Hoxie, 1988). Columbus's misidentification of the island and its people unfortunately categorized what was a heterogeneous society of different tribes and people occupying the Americas into a single homogeneous group. Columbus and his men, however, were not the only ones to group everyone under one label. Many other early explorers also paid little attention to the cultural diversity of the native peoples even though it is estimated that at the time of the European contact, the native peoples of North America spoke between 1,000 and 2,000 different languages, with each tribe speaking a different language from that of its nearest neighbors (Washburn, 1975). Each tribe had its own political organization, methods of subsistence, and beliefs and knowledge concerning its own existence that expressed its religion, world view, values, and historical roots.

\ These cultural and historical roots for Native Americans go back thousands of years to generations of ancestors—whose footprints in history left evidence of their societies in religious sites, mounds, and burial sites that have revealed pottery, clothing, basketry, ornaments, weapons, tools, and use of metals such as copper and gold. This material evidence clearly illustrates that most tribes had made use of the land and its resources. Indeed, tribes such as the Mayans and Aztecs had created great cities and had accomplishments in the arts and sciences that equaled or exceeded those of the Europeans.

The European conquest, which took almost 400 years, devastated the Indian tribes politically and economically. Although the Europeans tried to force Indian peoples into adopting the values and beliefs—economic as well as cultural and religious—of mainstream society, they were only partially successful. The net effect has been an "emulsion" of cultures rather than a smooth blending or mixing of peoples.

Native American families are currently present in every state and most major cities. Over 400 distinct tribal groups and villages are found in the United States, and these groups reflect quite diverse cultures, including "woodland Indians of the Northeast, the Pueblos of the Southwest, the coast communities of the Northwest, and the Eskimos of the Arctic tundra" (Northwest Indian Child Welfare Institute, 1987, p. 16).

Great diversity is found not only among tribes but also within each tribe and/or within extended families. The various members of most Native Ameri-

---

[1]Stories, rather than proverbs, are generally used by most Native Americans to express certain sociocultural values or world views. Mr. Old Coyote and Mr. Quetone, members of the Crow and Kiowa tribes, respectively, elaborated on some of these values at a child development seminar (cited in Morey & Gilliam, 1974, pp. 181, 183).

can families may have differing levels of acculturation and traditionalism. For example, the grandparents in one extended family may live on the reservation and speak predominantly the native language, while the younger generation may live in a city and speak predominantly English (Hoffman, 1981).

Furthermore, most Native American Indians today live in a bicultural world where they must live within the rules of the dominant society as well as the traditional ways (Joe & Miller, 1987). It is not uncommon to see a blending of traditional and nontraditional practices. For example, Indian families may observe birthday celebrations or acknowledge the "tooth fairy" in addition to some of their traditional tribal customs, such as "naming ceremonies." Indian babies today may also start out in a traditional tribal cradle board but soon be introduced to baby walkers, strollers, and disposable diapers.

Thus, a continuum of acculturation exists within Native American communities, ranging from individuals who hold to a traditional lifestyle to those persons who operate primarily within the dominant culture (Northwest Indian Child Welfare Institute, 1987). Families may move about on this continuum, becoming more traditional at times (e.g., after the birth of a child), and less so at other times. While many Native Americans are integrated into mainstream society, many still maintain their traditional beliefs and customs to varying degrees. Oral history, songs and dances, and ceremonial activities are still part of the culture of most contemporary Native Americans, and native languages are still used and taught in many tribal communities.

These cultural phenomena are extremely important because varying levels of acculturation affect the way Native Americans respond to non-Indian service delivery systems and the professionals who help provide these services. There are no sets of rules for identifying levels of acculturation, although there are communication protocols that will facilitate interaction between native and non-native peoples. The main purpose of this chapter is to describe briefly the historical background of Native Americans and some of the more common experiences, cultural practices, and beliefs that may influence Native Americans' communication and interaction with interventionists. The last section of the chapter briefly discusses some of the communication protocols of which non-native interventionists should be aware when working with a Native American family.

BACKGROUND

Historical Origins

1492–1800

Although the American continents were occupied by indigenous peoples, the arrival of the Europeans quickly depopulated the land (Washburn, 1975). The Europeans brought great destruction, both directly and indirectly, to the native peoples of the Americas. Warfare brought direct destruction, but indirectly, the most devastating impact was caused by the introduction of communicable diseases. Most native peoples had no resistance to these new infectious diseases such as smallpox and diptheria, and countless numbers died in each epidemic in one Indian community after another. Thornton (1987) estimated that the 1492 population of approximately 5 million Native Americans in North America had dropped to about 600,000 by the 1800s.

In the aftermath, the groups and tribes that survived the ravages of these epidemics were left with limited resources and with their social order destroyed and/or fragmented. These cycles of epidemics cost many tribes their healthy warriors as well as their children and their elders. The loss of the elders was devastating for some tribes because the elders served as the repository of cultural and historical knowledge. Conversely, the epidemics favored the economic and political aspirations of the Europeans in that many of the powerful tribal alliances were destroyed, making it easier to seize the land (Jennings, 1975).

At various times after 1492, when increasing numbers of European settlers arrived and demanded more and more land, warfare erupted between the settlers and various tribes of Indians all across the continent. The Indians put up a formidable resistance to the invaders. In the Northeast, the British and French were met with the formidable might of the Iroquoian nation. Confronted with this military power, some Europeans negotiated and dealt with these tribes as sovereign nations. Farther south in what is now Virginia, the Powhatan Confederacy, with its 30 tribal alliances, was also a military and political power source with which to be reckoned. In the Southeast, the Europeans encountered the Creek Confederacy, including remnants of the once-powerful aristocratic Natchez tribal society. The Europeans who ventured from South America and Mexico into the American Southwest, however, were not met by tribal coalitions. In California, the Spanish explorers met a succession of independent tribal bands that varied in size. In what are now the states of Arizona and New Mexico, the Spanish encountered resistance, and this resistance continued from the 16th to the late 18th centuries. In the latter part of the 19th century, a series of military campaigns against the U.S. government brought an end to the last of the fighting warriors of the Apache, thus closing the history on "Indian" wars. Most of these conflicts were about land, and once the Europeans discovered the riches of the Americas, the Native Americans were powerless to keep the Europeans from encroaching and taking over their land (Axtell, 1981).

The European perception of the natives and the European reason for coming to North America set the stage for the outcome of the interactions between natives and Europeans. For example, the Spanish colonial efforts quickly began to exploit the natives as a source of free labor to work the mines and/or to help build and support the missions; at the same time, the Spanish priests tried to win the natives' souls for the church (Dobyns, 1988). By the end of the 17th century, there was emerging a strong blend of Hispanic and Indian cultures; but early on, only a few Spanish–Indian marriages were approved by the Roman

Catholic Church because most Spaniards viewed the Indians as a pagan and inferior race.

The French, whose purposes in the New World were primarily economic, viewed the natives as valuable assets for helping them to achieve their goals. By the late 16th century, some French trappers and traders, for example, adopted Indian customs and lived among the natives. The French were able to expand and utilize this network of friendship to increase their fur trade. It was not uncommon for some French traders and trappers to marry members of Indian tribes. This is evident today in the many French surnames found in some tribes, although some of these surnames were assigned by census takers who were unable to pronounce or write the traditional Indian names of the Native Americans.

As the population of the English colonies expanded, many of the English who settled in the New World wanted little to do with the natives in North America. Seeking religious freedom and/or a chance to improve their economic lot, most English colonists came to the Americas to build permanent settlements and to transplant their way of life. They viewed the native peoples as barriers to this goal. Thus, their treatment of the native peoples was most harsh, and many viewed Indians as "savages" and pagans (Berkhofer, 1965). Because the native peoples were not Christians, and therefore not "human" in the eyes of most English colonists, the invaders believed that their Christian faith and alliance to the King (who had divine right) gave them the right to claim all the land in the New World. In many instances, the view of natives as "savages" served as a justifiable excuse for removing the natives from their land, dispossessing them, even killing them.

European immigrants, explorers, traders, missionaries, soldiers, colonists, and trappers changed forever the culture and world of the native peoples, and most of these changes were negative. With increasing numbers of Europeans migrating to the Americas, the hunger for land intensified, and most of the eastern tribes were pushed westward. Those who resisted with force were generally annihilated or forcibly removed by various means. Invariably, where tribal members agreed to live in peace with the Europeans, they were also pressured to denounce formally their "Indian-ness" and adopt the European lifestyle, manner, and values. These cultural converts, for example, had to prove that they were worthy of the effort by presenting various proofs such as church baptism records or evidence of knowing how to farm. Indian women had to demonstrate that they knew basic European-style homemaking skills. Those who passed these "tests" were granted land ownership and/or citizenship (Berkhofer, 1979; Peckham & Gibson, 1969).

1800–1900

During the late 19th century, the American government continued its mission to assimilate Native Americans, but this time the primary methods were in the educational arena and with the school-age population. The official policy on education mandated formal schooling for all Indian children. The government often sanctioned or encouraged religious groups to take Indian children and remove them to distant boarding schools modeled after similar schools in Europe. The school settings discouraged any tribal or cultural practices (e.g., children were not allowed to speak their native languages), and the curriculum fostered the European lifestyle and values. Similar orientations were held by the various government-sponsored classes aimed at the adult population in Indian communities.

With the drastic reduction in population and with most tribes safely contained on reservations, the Indian tribes no longer posed a military threat to the Europeans. In 1871, the U.S. Congress passed a law putting an end to treaty negotiations with tribes. This action signaled a new relationship with Indian tribes. Indian tribes were no longer accorded recognition as independent, sovereign nations. Thus, despite their drastic efforts to protect their ancestral lands, most tribes were caught in the web of conquest no matter where they lived. By the end of the 19th century, the final stages of the conquest ended with relocation of many tribes to isolated and unproductive patchworks of lands called "reservations." Although the reservations were justified by the U.S. government as "sanctuaries," such forced relocation not only broke the spirit of many once-proud Indian nations, but also destined them to a life of poverty and hopelessness—conditions that continue to haunt Native Americans today.

The lands set aside as communal lands or reservations, however, were not safe havens for long. The U.S. Congress enacted the Dawes Act in 1887, which allotted to each eligible Indian a few acres of the reservation land. The sponsors of the legislation thought that such individual land ownership was essential to becoming civilized or to taking up the ways of mainstream American culture. Although this individual land ownership policy was intended to help assimilate North American Indians into mainstream society, the subdivision of land merely provided another way to take more land away from Native Americans. The unassigned land that was left after the allotment was made available to non-Indians.

By the closing years of the 19th century, fewer than 250,000 Native Americans remained in North America (Thornton, 1987). As a conquered people, they were left almost totally dependent on the federal government for their survival. In the ensuing years, the isolation of many reservations or villages provided a measure of protection from mainstream society—but the clash with the non-Indian world continues, and thus shapes the world view and self-identity of most tribal groups today.

1900–Present

Despite governmental efforts to integrate them, most Native Americans continued to be strangers in their own land and they still had to prove themselves worthy of citizenship. During World War I, many Native Americans volunteered to serve in the armed forces; in 1919, citizenship was awarded to those Native Americans who had served in the war. Finally, in 1924, the Indian Citizenship Act was passed for the remaining numbers who were not previously eligible and who now desired United States citizenship. Granting citizenship, however, did not automatically guarantee Native Americans the right to vote. Because state governments maintained the power to grant voting rights, New Mexico and Arizona barred their Indian population from voting until after World War II. The Indians in these two states acquired the right to vote only after lobbying for their rights.

During the period of removal and relocation on reservations, the Native Americans responded to the loss of their tribal sovereignty and the relentless assaults on their traditional way of life in a number of ways. For example, when some tribal religious practices such as the Sun Dance were outlawed, or the use of alcohol prohibited, or multiple marriages condemned, and/or when Indian children were punished at school for speaking their native languages, the reactions consisted of either violent resistance, passive resistance, or escape such as fleeing to neighboring countries (Canada and Mexico). Today, the violent resistance to the pressure of assimilation has eased somewhat, but now cultural revival serves as a form of resistance combined with the adoption of more Anglo-European American–oriented models of political organizing and lobbying, particularly in the political arena in the federal government.

Shortly after the end of World War II, the federal policy favoring rapid assimilation of Native Americans once again emerged as a congressional issue. The plan was to relinquish or terminate federal trusteeship for tribes deemed by the Bureau of Indian Affairs (BIA) to be economically viable and ready for termination of ties. This policy had a major impact on the 10 tribes recommended for termination: the Osages, the Klamaths, the Menominees, the Flatheads, the Potawatomis of Kansas and Nebraska, the Chippewas of Turtle Mountain, the Six Nations of New York, and three small tribes in California. These tribes were terminated after the passage of House Concurrent Resolution 108 in 1953. Many Native Americans were thus forced into poverty: They lost their land and their homes because they were unable to pay taxes.

In addition to the advent of termination, the federal government also initiated other programs to push Native Americans into assimilation. One of these efforts included the relocation of many young Native Americans into the cities. These young people were often relocated into the urban ghettos at locations arranged so that the relocatees did not live near one another. While the relocation worked for some, many found themselves isolated and ill prepared to deal with the cultural shock of the impersonal urban lifestyles, and thus they returned home to the reservation. Many also experienced other hardships such as the lack of medical care and were forced to return to the reservation, where they were eligible for care through the Indian Health Service.

The aftermath of the termination policy for tribes released from federal trusteeship also proved disastrous. Within a few years, tribes like the Menominee, who appeared to have a strong economic base, were left bankrupt and on the brink of losing their remaining land base. Each year after termination, increasing numbers of Menominee families were forced to auction their homes or farmland to pay taxes and/or to apply for public welfare. Thus, the termination program increased poverty instead of eliminating it. In the 1970s, some of these 10 tribes began to lobby Congress to reverse their termination. Ultimately, the Menominee and Klamath tribes were successful in reversing their termination status.

In the late 1960s, participation of Native Americans in sporadic outbreaks of public demonstrations and civil disobedience were reported by the media. The occupation of Alcatraz island by a group of Indian college students and the "fish-ins" organized by the Northwest Coast tribal groups are but two examples of these protests. The fish-ins were staged by members of one Northwest Coast tribe to reaffirm their treaty rights to fish, while the purpose of the Alcatraz occupation was to ask for the return of federal surplus land to Indian tribes. Various other pan-Indian political movements also emerged in the 1960s. Some of the movements either revitalized old coalitions or sparked the formation of new coalitions such as state intertribal councils, the National Tribal Chairmen's Association (NTCA), the Alaskan Federation of Natives (AFN), and the American Indian Movement (AIM). Some of the impetus for this development also came from President Johnson's antipoverty programs under the Office of Economic Opportunity (OEO). The OEO enabled many tribes to receive direct federal funding and manage these programs without going through the BIA, a process that was unheard of in most Indian communities. The push for consumer participation under these programs helped the tribes to renew efforts for tribal sovereignty and self-determination. These efforts as well as the various public protests and political posturing by Indian organizations and their advocates during the 1960s led to some significant legislation in the 1970s.

Some of these legislative milestones came with the passage of the Indian Self-Determination and Education Assistance Act of 1975 (PL 93-638), the American Indian Freedom of Religion Act of 1978, the Indian Health Care Improvement Act of 1976, and the Indian Child Welfare Act of 1978 (PL 95-608). The Self-Determination Act, in particular, allowed Indian tribes to contract with federal agencies, such as the BIA, in order to take over the management and operation of programs in Indian communities. The Indian Health Care Improvement Act allocated extra resources for improving the health status of Native Americans on the reservation as well as in selected urban communities. The Freedom of Religion Act permitted Indian tribes to have access to their traditional sacred and religious sites on federal and other government lands. Finally, the Indian Child Welfare Act gave tribes increased jurisdiction over the placement and adoption of their children.

Native American communities continue to foster their own tribal identity and to remain separate and distinct from one another. However, their common experiences formed through colonization and the intertribal and pan-Indian alliances that have evolved in recent decades have forged agendas that are common to most, if not all, tribes. These common agendas include the right to self-government, equal access to quality health care and education, and an appreciation and encouragement for fostering their tribal language and culture.

Religious Origins

Because religion was never a separate institution for Native Americans, it is taken for granted that the origin of religion came with the emergence of mankind and/or the specific tribes. Religion or the spiritual side of man is perceived to be an integral part of every living thing. Thus, religion or spiritual beliefs are an integral part of every tribal culture. At the center of most of these religious beliefs is a deity or "Great Spirit," "Creator," "Grandfather," and/or other terms of respect that give this deity recognition. Another core concept is the notion that all things (natural and supernatural) are interconnected.

Language Origins

It is estimated that in 1492, there were slightly over 1,000 separate American Indian languages (Driver, 1961). Today, eight different ancient language group-

ings are used to categorize most of the Indian languages in use. Iroquoian, Muskogean, Caddoan, and Athapaskan are examples of these major groupings.

The various tribal languages have also been greatly influenced by cultural contact with the Europeans. For example, in the Southwest, Spanish words are incorporated into the tribal language for things that have been introduced into the culture (e.g., words for currency, days of the week). English, however, is the most common second language found today in Indian communities (Malach, Segel, & Thomas, 1989).

CONTEMPORARY LIFE

Despite efforts in the past to integrate American Indians and Alaska Natives into the mainstream culture, their numbers and their unique cultures are still separate parts of the American landscape. Contrary to the popular belief of the vanishing First Americans, Native Americans today live in all of the 50 states and are no longer confined to the existing 278 reservations and the 200 Alaskan native villages (Snipp, 1989).

In 1990, approximately 1.9 million people in the United States identified themselves as American Indians, Eskimos, or Aleuts (Johnson, 1991). Compared to other minority populations, however, Native Americans remain "invisible," as they only make up slightly more than 0.75% of the total United States population.

As discussed earlier, Native Americans or American Indians are not a homogeneous group. There is great diversity among tribes. Diversity starts with the size of some of the Native American groups. For example, tribes such as the Cherokees, the Navajos, the Sioux, and the Ojibiwas (Chippewas) have sizable populations. Other tribes such as the Cocopah, the Modoc, and the Chumush are very small tribes, numbering less than 1,000 each. Some tribes also may not have a tribal land base while others no longer reside on reservations because they have moved to cities. Other Native Americans migrate back and forth between the city and the reservation, many leaving the reservation during times of economic hardship to seek work in cities or towns. The out-migration from the reservations, however, has increased since the 1950s so that today over half of the Indian population resides in off-reservation communities or cities (Johnson, 1991).

Although there have been periods of intense pressures to assimilate, many Native Americans continue to hold onto their tribal ways while at the same time allowing for the adoption of many non-Indian ways. The diversity among Native Americans also continues to grow as a result of increasing numbers of intertribal marriages as well as intermarriage with persons from non-Indian cultures. For example, Olson and Wilson (1984) noted that only 105 of the 5,000-member Blackfeet tribe are full bloods. The rest are of mixed blood.

Just as there are intertribal cultural differences, there are also intratribal differences. Within most Native American families, the level of acculturation between members of the same extended family usually varies. In many families, the younger members are the most acculturated and the elders the least acculturated. In a number of cases, some small tribes have been completely assimilated and/or have forgotten the traditional ways of the tribe. However, despite the loss of language or customs, there still remains a sense of tribalism or tribal identity.

The profile of many reservation communities today parallels that of the developing countries. The population reflects a high proportion of young people—more than two fifths are under the age of 20. There are high birth rates as well as high mortality rates (Indian Health Service [IHS], 1990). Poverty is endemic. Plantz and Stinson (1986) indicated that more than one third of the Indian population were below poverty income in 1979. This cycle of poverty contributes significantly to the poor health and well-being of many Native American families.

VALUES

Although values are not always visible, easily articulated, or upheld in every situation, Stein (1985) posited that "people not only use values to help them and to decide among choices but also to help them constantly define who they are, whom they belong to, and who and what are to be regarded as outside" (p. 36). When a significant proportion of a cultural group shares a set of values, these shared values form that sociocultural group's value system. As the cultural group undergoes changes, certain values may be abandoned, replaced, and/or compromised so that the values that continue are constantly changing or being modified (Kluckhohn & Strodtbeck, 1961).

Because the learning of values is predominantly a cognitive process, it is not always possible to observe how an individual selects one set of values over another and/or decides what value is better or more right than another. Often it is possible to observe some of this process by noting what values are central or are constantly being reinforced as part of the early childrearing practices (i.e., which behaviors or expressions are rewarded or punished by the young child's family member). As the child grows and expands his or her association with others, some of these childhood values may be challenged and/or may continue to be reinforced by peers, experiences, and other social or cultural institutions such as churches or schools. Thus, the value system of the group is maintained through these informal and formal processes of socialization (Hilger, 1977).

Much of what is known about the value system of Native Americans emerges out of ethnographic studies, some of which date back to the colonial period. The aim of most early ethnographers, however, was not to focus on values but to capture the unique aspect of the culture and/or sometimes to record anything and everything so that there would be a holistic picture of that Indian society before that tribe vanished. Thus, specific studies on values of American Indians have not been central in many of these documentations (DuBray, 1985).

The few studies that have centered on the values of some tribes have focused on some common tribal values such as individual autonomy, the ability to endure deprivation, bravery, the proclivity for practical joking, and the belief in the existence and essence of a supernatural power (DuBray, 1985). On a broader scale, these values, or the different emphasis give to some of them by Native Americans, however, do not appear to differ greatly from those of the mainstream society—until they are juxtaposed with non-Indian values. In Table 5.1, some value differences between the non-Indian culture and the Pueblo Indians of the Southwest (whose values are similar to those of other Indian tribes) are summarized. With time and the ever-present pressure toward acculturation, some of the traditional Indian values may no longer be held by some of the younger generation of Native Americans, but they are still visible and upheld by others, especially the elders.

Harmony with Nature

The value of harmony with nature is still evident as many tribal communities continue to resist mining and mineral development on their land. These tribal groups continue to teach respect for the land and to forbid desecration of their ancestral lands. These groups also carry on various ceremonies and rituals to ensure harmony with as well as protection of the land (Mother Earth).

Cultural conflicts can arise when Indian people must choose between encouraging land development that will employ tribal members and maintaining the cultural values that emphasize protecting and not destroying the land. In times of economic hardship, the decision is often weighed toward survival, and

Table 5.1. Value comparisons between Indian and non-Indian cultures

Pueblo Indians	Non-Indian
Harmony with nature	Mastery over nature
Present-time orientation	Future-time orientation
Cooperation	Competition
Anonymity	Individuality
Submissiveness	Aggressiveness
Work for present needs	Work to "get ahead"
Sharing wealth	Saving for the future
Time is flexible	Time is not flexible

Adapted from Zintz (1963).

thus, land developers or mineral companies are allowed onto the reservations to build or set up mining operations.

Time Orientation

Another value frequently cited as differing from that of the majority culture is the preference many Native Americans have for present-time orientation (Lewis & Ho, 1975); that is, they view time in a "rhythmic, circular pattern" (Ho, 1987, p. 71). In the past, rather than marking time by months or years, Indian peoples may have marked time based on the seasons, with daily routines gauged by the position of the sun or the moon.

Similarly, the milestones used to mark human development were also based on varying tribal customs. For example, the developmental milestones may not emphasize when a child starts walking but rather when the child has his or her "naming ceremony," laughs the "first laugh," and/or accomplishes the vision quest or completes other puberty ceremonies. Thus, in some instances, obtaining data on child development may be confusing or incomplete.

In most Indian communities, today health programs and nutrition supplement programs such as WIC (Women, Infant, and Children Nutritional Supplemental Program) utilize various developmental tests to examine and follow the physical development of many young Indian children who are eligible for these public programs. Most Indian women who are seen for prenatal care are indoctrinated early to the need to bring their babies or other young children to the clinic for immunizations and/or scheduled well-baby visits. In addition, if Indian women deliver in the hospital (and most do), the newborn is also given a routine assessment at birth and again at discharge. Thus, many Indian children with congenital abnormalities are identified at an early age. With these mothers, there is usually more frequent follow up, and mothers are encouraged to note specific developmental milestones. In other cases, if the baby is at risk for or diagnosed with developmental delays, referrals may be made to specialists for early intervention and therapy.

Family Roles and Relationships

In most Native American families, the concept of family is defined broadly to include extended family members as well as the immediate family (Malach et al., 1989). Other members of the family's tribe may be included as well. In many cases, extended family members rather than the biological parents may hold primary responsibility for the care of the children. Often, childrearing responsibilities are assumed willingly by grandparents or other extended family members so that parents of young children can be employed. Further, parents may seek the advice and assistance of older family members and elders in the larger family network, given the value placed on age and life experiences. In interactions with interventionists, these extended family members may act as case managers for the child and family in obtaining needed services (Malach et al., 1989).

Case Example #1

A traditional Indian family whose 2½-year-old daughter had a repaired cleft lip and chronic otitis media were referred for early intervention services by a community clinic pediatrician. The pediatrician was concerned about the child's speech and language, as well as the child's behavior problems.

The early interventionist went to the home for the first visit in order to talk to the family and get a case history. She was told the mother and father lived with the mother's parents and an elderly aunt. During the first visit to the home, the children were very quiet. The elder aunt stayed in the kitchen and the grandparents were in town shopping.

The early interventionist introduced herself and explained why she was there. She began to ask questions on the case history. She was confused by the responses to questions regarding the child's development. The parents did not seem to remember when the child sat up or began walking. Although the doctor stated that the child was using single words to name things, the parents said the child was not talking yet. The early interventionist also asked if the parents had any concerns about the child's behavior. The parents said, "No". The early interventionist left after arranging to come back in a week.

The early interventionist went back to the clinic and asked a nurse who had been working in the community for 10 years if she would talk to her about this referral and the home visit. She asked why the parents did not seem to know about developmental milestones. The nurse explained that in this Indian tribe, developmental milestones are not valued as they are in the mainstream culture and that in the family's culture, other events are considered significant. For example, the day a child first laughs and the day a child is named are important events. Talking is considered important some time between the child's third and fourth birthday. If the child does not talk as much as other children at that time, then the family becomes concerned.

Next the early interventionist told the nurse about the pediatrician's concern about the child's behavior and the parents' lack of concern. The nurse explained that in more traditional Indian families, the responsibility for discipline often belongs to the elder aunt or grandmother. In the Indian culture, age and life experience are essential for childrearing. The parents are not considered to have the years of experience necessary to raise their children alone. In this family, the children were well behaved in the presence of elder family members although the parents had difficulty when they were out with the children and the elders were not around.

When the early interventionist went back the next week, she asked some different questions. She asked the parents to tell her about when their daughter first laughed. They told her about the event and subsequent party with enthusiasm. Then the early interventionist asked them who was responsible for disciplining the children and how it was done. She then asked what they did when an elder was not around. They stated it was difficult. The early interventionist asked if they would like help. The mother indicated that they would, but that they could not take away the elders' role and responsibility. After discussion, it was decided that the parents would talk with the elders about the parents' learning behavior management skills outside the home in situations when an elder was not around.

Group Orientation

Another value of Native Americans that has received considerable attention is the value of being part of a group that emphasizes collateral relationships with others rather than individualism. Group consensus is a major value in most important decision making; usually sufficient time is allowed (even hours) to discuss and examine an issue until a consensus is reached.

This emphasis on group consensus has some interesting consequences Native American children, for example, are not likely to want to draw attention to themselves as individuals, but usually prefer to be part of a group. Educators often mistake this behavior as evidence that Indian children are passive or do not want to compete for top grades. Conversely, Indian children who display the aggressive or individualistic behaviors common to the mainstream culture are often taunted or teased by their peers.

Acceptance

The general tendency of the non-Indian culture to take charge and/or to manip-ulate nature to fit its needs has also frequently been contrasted with the Indian value of accepting natural and sometimes unnatural events as they are. This value of acceptance of things as they are has often been described for Indians as being-in-becoming in contrast to the non-Indian value of doing something about the situation (Kluckhohn & Strodtbeck, 1961). This acceptance of natural and unnatural events is representative of the Indian belief that these events occur as part of the nature of life and that one must learn to live with life and accept what comes, both the good and the bad (Coles, 1977). In some instances, non-Indians have viewed this value of acceptance by Indians as an explanation for why Native Americans do not want to impose themselves or their views on others when they are not asked (Good Track, 1973). Acceptance relates back to the traditional value of many tribes that called for respecting all living things and for not interfering with the nature of life events without cause (Bopp, Bopp, Brown, & Lane, 1984).

Self-Reliance and Autonomy

Whether in the city or on the reservation, many Native American parents still socialize their children based on their own cultural prerogatives. Some of these prerogatives may mean teaching an Indian child to be self-sufficient at an earlier age. Miller's (1979) comparison of certain tasks accomplished by white, African American, and Native American children illustrates this point (see Table 5.2). As Table 5.2 illustrates, most Native American children assume responsibility for self at an earlier age than do children from other groups. This is because most Native American children are reared in an adult-centered world and as soon as they can master self-care skills, they are encouraged to do so. In fact, any imitation of acceptable adult behavior is encouraged and praised. For example, a young child who can help with chores around the home is praised for her or his willingness to take on responsibilities without being asked. Similarly, children are asked about their opinion in important family decisions.

BELIEFS

The belief in the interconnectedness of all things, living and nonliving, is central to many Native American belief systems. The idea that human beings are but a small part of the larger fabric of the universe is a theme frequently heard in many tribal stories and legends (Neihardt, 1961). For example, among a number of North Central tribes, the four principles of the Medicine Wheel incorpo-

Table 5.2. Developmental milestones across cultures

| | Age accomplished (in years) | | |
Skill	White	African American	American Indian
Dress self	3.7	4	2.8
Do regular chores	6.1	6.3	5.4
Go downtown alone	13.5	12.8	10.6
Left alone in evening	14.4	13.6	9.2
Take care of younger sibling	13.1	12.9	9.9
Go on dates	16.4	16.5	15.7

Adapted from Miller (1979).

rate the four aspects of human nature—the physical, the mental, the emotional, and the spiritual (Bopp et al., 1984). The belief is that to have good health or harmony, all four of these elements have to be in balance, or harmony. Many of the curative as well as preventive ceremonies are therefore aimed toward maintaining or regaining harmony.

Among some other tribes, similar ideas may be expressed as the four cardinal directions, the four grandfathers, or the four winds—each symbolizing different concepts such as wisdom, growth, or generosity. Among the Hopis (a Pueblo tribe in northern Arizona), there is a belief that the original spiritual "being" shared with the Hopi people certain rules of life and placed spiritual helpers—the Kachinas—near the tribe to protect and help them maintain a certain way of life. The Kachinas, therefore, help teach and guide the Hopis with their songs, prayers, and ceremonies (Titiev, 1972). Among the Apaches, the Mountain Spirits have a similar role. Appropriate members of the respective tribe impersonate these deities during special ceremonies. Additionally, the social structure of some Pueblo tribes of the Southwest have moieties whose ceremonial activities also function to ensure harmony and/or community welfare.

Many non-Indians today continue to misunderstand the importance of the traditional beliefs that are a part of these ceremonies. They may fail to understand the ceremonies that are performed to bless a new baby, to offer prayers for rain, or to offer thanksgiving for a good harvest. Indian children often participate in the rituals and ceremonies as soon as they are able to sing or dance. Special gifts may be made in a child's honor when she or he first dances or participates in an important ceremony. Family members and/or clan members may also honor a child by making appropriate clothing for him or her to wear during these occasions. A sacred pipe, for example, may be given to a young Native American when he comes of age and is being indoctrinated into a special society. There is a strong belief in the proper preparation for someone who is to take on important responsibilities such as participating in the Sun Dance.

Wellness and Unwellness, Causation and Disability

Most Native American belief systems incorporate ideas of multiple causality of illness and misfortune; some of these beliefs concerning causes of illness, misfortunes, or disabilities may be attributed to supernatural or natural causes. The supernatural causes may link etiology to witchcraft, spirit loss, spirit intrusion, spells, and various unnatural forces. In the natural category, the causes may be attributed to various disturbances of balance or equilibrium brought on by such actions as breaking a cultural taboo, acculturation, and/or accidents that are not instigated by witchcraft or the harmful wishes of others.

Indian families or parents who have children born with handicapping conditions may be told by medical professionals that the disability is due to a genetic disorder. The parents may not dispute this diagnosis because it explains *how* the condition occurred, but these parents may also turn to their cultural resources to find out *why* the disability occurred. This sociocultural explanation may represent a breech of cultural taboo. In order to prevent the condition from worsening and/or to prevent future misfortune, the parents or family may turn to tribal healers or practitioners for assistance while at the same time continuing to take the child to physicians or to other specialists for treatment and follow up. Sometimes the family or parents may utilize their tribal healers to help enhance the treatment or therapy provided by the physician or by modern medicine.

When a family member has a disability or illness, traditional ceremonies are conducted to begin the healing process and to protect the individual and the rest of the family from further harm. For that reason, an Indian family may want to complete traditional ceremonies before they seek or become involved in a regime recommended by physicians or other service providers. For example, when a child is born with a disability that is not immediately life threatening, the family may seek the consultation of a tribal healer before consenting to other interventions. Unfortunately, some families may not volunteer this information for fear that their wishes may not be respected by the service providers.

The type of ceremonies utilized to help the child, the family, and the extended family will vary from one tribal group to the next. Sometimes various ceremonies or rituals are performed to ensure safe and healthy pregnancies and/or deliveries. In some tribes, the mother and child may have to observe a strict postpartum regime. The child and mother may be sequestered until the appropriate number of days have passed and the newborn is formally introduced to the appropriate religious deities of the tribe as well as to other members of the community. Some of these rituals may require the mother to undergo certain purification ceremonies to prepare her to raise her child.

Childrearing

In many Indian families, the childrearing activities may rest with other family members; in many instances, the grandparents are responsible for the children. Aunts and uncles also are likely to be involved, especially if the family resides on the reservation and not in an urban area. Indian families who live in the city tend to have nuclear households, whereas families on the reservation tend to include extended family members. In fact, in some tribes, the uncles instead of the parents may provide most of the discipline, while grandparents provide most of the spiritual guidance and teaching.

The advent of cultural change (mainly the change from a subsistence lifestyle to a wage-labor lifestyle) and the implementation of a number of government policies have disrupted this normal order of childrearing and family relationships for most tribes. The role and even the existence of extended family and nuclear family structures also have been changed drastically by various policies over the years. Social programs (e.g., Aid to Families with Dependent Children [AFDC]) have forced many Native American families into nuclear

Example #2

An Indian child with Down syndrome and his family received early intervention services for 2 years. At age 3 years, he was ready to transition into a
public school program. The child lived with his single teenage mother and
grandmother. Extended family lived nearby and were closely involved in decisions regarding childrearing. The mother believed that the public school
would provide her son with a good program and she was looking forward to
a break from child care. She also wanted to take classes so that she could get
a good job eventually.

The extended family did not support the decision to send this 3-year-old
child to school. They believed it was the mother's responsibility to care for
him. They believed the child was still ill and that he had suffered enough
because of his illness and should be kept at home and protected. They
trusted the early interventionist who had been visiting the home weekly for
2 years and wanted her to continue to see the child until he was at least
6 years old or when they decided he was ready for school. The family was
upset that the early interventionist would not continue to provide services.

The early interventionist met with the family and explained that she
would help the family learn about the preschool programs available to them.
That meant she would go with them to visit the programs and meet with the
school staff. She would answer their questions and help them to make a list
of questions they wanted to ask the school.

The family agreed and everything seemed to go smoothly for a while.
The interventionist planned two follow-up visits after the child started in the
school program to make sure everything was going smoothly. The school
reported the child had adjusted to the classroom and was doing well. The
mother enrolled in a class at the local community college. Three weeks after
school started, the mother called the early interventionist to say that the family was again questioning the decision. The early interventionist went to the
home and met with the grandmother and aunt. They expressed their concerns and restated their cultural beliefs that the mother should be home caring for her child. At the end of the discussion, they told the early interventionist that they trusted her but not the school, and they wanted her to
continue to visit the child at school and them at home every week. The early
interventionist told them she could not do that weekly, but that she could
visit twice a month.

For the next few months, the family continued to need support in their
decision. After 2 months, the visits were extended to once a month. Efforts
were made to help the family build a relationship with the teacher, school
counselor, and other families who had children in special education. Four
months after school started, the mother met another Indian mother of an
older child with Down syndrome who shared many concerns and understood her situation. As the two families began to provide each other mutual
support, the early interventionist extended the time between visits to 6 weeks.
In the spring, she helped the family prepare for the individualized education
program (IEP) meeting to plan for the next school year. She did not accompany them. After that meeting, she let the family know that she would not
schedule regular visits but that they could call her if they wanted her help.

households and/or forced the establishment of one-parent households. In other cases, young Indian families who relocate to the cities in search of jobs often leave behind their much-needed family and extended family support network.

ISSUES OF LANGUAGE

Language and Education

After the conquest by the Anglo-Europeans in the 19th century, speaking tribal languages and performing tribal dances or ceremonies were not permitted in most public schools, and children who broke these rules were severely punished. It has only been recently that this trend has changed.

Presently, because Native American societies must live in a bicultural world, a number of formal institutions (e.g., Head Start) that serve Native American children offer bicultural and sometimes bilingual education. Robert W. Rhodes, while discussing learning styles, noted that many young Indian children "prefer a more holistic observational technique, whereas the Anglo process of categorization lends itself to a linear approach" (cited in Felciano, 1990, p. 1).

Foremost in these programs is the attention given to the continuation of the tribal languages. For example, the Navajo Nation's educational policy states:

> The Navajo language is an essential element of the life, culture and identity of the Navajo people. The Navajo Nation recognizes the importance of preserving and perpetuating that language to the survival of the Nation. Instruction in the Navajo language shall be made available for all grade levels in all schools serving the Navajo Nation. Navajo language instruction shall include to the greatest extent practicable: thinking, speaking, comprehension, reading and writing skills and study of the formal grammar of the language. (Navajo Division of Education, 1985, p. 9)

According to Reyhner (1986), the Northern Utes of Utah also have a tribal resolution that declares the Ute language as the official language of their nation. The resolution, in part, states:

> The Ute language is a living and vital language that has the ability to match any other in the world for expressiveness and beauty. Our language is capable of lexical expansion into modern conceptual fields such as the field of politics, economics, mathematics, and science. (Northern Ute Tribal Business Council, 1985, p. 16)

As mentioned earlier, prior to the mid-1940s, the federal government did not favor cultural diversity and bilingual education for Native Americans. Formal schooling was seen as an important vehicle for assimilating and detribalizing Native Americans (Reyhner, 1986). To speed up the assimilation process, Indian children were taken (sometimes forcibly) from their homes to boarding schools, where they were to think and speak only in English. This process in the long run did not assimilate Native American children; it only served to disrupt their culture (Reyhner, 1986).

Prior to European contact, most Native Americans educated their children informally at home with the help of relatives and/or formally by means of arranged apprenticeships. For example, a young tribal member who desired to learn to be a medicine person often sought out a teacher or mentor, and the family arranged payment and the terms of the training program. In other instances, the clan or society took on the responsibility for training and preparing the child for participation in the clan or the society's activities. Some of this training included learning the sacred songs, prayers, or dances. Thus, children were taught to assume adult roles and to provide themselves with a livelihood.

In addition to basic language and communication skills, boys and girls were taught about plants, herbs, animals, seasons, hunting, food preparation, child care, and religion. Kinship, values, and other moral teachings were often shared by the whole family or community. Evenings were often reserved for storytelling, and each story invariably had a lesson to impart.

The teaching philosophy of most Native Americans also reinforced the value that each child was a distinct person taught to do or warned against doing certain things, not because they were right or wrong, but because the act or failure to act was for his or her advantage or disadvantage in the afterlife. The child's pride and ambition were appealed to, and appropriate role models were pointed out for emulation.

Most Native Americans in the past as well as today are not against formal education, but when many young Native American children enter the classroom, they frequently find themselves in foreign environments where familiar words, values, and lifestyles are absent. As the classroom activities and language become increasingly different from the familiar home environment, the students suffer a loss of confidence and self-esteem, a loss that is sometimes irreparable.

Thus, bilingual and bicultural education programs are sought by tribes to remediate these difficulties. Bilingual teachers (and teacher aides) who can teach and write the native language of the children's cultural group are crucial, as are new curriculum materials that incorporate the oral history, legends, and language structures.

Language and Communication Issues

Some English words have no equivalent in the native tribal language, and this creates difficulties. For example, an interventionist was asked to work with an Indian family whose 6-month-old son was diagnosed with profound bilateral hearing loss (Malach, 1991). When the interventionist tried to explain the diagnosis to the family, the translator used the term "without ears" because there was no equivalent word for hearing loss. The elders in the family said that they did not see a need for intervention if the child could not hear at all. The child's mother, however, wanted some intervention because she said she wanted her son to learn to talk eventually. Her decision, however, had to be supported by the aunts and grandparents. Because it was learned that there had been a translation problem, another attempt was made to explain the facts to the family, using a different interpreter. The interventionist also brought an audiometer and demonstrated the different degrees of hearing loss. She also showed the family a videotape that illustrated the various types of therapeutic activities that would be prescribed for the child. The family finally understood about the hearing loss, but they wanted the intervention delayed until the child was taken to a traditional healer to prepare the child for the therapy sessions. In other words, the family wanted to ensure success with the intervention by seeking and receiving the appropriate blessing from the traditional healer.

Communication style differences may exist between professionals and families, and differences are noted between non-Indians and Indians. Typically, non-Indian professionals ask many different questions and view eye contact as a sign of listening and respect. In contrast, some Indian people are brought up to show respect for people of knowledge and authority by not asking direct questions and not giving eye contact. Also, within many Indian cultures it is appropriate in certain situations to communicate an issue with a third person who assists in giving the information to the intended recipient. Sensitivity to differences in language and communication style will enable the interventionist to establish more supportive and effective exchanges with family members.

SUMMARY AND RECOMMENDATIONS

Summary

The life of an Indian family with special needs is frequently touched by many individuals and institutions. For some families, the touch may be sensitive and caring while for others the touch may be insensitive and uncaring. Sometimes, the Indian family and the interventionist will work together to maximize the client's potential; at other times, each may work at cross-purposes and thereby fail to bring about the expected results.

In Native American communities, as in other communities, there are various formal and informal systems such as the family, the education system, and the health care system that are involved in serving and protecting the well-being of community members. Families generally know how to access or integrate these systems for their own well-being. Unfortunately, because of poverty and other social problems in many Native American families, there may be an overwhelming sense of powerlessness and hopelessness. These families require and need an interventionst—not just to provide help, but also to provide advocacy and encouragement.

Many Native American families distrust public agencies because of previous negative experiences, including racism, discrimination, and/or cultural insensitivity. Many may have experienced the degrading and dehumanizing rituals of public agencies when they go to apply for or to receive public assistance.

The workers in these institutions may see them as lazy and unworthy of the agency's time and money. Further, Native American families may not seek help for fear they will be refused and/or feel intimidated by the time-consuming schedule that requires them to visit four or more agencies. In addition, because of rural isolation and limited experience, many Native American families do not know how to access services or specialists. It is critical that interventionists help coordinate and advocate for a more integrated or comprehensive community-based approach to working with families.

Recommendations for Interventionists

The following recommendations provide some general guidelines for interventionists working with Native American families. These considerations are of particular value to interventionists from non-Indian cultures.

Recommendations Regarding Inclusion of Family Members

- Ask parents whom they want to include in meetings. Do not assume that all Indian parents want to include extended family members or that those family members will want to attend all the meetings. Explain to the parents that all family and nonblood relatives whom they choose to include are welcome. Some families may want to include extended family in meetings while other families will meet with the professionals and then go back and talk to other family members. During home visits, family members may actively participate, while in other homes they may watch or listen from another room.
- When extended family members participate in a meeting, communication should be directed to the entire group, not just to the parents, interpreter, or spokesperson for the family. This shows respect for the entire family.
- Always show respect and provide emotional support to the family. That is done by listening to the family's ideas, acknowledging their concerns and feelings, and including interested family members. This approach allows the family to be an integral part of the intervention plans.

Recommendations for Improving Communication and Interactions

- Take time to learn about the communication style of the Indian families in the communities in which you are providing services. Identify a contact person who can advise you and answer your questions. Be sensitive to the communication interaction styles. For example, an early interventionist who describes herself as a talkative and bubbly person found that in one Indian community she needed to be more reserved and quiet until the families felt more comfortable with her in their homes. She allowed periods of silence to occur and made an effort to talk more slowly.
- When first establishing contact with a family, it is essential to proceed at a pace that is comfortable for the family. Take some time at the beginning of

each visit for "small talk." Ask how they are, comment on the weather, talk about the roads, share an appropriate personal experience (e.g., you were glad to have rain for your own garden), or find things you have in common. This time provides an opportunity for the family to get to know you as a person, and it forms a foundation for developing rapport with the family.

- Ask each family if they want assistance in explaining complicated information (e.g., the results of an evaluation) to other family members. You can offer to meet with those family members or together with them identify an interpreter who can explain the technical information in their native language.

- If the family members speak English as a second language, no matter how good their English language skills are, always offer the services of an interpreter. Most people for whom English is a second language prefer to hear new or technical information in both their native language and English. Even if a family is comfortable talking in English during regular intervention visits, when an evaluation is done or a new treatment procedure is explained, offer the services of an interpreter.

- Always discuss the choice of interpreter with each family first. You may think you have a great interpreter who speaks the language and comes from the same community. However, because the family knows the interpreter, they may not want that person to know their personal business, so they may talk less and be uncomfortable in his or her presence. In some situations, you may need the expertise of a particular interpreter who can translate specific technical terms or information. Tell the family the reason you want to use that interpreter and review the information later after the interpreter is gone.

- When you need to ask a lot of questions (e.g., when obtaining case history information), first explain to the family that you will be asking them questions, what types of questions, and how you will use the information. Tell the family that it is okay for them to ask you questions at any time they do not understand a question or do not understand why you are asking it. Let them know that it is okay if they need to discuss a question with other family members before they answer. Ask them to tell you if they want to think about a question or discuss it with other family members before they answer.

Recommendations Regarding Traditional Beliefs and Practices

- Do not assume an Indian family is or is not practicing its tribal religion and/ or consulting tribal healers. You should ask if they are considering such alternatives so that evaluation or other interventions can be scheduled when it is convenient for the family and child.

- Unless the family volunteers, do not ask a lot of questions about these tribal ceremonies. If you need to notify other co-workers about healing ceremonies that have been planned, ask the family permission and how best to explain it. Some families may consider this information confidential.

- If a child is wearing amulets or certain markings on his or her body, do not remove them without discussing it first with the family. These things may have been given to the child to protect him or her from harm. If they must be removed, explain the reason why and allow the family members to decide who should remove them. If amulets are removed, give them to the family for safekeeping.
- Do not be embarrassed to admit that you know little or nothing about the family's culture. Let the family know that you respect their culture and ask them to let you know if you do or say something wrong. Sincere efforts to learn the culture are appreciated in most instances.

Recommendations Regarding Intervention Procedures

- When doing a home visit, always ask the family if it is a good time to visit before you step in the door. If the family says "no," do not ask why. They may be attending to some religious ceremonies. Respect their privacy, and arrange for a re-visit.
- Explain all timelines and time limitations to families. Tell them the reasons why and the options. Families should know if they need to make a decision by a certain date because of potential medical complications or financial arrangements. Discuss the options and the consequences of each choice.
- Explain medical and other procedures in detail and allow the family to discuss their concerns regarding these procedures. Some may have strong taboos about certain interventions such as transplants, amputations, and/or transfusions.
- When explaining procedures that involve internal organs, ask if models, diagrams, or pictures would be helpful to the family.
- When using visual or treatment aids such as dolls or pictures, discuss with the family any cultural beliefs regarding these that might make them feel uncomfortable.

Recommendations Regarding Case Management

- Whenever possible, the family should have the option to select a case manager whom they know and trust to assist them in accessing services for their child with special needs.
- When changes in staff occur, allow time for transition. Since relationships with individuals are so important, families often feel uncomfortable when they are assigned a new interventionist or case manager without time for transition.
- Families should be given opportunities to talk to other parents who have children with special needs. This suggestion should be offered more than once. Some families have stated that when they were ready, they would have

liked to have known that the opportunity to talk to other parents was still available (Malach, 1991).

Conclusion

In working with Native American families, interventionists must use strategies that are flexible enough to include extended family members if the family so desires and are open enough to incorporate relevant beliefs and values. If interventionists are not from the families' cultures, they should include persons who are knowledgeable about the culture and languages. If there is one recommendation that stands out above all others, it is the need to respect families. When interventionists show respect, all other shortcomings, such as not knowing the culture or language of the family, become secondary.

REFERENCES

Axtell J. (1981). *The European and the Indian: Essays in the ethnohistory of colonial North America*. New York: Oxford University Press.

Berkhofer, R.F., Jr. (1965). *Salvation and the savage: An analysis of Protestant mission and American Indian response, 1787–1862*. Lexington: University of Kentucky Press.

Berkhofer, R.F., Jr. (1979). *The white man's Indian: Images of the American Indians from Columbus to the present*. New York: Vintage Books.

Bopp, J., Bopp, M., Brown, L., & Lane, P. (1984). *The sacred tree*. Lethbridge, Alberta, Canada: Four Worlds Development Press.

Coles, R. (1977). *Children of crisis: Vol. IV. Eskimos, Chicanos, Indians*. Boston: Little, Brown.

Dobyns, H.R. (1988). Indians in the colonial Spanish borderlands. In F. Hoxie (Ed.), *Indians in American history*. Arlington Heights, IL: Harlan Davidson.

Driver, H.E. (1961). *Indians of North America*. Chicago: University of Chicago Press.

DuBray, W.H. (1985). American Indian values: Critical factor in casework. *Social Casework*, *66*(1), 30–37.

Felciano, R. (1990). Bridging both worlds. *Children's Advocate*, *XVIII*(5). (Available from Action Alliance for Children, Oakland, CA).

Good Track, J.G. (1973). Native American non-interference. *Social Work*, *18*, 30–34.

Hilger, S.M.I. (1977). *Chippewa child life and its cultural background*. (Bureau of American Ethnology Bulletin 146). Washington, DC: The Smithsonian Institution.

Ho, M.K. (1987). *Family therapy with ethnic minorities*. Beverly Hills: Sage Publications.

Hoffman, F. (Ed.). (1981). *The American Indian family: Strengths and stresses*. Isleta, NM: American Indian Social Research and Development Association.

Hoxie, F. (Ed.). (1988). *Indians in American history*. Arlington Heights, IL: Harlan Davidson.

Indian Health Service. (1990). *Trends in Indian health*. Washington, DC: U.S. Department of Health and Human Services.

Jennings, F. (1975). *The invasion of America: Indians, colonialism, and the cant of conquest*. Chapel Hill: University of North Carolina Press.

Joe, J.R., & Miller, D.L. (1987). *American Indian cultural perspectives on disability*. Tucson: University of Arizona, Native American Research and Training Center.

Johnson, D. (1991). *1990 census: National and state population counts for American

Indians, Eskimos, and Aleuts. Washington, DC: U.S. Department of Commerce, Bureau of the Census.

Kluckhohn, F.R., & Strodtbeck, F.L. (1961). *Variation in value orientation*. Evanston, IL: Row Peterson.

Lewis, R.G., & Ho, M.K. (1975). Social work with Native Americans. *Social Work*, *20*(5), 379–382.

Malach, R.S. (1991). Unpublished manuscript, Southwest Communication Resources, Bernalillo, NM.

Malach, R.S., Segel, N., & Thomas, T. (1989). *Overcoming obstacles and improving outcomes: Early intervention services for Indian children with special needs*. Bernalillo, NM: Southwest Communication Resources.

Miller, D.L. (1979). *Mother's perception of Indian child development*. Unpublished research report, Institute for Scientific Analysis, San Francisco.

Morey, S.M., & Gilliam, O.L. (1974). *Respect for life: Traditional upbringing of American Indian children*. Garden City, NY: Waldorf Press.

Navajo Division of Education. (1985). *Navajo Nation: Educational policies*. Window Rock, AZ: Navajo Division of Education.

Neihardt, J.G. (1961). *Black Elk speaks*. Lincoln: University of Nebraska.

Northern Ute Tribal Business Council. (1985). Ute language policy. *Cultural Survival Quarterly*, *9*(2), 1–3.

Northwest Indian Child Welfare Institute. (1987). *Cross-cultural skills in Indian child welfare: A guide for the non-Indian*. Portland, OR: Author.

Olson, J.S., & Wilson, R. (1984). *Native Americans in the twentieth century*. Chicago: University of Illinois Press.

Peckham, H., & Gibson, C. (Eds.). (1969). *Attitudes of colonial powers toward the American Indian*. Salt Lake City: University of Utah Press.

Plantz, M.C., & Stinson, F.S. (1986). *Indian people in Indian lands, 1980: Profiles of American Indian and Alaska Native populations in various settings*. Washington, DC: U.S. Department of Health and Human Services, Assistant Secretary for Planning and Evaluation.

Reyhner, J. (1986). *Teaching the Indian child: A bilingual/multicultural approach*. Billings: Eastern Montana College.

Snipp, C.M. (1989). *American Indians: The first of this land*. New York: Russell Sage Foundation.

Stein, H.F. (1985). Therapist and family values in a cultural context. *Counseling and Values*. *30*(1), 35–46.

Thornton, R. (1987). *American Indian holocaust and survival: A population history since 1492*. Norman: University of Oklahoma Press.

Titiev, M. (1972). *The Hopi Indians of Old Oraibi: Change and continuity*. Ann Arbor: University of Michigan Press.

Washburn, W. (1975). *The Indian in America*. New York: Harper & Row.

Zintz, M. (1963). *Education across cultures*. Dubuque, IA: William C. Brown.

APPENDIX A
CONTRASTING BELIEFS, VALUES, AND PRACTICES

American Indian	Anglo-European American
Group life is primary.	Individual is primary.
Respects elders, experts, and those with spiritual powers.	Respects youth, success, and high social status.
Time and place viewed as being permanent, settled.	Time and place always negotiable; plans for change.
Introverted—avoids ridicule or criticism of others if possible.	Extroverted—seeks analysis and criticism of situations.
Pragmatic, accepts "what is."	Reformer, change or "fix" problems.
Emphasizes responsibility for family and personal sphere.	Emphasizes authority and responsibility over a wide area of social life.
Observes how others behave; emphasis on how others "behave," not on what they say.	Eager to relate to others, emphasis on how others "feel" or "think."
Incorporates supportive nonfamily or other helpers into family network.	Keeps network of family, friends, acquaintances separate.
Seeks harmony.	Seeks progress.

From Joe, J.R., & Miller, D. (1987). *American Indian cultural perspectives on disability* (p. 4). Tucson: University of Arizona, Native American Research and Training Center, reprinted with permission.

APPENDIX B
CULTURAL COURTESIES AND CUSTOMS

As previously mentioned, cultural diversity influences the variation of interaction customs. The following examples highlight some of the variation and the differing courtesies and customs interventionists may encounter among some Native American groups:

- It is acceptable to compliment a family on their baby, but it is deemed inappropriate by some families to give a lot of compliments, and thereby draw attention to the child. The child's family may believe that this behavior might bring harm to the child.
- Cradle boards or swings are used by many Indian families. It is important for you to discuss with the family their wishes with respect to removing a child from the cradle board or other child-tending device for intervention activities.
- Certain animals, dolls, and so forth may be considered bad luck or evil in certain Indian tribes. When the intervention therapy for a child requires toys or pictures, you should consult the family to see if the toys or images selected are appropriate. For example, one Indian family came from the reservation to keep a medical appointment, but when the interventionist suggested they eat lunch nearby at the "Owl Cafe," the family became very upset. In this family's culture, owls are considered the sign of a bad omen or evil force.
- Sometimes when a child is in the process of or has completed a healing ceremony, there may be markings or objects (considered sacred) placed on the child's body to protect and/or to ensure healing. If it is necessary to remove any of these objects, you should do this in consultation with the family. The family should be given the option to remove the objects and when objects are removed, they should be returned to the family. In addition, it may be necessary to wash or cleanse an area on the child for certain procedures. If the child has markings, the family again should be asked and their wishes respected.
- Because of distance and socioeconomic hardship, many Indian families living in remote rural areas do not have telephones so some of the home visits made by service providers may not be expected. In these situations, it is customary to drive up and honk the car horn to announce yourself. Because you were not expected, it is also customary that you wait until someone comes out to inquire about the purpose of the visit and with whom the visit is to be made.

    It is always respectful to ask if it is convenient to visit and not assume that because an appointment was made for the home visit that the timing

(continued)

was good. Sometimes no one may answer door knocks even though someone appears to be home. This usually means the family is either busy or is not ready to receive a visitor. Sometimes, ceremonial activities may be taking place and it would be inappropriate for the family to leave the house or be interrupted.

- During home visits, especially the first one, ask the family where they would like you to sit. Do not assume a certain location is best. The family will feel more comfortable if you ask them.
- It is not uncommon during home visits to have family members or other relatives coming and going; they may be participating in the discussion. If confidential matters need to be discussed, it may be better to ask the family to come to the agency.
- When conducting a home visit or carrying out therapeutic activities in the home, it is customary to address all those who are present.
- Oftentimes during home visits, you may be offered food or coffee. If you have just eaten, you may explain this and ask if you can take a little bit of the food with you or if you can have water instead of coffee. To refuse without explanation is considered rude.
- Although it is not expected, it is also permissible to reciprocate and bring cookies or a small treat for the child or children if you wish to do so.
- As discussed elsewhere in this chapter, some families may follow the traditional tribal childrearing practices, and therefore, grandparents, not parents, may have the primary parental role. Other family members may serve as disciplinarians. In some homes, children with special needs may not be disciplined because it is felt that they have suffered so much already. These issues need to be discussed with the family so that the roles of the family and the interventionists are clear.
- Sometimes rapport with a family happens immediately, but if it does not, it is important to be patient and to continue to be available and follow through on plans made with the family. Once trust has developed, in most instances, the service provider often becomes included in the family network.

APPENDIX C
SIGNIFICANT CULTURAL EVENTS/HOLIDAYS/PRACTICES

There is a great variation from Indian tribe to Indian tribe with respect to cultural events, particularly those related to childrearing, health, and healing practices. Within some tribes, a number of ceremonies can take place only at certain times. The ceremonial cycles may follow the season or be determined by the family's resources. In some ceremonial activities, the family must pay for the ceremony with money and gifts, while other ceremonies may require only gifts. In some instances, certain ceremonies also may be scheduled by elders with limited prior notice. For example, a family may not know until the day of the ceremony that their child has been scheduled for the ceremony.

Because of the diversity among families and the continuum of acculturation within tribal groups and families, the interventionist should learn about the customs of his or her clients. If a tribe has a ceremony that prohibits interaction with outsiders for a week or two, it would be inappropriate for a service provider to schedule a home visit during this time. Such isolation, however, is not usually called for in most of the ceremonies, but it is important to ask prior to any home visit if it is convenient for the family.

Some cultural events that are common to many tribes include ceremonies related to the birth of a child, the celebration of the child's first smile/laugh, puberty, marriage, blessing of new homes, death, and/or the end of a mourning period. In addition to these more common ceremonies, during times of misfortune or illness, healing ceremonies may take place; these also may occur prior to a significant intervention, such as surgery. Children with disabilities may undergo a number of healing ceremonies, depending on the diagnosis and cultural orientation of the family.

While most of these ceremonies are tribally specific, most Indian families today also celebrate the national holidays, such as Christmas and Easter, and depending on the religious affiliation, religious holidays such as certain saint days may be observed with tribal dancing or ceremonies. In some communities, the Fourth of July celebration may consist of a rodeo, traditional tribal dances, and carnival rides.

Within some Indian communities, there also are other events that may not be culturally related but are nevertheless customary and may influence intervention activities. These may include hunting season, harvesting or planting, and "check day." The latter is usually when the public assistance check arrives, or it is pay day at work, and/or it is per capita distribution day. These days are usually busy for most Indian families who live in rural communities because it may be the only time they go into town to shop or do a variety of other things such as have the car fixed, do the laundry, take the children to the dentist, keep doctor's appointments, and so forth.

chapter 6 _____

FAMILIES WITH AFRICAN AMERICAN ROOTS

Winnie Willis

> In the fear of the Lord is strong confidence: and his children shall have a place of refuge.
> —Proverbs 14:26

> Know where you came from and you'll always know where you're going.

> Boast not thyself of tomorrow; for thou knowest not what a day may bring forth.
> —Proverbs 27:1

> Don't be fooled by a whole lot of show.

African Americans and the richness of their culture have been a part of the United States since its founding. Although much of their history has only recently been told, African Americans have contributed to every aspect of the country's development. Of all of the diverse groups that make up the United States, African Americans are unique in their history of immigration. Although some Africans entered the United States as free men and women, the majority were forcibly taken from villages in Africa, held captive on ships for the long journey across the Atlantic, and sold into slavery on southern colonial plantations. The long path to freedom and equality has influenced the lives of African Americans in the United States just as their cultural heritage and accomplishments have helped to shape the nation. This chapter highlights aspects of history, contemporary life, and the values and beliefs that are important for interventionists to be aware of as they serve African American families.

BACKGROUND

Geographic Origins

The people called African Americans originate from the continent of Africa. They come from several racial stocks and tribes including Mandingo, Ibos, Efiks, Hausas, Krus, Yorubas, Ashantis, and Sengalese (Bennett, 1966).

Historical Origins

The following overview of African American history does not provide a myriad of detail about numerous significant historic events and people, but enough is included for the reader to identify historical trends and events that have shaped the lives and culture of all Americans, particularly African Americans. With a history of migration to this country unlike that of any other racial or ethnic group, and through years of slavery and denial of basic "inalienable" rights, African Americans continue to survive, adapt, and even prosper, within a cultural identity that has been shaped by Africa and by America.

17th Century

By far the majority of African American people spring from ancestors who came to America as slaves, against their will. The transporting of slaves across the Atlantic from the West African coast is described as the "greatest migration in recorded history" (Bennett, 1966, p. 30). Of the estimated 40 million Africans forcibly removed from their homeland between the 16th and 19th centuries, 20 million came to the New World, including South and Central America, the West Indies, and North America. The 4 million who came to North America are the genesis of today's African Americans.

By the beginning of the 18th century, 50,000–100,000 Africans each year were being moved across the Atlantic to Europe and the Americas. In fact, European and American economies were totally intertwined with and dependent upon the slave trade. Although it appeared that the plantation system in America was the economic sector most heavily dependent upon slavery, the mercantile system based in New England also could not have existed without slavery. African labor kept the rum, sugar, and molasses trade going; supported the industries that developed around tobacco, hemp, fishing, railroading, and distilling; and supplied the artisans (Genovese, 1974).

It is an important part of African American history to note, however, that some few Africans who came to America were not slaves. The first recorded landing of Africans on American soil took place before the slave trade was at its height, in 1619. Prominent historian Lerone Bennett (1966) stated that their arrival in Jamestown, Virginia, occurred "one year before the Mayflower, 113 years before the birth of George Washington, and 244 years before the signing of the Emancipation Proclamation" (p. 29). These Africans came to sell their services for a specified number of years as indentured servants, which was also common practice for whites who were looking for a new life. In the subsequent years, a small number of free men and women from the West Indies and Africa also immigrated to America.

18th and 19th Centuries

Whether slave or free, Africans were as integral a part of the building of pre- and post-Revolutionary America as the whites; and if bloodshed and sweat are weighted, some would say more so. Their contribution to trade, industry, and agriculture was significant and immeasurable, and they distinguished themselves in the major wars of their new land as well. They fought side by side with whites in the American Revolution and the Civil War—in the hope that changes that took place would afford them the status of being "created equal" with "certain inalienable rights."

Crispus Attucks, a former slave, was the first man to die in 1770 during the Boston Massacre, the event that crystallized the colonies' commitment to severance from the British Empire. African American soldiers from all of the original 13 states fought bravely in most of the major battles of the Revolutionary War; and some 100,000 slaves did receive their freedom as a direct result of the war (Bennett, 1966).

During the Civil War, African Americans were originally barred from military service by the Lincoln Administration; however, they were finally recruited and recognized, if not warmly accepted, when it became apparent that the confederacy would be a formidable opponent for the Union Army. By the end of 1863, the year in which the Emancipation Proclamation was signed, some 50,000 African American soldiers were in the Union army. It was during that summer that they demonstrated the strength of their commitment to the cause and the skill and bravery with which they were willing to carry it out. The battles of Port Hudson, Milliken's Bend, and Fort Wagner signify the honor African American men gained in fighting for freedom (Bennett, 1966).

Neither the dreams inspired by the American Revolution nor the hopes built upon the Emancipation Proclamation and the uniting of the states were to be so easily realized. African Americans were tolerable as slaves, but as free people they were viewed as a threat to the way of life of the whites. What to do with them became the conundrum of the day: Too many of them were walking around free, and no plans for getting rid of them had been proposed. Years of racial hatred ensued that saw the advent of contradictory social forces: the Reconstruction Era, the Freedmen's Bureau, the Ku Klux Klan, and the Black Codes. The Reconstruction Era spanned the years 1867 to 1877, during which time the South Carolina House of Representatives had an African American majority; and postmasters, policemen, judges, and bishops were African American. The Freedmen's Bureau lasted 5 years (1865–1870), during which time it gave aid and assistance to freedmen and poor whites in the areas of medical care and education. The Ku Klux Klan, organized in 1866 as a white supremacy group devoted to committing atrocities against African Americans, and to whom the institutionalization of the practice of lynching can be credited, has continued to the present day. The Black Codes (1865–1866) were harbingers of many years of systematic disenfranchisement of African Americans. In 1896, the U.S. Supreme Court wrote the doctrine of racial separation and classification into law (*Plessy v. Ferguson,* 1896). It gave states the sanction and power to establish "separate but equal" accommodations and institutions for the races. Segregation had officially begun and the spark ignited the profusely spread kindling of the post-Civil War and Reconstruction Era racial discontents.

Beginning in the 1890s and continuing through World War II, many African Americans migrated from the South to the North in search of greater opportunities. However, there migrations coincided with considerable crowding in northern and eastern cities occasioned by the influx of European immigrants (Leigh & Green, 1982). Although charity organizations with mostly affluent, white volunteers provided services to the newly arrived European immigrants, African Americans were viewed as "a group apart—a caste—physically present in American society but culturally distinctive because of appearance, origins, and the experience with slavery" (Leigh & Green, 1982, p. 95). Therefore, except for the settlement house movement of the 1880s, little was done to assist African Americans to obtain education, housing, and employment. As a result of the prejudice encountered in the North, urban ghettos with slum conditions grew up and became the homes for many African Americans. The impact of prejudice, poverty, and urban ghettos continues to affect many African Americans disproportionately to the present day.

20th Century

By 1901, laws dealing with "Jim Crow," a term that had become synonymous with African Americans, had become the fabric of how the races would relate to one another. It was clear that the relationship would be based on skin color and myths of genetic superiority for whites and inferiority for African Americans. Considerable time and energy of the states were expended in the implementation of laws separating the races in schools, housing, jobs, public facilities, and services. Miscegenation, the mingling of the races sexually, was seen by many as the real motivation for most of what Jim Crow signified (Bennett, 1966). The culmination of Jim Crow, however, was seen in the systematic and extreme measures taken by states to deprive African Americans of the right to vote, which had been theirs since the Emancipation Proclamation. "Grandfather" clauses, literacy tests, "white" primaries, and poll taxes were the most commonly used methods of disqualifying African American voters, while maintaining sufficient loopholes for whites. For a period of about 40 years, white Americans went about the business of pursuing the American Dream— getting an education, participating in meaningful work, marrying, raising a family. Whether any dream at all was present in the African American community was of concern to African Americans only—because of the stranglehold of Jim Crow, they could not partake of the vast resources and opportunities of that period.

Two major historical events became the catalysts for change. During World War II, after considerable pressure from organized African American groups, the military was officially desegregated. And, in 1954, the Supreme Court struck its most significant blow to the Jim Crow rampage with the *Brown v. Board of Education* decision. The decision concluded that "separate but equal" had no place in the American system of education and stated that separate educational facilities were inherently unequal (Bremner, 1974). However, the legacy of the incredible wall of Jim Crow, the pervasive, deep-seated warping of attitudes of whites toward African Americans, was not to be removed by a decree of the Supreme Court. Negative attitudes, instilled by years of institutionalized breeding of fear and contempt, are still evident. In 1991 it may be masked under the guise of preference to share life experiences with people of "one's own kind." However, there are multiple, recent examples where the surface veneer has been scratched and hatred and violence, for no other reason than race, have erupted to the surprise and consternation of those who witness it as well as those who are caught up in it. The recent murder of an African American youth visiting an all-white neighborhood to purchase a car (Mandulo, 1991), the videotaped beating of an African American man by a group of Los Angeles Police Department officers ("Reassuring a Troubled Citizenry," 1991), and the resurgence of activity within the Ku Klux Klan all underscore the continued existence of racial prejudice and hatred.

Throughout all the years of adversity, however, there have been African American heroes who are bigger than life, distinguishing themselves in politics, medicine, the arts, religion, education, and in the development of a social/community order. They have stoked the pride, the will to survive, and the determination to gain equality of opportunity for their people during some of the darkest hours. African Americans from W.E.B. Dubois to Mary McLeod Bethune, Marcus Garvey to Gwendolyn Brooks, Duke Ellington to Marion Anderson, Thurgood Marshall to Autherine Lucey, and Martin Luther King, Jr. to Alice Walker have served as examples for the African American community as well as the world.

African American leadership organizations influenced the lives of these individuals, and their contributions to the viability of the organizations is undeniable. The National Association for the Advancement of Colored People (NAACP) was founded in 1909, and the Urban League was founded in 1910. The National Council of Negro Women began in 1935, the Congress of Racial Equality (CORE) in 1943, the United Negro College Fund (UNCF) in 1944, and the Southern Christian Leadership Conference (SCLC) in 1957. During the 1960s, new groups such as Operation Push and the Student Non-Violent Coordinating Committee (SNCC) attained prominence as activist organizations.

Martin Luther King, Jr., after several years of involvement in the civil rights struggles of the late 1950s and the early 1960s, became the central charismatic leader around whom the committed workers of all races united. The civil rights workers from the sit-ins, freedom rides, and voter registration drives, as well as ordinary people of conscience, coalesced as a dynamic, nonviolent force that could not be ignored. The efforts of years of action by people at the grassroots level came together under the banner of the movement for civil rights and racial equality. There existed a spirit of readiness, and the galvanizing leadership of Martin Luther King, Jr. was the spark that was needed.

Who, of age, cannot remember the excitement, hope, and the call to action engendered by the historic March on Washington in 1965? Everyone was there by way of television; it, therefore, had a far wider impact than would have otherwise been afforded. This nationwide visibility, as well as the televising of the civil unrest, peace demonstrations, and the violence attendant to the attempts of African Americans to gain admission to formerly segregated institutions, provided a large segment of the American population with a first hand look at the pervasiveness of the problem of race relations in a society where many people had thought the problems no longer existed.

The Civil Rights Act and the Economic Opportunity Act of 1964, and the Voting Rights Act of 1965, as well as other landmark legislation affecting the quality of life for African Americans, were passed during the transition years of the Kennedy to Johnson Administrations. These pieces of federal legislation gave the government the power to intervene in cases of discrimination within the individual states, without which school desegregation and other discrimination and criminal cases affecting African Americans could not have been settled.

Religious Origins

Early African religion was centered on the concept of a supreme God who created the Earth, and that this Creator had a life force that was present in all things. The worship of ancestors and the spirits of nature existed simultaneously. Ancestors were venerated and deified upon their deaths, and it was believed that the ancestral spirit remained with the family as protector. The earliest ancestors were seen as having the greatest influence and power, and therefore were most devoutly worshiped. Rituals of ancestor worship were conducted by the eldest family member because that person had the closest connection to the ancestors. Religion and family were thus inextricably woven.

This link was best observed in the elaborate funerals provided to family members, where special attention to ritual was the family obligation as a show of respect for the spirit of the deceased. The worship of spirits of nature, such as the land, trees, and terrestrial bodies, was also common. Sacred objects were made of wood, rock, or other minerals and ancestral bones. Sometimes animals and prisoners were sacrificed to appease the gods. Ceremonies also included the drinking of specially prepared beer, wine, and other libations (Bennett, 1966; Franklin, 1967).

The influence of Islam and Christianity on the early African tribes has been greatly exaggerated, according to Franklin (1967). Neither ever supplanted tribal religious practices, although they clashed in a struggle for the souls of Africa. Islam offered opportunities for cultural and economic advancement. Christianity contained major contradictions for many Africans who saw, on the one hand, that the religion did not condemn the brutality of the slave trade, while, on the other hand, it preached brotherhood and equality.

In the New Land, slaves were not allowed to practice their religion openly because by its very nature religion is collective, and any collective activity not supervised by the slaveowner was thought to be seditious. However, some slaveowners did permit their slaves to hear the Gospel as long as the central message was that from Ephesians 6:5, which preached obedience of the servant to the master (Bennett, 1966). Of course, slaves did, in secret, practice the religion they brought from Africa, and they sang openly. They sang the songs of hope, of joy, and of tears. Songs were a means of communication with God, and with one another in a collective experience, and were also a source of individual comfort. These spirituals, in their purity and intensity, continue to be the foundation of African American worship and a dynamic part of African Americans' proud heritage.

The organized church in African American life was established after the Revolutionary War, in 1787, by Richard Allen and Absalom Jones, in Philadelphia. It was called the Free African Society, and out of it came the African Methodist Episcopal (AME) Church. About the same time, the African Methodist Episcopal Zion (AMEZ) Church was established in New York City. It should be noted that this was about 75 years before the Emancipation Proclamation. During the early years of the entrenchment of Jim Crow, around the start of the 20th century, there was a surge in the quality of the group life of African Americans, because the African American church had become a vital and dynamic institution. The AME, AMEZ, and the Baptist churches had increasing memberships and thereby increased financial bases and power. The churches were the places where most African Americans saw and participated in leadership and organizational experiences (Bennett, 1966; Billingsley, 1974).

Language/Linguistic Origins

Many different languages were spoken in Africa, but there were commonalities. Most were not written, but Egyptian, Ethiopian, Berber, and a language of the Vai people in Liberia had written forms before white people ever came to the continent. It is believed that Swahili, the pan-African language, has been in written form since the 12th century (Maquet, 1972). Although new slaves were required to take on new names and to learn pidgin English, scholar Lorenzo Turner (cited in Bennett, 1966) has found evidence of the survival of Africanism in the language of the United States, especially in the South. For example, the word goober is used for peanut, gumbo for okra, tote for carry, and yam for sweet potato. African names also abound in many African American families of the 1990s.

Some African Americans use a dialect called "Black English." Black English is influenced by some retained African language patterns, social factors such as socioeconomic status (SES), and geographic region. It may serve a symbolic function of uniting its speakers (Hannerz, 1969; Kochman, 1972; Labov, 1972; Mancini, 1980). Black English, like any dialect, serves as a bond between African Americans and is usually not spoken by others (Tiedt & Tiedt, 1990). Dillard (1972) estimated that as many as 80% of African Americans use Black English. He also stated that the amount and place of use is highly associated with SES, with generally wider use among African Americans of lower SES and selected use by those of higher SES. He cautioned that an understanding of Black English use, or the use of any other dialect, can only be gained when efforts to compare it to Standard American English in a pejorative manner are abandoned. Black English and slang are *not* the same.

Black English is most different from Standard American English in its linguistic syntax, including the way verbs are used; its features also include ambiguity and double-entendre. According to Genovese (1974), the ability to code switch (i.e., to move back and forth between Standard American English and Black English) has served its users well throughout the years. For more information about Black English, the reader is referred to J.L. Dillard's *Black English* (1972), Burling Robbins's *English in Black and White* (1973), or other books listed in the reference section of this chapter.

CONTEMPORARY LIFE

Lerone Bennett (1966, p. 24) described the person who came out of Africa as a "courageous individual" who was used to hard work and a well-organized social life. John Hope Franklin (1967) stated that African experiences are so deeply rooted that the customs and traditions still exist today. With these influences and a history of struggle on the American soil, African Americans have kept their faith; their sense of family, community, and country; and an abiding commitment to achievement, despite the problems that exist within some segments of the African American community.

African Americans made up 12% (30,326,000) of the population of the United States in 1988. They are heavily concentrated geographically in the southern Atlantic area of the United States (21.0%). The next highest concentration is in northern, midwestern, and western urban centers. Thirty-seven percent have completed 4 years of high school as compared to nearly 40% of whites. Fifteen percent have completed 1–3 years of college and 11.3% have completed 4 or more years of college (U.S. Bureau of the Census, 1990). Occupationally, the percentage of African American males in the professional-managerial classes was 17.4% in 1980, as compared to 31.4% for white males (Allen & Farley, 1986). The percentage of professional-managerial African American females was 18.5% in 1980, as compared to 24.4% for white females, reflecting less disparity than among males.

Many African American families are doing well and thriving, with increasing numbers completing their education and entering the professions;

most are ordinary people who are making it day to day without fanfare. However, major inequities in income, health, and quality of life between African Americans and whites continue to exist, and are increasing. In 1988, the median household income for African Americans was $16,407, 57% of the median income for whites and 80% of the Hispanic median income (U.S. Bureau of the Census, 1990). Twenty-eight percent of African American families had incomes below the poverty level, which is over three and a half times as many as whites (7.9%), and somewhat more than Hispanic families (23.7%) (U.S. Bureau of the Census, 1990). According to U.S. Census Bureau (1986) figures, one out of two African American children live in poverty, compared with one in every five for all children in the United States—even though 53% of the mothers of African American children under age 6 work, as compared to 45% of white mothers with children under age 6 (McAdoo & McAdoo, 1985). Almost 43% of children from African American families live in homes in which the father is absent, and 67.1% of these households are poor (U.S. Bureau of the Census, 1987).

> The rising tide of opportunity brought by the Civil Rights Movement was neither long enough nor strong enough to enable most Black children to gain the opportunities that so many white children take for granted. . . . Black children, youth, and their families remain worse off than whites in every aspect of American life. (McAdoo & McAdoo, 1985, p. 74)

African Americans make up the majority of the population in major inner-city areas of the United States, where crime, poor housing, unemployment, and lack of access to services is widespread (U.S. Department of Health and Human Services [DHHS], 1985). The urban slum conditions that were a result of prejudice encountered by African Americans in education, job opportunities, and housing in their migrations north and to larger cities persist in the 1990s. In these environments, where problems of poverty, overcrowding, violent crime, illegal drug trafficking, and lack of services are widespread, children and families are at considerable risk for high infant mortality, poor health, and psychological problems (Allen & Majidi-Ahi, 1989; Randall-David, 1989).

In inner-city areas of the United States, homicide is the leading cause of death for young adult males under 25 with the African American–white ratio being 5.88:1 (DHHS, 1985). Accidental death and injury are also common. In 1982, the estimated life expectancy for African American males was 7 years less than that for white males; heart disease (African American–white ratio of 1.29:1) and cancer (African American–white ratio of 1.32:1) continue to claim the lives of both males and females disproportionately (DHHS, 1985). Infant mortality is 20 per 1,000 African American live births versus 10.5 per 1,000 white births; low birthweight is a factor in 12% of African American infants versus 6.8% of white infants—a ratio of nearly 2:1. Death from nutritional deficiency in infancy is more than 10 times as likely as for whites, death from sudden infant death syndrome is twice as likely to occur, and one in eight Afri-

---

Case Example #1

When the interventionists received the referral for Tanya, they felt overwhelmed by the problems that they thought that her family would present. The referral information included the following. Tanya was born at 36 weeks gestation with myelomeningocele. She has had several surgeries to repair the opening, but has not had to have a shunt implanted. At this point in her life (8 months adjusted age), she has spent more time in the hospital than at home; although she is now medically stable and beginning to grow and gain weight. Her mother, Shareen, is 17 years old, single, and she dropped out of high school. She became involved in illegal drug use when she was 16, and continued to use drugs until she was admitted to a treatment program that would accept a pregnant teenager. Shareen is unemployed, unskilled, and does not have her own housing. Tanya's father was a street acquaintance of Shareen's, and he has since disappeared.

The referral records for Tanya and her mother painted a very bleak picture; like many agency records, they described the weaknesses rather than the strengths and focused on dysfunction rather than resilience. The records did not include the following. Shareen was a bright student who had been doing well in high school until her father died unexpectedly of a heart attack. After his death, she became severely depressed and began to experiment with drugs. When she discovered that she was pregnant, she sought help from her mother, aunt, and a school counselor with whom she had a strong relationship. During the drug treatment program, she began to study for the GED exam to complete high school, and she will be able to take the exam in 2 more months. In anticipation of having her high school equivalency diploma, Shareen has begun to explore community college options that would allow her to work and begin a degree program. She is also attracted to the local community college because there is cooperative child care on campus that would accept Tanya. The program would also give her a chance to learn more about parenting and child development. Currently, Shareen and Tanya are living with her mother and aunt who are supportive and nurturing. Their home is comfortable, safe, and they are surrounded by family and friends who are available if needed. In addition to studying, caring for Tanya, and helping at home, Shareen works 20 hours per week in a local social service agency as a clerical assistant. Despite her medical problems, Tanya has become a happy, engaging baby; her prognosis is very good.

Clinical records often do not tell the whole story. This may be especially true when families of color are referred for services. This case example illustrates the differences between records and reality and how important it is to avoid stereotyping individuals and families.

---

can American children under the age of 6 has an elevated blood lead level (McAdoo & McAdoo, 1985; DHHS, 1985).

These statistics have numerous implications for interventionists. The environments in which many poor, African American families live and rear their children are ones in which survival is paramount. Protecting themselves and their children from violence, locating affordable housing, keeping their children healthy, obtaining medical care when illness occurs, providing food, and paying the rent are major stressors in the lives of these families. These stressors, combined with continued discrimination and rejection that may result in feelings of rage, worthlessness, and hopelessness, underscore the importance of family-focused interventions (Randall-David, 1989). To be effective, services must consider the child's ecological context and the needs of the total family, not just the child who is disabled or at risk (Allen & Majidi-Ahi, 1989). Interventionists must recognize and utilize the strengths of African American families—such as the support of kinship networks and strong work orientation in support of family ties—and help families to regain a measure of control over their own lives. It is also important for the interventionist to recognize the difference between cultural/ethnic/racial differences and differences that are attributable to poverty. Being poor in an affluent society whose symbols of wealth are everywhere may result in coping strategies that seem self-defeating, but it is the interventionists' role to help combat the racism that these families encounter rather than assume that it is the family that is pathological (Allen & Majidi-Ahi, 1989). The deficit model that has been used to explain differences in poor African American families must be replaced by an awareness described by Leigh and Green (1982):

> Poverty, even where blatantly apparent, does not exist simply because some have worked hard to change their lot in life and others have not. Poverty always serves social purposes. That is, the interests of someone, somewhere, are being met through the disadvantage of others. (p. 119)

VALUES

Family

"My family," "my folks," "my kin," "my people" are terms used by African Americans to identify blood relatives and to denote relationships with special friends or "cared for" individuals who are not related. Thus, family is a group of people who feel they belong to each other, and they may or may not live in the same house (Billingsley, 1974). Values related to family are rooted in African traditions. Billingsley (1968) described the importance of marriage in West African society as a way to link lineages and villages. The family and kin relationships that resulted were governed by complex rules that guided interactions and ensured that physical necessities and support were available to all (Leigh & Green, 1982). Although slavery disrupted the traditions and family relationships that Africans had grown up with, it did not eliminate the value of kinship. In fact, kinship bonds became a major means of support for slaves. Because both men and women had to work on the plantations and tend their own plots to supplement the food provided by their owners, young children were often cared for by older women or older children; often, the biological parents had little time with or direct involvement in the child's upbringing. However, within the rigid constraints of plantation life, men established close, affectionate bonds with their wives and children and asserted their domestic authority to the extent possible. Women nurtured and socialized their children and tended to their husbands. Despite the facts that formal marriage among slaves was not recognized and family members were routinely separated from one another through sale to another plantation, family bonds and kinship ties remained strong (Leigh & Green, 1982). The stereotype that African American families were disorganized by slavery and that such disorganization persists is not supported by historical fact (Leigh & Green, 1982).

The fact that African American family members may or may not live together is of fundamental importance to interventionists because it means that a demographic status such as "female single head of household" does not in many instances credit the existence of this individual in a kinship group of people who care about each other and feel that they belong together. Although times have changed and African American lifestyles are undergoing tremendous evolution, the extended family is still quite viable for many.

The family is the source and the reflection of the African American culture. The culture of a people is the way in which they live their lives, the way

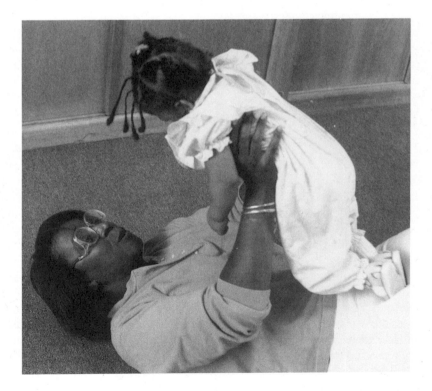

they express their beings. African Americans value communication, both verbal and musical. Kochman, as cited by Genovese (1974), suggested that prestige associated with African American speech behavior relates to patterns of speaking that have been used successfully to manipulate and control situations—an art and a skill with high value in settings in which one has few other options. Genovese (1974, p. 432) pointed out that "even today in the black urban ghettos verbal ability contributes at least as much as physical strength to individual prestige." In the culture, verbal communication includes making particular use of phraseology and rhythmic cadence of expression; it is reaching out, keeping the lines open, and showing interest in what the other person thinks and feels.

Music is an integral part of life. It is experienced either interactively by following the words, dancing, tapping, or bobbing to the rhythm; or it may be experienced passively as a part of the environment, like sunlight or wind, or as a part of life, like a heartbeat. However the individual prefers to experience it, it is a vital and living aspect of African American culture. Because of the relatively continuous presence of words or music among African Americans, some people would characterize them as "loud" or shallow. These pejorative terms reflect perceptions stemming from a different set of cultural values, as well as a lack of understanding of African American values. The lesson is that both value systems have legitimacy, and recognition of differences opens the door to a better understanding between groups, or between interventionists and clients.

The family has kept the culture alive because information about it was either not available or distorted in school or in the larger society (Billingsley, 1974). American history as taught in the schools has typically neglected the contributions of African Americans to the building of this country, as well as their influence on the manner in which all Americans live and work today. However, African American history and culture are increasingly being included in school curricula, which extends what children learn in the family and community.

The family also has been the source of strength, resilience, and survival. The value of group effort for the common interest is taught as a more enduring strategy for the survival of the African American community, as opposed to individual effort for private gain (Billingsley, 1974). Private gain is well respected, but there is an expectation among many African Americans that it will be shared in reasonable measure with the larger community. An important part of the message about survival that is instilled within the context of the family is the value of independence—the ability to stand on one's own feet, to have one's "own thing." This may seem at first to be in conflict with the group-effort ethic, but it actually extends that ethic. It has to do with the empowerment that comes when as many as are able can earn a living, meet their family's basic needs, and have a little bit left over to help others in the extended family who may need temporary assistance. As the extended family circles widen and overlap, the entire community would theoretically be covered. In addition to contributions, it is common practice within African American families to make small loans with token or no interest to one another on a short-term basis. The ability "to get it from each other" is highly valued because underlying the exchange of funds is the strength that comes from self-reliance and the demonstration of trust between family members.

The family also provides socialization, guidance, and inspiration (Billingsley, 1974). The most primary socialization task of the African American family is instilling in its members a sense of who they are. This includes knowledge of the African heritage, the history of the American experience, and how the two sources have blended to produce the contemporary African American. According to Billingsley (1974), each is complex and varied, but highly interrelated. The process is all about pride and the development of competent individuals. Billingsley (1974) further stated that the process of socialization enables the individual to develop an African American consciousness, which is an awareness of a common history, common heritage, and common predicament. The instilling of this consciousness is an important part of each child's socialization.

Many white people feel that African Americans are overly sensitive and that they imagine slights and offenses where none exist. It is the institutionalization or normalizing of prejudice against African Americans that makes prejudice invisible. In other words, if it is the norm, then it is acceptable, unremarkable, and most critically, unrecognizable—except by the person on the receiving end. Many African Americans have tried to explain to white friends and colleagues the validity of their sensitivity to prejudice activated by the African American family socialization process. A cornerstone in this process of prejudice barrier education has to do with teaching the individual how not to waste valuable energy on knee-jerk responses to "minor" incidents reflecting prejudice.

Fairly universally, whites have trouble relating to this because they have never experienced discrimination on the basis of the color of their skin. Even for those African Americans who have an education and have attained a certain economic status, the salient characteristic of African Americans is their skin color. Those whites who need to test this statement for its validity should go to a restaurant in a predominantly African American neighborhood, eat their meal there, and then describe their feelings about being noticed because of the color of their skin. This exercise, undoubtedly, will contribute significantly to a better understanding of color consciousness in American society. Further, it is vital that interventionists understand why prejudice barrier education is a fundamental building block in the socialization of African American children.

Respect for Elders

Although changes in African American families, like changes in all families in the United States, have diluted the importance of elders, many African American families continue to place a high value on respecting and obeying elders (Randall-David, 1989). Elderly persons are seen to have wisdom and hindsight. They have seen things "come around" and "go around," and they have witnessed a lot of what the younger generation calls history. In the South, titles of respect, such as "Ma'am" or "Sir" are still widely used. Just as in the early African religions, the oldest are also believed to have a special status and an ability to communicate with God; therefore, they are routinely in charge of prayers. In addition to honoring the special status of elderly persons, there is a high value placed on obedience to parents as well as other older persons, including an older sibling. The learning of obedience and respect for elders is the child's earliest contribution to family maintenance and cohesiveness.

Education

The attainment of one's potential through the acquisition of education, life skills, and personal competence is a major goal and desired achievement among African Americans. The family nourishes and supports individual ability through a strong belief in education as the means to a better life. The promise of education is and has been a beacon for many African American families, and individuals who have attained high educational goals come not just from the so-called better, stronger families, but from families with a variety of statuses and fortunes. With regard to educational attainment, the difference between ordinary and extraordinary people is often opportunity—something that has not been consistently available to African Americans (Billingsley, 1974). Families often tell their children that times and situations may change, but a good education is something no one can take away. Education enables the individual to weather changing times.

Humor

In describing plantation life, Genovese (1974) said that "the songs, often made up on the spot, bristled with sharp wit, both malicious and gentle. . . . but the songs also turned to satire . . . they [the slaves] turned their wit and incredible talent for improvisation into social criticism" (p. 317, p. 318). For many African Americans, humor continues to be a way of keeping the spirits up and a way of interpreting the reality of their world—the world "according to us."

The gift of people who are humorous may not always be in the raucous funniness of the situation itself, but as much in the act of telling the story or delivering the line. The "world according to us" is a good title for humor that African Americans use to reinterpret or find new meaning in situations acted out in the larger society. For example, it would involve the stripping of the "fancy language" from a political speech and replacing it with "plain talk," and "here's what he really means" from the African American perspective. Ordinary conversations are often embellished by a liberal sprinkling of metaphors and descriptors, and body language and motion are used by the more gifted storytellers to illustrate or emphasize points.

Interventionists need to keep in mind that this kind of humor provides a healthy release of feelings and concerns. It does not mean that the humorist is making light of the situation or that he or she does not see its seriousness. In fact, satire and social criticism are extremely serious and sophisticated forms of humor that allow everyone involved to see the world from a different perspective.

Religion

Religion is a confirmation of identity, a confirmation of being God's children (Billingsley, 1974). African Americans may belong to one of several different organized religions, but more important than the particular denomination is the place of religion in the life of the family and community. Religion has traditionally been the source of spiritual sustenance in the African American family whether the family regularly attends church or not (Randall-David, 1989). It is important to sanctify life events such as marriages, births, and deaths in the church because it validates their meaning in the family and community. Although the organized church of today is somewhat less influential than in the past, the spiritual resources of the community have had a direct impact on the lives of most African American people of substance (Billingsley, 1974). Children are taught early on that they must "believe in something" (have faith) in order to have a good (meaningful) life.

From its inception, the African American church has been the place where community members learned the values and responsibilities of leadership and organizational skills, since in the past these experiences have not been available to African Americans in the larger society. The church is a complex organization that has the responsibility for producing a weekly worship service, with all its component parts such as choir, ushers, and Sunday School; and the responsibility for outreach, missionary programs, and community-based activities such as visiting parishioners who are sick, providing food for those who are poor, and conducting educational and recreational programs. Young and inexperienced people are mentored by the elders. It is also where many children and young adults identify role models. Among the values stressed by the church are humaneness and sympathy for others, as well as offering a helping hand when needed.

Interventionists should learn about the importance of religion or an organized church to each of the African American families that they serve. In some instances, with the family's permission, their minister or other church members may be important allies in the intervention (Randall-David, 1989). The informal support network provided through these channels may be far more valuable than referrals to a multitude of bureaucratic agencies.

BELIEFS

Childrearing

African Americans believe that children are the future. Children need to know that they are loved and that they belong. Children need adult protection and guidance. They must be disciplined, and all responsible adults in the community take part in the training and discipline of the child. Children must have a good education, good food, and a place to play. Once young children are able to speak and understand, they are expected to obey the family rules, to treat others as they want to be treated, and to do their schoolwork to the best of their ability. Although these beliefs are not acted upon by all African Americans because of their life circumstances, they form a core set of beliefs that continue to be valued by many.

African Americans are firmly committed to developing the child's knowledge of his or her kinship and of who his or her people/family are. As the knowledge is instilled, so is a sense of curiosity and caring about family relationships. It is quite rewarding to see a child's first awareness that "Momma's sister" is "my aunt," or that Sandra is "my sister." As children place themselves within this circle of people they care about and who care about them, their experience of the meaning of family and their sense of belonging is heightened. Some African American families tend not to be especially verbal with the ex-

---

Case Example #2

Andrew and Beth are attorneys in Washington, D.C. He is employed by the Children's Defense Fund, and she is a deputy prosecutor. Their one child, Jesse, is 3 years old. Jesse is visually impaired and has been involved in early intervention programs and services since his first year of life. He is active, mobile, and can see large print and pictures. Except for slight delays in gross motor functioning, Jesse is above average. His parents are eager to enroll him in a private preschool program that also provides extended day care, but the program director has said that she is concerned that the preschool environment is not safe for a child with Jesse's "handicaps."

In this case example, Jesse's parents enlisted the help of the interventionists who had worked with Jesse since the early months of his life. Together, they talked with the program director at the preschool, showed her videotapes of Jesse's performance with his peers, and offered to provide follow-up consultation to her staff if it was needed. Through this parent–professional team approach, the private preschool director was convinced that Jesse could be accommodated in her program.

pression of love, because they believe that actions, such as concerned caregiving and attention to others' well-being, speak louder than words.

The setting of limits, or disciplining children, is part of the socialization process of the child and is seen in two ways: 1) as a means for the child to learn to be sensitive, and 2) so that when the child encounters the system existing outside the home he or she will understand how to follow the rules in order to avoid confrontation with authorities. According to Allen and Majidi-Ahi (1989, p. 157), "a final socialization issue, which exemplifies all that is distinct about the Black experience in America, is teaching children how to cope with racism." The latter is seen as particularly critical for male children due to the high incidence of racially biased arrests of young African American males. In the first instance, it is believed that the building of self-respect derives from learning respect for the rights of others. This lesson starts early, and at home. In fact, the permissive childrearing practices common in many white, middle-class households in which discipine is seen as stifling creative expression would not be tolerated in most African American families.

Although less true now than in the past, the African American community still maintains a belief that all responsible adults are expected to act *in loco parentis* for the children of the community. The presence of an adult has traditionally been enough to deter the young African American child from too much wrongdoing because the the nonparent adult in whose presence the child is acting will usually comment on or correct the obvious problem behavior. Things have changed somewhat from the days when nonparent adults could "take a switch" to the child, but a considerable amount of behavioral observation and advice about appropriate punishment is alive and well in the African American community.

The belief in eating well, feeding one's family well, and having good food to offer one's guests is an abiding value in the African American family—although it is one that is difficult, if not impossible, for families living in urban poverty to maintain. Among middle-class families, the diet is generally rich in nutrients due to a particular preference for dark green leafy vegetables, red meat, and cheese. Potatoes, rice, and bread are staples, and a variety of fresh and dried fruits are liked and used. The primary problems with diet arise from the use of too much salt and a reliance on frying as a preferred method of cooking, although messages in the media may be modifying this behavior somewhat. Children are switched from baby foods to the same food as the rest of the family around 1 year of age, and the same attitude about the importance of good food to strength, stamina, and health prevails in the feeding of children. Mealtimes in some African American families may differ from those familiar to the interventionist. Although a common mealtime is still the norm, prepared food may be "left on the stove" and available for family members to take when they are ready to eat.

Another belief about health for children has to do with the importance of

play. Play is seen as important for both social (to have friends and fun) and physical (to have a strong body) well-being. In contrast with cultures that push children toward early adulthood, in African American families there is an attempt to give the child an opportunity to be a child, and to enjoy the care and protection of responsible adults until such time as he or she is maturationally ready for a broader role.

Medical Care

Medical and preventive health care, knowledge about treatment, and types of treatment that may be preferred vary widely within the African American community, particularly between middle-income/upper income families and families living in poverty. Most African Americans use the local private physician for basic health needs, and many are involved in work-related health plans that utilize health maintenance organizations as providers. For these families, health care is no different from any other mainstream, U.S. family.

Some African Americans, particularly those with strong ties to the rural South, may prefer holistic, natural approaches to health. There is an oral compendium of herbs, teas, roots, over-the-counter preparations, and foods that have preventive health and healing properties. Many families still rely on or have their own versions of Vicks VapoRub, castor and cod liver oil, sassafras tea, dried peaches and apricots, and "pot liquor." Some older people can discuss the variety of health uses of tallow, sulfur, and vinegar and water; and African American physicians of the "old school" may dispense advice and

---

Case Example #3

Marshall was 6 years old and had Down syndrome. Although he was making good progress in many areas, his language lagged behind many of his other skills. His parents seemed concerned about this, and it was decided that his teacher and the speech and language therapist would suggest some activities that his family could use at home to encourage Marshall to use more words and longer sentences. The major suggestion presented to the family was for each family member to direct one or two questions or comments requiring a longer response to Marshall when they were gathered at the dinner table. This would give him lots of opportunities to practice in a natural context and could be worked into the daily routine without causing disruption in the family. At least this is what the interventionists assumed.

In about 3 weeks, the teacher called Marshall's mother to ask how the suggestions were working. His mother said that they hadn't gotten around to trying the dinner table suggestion, then went on to say that she was not sure that they ever would. "You see," she said, "we just don't have dinner that way. People are always coming and going. I just keep the stove on, and everyone gets what they want when they want it."

To resolve the issue, they asked Marshall's mother whether there was a time during the day when something like that might work. She said that there were few times when they were all together, but that each family member could easily use the idea when they were playing with Marshall, helping him with his bath, or putting him to bed. In this example, the interventionists had developed an intervention that did not match the family's lifestyle, and was therefore not workable. But, with family consultation, a new strategy was devised that promised to be more effective.

---

counsel based on knowledge of the individual and his or her family context as well as standard medical treatments.

High-technology medical care is viewed by some less-educated or low-income families as care that is used in trauma situations. This observation is based on the reality that violence and accidental death and injury are at the top of the list of leading causes of morbidity and mortality in the African American community (DHHS, 1985). High-technology care is also encountered all too frequently in neonatal intensive care units, because of the disproportionately high numbers of African American babies born with conditions such as low birthweight, prematurity, and the effects of anti-health behaviors and lifestyles.

While there are many healthy African Americans who live in ways that support and stimulate good health, there are many—who tend to live in the inner city—who lack opportunities for employment and live in poverty, and for whom the societal institutions of mainstream America have not worked. Among the families living in poverty, the wide range of health provider options, the variety of third-party payers, the potential for publicly funded programs, or even the process for locating and selecting a doctor are not universally well understood. Likewise, the facts about current health problems relevant to African Americans, such as infant mortality, cancer, heart disease, and AIDS, are not well known to these families which results in a lack of perception of the common major threats to health. Publicly funded clinics and programs serve some who cannot pay or who can pay only a sliding or income-adjusted fee; but there are significant numbers who have no health care access due to lack of knowledge, lack of money, lack of financial and motivational resources to get care, or lifestyles and behaviors that prevent them from gaining access. Among these individuals it is, however, common knowledge that a hospital emergency room can be used when one does not know of or does not have access to any other options; in fact, many poor, inner-city families use emergency wards for all of their health care needs.

Due to the increasing proportion of African American families who live in poverty, or who are found among those who are working but poor, more families are compelled to wait for an illness to occur before seeking medical attention. Preventive health visits, including routine gynecological care for the women in the family, routine physical checkups for the entire family, and especially dental care, will not be sought. Even though visits for infants and children may also be less frequent, the family will usually ensure that children get the basics of whatever care they need. Even parents who may handle their own health in a cavalier manner by utilizing episodic care, are motivated to get care for their child—although they may find the eligibility procedures drawn out, tedious, and sometimes even offensive.

The challenge to the society at large is to make the ineffective institutions work for people who are difficult to reach. The onus is on the larger society, because fragmented, finger-in-the-dike demonstration programs are short lived and rarely become institutionalized. Although the short-term result is good, there is nothing left behind to meet the expectations raised by the quick-fix programs. The challenge to the interventionist is to help make the system responsive to children and families and to work with the family to provide health education, support in seeking and using care, and assistance in maximizing the effects of treatment. An example of the final point is a continuing practical problem related to medications. Many poor and under-educated African Americans do not comply with medication regimens. They may not follow the directions for administration, may over medicate, or may prematurely discontinue treatment when the pain is gone or when they are feeling better. Although misuse of antibiotics is a typical example, this behavior translates into all therapeutic interventions and regimens. To counteract these problems and to encourage adherence to therapeutic programs in the home, the interventionist should: 1) make the initial teaching and take-home materials simple, uncluttered, and practical for home use; 2) ensure that at least two family members understand how the therapy is done; 3) ensure that the family can obtain the necessary equipment and materials; and 4) check up on the progress and problems encountered by the family in order to make appropriate adjustments. These suggestions, although made in the context of working with African Americans of low socioeconomic status, are equally applicable to many families with whom interventionists work.

Causation

According to Randall-David (1989), religion and beliefs about illness are intertwined among African Americans. Therefore, some African Americans may attribute the cause of illnesses to punishment for disobeying God, to the work of the devil, or, in some instances, to evil spirits. However, as with any diverse group of people, beliefs will vary from individual to individual and from family to family. Although some may take a fatalistic view of the world in terms of life and death, African Americans are typically amenable to doing things that can influence the course of their life.

Disability

Disability is often interpreted in one of two ways: 1) as bad luck or misfortune, and, less so, 2) as the result of "sins of the fathers." The experience of most African Americans with disabilities is by way of the elderly. The larger group of people with disabilities were not very visible in the African American society, as in the society at large, until recent years. The young are taught not to stare at people with disabilities because it is rude; as has been shown in the larger society, this approach may have had the backlash of teaching individuals to "look right through" people with disabilities. This sets up a poor interactional dynamic between those who are disabled and those who are not. Attempts are also made to assist young children to view people with disabilities as they view nondisabled people. For the most part, African Americans do not exhibit any particular prejudice toward people with disabilities although they, like many people, have not had enough interaction with people with disabilities to appreciate fully that the only dimension on which they differ is that of the disabling condition. There is one exception to the lack of visibility of people with disabilities mentioned above, and that is the case of individuals who are mildly or moderately mentally retarded. Many African American families and communities have lived with and incorporated these individuals into all aspects of their lives.

Because African Americans are practical people, neither of the attitudes about causation of disability has any real effect on how they interact with families who have a disabled member or on how a family with a disabled member conducts the business of living. Initially, the assigning of blame to bad luck or to a family member's foibles may have to be acted out and assistance and counseling provided. However, that phase may be short relative to the subsequent phases that revolve around the securing of necessary health, medical, social, and educational services, and coping with the challenges of the disabled person's developmental and maturational needs.

ISSUES OF LANGUAGE

As noted earlier in this chapter, African Americans may speak Standard American English or a variety of "African Americanisms," which have been called Black English. These "African Americanisms" range from the use of mostly Standard American English with minimal injection of dialectical words and phrases; to the use of urban street language; to a typically southern usage of about half Standard American English and half southern African American vocabulary; all the way to dialects such as Gullah, spoken on southern U.S. coastal islands of Georgia and South Carolina. For many African Americans, the language that is used is often highly contextual, and they may choose to speak quite differently in different situations. However, among African Americans who have not been educated, those living in poverty, those who have remained in somewhat isolated coastal and island areas, and those who have recently immigrated to the United States from parts of the Caribbean, dialects other than Standard American English are more prevalent.

Language for African Americans is another manner of identification, because those who speak the same language or dialect have something in common with one another. Critically, as one identifies, so one thinks. Values underlie the thought process, so the circle of language, identity, values, and thought is completed. Researchers in education have shown that African Americans have a preference for the aural mode of presentation in their learning (Shade, 1984); African Americans report that they learn better via the spoken word. Shade also described the importance of teaching African American children by incorporating movement and touch. She cited other researchers who have hypothesized that African Americans' distinctive body language and "kinetic" idiom have developed as a result of a preference for learning through interaction with the environment rather than for learning through introspection. Pasteur and Toldson (cited in Shade, 1984) stated that the essence of African American culture is the development of somatic perceptions as a way of experiencing and expressing reality. A great deal of credence is given to gut feelings. Verbal as well as nonverbal communication is a fine art for African Americans, for throughout their history they have had to communicate so much within the confines of a dominant "overseer." In contemporary life, there is a liberal use of the full body, not just facial expressions, to convey a variety of feelings. African Americans are high-context communicators who use shared experience, nonverbal cues and signals, and the situation itself as a large part of the communicative process. Interventionists need to be sensitive to this style of interaction and avoid overexplaining when feedback from African American clients is different from that with which they are familiar.

Interventionists should also look for cues that indicate a shutdown of communication or learning. These might include behaviors such as: a completely bland face; the standard arms folded across the chest; totally intense, almost frantic involvement in the task being done, yet repeated inability to accomplish it (due to a blocking out of ongoing instructions and corrections that may be seen as harassing); or a range of expressions of exasperation—eye rolling, exhalations of air, and looking toward heaven (as if looking for divine intervention). Although some of these clues may be delivered reflexively, they may also be well planned to display dissatisfaction openly. Other families may be less expressive and will provide few if any clues to the fact that they do not find the intervention helpful, practical, or understandable. When working with African American families, interventionists may want to seek advice and assistance from African American interventionists or other team members to help them find ways in which the intervention might be modified to increase its likelihood of success.

SUMMARY AND RECOMMENDATIONS

Summary

This chapter has reviewed the origins and history of African Americans as they influence the values and beliefs of today. It has reviewed events that make up their rich heritage on both the African and American soils—a heritage built upon a strong sense of family, community, and culture as well as a will to survive and to progress. In spite of historical constraints, most African American families are dong well within the societal milieu that they value and select. Other families are not making it, partly due to the inability of the major societal institutions to meet their complex needs. Whatever their level of education or attainment as viewed from the larger society, African Americans "act out their being" within a circle of kinship that reinforces the knowledge that they belong, they have roots, and they have a future.

Recommendations for Interventionists

- Capitalize on kinship bonds, and focus on family strengths rather than weaknesses in developing and implementing interventions. If extended family members are primary caregivers or highly involved with the child and family, include them in the intervention.
- Use informal support networks such as the church, neighbors, or friends whenever possible and permitted by families to increase the effects of intervention or to reduce the need for formal interventions.
- Address family members formally, using titles and last names, until given permission to be more informal.
- Determine families' attitudes and beliefs about health and medical care, and work to match their preferences to appropriate treatment regimens.

- Become familiar with the resources in the African American community in your area and use those resources.
- Adapt therapeutic interventions to the learning style and lifestyle of the family, and do periodic evaluations to determine their effectiveness, progress, or the need for redirection.
- Critically assess the effects of poverty on families and determine which issues are related to culture and which are related to socioeconomic status. To help understand this, consider the effects of significant economic or social decline in your own family by answering the following questions: How many months could your family weather unemployment without going under? What things would you have to do without if your monthly family income was cut in half? Where would you go if you had a problem with substance abuse? What would you do to protect your children from harm if they attended a school where some of their schoolmates routinely brought a weapon to school? Issues of personal discomfort, lifestyle change, insecurity, loss of personal power, self-esteem, trust, and fear must be taken into account by the interventionist.
- Recognize that poverty does not equate with dysfunction. Many impoverished families manage to provide strong, nurturing care for their children.
- Avoid stereotyping all African Americans based on the behavior or lifestyles of a subset.
- Recruit ethnically diverse staff members for your program.

REFERENCES

Allen, L., & Majidi-Ahi, S. (1989). Black American children. In J. T. Gibbs & L.N. Huang (Eds.), *Children of color* (pp. 148–178). San Francisco: Jossey-Bass.

Allen, W.R., & Farley, R. (1986). The shifting social and economic tides of black America. *Annual Review of Sociology, 12,* 277–306.

Bennett, L., Jr. (1966). *Before the Mayflower.* Baltimore: Penguin Books.

Billingsley, A. (1968). *Black families in white America.* Englewood Cliffs, NJ: Prentice-Hall.

Billingsley, A. (1974). *Black families and the struggle for survival: Teaching our children to walk tall.* New York: Friendship Press.

Bremner, R.H. (1974). *Children and youth in America: A documentary history.* Cambridge, MA: Harvard University Press.

Brown vs. Board of Education, 347 U.S. 483, 493 (1954).

Dillard, J.L. (1972). *Black English: Its history and usage in the United States.* New York: Random House.

Franklin, J.H. (1967). *From slavery to freedom* (3rd ed.). New York: Vintage Books.

Genovese, E.D. (1974). *Roll, Jordan, roll: The world slaves made.* New York: Pantheon Books.

Hannerz, U. (1969). *Soulside: Inquiries into ghetto culture and community.* New York: Columbia University Press.

Kochman, T.E. (1972). *Rappin' and stylin' out.* Urbana: University of Illinois Press.

Labov, W. (1972). *Language in the inner city: Studies in the Black English vernacular.* Philadelphia: University of Pennsylvania Press.

Leigh, J.W., & Green, J.W. (1982). The structure of the black community: The knowledge base for social services. In J.W. Green (Ed.), *Cultural awareness in the human services* (pp. 94–121). Englewood Cliffs, NJ: Prentice Hall.

Mancini, J.K. (1980). *Strategic styles: Coping in the inner city.* Hanover, NH: University Press of New England.

Mandulo, R. (1991, April 23). The eighth and last defendant in the Bensonhurst racial attack . . . . *UPI News Release.*

Maquet, J. (1972). *Civilizations of black Africa* (J. Rayfield, Trans.). New York: Oxford University Press.

McAdoo, H.P., & McAdoo, J.L. (Eds.). (1985). *Black children.* Beverly Hills: Sage Publications.

Plessy v. Ferguson, 163 U.S. 537 (U.S. Supreme Court, 1896).

Randall-David, E. (1989). *Strategies for working with culturally diverse communities and clients.* Washington, DC: Association for the Care of Children's Health.

Reassuring a troubled citizenry. (1991, March 15). *Los Angeles Times,* Metro p. 6.

Robbins, B. (1973). *English in black and white.* New York: Holt, Rinehart & Winston.

Shade, B.J. (1984, August). *The perceptual process in teaching and learning: Cross-ethnic comparisons.* Paper presented at the annual meeting of the American Psychological Association, Toronto, Canada.

Tiedt, P.L., & Tiedt, I.M. (1990). *Multicultural teaching* (3rd ed.). Boston: Allyn & Bacon.

U.S. Bureau of the Census. (1986). *Statistical abstract of the United States, 1987* (107th ed.). Washington, DC: U.S. Government Printing Office.

U.S. Bureau of the Census. (1987). *Statistical abstract of the United States, 1988* (108th ed.). Washington, DC: U.S. Department of Commerce.

U.S. Bureau of the Census. (1990). *Statistical abstract of the United States, 1990* (110th ed.). Washington, DC: U.S. Department of Commerce.

U.S. Department of Health and Human Services. (1985). *Health status of minorities and low income groups* (DHHD Publication No. [HRSA] HRS-P-DV 85-1). Washington, DC: U.S. Government Printing Office.

APPENDIX A
CONTRASTING BELIEFS, VALUES, AND PRACTICES

African American culture	Mainstream culture
Collective orientation	Individual orientation
Kinship and extended family bonds	Nuclear and immediate family bonds
High-context communication	Low-context communication
Religious, spiritual orientation	More secular orientation
More authoritarian childrearing practices	More permissive childrearing practices
Greater respect for elderly and their role in the family	Less respect for the role of elderly in the family
More oriented to situation than time	More oriented to time than situation

APPENDIX B
CULTURAL COURTESIES AND CUSTOMS

- Do not address the African American client by his or her first name unless given permission. It is not seen as friendly, but instead implies disrespect.
- Do not tell African Americans they are "too touchy" about race.
- Do not make assumptions about the individual from knowledge of a particular demographic profile (e.g., single female head of household). This has very little meaning in the absence of a direct professional assessment.
- Do not tell ethnic jokes about any group—not even your own. African Americans feel that were they not in the room, the joke would have been about them.
- Do not converse with co-workers about personal matters, such as husbands, vacations, boyfriends, new cars, and so on while providing care to African American clients. African Americans will lose faith in your professional ability because chit-chat in a professional setting is seen as "your mind is not on your work," and they may feel that you are not a competent caregiver.
- Remember that poverty does not equate with dysfunction.

APPENDIX C
SIGNIFICANT CULTURAL EVENTS/HOLIDAYS

Event/holiday	Date	Description
KWANZAA	December 26 through January 1	Started in 1966 by Dr. Maulana Karenga. The purposes of the celebration are to: reinforce African American identity (the bonds between African Americans and community), to celebrate African American life and achievement, and to inform society at large of the contributions of African Americans to human history. It emphasizes the core beliefs of Nguzo Saba (the seven principles or values): unity, faith, self-determination, cooperative economics (familyhood), collective work and responsibility, creativity, and purpose.
Martin Luther King Jr.'s Birthday & Human Relations Day	January 15	A national holiday celebrating the life of Martin Luther King, Jr. and his contributions to the world community in the area of civil and human rights.

APPENDIX D
LANGUAGE

Black English differs from Standard English in several ways. The summary of differences presented below is based upon descriptions provided by Tiedt and Tiedt (1990) and Genovese (1974).

Differences in Black English	Standard American English	Black English
The verb "to be" is often omitted.	• Where are you?	• Where you?
Where contractions are commonly used, the verb will be omitted	• Why're you leaving?	• Why you leaving?
Multiple negatives are used.	• It won't do you any good.	• It won't do you no good.
Consonants that occur at the end of words and suffixes tend not to be voiced.	• I need to rest. • It is finished. • These are my folks.	• I need to res. • It finish. • These my folk.
The "th" sound in the final or middle position in a word is often sounded as an "f," "t," "v."	• I am going with you. • Lather the soap.	• I go wit you, or I go wif you. • Laver the soap.
Gender is not differentiated.	• He, she, and it are used to mean very specific and different things.	• He, she, and it can be used to refer to the same person or thing.
Concepts and their meanings may vary.	• Good = good	• Bad = good

chapter 7

FAMILIES WITH LATINO ROOTS

Maria E. Zuniga

No hay mal que por bien no venga. (There is nothing bad out of which good cannot come.)
[Helpful for enabling a client to reframe a painful situation such as the birth of a child with a disability]

Dios es muy grande. (God is very big.)
[Helpful for instilling in a client a sense of hope that maybe in the arena of life there will be room for some resolution of a major difficulty]

La verdad no mata, pero incomoda. (The truth doesn't kill you but can make you uncomfortable.)
[May be used to point out the difficulty of hearing things that are painful]

Helping families address the various issues they experience when an infant is born with a disability demands knowledge and insight about the complexities of family life. When families come from culturally diverse backgrounds, the complexity theme is compounded. This chapter focuses on the complexity of working with Latinos who have young children with disabilities. The core underpinning of this chapter is the critical nature of individualizing for each Latino family system and discussing to what extent cultural themes are pertinent.

BACKGROUND

The Latino population in the United States is characterized by its diversity. Latinos come from different Spanish-speaking countries, each of which has its own political history and unique immigration pulls and pushes. Particular settlement patterns and different acculturation rates also contribute to this diversity.

Currently, Latinos constitute approximately 8% (19.4 million) of the population in the United States (U.S. Bureau of the Census, 1988). Latinos of Mexican origin make up the largest group, with 12.1 million or 62.3% of Latinos. They are followed by Puerto Ricans, who constitute 2.5 million and 12.7 % of the Latino group. Central and South Americans are 2.2 million, or 11.5% of all Latinos. Persons from Spain or those who refer to themselves as Hispanic in a generic sense make up 1.6 million, or 8.1% of the Latino population. Cubans make up 1.0 million, or 5.3% of the Latino population.

Geographic and Historical Origins

Mexico

Mexico has a unique tie to the United States because it lost a significant mass of its territory to the United States in the Mexican War of 1848, areas that include what are now California, New Mexico, Texas, and Colorado. Mexico shares the most extensive border with the United States and has economic ties that have been the impetus for mass migrations to the United States, such as the Bracero programs of the 1950s that recruited workers from Mexico to harvest U.S. crops. Yet, many Mexicans in the United States are not immigrants. They have lived in this country for generations in areas such as California and New Mexico where ancesters can be traced to the 1700s.

The economic tide in Mexico has an impact on the rate of undocumented immigration. Although the Simpson-Mazzolli Immigration Act of 1985 (Russell, 1985) proposed to stem this flow of undocumented immigration, Mexico's economic woes have pushed Mexicans across its borders continuously. Census data indicate that about 2 million undocumented aliens reside in the United States; Mexico contributes 45% or 900,000 of these individuals, with Latin America and the Caribbean area accounting for 23% or 480,000 of undocumented residents (U.S. Bureau of the Census, 1988).

Puerto Rico

Puerto Ricans, the second largest Latino subgroup, have a political history that has resulted in U. S. citizen status, so that their migration issues have a distinct flavor from those who are Mexican. The U.S. invasion of Puerto Rico during the Spanish American War ended 400 years of Spanish rule. The United States retained Puerto Rico as an unincorporated territory and imposed its citizenship on Puerto Ricans (Montijo, 1985). The political issue that is coming to the fore for the Commonwealth of Puerto Rico is whether it should seek the status of a state, causing political polarization for many Puerto Ricans.

Puerto Ricans thus can migrate from the island of Puerto Rico with ease, contributing to the constant flux to and from the U.S. mainland. Many leave the island to seek economic advancement, since poverty affects its population to great degrees. The major immigration movement began after World War II, when Puerto Ricans came to work in the industrial centers since there was a need for manufacturing, industrial, and service workers (Inclan, 1985). These employees settled in the eastern seaboard states: New York, Massachusetts, New Jersey, and Connecticut. On the West Coast, the major settlement of Puerto Ricans is in San Francisco, although they may be scattered in small numbers throughout cities in California, many staying on after military service draws them to the West Coast.

The culture shock first encountered during the massive wave of immigration in the 1940s resulted in the establishment of barrios where Puerto Rican culture and the Spanish language could be maintained. For second-generation Puerto Ricans, their experiences were different; they were schooled in the United States, often living in urban slums and exposed to mainstream values. Yet, lack of educational and occupational opportunities, coupled with cultural insensitivity and racism, contributed to the many social problems that still plague this subgroup. In 1982, Puerto Rican families had the lowest median income, $11,000 compared to $16,000 for Mexican-origin families and $19,000 for Cuban families (Center on Budget and Policy Priorities, 1988). Puerto Ricans have the highest poverty rate among Latinos, 40.3% in 1987 (Center on Budget and Policy Priorities, 1988).

Cuba

The first wave of Cuban immigrants were refugees who were escaping the political upheaval that began in their country in 1959. Prior to this time, approximately 30,000 Cubans resided in the United States. In contrast to the Puerto Ricans, who experience a fluid migration to the United States, the Cuban subgroup is characterized by distinct waves of immigration that began with the Cuban Revolution and the reign of Fidel Castro in 1959. As Castro took over, many Cubans of the professional and upper classes fled Cuba on commercial flights, the estimate being about 248,070. After the Cuban Missile Crisis in 1962, another 55,916 fled in small boats, rafts, and any other available craft. Between 1965 and 1973, U.S. airlifts transported another 297,318. In the last three stages, the biggest group comprised those who came in the Mariel boatlift to Key West, about 124,789 Cubans (Szapocznik & Hernandez, 1988). By 1988, the Cuban population in the United States was 1.0 million, or 5.3% (U.S. Bureau of the Census, 1988).

Cubans, in contrast to Puerto Ricans and Mexicans, have been recognized for their distinct economic success. The economic, social, and political know-how of the first waves of immigrants offered significant contributions to the Miami, Florida, economy and later spread to other areas such as New Jersey. A central outcome is that Miami has become a cultural and economic magnet for Latin Americans, bolstering the Latino culture in this area and offering a bicultural environment (Szapocznik & Hernandez, 1988). However, this does not mean that the stresses of acculturation and displacement have not had an impact on this group. For many Cuban immigrants in the first wave, the belief that they would be able to return eventually to a free Cuba constrained some of their acculturation achievements.

Central America

In the last 10 years, as the wars in Central America have cost lives and freedom, there has been a steady increase in the legal and undocumented immigration of political refugees from war-torn countries such as El Salvador and Nicaragua. These immigrants are found dispersed in various parts of the United States. Some have settled in Florida, where usage of the Spanish language provides an important support; others have flocked to areas where relatives live or where enclaves of their countrymen have settled (e.g., New York, San Francisco, Los Angeles). The experiences of war and conflict burden their emotional well-being, and, like the other subgroups, attending to the culture shock they encounter drains important energies.

Stages of Migration

Sluzki (1979) warned human services workers to be cognizant of the various stages of migration that Latino immigrants are experiencing since these stages may pose particular stresses and symptoms that can contribute to presenting problems. In illustration, these stages include the following:

1. *Preparatory Stage*   How was decision to move made? Were all members of the family involved in this process? Did they say goodbye to family and friends? Were there any rituals to mark this event, or was it characterized by emergency decisions to move without preparation—emotional or otherwise?

2. *Act of Migration*   What was the process like—did it involve an atmosphere of fear, exploitation, life endangerment? Were there tragedies wherein a family member had to be left behind; robbery, rape, or other trauma?

3. *Period of Overcompensation*   As recognition of the massive changes are realized, members may begin to doubt their own senses, their values, and their judgment. This is reinforced by incongruence between old and new realities. Families may choose to stay entrenched in their old culture with exaggeration of family rules or style.

4. *Period of Decompensation*   This is a time during which conflicts, symptoms, problems, and crises arise for the family. Inverse role relations may appear when women are more able than men to find employment, contributing to reversal of traditional sex roles. This has an impact on the spousal system, in particular.

5. *Transgenerational Impact*   With time, issues and conflicts arise between generations, especially as the young people become more acculturated than those who are older, especially their parents.

For interventionists attending to the issues of a child with special needs, their job is not to address these themes as would a family therapist. However, if the parents or family are grief-stricken by the birth of a child with a particular disability or life-long illness, this may activate buried grief related to the immigration process. For example, the sense of loss that an immigrant Latino family may experience in leaving relatives behind in the country of origin, which has not been expressed, may come to the fore in relation to the sorrow surrounding the birth of an infant with a disability. This compacted grief process may need to be addressed in family treatment. Thus, it may be appropriate to make a referral to a bicultural therapist or to a priest or minister who may enable the family to acknowledge the various grief themes they are experiencing.

Attendance to this familial need must be considered so that the work and the emotional unveiling that must be addressed related to the child with special needs can be the arena of intervention focus. Often, this focus must entertain the religious belief system of the family so that the interventionist will have perspectives on how the family perceives the child and his or her disability.

Religious Origins

Due to the influence of the Spanish heritage, the majority of Roman Catholics in the world are Latinos. Thus, many of the Latino families encountered by human services workers will adhere to different forms of Catholicism, the unique aspects stemming from each country's own cultural and indigenous influences. It is important, however, that human services workers realize that not all Latinos are Catholics. In reality, there is a growing influence of Protestant sects, both in Latino countries and in the United States (Abalos, 1986). Thus, an interventionist should determine to which religion a family belongs. Furthermore, the importance of assessing the extended family's or grandparents' religious system is not to be overlooked since it may have implications for rituals or resources on which the immediate family may rely in dealing with the child's disability.

For Mexican-heritage families, the importance of Our Lady of Guadalupe as a patron saint and as the "Virgin Mother" of Mexico is a prominent feature in their practice of Catholicism. It is not uncommon for a parent to implore the Virgin Mary to intercede for him or her to cure a child of a disease or disability. The use of *mandas* (a promise or offering in return for God's intervention) is another aspect of this intercession. For instance, a parent commits to carry out a tradition or ritual in return for the intercession of a saint or the Virgin Mary. This may mean not cutting the child's hair until the parent can visit a shrine in Mexico, such as the Basilica of Our Lady of Guadalupe. Or it can mean dressing the afflicted child in robes, similar to St. Martin de Porres, for example, as a bartering gesture (Smith-DeMateo, 1987). Sometimes parents feel that the disability is the cross that has been sent to them as part of God's will and thus must be borne as part of the pain of the human condition. Others will respond with less acceptance, may feel they are being treated unjustly, or feel that they are being punished for a previous wrongdoing. Each of the child's parents may have individual reactions.

For Cubans, religious beliefs and practices are also not homogeneous, although the majority of Cubans are Catholic. In Latin America, especially in those countries where there is a significant African and/or Indian heritage (e.g., the Carribean, Mexico, Central and South America), Christ, the Virgin Mary, and Catholic saints are fused with the deities and rituals of the Indian and African populations (Rubinstein, 1976).

Puerto Ricans and Cubans, in particular, often practice Santeria, which is a syncretism of Catholic saints and African orishas or saints. During the time of the Spanish colonies, Yoruba slaves, from Nigeria, identified their saints with those of the Catholics, endowing the latter with the same supernatural powers of the African deities. This syncretism, while mainly practiced by illiterate Catholic masses in these countries, has also been taken on by Anglo-European Catholics (Ortiz, 1973).

In Cuban culture, Santeria tends to promote and strengthen traditional family ties since the religion models a pantheon of saints and deities that interact as a "sacred family." The most influential of all African demigods are Chāngó and Obatālá, who are ascribed with miraculous powers. Reflections of this religion may be encountered in homes where a Catholic statue such as Our Lady of Mercy stands next to a food offering to Ochún, the Santeria saint who is the patron of love, marriage, fertility, and gold (Gonzalez-Whippier, 1989).

Interventionists thus may find different manifestations of these religious belief systems related to a child's disability: a *manda* made by Catholics, for example, in not cutting a child's hair as an imploration to God for healing; altars that are syncretisms of saints and food offerings in Santeria, wherein the powers of certain deities may be called on to help the child; or the placement of a glass of water or a Santeria idol under a child's bed to protect the child.

These religious symbols represent the family's belief that a cure is possible or in the hands of supreme powers. Interventionists must recognize these belief systems as part of the family's cultural context so that intervention efforts do not directly challenge or disregard the family's need to use a spiritual frame for comprehending the disability of their child or to support a sense of hope. In working with Latino families comprehension of their attitudes and assessment of their situations will also demand knowledge of how their Spanish language affects their communication process.

Language/Linguistic Origins

Spain's colonization of the New World imposed the Spanish language as the central political and economic communication mode. Thus, a major unifying factor for Latinos is their use of the Spanish language, albeit reflected uniquely in each country and region via indigenous idioms or rates of speech. Often the Spanish spoken in the United States by the various subgroups mirrors English expressions. For example, the Spanish spoken in Miami differs somewhat from the Spanish spoken in Los Angeles (Rubinstein, 1976). Mexican Americans classify this Spanish–English syncretism as *pochismos* or Americanized Spanish. For all Latino groups in the United States, the degree of fluency in Spanish will vary, especially with acculturation rates.

Third-generation Chicanos or U.S.-born Mexican Americans often lose the use of Spanish while their grandparents may only be Spanish speaking, resulting in communication estrangement in family systems. Commonly, Chicanos use Spanish for informal, ingroup, familial, and personal interactions and then use English for communicating with outsiders (Gomez, 1977). Awareness of this tendency to code-switch, or shift from one language to another, should be understood as reflecting these interactional predispositions. An interventionist may misunderstand a family member's switching to Spanish with another member, deeming it as a way to hide data from the worker when it is often just tied to language predispositions.

When an interventionist does not speak Spanish and the family is only Spanish speaking, translators must be utilized to ensure viable communication. Using the children in the family to translate should be avoided if at all possible. This shifts the family structure by placing the child in a superior position, and parents may be hesitant to discuss emotion-laden content in front of their child. Equally important, this kind of translating places a great burden and pressure on a child to be accurate, or it may expose the child to the parent's pain, resulting in the child taking on the responsibility for the family's burden (Garcia-Preto, 1982; Mizio, 1974). When translators are used, Latino adults are preferable. However, the interventionist must be sensitive to the possibility of distortions that can result in this communication medium (Abad & Boyce, 1979).

If the interventionist is Spanish speaking but not of the client's culture, familiarity with that culture will enable an understanding of the nuances of communication used by each family (i.e., colloquialisms or nonverbal expressions). For example, among Cubans, the impact of African cultures on Cuban history and social institutions is reflected in language expressions. Many Cubans use such expressions as *mi negro(a)* (i.e., my black one) to manifest comradeship or familiar affection and love (Szapocznik & Hernandez, 1988).

Also, it should be noted that not all Spanish-speaking persons are literate in the written form. For instance, many Mexican Americans, although they speak Spanish well, may have had no formal education to support reading and writing it in a viable way. In particular, an interventionist must be on guard to whether a monolingual Spanish-speaking parent is literate in Spanish. For example, health care workers have left medical regimens written in Spanish for parents to follow, not realizing that the parents could not read or write in Spanish. Often parents will be hesitant to reveal their lack of reading ability due to embarrassment.

CONTEMPORARY LIFE

Due to the large flow of immigrants of Latin descent, about one third of the Latino population in the United States in 1980 was foreign born. The numbers may be even higher in 1990 due to the amnesty process, which enables undocumented immigrants to obtain legal immigration status.

Among the various subgroups, those from South and Central America are the fastest growing group of Latinos, with a 40% increase in their numbers between 1982 and 1987. The number of residents of Mexican descent grew by 22% while Puerto Ricans increased by 11% and Cubans by 7% ("Hispanic population," 1987).

The current recessionary trends have affected Latino families adversely. About 1.2 million (25.8%) of the 4.6 million Latino families in the United States live below the poverty line. The labor force participation for Latina women increased from 48% in 1982 to 52% in 1988, while the participation rates for Latino men decreased from 81% in 1982 to 79% in 1988. The Puerto Rican subgroup had the highest poverty rate of 40.3% in 1987; the Central and South Americans a rate of 18.9%; and the Cubans had a rate of 13.8%. Latino married couples decreased between 1982 and 1988 from 74% to 70%. Thus, Latino families headed by single parents increased from 26% to 30% (U.S. Bureau of the Census, 1988).

Acculturation Process

The process of migration is a relocation to an unfamiliar context. Immigrants face an environment in which the habits, values, and socialization processes from their country of origin are no longer applicable. Migration involves stressful experiences including culture shock, acculturative stress, and cultural fatigue. The conflicts characteristic of cultural shock typically continue until the immigrant incorporates both his or her culture of origin and the host culture into an integral approach to his or her existence in the new society. This process is the acculturation process. It involves the conflict-ridden, decision-making process in which the immigrant trades off his or her indigenous attitudes, values, and behaviors for those of the host group, until she or he achieves a mixture of old and new that is deemed optimal (Salgado de Snyder, 1987). Some resist this change process and underacculturate, resulting in less adaptation to their new environment. Children who attend school or adults who obtain employment may be more exposed to acculturation pushes, which may result in uneven acculturation levels among family members, incurring disagreement about values and behaviors. In this situation, the interventionist may not be able to intervene directly, but may consider referring to therapists or community agencies that can address these familial and acculturation strains.

Social Supports

An important factor in noting the immigrant status of a family is the designation of available support networks. The social support received from these networks helps to alleviate stress and contributes to the immigrants' adaptation. Thus, migration success is not only based on the learning of new sociocultural norms

Case Example #1

A bilingual, bicultural worker from a regional center in a Latino populated area of Southern California had five Latina immigrant mothers on her case-load, all of whom had a child with spina bifida; the children ranged in age from 6 months to 6 years. The mothers were from low socioeconomic levels and most were single. They were not used to talking about their feelings or expressing their needs directly. Their ages varied from 20 years to 38 years.

Common themes for them included their sense of isolation, lack of sup-ports, lack of transportation, and stresses related to acculturation and the diagnoses of their children. They were mainly overwhelmed; they also dis-played a lack of confidence in their abilities to meet the needs of their chil-dren with disabilities.

The interventionist contacted various Latino and community resources to discern if a related support group was available in Spanish for these women. Despite the large Latino population, Spanish-speaking support groups were not common. The interventionist approached her agency direc-tor and advocated for the resources needed to begin a support group.

Initially, the support group met every 2 months. Talking about their needs and recognizing the generalized issues they all shared as immigrant parents of children with disabilities influenced the mothers' self-esteem in a positive way and enabled them to begin expressing themselves with more confidence. The effects were so dramatic that other Spanish-speaking moth-ers with infants with other diagnoses were also included. The group asked to meet monthly. Apart from their mutual support processes, they requested speakers so they could be better informed about their infants. They also set the monthly agenda, depicting an empowerment theme that was critical to their sense of themselves as mothers. From this support group, two of the mothers with more English fluency participated in the training of the Valley Support Group and have learned to function as advocate volunteers for other Spanish-speaking parents of children with disabilities.

Interventionists may need to help Latino parents to empower them-selves so as to be better equipped to advocate for their children. Support groups contribute to this process, enabling the interventionist to reach more of these needy parents, and to facilitate the kinds of change that character-izes group process. Lack of support groups for Latino parents of special needs children is a dramatic need that must be addressd (Arias, 1990).

and behaviors, but is also reliant on the social support from co-nationals and the social acceptance of the host group (Boekestijn, 1984).

Designation of ethnic social networks is important because often it may be the only source of support during times of crisis. Ethnic networks are composed of co-culturals with whom the immigrant may be more inclined to have a more personal relationship. Immigrants can ask questions, discuss the beliefs and values of the host culture, and still obtain reaffirmation of the norms and values of the native culture in a supportive environment.

Ethnic networks may provide the brokering process wherein the new immigrant is taught about the resources, procedures, and mechanisms needed to survive. For a family with an infant or young child with special needs, having this kind of network available may help to mitigate the stress, confusion, and pain related to addressing the issues of a child's disability. Especially for immigrant Latina women, ethnic networks that can offer confidante support are of particular value since these women may not have the natural familial or community networks that existed in their country of origin. If confidantes are not available, the immigrant woman may be in jeopardy of depression or other symptomatology (Vega, Kolody, & Valle, 1988).

The interventionist needs to assess this natural support arena. Another area to include in this evaluation is the presence of a religious system that may provide spiritual resources. Often, Latino immigrants may gravitate to a barrio church with a Latino congregation and Latino priests/ministers. This would be one area for the interventionist to suggest as an emotional resource for a family stressed or grieving about a child with a disability.

Although many communities may offer support groups for parents with children with such disabilities as cerebral palsy or Down syndrome, there is a paucity of Spanish-language support groups for Latino families. Interventionists should nonetheless discern if any do exist. In large metropolitan areas like Los Angeles, Regional Centers, California's comprehensive service agencies for individuals with developmental disabilities, may be the agencies to call to make that determination.

Aside from the stressors related to immigration, a critical stressor for many families is related to illegal immigrant status. These families suffer the daily torment of never knowing when and how they may be discovered and subjected to deportation. Families in this situation may be hesitant to seek out resources for their child. Moreover, they may feel that interventionists who come to help with the child may use the information about their illegal status to inform the Immigration and Naturalization Services. It is critical that the interventionist inform them that his or her job is not to call their illegal status into question. The interventionist may need to state very explicitly that she or he will not call authorities. Moreover, the worker will need to know what resources can be used for illegal immigrants and which resources, if used, could jeopardize their legal immigration application at a later time. Helping the family to understand what options are available and which options could work against future legal application plans is an invaluable service to the family. This will help to heighten the trust level with the interventionist while also undercutting the stress related to lack of information about this crucial area (Salcido, 1982).

VALUES

The role of the Latino family as the central operating principle in the life of this population is duly supported (Bernal, 1982; Garcia-Preto, 1982; Zuniga, 1988b). However, the static traditional role configurations often ascribed to Latino families is being called into question (Vega, Hough, & Romero, 1983). In illustration, the traditional family has been described as exhibiting male supremacy, the submissiveness of the mother, and strict sex role delineations, with childrearing the exclusive domain of female members and with aloof fathers. Latino social scientists have noted that Latino families are not static; they are typically in transition stages, so that it is difficult to discern what a normative Latino family is like (Levine & Padilla, 1980; Montiel, 1975; Vega, 1980). Being foreign born or native born, regional differences, acculturation stages, upward class mobility, outmarriage rates, and other characteristics all produce a variation of Latino family configurations with a mix of structures, values, styles, and preferences.

One of the crucial themes to recognize is that class variations are often misinterpreted as culture variations. Class phenomena may provide more insight about a family related to its world view and experiences with freedom and self-identity. Abalos (1986) questioned whether the "passiveness or fatalism" often ascribed to Latinos is not more specifically an outgrowth of class dimensions. Persons who are poor and minimally educated may have a limited sense of options. They may have few experiences with self-empowerment due to the economic constraints under which they have lived. Moreover, their lack of political freedom, especially for those from South and Central American societies, may contribute to their accustomed stance of allowing those in power or those with status to make decisions for them. If an individual is poor, of lower status, and socialized to be powerless, she or he will be less prone to take the lead or to be assertive in interpersonal interactions—especially with regard to decision making. Thus, the interventionist should discern how class realities affect a particular family system (Montijo, 1985). For example, an immigrant Mexican family from Mexico City from a middle-class milieu may be more similar in its values and behaviors to U.S.-middle-class families than a U.S.-born Mexican family of low socioeconomic status.

This is not to say that there are not cultural frames around which the family organizes itself and functions. However, the traditional format is changing. Interventionists must individualize each Latino family system to discern to what extent it follows these cultural formats. Ramirez and Arce (1981) noted that the concepts of *machismo,* an absolute patriarchy of the father, were having less of an influence on the dynamics and structure of contemporary Mexican American families. Others (Ybarra-Soriano, 1977) have also found that the Mexican American family is often characterized by joint decision making and greater equality of male and female roles. One significant contribution to these changes is the increasing influence of women's employment outside the home. This has enhanced the wife's position and supported her role in decision making (Cromwell & Ruiz, 1979; Ybarra-Soriano, 1977).

Moreover, as Latino family members become more highly educated, acculturation changes occur that further weaken traditional stances, especially around sex roles. Census figures note that in 1970 only 45% of Latinos in the United States were high school graduates. In 1988, 51% had graduated. Similarly, in 1970 only 5% of Latinos had graduated from college, but by 1988 that figure had doubled to 10% (Center on Budget and Policy Priorities, 1988; U.S. Bureau of the Census, 1988).

If families are immigrants, the country of origin may influence the family's adaptation or acculturation to the new country. For instance, a rural context would imply that the family will have fewer skills and more stress in adapting to the fast-paced urban context of the United States.

However, even when Latino families become acculturated to U.S. values, one of the last value stances they give up is their sense of familialism and family loyalty. In many non-Western cultures, the guiding framework is a collective orientation that supports family and community life (Roland, 1988). Latinos, as a whole, adhere to this collective sense, which often results in extended family configurations that often offer valuable support services (Vega et al., 1983). Although many Latino families now live in nuclear households, support may emanate from each household to the other. Moreover, the godparent system or compadre system offers support through additions to the family through marriage, and the consequent uses of godparents at baptism, confirmation, and at the *quinceañeras* (15-year-olds' coming-out celebrations) of daughters.

Thus, many families may have these resources to call upon for help in child care or babysitting. Interventionists can discuss this area with families, particularly when there is a need for the parent to obtain some form of respite from a child with a disability, for example from demands for extensive attention and caregiving. Likewise, the parents may be asked to designate certain family members to be trained along with them in special medical regimens for the child.

As noted previously, examination of central tendencies in family life among the Latino subgroups denotes traits that are often attenuated by class, migration, and acculturation phenomena. The legacy received from the Spanish culture contributes to viewing the man as the provider and the woman as the main one who takes care of the children. In speaking about Cubans, Bernal (1982) noted that when the wife has to work outside the home, this affects the power balance of the family and may undercut the male's role. If the man is unable to obtain work, he loses face, self-esteem, and respect, and marital and intergenerational difficulties will likely develop.

Most Latino families remain two-parent families throughout their lives.

The divorce rate (6.9%) for this population is lower than for the Anglo group (Alvirez, Bean, & Williams, 1981; U.S. Bureau of the Census, 1988). The fact that most Latinos are Catholic may influence this disinclination to divorce (Ho, 1987). Yet, in urban centers, the single-parent household is not uncommon for Latinos (Fitzpatrick, 1981) and appears to be growing.

Another Spanish legacy is the emphasis on female virginity prior to marriage and fidelity to her spouse thereafter. This purity theme is then reinforced by religious ideology. Consequently, childrearing patterns highlight the protection of girls and restriction of their freedom. For Cubans, Bernal (1982) noted that sexuality, virginity, and machismo themes are difficult areas to address with most families. Given the similar Catholic and role expectations, these issues would also be awkward to address in other Latino subgroups.

The collective and familial stance for Latinos also influences the world view of these individuals. Research has found that Mexican American children have a more field-sensitive cognitive style than children of other ethnic groups. This field dependence implies a high sensitivity to nonverbal indicators of feelings and is operationalized in the Latino cultural concept of *personalismo* (Ramirez & Price-Williams, 1974). This concept is predicated on warm, individualized attention and responsiveness in interpersonal interactions. This concept is coupled with interpersonal respect (Gomez, 1977) and supports the value stance of the various Latino groups.

In order to respect Latino values, the interventionist must consciously work at a humanistic orientation that first considers the interpersonal interaction versus the task-oriented style so readily adhered to by some human services professionals. The cultural practice of *platicando* must be incorporated into the interventionist's style of relating to Latino clients. This involves friendly, informal, and leisurely chatting that establishes the *ambiente* or atmosphere in which the work will take place. The interventionist who can incorporate this style will be admired by the Latino family and may attract greater familial cooperation and trust. The trust of families will also be engendered when the interventionist is able to comprehend rather than reject the belief systems that these families espouse. Knowledge about differences in childrearing practices, use of medical care, and views on what causes disabilities will help to support the interventionist's delivery of services.

BELIEFS

Childrearing

In Latino cultures, one marries for the purpose of having children. Children validate the marriage. The parent–child relationship has more importance than the marital relationship. Parents tend to be very nurturing toward their children as well as permissive and indulgent with young children. The attitude toward the young is to placate them, not to push for the achievement or developmental milestones that are often valued in Anglo families. This relaxed attitude toward the attainment of early skills may be related to a value thrust that supports a family member's interdependence with the family as opposed to the focus on the family member's independence and individuation (Roland, 1988).

Juarez (1985) related the importance of recognizing different norms around childrearing that exist for many Latino families as compared to Anglo families. In illustration, Latino families find it acceptable for preteens to sit on the mother's lap. Preschoolers who drink from a baby bottle may not be admonished. Moreover, it is normal in these families for members to sit close to one another and to have direct physical contact regardless of age. Anglo professionals might view this closeness as symbiotic behavior and as unacceptable.

Torres-Matrullo (1982) noted that while positive emotions are elicited among Latino women and children, emotions such as anger, aggression, and other negative feelings are not acceptable. Mothers may teach their sons to be dominant and independent, with the eldest son typically having more authority than younger male brothers (Kluckholn & Strodtbeck, 1961). Siblings share close emotional ties, and parents discourage infighting (Goodman & Beman, 1971).

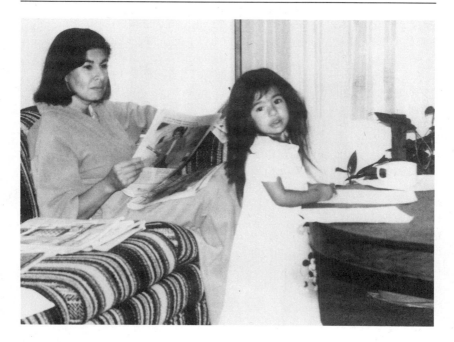

Research on the cognitive styles of Mexican American children has found that their field-dependent style may be attributed to various dimensions, including more traditional childrearing practices in Mexican culture. These practices emphasize adherence to convention, respect for authority, and identity with the family (Romero, 1983). This traditional childrearing includes teaching children respect for their elders, and should result in a child who is *bien educada* or well educated. *Una persona bien educada* (a well-educated individual) is one who has been taught skills in human relationships, and who understands the importance of interacting and relating to others with respect and dignity (Zuniga, 1988a). Thus, a person who calls a child *mal educado* is noting that the parents have not provided him or her with the education that is expected in Latino families.

An important aspect for children is the expectation that they will take up work roles within the family, whether this includes babysitting, helping with chores, or actually working with other family members. Often this expectation of more responsibility for children may be class related; for many poor families, the theme of survival may demand that all members participate for the good of the family.

Insights on childrearing are many, and may take on different hues depending on the particular Latino subgroup. It is important that interventionists individualize these practices for each family, recognizing that factors such as class, region, and acculturation stage may contribute to more or less traditional formats for childrearing. Readings on culturally diverse children should be sought to strengthen interventionists' knowledge bases in this area (e.g., *Children of Color* [Gibbs & Huang, 1989] or *The Psychosocial Development of Minority Group Children* [Powell, Yamamoto, Romero, & Morales, 1983]).

Importantly, the interventionist must realize that cultures that value a collective style versus an individualistic style and a cooperative mode versus a competitive mode will result in the socialization of children who may have different goals and different learning processes from those raised in the majority Anglo culture. Although these differences contrast to the modes and styles of the majority cultural group, one must not assume that they are inferior or dysfunctional. For example, a family that does not focus on the developmental milestones referred to earlier may not comprehend the interventionist's concern for teaching a child with a disability processes to ensure that his or her development does not become too delayed. If the family does not follow through immediately on recommendations, the interventionist may need to consider the family's perspective. The interventionist will need to recognize that developmental goals may have to be addressed in alternative modes that may enable the family to realize the need for these developmental processes.

Medical Care

One of the traits often ascribed to Latino families is their use of natural healers as a preferred medical alternative. Again, class issues may dictate what resources a family uses. Use of natural healers often occurs since they are geographically accessible, the charges are minimal, and often families cannot afford or do not have access to Western resources. Mexicans will use *curanderos (as)* or Puerto Ricans will rely on spiritists because they value and believe in the religious/spiritual aspects that surround these healers. Although folk beliefs about medical and psychological interventions may be characteristic of the more traditional and less acculturated Latinos, there is evidence that even modern-day Chicanos are influenced by these beliefs and practices (Gomez, 1977).

For many Mexican-heritage persons, medical folk beliefs include *mal ojo, susto,* and *mal puesto. Mal ojo* (evil eye) is believed to be the result of excessive admiration or desire on the part of another. Mothers may isolate their children for fear of having one become victim of *mal ojo* (Gomez, 1977). *Susto* (fright) is a syndrome that is a result of an emotionally traumatic experience: A simple scare or witnessing an accident could result in *susto*. Symptoms of *susto* would include restlessness during sleep, loss of appetite, disinterest in personal hygiene, loss of strength, weight loss, and introversion (Gomez, 1977). *Mal puesto* is an evil hex or illness willfully put on someone by a *curandero(a)* or a *brujo(a)* (witch). The hex may be given through food or one's photograph. Often the hex is motivated by jealousy or vengeance. When a child is born with a defect or disability, this may be interpreted as being caused by someone in the family's ecological context who is at odds with the parent or family. For exam-

Case Example #2

A Mexican-heritage mother had a 20-month-old infant who was diagnosed with Down syndrome. She was from a rural part of Mexico, had 4 years of schooling in Mexico, and had gone to English classes in the United States for 1 year. She had a brother and sister-in-law who lived in the area and who often offered their ideas on child care since they had four children.

The mother had noted that her infant had been restless and seemed to be uncomfortable. She felt the top of his head and noted that it was particularly soft. Sometimes parents who cannot ascribe a specific illness to a child who is fretful may say, "*Se ha caido la mollera,*" which implies that the child's fontanel has fallen, causing the discomfort.

This mother had heard her brother describe the interventions: one was to break an egg over the child's head; the other was to push on the roof of the child's mouth to address the problem. The mother held the child upside down and placed her hand in the child's mouth to push the *mollera* back up so as to bring relief to the child. Instead, the child began choking and almost stopped breathing. That same day the visiting nurse heard about this episode and made a referral to a worker who was bilingual. When the mother explained she was concerned that the child had problems with his *mollera* and that her relative's prescriptions or interventions were being followed since he had more experience with children, the interventionist assessed her other practices with the child. The outcome was that this mother was not intending to be abusive and was only following a folk belief.

The interventionist provided important educational inputs regarding the danger of the manual intervention. An appointment with the physician was scheduled to discern what the difficulty was with the child.

The interventionist also had to explain and work with this mother about the special needs of her infant. She helped to refocus her folk beliefs so they would not present a danger to the child. Importantly, she educated the mother about U.S. laws on child abuse and how sometimes good intentions can become confused by authorities. The interventionist acknowledged how important it was for this mother to have family support, but underlined the special needs of her child and asked the mother to call her for consultation before proceeding with any interventions.

ple, a Mexican child born with severe retardation and with extreme facial distortions was viewed by the mother as being born with that disability because she felt that her husband's family put an evil eye on the child (G. Federico, personal communication, October 10, 1990).

Parents may take a child with a disability to a *curandero(a)* to seek a *cura* (cure). Most Latino communities have healers or other specialists like a *sobador* (person who heals through massage). It is not unusual, for example, for a family to seek a *sobador* for help with a child diagnosed with cerebral palsy. Or a family may take a seriously afflicted child to a healer to seek a second opinion. Families who live close to Mexico may make the effort to seek out healers who are available in border towns like Tijuana. For example, a family may travel all the way from Los Angeles to obtain such a second opinion (A. Dunn, personal communication, October 15, 1990).

Delgado (1988) explained that many Puerto Ricans turn to spiritists to seek healing, to dispel evil spirits, or to obtain spiritual protection. Spiritism is a highly ritualized intervention that uses various paraphernalia to provide a healing environment (Delgado, 1977). Statues or pictures of saints, flowers, cigars, and so forth may be part of the assortment of resources needed to perform healing ceremonies. The principle is that multiple stages of spiritist practices offer various stages of intervention: 1) setting the atmosphere, 2) discovering the reason through a spirit medium for what is causing the physical or emotional discomfort, and 3) *despojas* (cleansing ceremonies) to take away the symptoms. These stages are similar to those that Western social workers are taught for interventions: 1) develop the relationship, 2) assess the client and situation, and 3) offer a plan to dispel the problem (Hepworth & Larsen, 1990).

Interventionists must acknowledge these belief systems rather than ridicule them; this results in the act of "joining" the family in its desire to seek a cure for an afflicted infant or child. However, the issue of curative modes based on folk beliefs must be examined to ensure that the child's safety is protected and to minimize contra-indicated interventions or medications. Direct but sensitive questioning about the folk modes, cures, procedures used, or medications offered should be carefully posed. The interventionist can frame the questioning in a positive manner to learn what the healer is providing—without putting the family on the defensive. Also, neighbors may offer their own medication prescriptions if symptoms are similar, as a gesture to aid the afflicted family. Again, assessment needs to be made and indicated educative inputs offered to protect the child (Smith-DeMateo, 1987).

Causation and Disability

The belief in folk remedies is very much tied into religious beliefs for many Latinos. For instance, all these groups believe in the powers of good and evil, often reinforced by Catholic traditions. The Catholic belief that holy water can be used to ward off evil and to bless the person lends credence to indigenous themes about "warding off evil." The underlying principle is that illness or problems can occur due to the presence of evil in one's environment. Certainly the idea of the evil eye illustrates this theme, and is a common belief that runs through the various Latino subgroups.

The birth of a child with a disability can be interpreted as a curse put on the child by someone or the effects of an evil spirit. Thus, amulets may be placed around the neck of the child to ward off evil. An interventionist may find a Cuban infant with a semiprecious black stone worn around the neck or wrist.

This is an *azabache* used to ward off evil and means that this parent may adhere to this type of folk belief system. If the stone shows chips, this is interpreted as demonstrating that the evil eye has been warded off (M. Sardinas, personal communication, September 15, 1990). Thus, the theme is that evil is a powerful force and one has to utilize the various means for contending with this force, often through symbolic rituals like the use of amulets. However, there are pathways to address evil or to remedy its effects.

As noted earlier, interpretations on what causes disabilities or birth defects for children may result from an array of influences: belief in a punishing God, folk beliefs about the power of evil, or beliefs that life is laden with tragedy and one accepts the good with the bad. There may be families wherein a fatalistic view works to enable them to address a difficult situation with less emotional trauma. However, this kind of view may hinder the family's need to work aggressively in helping the child with his or her disability. A mother's family may argue that the disability was caused because the mother was not careful during her pregnancy. For example, one fairly acculturated Mexican American family felt that a child born mentally retarded was harmed during the pregnancy because of the mother's bowling.

Folk beliefs may play a role in the definition of many disabilities or defects. For example, one such belief is that a pregnant woman must be careful when using scissors or sharp objects while pregnant or else the child can be born with a cleft palate. Another is that if the mother knits clothes for the child, she cannot wind the yarn into balls or the child will be born with the cord wrapped around his or her neck (Smith-DeMateo, 1987).

Interventionists will encounter variations in the interpretation of the disability. Those families who are middle class or more educated may have a more sophisticated view. Social class can also influence a reverse reaction. Smith-DeMateo (1987) argued that often the higher the socioeconomic status, the more likely that a disabled family member, especially one who is mentally retarded, will be kept hidden from society at large. Another view is that in folk cultures disabilities like mental retardation are more readily accepted. Thus, an immigrant family from a rural area in their country of origin may be more predisposed to accept this kind of child and less likely to feel embarrassed by this "act of God." The central principle is to view each family as an individual unit to ascertain what meaning they ascribe to the illness or disability. Assumptions should not be made without first getting to know the family since so many variables contribute to views on causation and disability, particularly related to children.

ISSUES OF LANGUAGE

Although the various groups referred to in this chapter are Spanish speaking, the interventionist needs to use caution in working with the various immigrant

Case Example #3

A Latina mother from Central America gave birth to a female child with a stomach disorder that the teaching hospital was having difficulty diagnosing. The child could not eat normally and had to be tube fed. The mother's first two children, ages 4 and 2, had been born healthy. The child remained in the hospital for over 2 months; assessment indicated that the child would have long-term medical difficulties.

It was expected that the mother would visit frequently so that she could learn the complicated feeding procedures, since the child's discharge from the hospital was imminent. The mother would agree to visitation schedules so one of the staff could instruct her. However, she would typically miss two visits out of three. The staff felt she was not bonding with the child since visitation had always been infrequent.

A social worker was asked to take on the case and to attend a staffing with the multidisciplinary team and the mother. Staff members spoke in English about the mother, noting that they felt there were potential child abuse issues present in view of her lack of participation. They described the mother as uncaring and unnurturing.

Review by the bilingual/bicultural social worker uncovered the following: 1) the mother, although she had lived in the United States for 5 years, had few friends and no relatives in the area, was a single parent, and had no one who could provide child care for her two other children, as well as no money to pay for child care; and 2) she lived more than an hour's distance from the hospital, in a rural area where bus transportation was infrequent and meant several bus transfers. The mother related to the social worker that lack of child care and money kept her from visiting her daughter. It was painful for her not to be able to see her daughter more often. Also, when she did come, the nurses acted very cold with her and she felt unwanted, and disrespected by staff. Moreover, instructions were often in Spanish that was hard for her to follow; she had made mistakes in trying to learn the complicated feeding instructions, resulting in her feeling incompetent as a mother.

The interventionist explained these considerations to the staff. The staff asked why the mother had not told them of her problems. The mother answered in Spanish that no one had ever asked her. Intervention by the social worker included educating the staff about this mother's embarrassment about her poverty, and her lack of education and communication skills, as well as her reticence in interacting with professionals. Child care and transportation were obtained and further monitoring noted no child abuse present.

groups because the recent immigration trends have produced some interesting differences in dialect. For example, in the last 5 years, Southern California has received many immigrants from the state of Oaxaca in Mexico, many from very small towns in the interior where Indian dialects are prevalent. Thus, many of these immigrants are bilingual in their Indian dialect and Spanish, but may feel more comfortable in their indigenous dialect. Thus, even Spanish-speaking interventionists must be cautious in their communication to ensure that they do not use idioms or concepts that immigrants may not comprehend. For example, the interventionist may ask if an Indian language is used by the client; she or he may then use this as a reminder to ask if the client has understood his or her communication or to ask questions of the client to assess if comprehension has occurred. She or he may need to communicate the same idea or theme in various ways to ensure better comprehension.

Another theme related to communication is the field-dependent aspects of Latino culture. This implies that Latino persons are very sensitive to interpersonal relations and may pick up communication cues that are nonverbal as a normal way to assess their interaction with others, particularly in relation to an authority figure or in relation to someone with status. Thus, the interventionist must be conscious of his or her reactions, for example, to aspects of the client's culture that are novel, curious, or even frightening to him or her. The interventionist's affect or body language can convey to the Latino client or family a view of the interventionist as a caring and respectful helper or someone who disrespects their style of coping and living.

SUMMARY AND RECOMMENDATIONS

Summary

The diversity theme presented at the beginning of this chapter highlights the variety of factors that can influence each Latino family system. The range of countries from which Latinos come contributes to the differences that are often present. Yet the language commonality and the influence of Spanish traditions, particularly around family life and expectations for children, offer some insight into the values and beliefs that may underlie how children are viewed and how disability may be addressed.

A critical theme is the influence of class on the Latino view of family life, sex roles, and roles of children. Moreover, class status may also influence the extent to which families rely upon folk beliefs. Folk beliefs influence families' views of causation and disability. Yet, every family and parent will need to be addressed as individuals for their particular reactions and perspectives on the disabilities or illnesses that affect their children. Moreover, assumptions cannot be made about a family's cultural stance. The interventionist is responsible for individualizing each family or parental system to determine what cultural traits fit. If families do in fact subscribe to the use of healers, the interventionist is cautioned to respect this fact while at the same time ensuring that there are no contraindicated interventions occurring that may harm the child.

Language themes will be particularly pertinent if a family is not English speaking. The interventionist must be careful in the selection of interpreters and recognize that communication can be foiled in the interpretation process. Last, interventionists must be conscious and sensitive to how they use themselves as interventionists so that they humanize their relationships and acknowledge the value placed in Latino cultures on interpersonal respect.

Recommendations for Interventionists

The importance of use of self cannot be overstated. The interventionist's effectiveness with Latino families with children with disabilities will depend in a very significant way on the extent they are open to discerning how they handle ethnic, cultural, and racial differences. The following directives are offered to help the practitioner recognize these issues and also to consider the particular implications of the information offered in this chapter.

- Examine your experiences with diversity, both culturally and racially. Were you socialized to accept and appreciate cultural and racial differences? Did you have negative experiences in your socialization that presently affect how you interact with a culturally diverse person? Do you have a need to "hide" your prejudices or to rationalize them? Can you uncover these "isms" and work on eradicating them? Can you make a commitment to unlearn prejudices or ingrained aspects of racism? These negative residues can only undermine your ability to be effective with client systems that are culturally diverse and can actually be harmful to clients (Devore & Schlesinger, 1987).
- You must assess your normal style of interacting with people in general, and clients in particular. If you are always constrained by time, you may need to retune your timing mechanisms so that a Latino client does not receive the message that you are in a hurry and thus interprets this as your giving him or her less respect or concern. This is especially important in light of the Latino's sensitivity to interpersonal cues (Davis & Proctor,1989).
- If the family has recently immigrated, you must assess its adaptation processes to discern if and where problems may be present that could cloud the family's ability to focus on the needs of the identified infant or child (De-Anda, 1984).
- If the immigrant family members come from a rural region of their country of origin, you must assess basic issues, such as whether they know about childproofing their home. They may not recognize the need to have covers for electrical outlets since wiring in their previous country may have been structured differently.
- Do not assume that a family or parent is literate in English or Spanish. Carefully assess this so that education inputs will be used appropriately.
- For poor and immigrant families, assess their feelings about going to doctors' offices or large urban centers for examinations. It may be necessary to accompany them and role model for them on how to use elevators, or what the protocol is when entering a reception area in a doctor's office.

- Does the family have transportation for following through on a referral that you make? They may gladly agree to all your plans but may be embarrassed to inform you that they have no means of transportation. Or they may not know how to traverse freeways that you assume everyone can negotiate.
- Learn about the class/economic backgrounds of families who are immigrant since their status in their country of origin may support a more Western view than you may realize.
- If a family comes from a Latino culture with which you are unfamiliar, such as from El Salvador, assess what resources may exist in your community that can offer you consultation, readings, or perspectives so that you can become better informed.
- In your city, identify the Latino community networks and agencies that exist so that you will know what is available for referral purposes and whom you can call on to support your work or to offer you consultation. Attend Latino community celebrations as another avenue for you to gain respect for and knowledge of different Latino cultural rituals and practices.
- Given the growing presence of Latinos, you must begin or continue to read about this population. There are presently many publications, journals and texts available. The *Hispanic Journal of the Social Sciences* is an excellent resource that can be obtained from Sage Publications.

In conclusion, it is important to realize that learning about cultural diversity is a lifelong process, just as enhancing one's competency as an interventionist is similarly lifelong. The variety of knowledge that you are being asked to consider can be overwhelming. Do not react by shutting off emotionally, but reframe your reaction so that you view this as an avenue for broadening your appreciation for how different cultures live life, thus broadening your world view.

REFERENCES

Abad, V., & Boyce, E. (1979). Issues in psychiatric evaluations of Puerto Ricans: A sociocultural perspective. *Journal of Operational Psychiatry, 10*(1), 28–30.

Abalos, D.T. (1986). *Latinos in the United States: The sacred and the political.* Notre Dame, IN: University of Notre Dame Press.

Alvirez, D., Bean, F., & Williams, D. (1981). The Mexican American family. In C. Mindel & R. Habenstein (Eds.), *Ethnic families in America* (pp. 269–292). New York: Elsevier Press.

Arias, A.M. (1990, September). Casa Colina. *Hispanic: The Magazine for and about Hispanics,* p. 60.

Bernal, G. (1982). Cuban families. In M. McGoldrick, J. Pearce, & J. Giordano (Eds.), *Ethnicity and family therapy* (pp. 187–207). New York: Guilford Press.

Boekestijn, D. (1984, September). *Intercultural migration and the development of personal identity: The dilemma between identity maintenance and cultural adaptation.* Paper presented at the XXIII International Congress of Psychology, Acapulco, Mexico.

Center on Budget and Policy Priorities. (1988). *Shortchanged: Recent developments in Hispanic poverty, income and employment*. Washington, DC: Author.

Cromwell, R., & Ruiz, R.A. (1979). The myth of macho dominance in decision-making within Mexican and Chicano families. *Hispanic Journal of Behavioral Sciences, 1*, 355–373.

Davis, L., & Proctor, E. (1989). *Race, gender and class*. Englewood Cliffs, NJ: Prentice Hall.

DeAnda, D. (1984). Bicultural socialization: Factors affecting the minority experience. *Social Work, 29*, 101–107.

Delgado, M. (1977). Puerto Rican spiritualism and the social work profession. *Social Casework, 58*, 451–458.

Delgado, M. (1988). Groups in Puerto Rican spiritism: Implications for clinicians. In C. Jacobs & D. Bowels (Eds.), *Ethnicity and race: Critical concepts in social work* (pp. 71–83). Silver Spring, MD: National Association of Social Workers.

Devore, W., & Schlesinger, E. (1987). *Ethnic sensitive social work practice*. Columbus, OH: Charles E. Merrill.

Fitzpatrick, J. (1981). The Puerto Rican family. In C. Mindel & R. Habenstein (Eds.), *Ethnic families in America* (pp. 189–214). New York: Elsevier.

Garcia-Preto, N. (1982). Puerto Rican families. In M. McGoldrick, J. Pearce, & J. Giordano (Eds.), *Ethnicity and family therapy* (pp. 164–186). New York: Guilford Press.

Gibbs, J.T., & Huang, L.N. (Eds.). (1989). *Children of color: Psychological interventions with minority youth*. San Francisco: Jossey-Bass.

Gomez, E. (1977). *Chicano culture and mental health: Trees in search of a forest*. San Antonio, TX: Our Lady of the Lake University of San Antonio.

Gonzalez-Whippier, M. (1989). *Santeria, the religion*. New York: Harmony Books.

Goodman, M.E., & Beman, A. (1971). Child's-eye-views of life in an urban barrio. In N. Wagner & M. Haug (Eds.), *Chicanos: Social and psychological perspectives* (pp. 109–122). St. Louis: C.V. Mosby.

Hepworth, D., & Larsen, J. (1990). *Direct social work practice: Theory and skills*. Belmont, CA: Wadsworth.

Hispanic population up 30% in U.S. since '80. (1987, September). *San Diego Union*, p. A-22.

Ho, M. K. (1987). *Family therapy with ethnic minorities*. Beverly Hills: Sage Publications.

Inclan, J. (1985). Variations in value orientations in mental health work with Puerto Ricans. *Psychotherapy, 22*, 324–334.

Juarez, R. (1985). Core issues in psychotherapy with the Hispanic child. *Psychotherapy, 22*, 441–448.

Kluckholm, F., & Strodtbeck, F. (1961). *Variations in value orientations*. Evanston, IL: Row and Peterson.

Levine, E., & Padilla, A. (1980). *Crossing cultures in therapy: Pluralistic counseling for the Hispanic*. Monterey, CA: Brooks-Cole.

Mizio, E. (1974). Impact of external systems on the Puerto Rican family. *Social Casework, 55*(1), 76–83.

Montiel, M. (1975). The Chicano family: A review of research. *Social Work, 18*(2), 22–31.

Montijo, J. (1985). Therapeutic relationships with the poor: A Puerto Rican perspective. *Psychotherapy, 22*, 436–440.

Ortiz, F. (1973). *Los Negros brujos* [The Negro witches]. Miami, FL: New House Publishing.

Powell, G., Yamamoto, J., Romero, A., & Morales, A. (Eds.). (1983). *The psychosocial development of minority group children*. New York: Brunner/Mazel.

Ramirez, M., & Price-Williams, D. (1974). Cognitive styles in children: Two Mexican communities. *InterAmerican Journal of Psychology, 8,* 93–101.

Ramirez, O., & Arce, C.H. (1981). The contemporary Chicano family: An empirically based review. In A. Baron, Jr. (Ed.), *Explorations in Chicano psychology* (pp. 3–28). New York: Praeger.

Roland, A. (1988). *In search of self in India and Japan: Towards a cross-cultural psychology.* Princeton, NJ: Princeton University Press.

Romero, A. (1983). The Mexican American child: A sociological approach to research. In G. Powell, J. Yamamoto, A. Romero, & A. Morales (Eds.), *The psychosocial development of minority group children* (pp. 538–572). New York: Brunner/Mazel.

Rubinstein, D. (1976). Beyond the cultural barriers: Observations on emotional disorders among Cuban immigrants. *International Journal Mental Health, 5*(2), 69–79.

Russell, G. (1985, July 8). Trying to stem the illegal tide. *Time,* pp. 50–53.

Salcido, R.M. (1982). Use of services in Los Angeles County by undocumented families: Their perceptions of stress and sources of support. *California Sociologist, 5*(2), 119–131.

Salgado de Snyder, N. (1987). *Mexican immigrant women* (Spanish Speaking Mental Health Research Center, Occasional Paper 22). Los Angeles: University of California at Los Angeles.

Sluzki, C. (1979). Migration and family conflict. *Family Process, 18,* 379–390.

Smith-DeMateo, R. (1987, February). *Multicultural considerations: Working with families of developmentally disabled and high risk children: The Hispanic perspective.* Paper presented at the conference of the National Center for Clinical Infants Programs, Los Angeles.

Szapocznik, J., & Hernandez, R. (1988). The Cuban American family. In C. Mindel, R. Habenstein, & R. Wright, Jr. (Eds.), *Ethnic families in America* (3rd ed., pp. 160–172). New York: Elsevier.

Torres-Matrullo, C. (1982). Cognitive therapy of depression in the Puerto Rican female. In R.M. Becerra, M. Karno, & J. Escobar (Eds.), *Mental health and Hispanic Americans: Clinical perspectives* (pp. 101–113) New York: Grune & Stratton.

U.S. Bureau of the Census. (1988). *The Hispanic population in the United States: March, 1988 (Advance Report* [Current population Reports, Series P-20, No. 431]). Washington, DC: U.S. Government Printing Office.

Vega, W. (1980). Mental health research and North American Hispanic populations: A review and critique of the literature and a proposed research strategy. In R. Valle & W. Vega (Eds.), *Hispanic natural support systems* (No. 620047, pp. 3–14). Sacramento: State of California Department of Mental Health.

Vega, W., Hough, R., & Romero, A. (1983). Family life patterns of Mexican Americans. In G. Powell, J. Yamamoto, A. Romero, & A. Morales (Eds.), *The psychosocial development of minority group children* (pp. 194–215). New York: Brunner/Mazel.

Vega, W., Kolody, B., & Valle, R. (1988). The relationship of marital status, confidant support, and depression among Mexican immigrant women. *Journal of Marriage and the Family, 50,* 391–403.

Ybarra-Soriano, L. (1977). *Conjugal role relationships in the Chicano family.* Unpublished doctoral dissertation, Department of Sociology, University of California, Berkeley.

Zuniga, M. (1988a). Chicano self-concept: A proactive stance. In C. Jacobs & D. Bowles (Eds.), *Ethnicity and race: Critical concepts in social work* (pp. 71–83). Silver Spring, MD: National Association of Social Workers.

Zuniga, M. (1988b). Clinical interventions with Chicanas. *Psychotherapy, 25,* 288–293.

APPENDIX A
CONTRASTING BELIEFS, VALUES, AND PRACTICES

Latino cultures	Mainstream culture
Collective orientation	Individual orientation
Interdependence	Independence
Collective, group identity	Individual identity
Cooperation	Competition
Saving face	Being direct
Relaxed with time	Time sensitive
Emphasis on interpersonal relations	Emphasis on task orientation
Spiritual/magical belief orientation	Rational/empirical orientation
More recent agrarian influence	More urbanized/industrialized mode
Tendency toward more patriarchal family structure	Tendency toward more democratic family structure
More relaxed with child development	Strong expectations for child development
More overt respect for the elderly	Less value/respect toward the elderly
Extended family systems more pronounced	Nuclear family systems more pronounced

APPENDIX B
CULTURAL COURTESIES AND CUSTOMS

It is inappropriate for the interventionist to:

- Speak to the wife before the husband, when both are present
- Not ask whether the father is in agreement with the recommendations or plans, even if he is not at the session or meeting
- Decline a beverage or food offering
- Begin on work or tasks immediately, before any informal and relaxed exchange with the client has taken place
- Use a tone of voice that is harsh and authoritarian
- Show impatience or to present him- or herself in a very hurried manner

APPENDIX C
SIGNIFICANT CULTURAL EVENTS/HOLIDAYS

Event/Holiday	Date	Description
Dia de los Muertos; All Souls Day for Catholics	November 1 for children who have died; November 2 for adults who have died	Celebrated by Mexicans and contains aspects of Indian ancestor worship coupled with Catholic prayer rites for the deceased. Mexican families may build altars to commemorate the dead. Altars have statues, pictures of the dead, food offerings, decoration of skeletons, candied skulls with the names of the deceased, candles, and so forth.
Noche Buena	December 24	Celebrated by preparing foodstuffs for the holiday, such as tamales for Mexicans, then attending midnight Mass.
Nuestra Senora de la Caridad del Cobre	Eve of September 8th in New York's St. Patrick Cathedral	A celebration by those from Cuba and the Carribean honoring the Patron saint of Cuba and Ochún in Santeria. After Mass, the statue of this saint is paraded in the church and those present wave yellow handkerchiefs in the air (Gonzalez-Whippier, 1989).
Feast of St. Francis of Assisi or Orúnla, *the syncretized Santeria deity*	October 4	Coconuts are brought to the house of the *babalawo* who is a high priest in Santeria. The coconuts are *derechos* (rights) that his godchildren bring as offerings (Gonzalez-Whippier, 1989).

Appendix D
Vocabulary

English	Spanish spelling	Pronunciation
Mother	Madre	măthray
Father	Padre	pa-thray
Family	Familia	fah-mee-lēah
Hello	Buenos dias	bway-nōs dee-ahs
Goodbye	Adios	ah-dee-ōs
Thank you very much	Muchas gracias	moo-chahs grră-sē-ahs
Please	Por favor	poŏr fah-boŏr
With your permission	Con su permiso	cön su pār-mèso

chapter 8

FAMILIES WITH ASIAN ROOTS

Sam Chan

Chinese

A journey of a thousand miles begins with the first step.

A boy is born facing in; a girl is born facing out.

What is happiness? Grandfather dies, then father dies, then son dies.

Korean

Don't even look at a tree you cannot climb!

You can fall down seven times; but you'll stand up after the eighth.

Vietnamese

Birds have nests. People have roots.

Handle me as a fragile egg, cherish me as a delicate flower. (children's saying)

Curve your tongue three times before you speak.

Japanese

Better to cover the fish than to chase the cat.

The nail that raises its head is hammered down.

A slip of the tongue cuts deeper than the sword.

What is left unsaid is rich as flowers.

In honoring the spirit of collective endeavor, the author of this chapter and Chapter 9 wishes to express his deep appreciation for the contributions of several friends and colleagues and their long-standing dedication to serving Asian Pacific families and communities. They provided valuable input, materials, and consultation for numerous aspects of each chapter. He is especially grateful to Drs. Sam Lo, Chung Suh, and Kristy Kim; Yen Nguyen; Lillian Lew; Erica Hagen; and Nancy Spiegel for their assistance on the "Families with Asian Roots" chapter. He also thanks Drs. Jonathan Okamura and Ben Marte, Royal Morales, Helen Brown, Nathan Fuentes, and Carolyn Yano for their special contributions to the "Families with Pilipino Roots" chapter.

In honoring his family, the author wishes to thank his parents (Sam and Lola Chan) for giving him such strong roots and his wife and sons (Nachi, Aki, and Kenji) for the countless hours of support and sacrifice they offered throughout the many months and weekends it took to get the job done.

Asian Americans have emerged as the fastest growing ethnic minority group in the United States. The current Asian population of over 7 million has doubled since 1980 and is projected to grow to nearly 10 million by the year 2000 ("Asians in America," 1991; Bouvier & Agresta, 1985; Gardner, Robey, & Smith, 1985). This accelerated growth has been largely attributed to the continuing waves of Asian immigrants and refugees since the Immigration and Nationality Act Amendments of 1965 and the withdrawal of the United States from Vietnam in 1975. In fact, more refugees and immigrants have come to the United States from Asia than from any other region in the world; they currently constitute half of all annual admissions (Arnold, Minocha, & Fawcett, 1987; U.S. General Accounting Office, 1990).

The Asian American population is further characterized by considerable diversity and originates from three major geographic areas:

East Asia: China, Japan, Korea
Southeast Asia: Cambodia, Laos, Vietnam, Burma, Thailand, Malaysia, Singapore, Indonesia, the Philippines
South Asia: India, Pakistan, Sri Lanka

Differing political and economic conditions in these respective countries of origin, time of arrival, and varying modes of adaptation to the host society have thus shaped the unique experiences and lifestyles of recent Asian immigrants (Fawcett & Arnold, 1987). The diverse ethnic, sociocultural, and linguistic characteristics of the immigrants themselves further contribute to the extreme heterogeneity of this population (Leung & Sakata, 1988).

Despite their rapid growth, increasing visibility, and diversity, Asian Americans have remained one of the most poorly understood minorities. Throughout their respective histories of experience in the United States, Asian immigrants have been persistently confronted with stereotypic, undifferentiated, and often hostile perceptions. Today's Asian Americans find themselves celebrated as America's "model minority." Yet they have also been victimized by an explosion of hate crimes and violence, fueled by a new wave of "yellow peril" sentiments (Attorney General's Asian and Pacific Islander Advisory Committee, 1988).

Thus, successive groups of Asians in America and their ancestors have been considered both threatening and "enigmatic." Just as earlier immigrants were seen as a monolithic race, originating from the "mysterious East," the new Asian immigrants still find themselves viewed and treated as "strangers from a different shore" (Takaki, 1989, p. 18). This perception serves to disguise the reality of unique customs, traditions, values, beliefs, and familial systems based on political and religious foundations that are thousands of years old (Shon & Ja, 1983).

Acknowledgment and appreciation of such rich histories are critical in the delivery of human services to increasingly diverse Asian immigrant populations. In particular, the effectiveness of early intervention programs and providers is significantly enhanced by an understanding of the distinct historical, social, and political experiences of the individual ethnic clients and communities that are served. Viewing children and families within an ecological context further entails specific knowledge of: traditional values, beliefs, and practices pertaining to family, religion, childrearing, education, health, mental health, and disability; language characteristics and communication styles; and cultural orientations and behaviors related to service utilization (Chan, 1986).

This chapter addresses these topics in relation to selected Asian ethnic groups: Chinese, Koreans, and Southeast Asians (specifically, Cambodians, Laotians, and Vietnamese). In contrast to other immigrants such as Asian Indians and Pilipinos (who are generally proficient in English), the most recent Chinese and Korean immigrants as well as Southeast Asian refugees are predominantly non–English speaking. They have also typically concentrated their economic resources and primary social and cultural institutions within their respective ethnic communities or enclaves. These particular Asian immigrant and refugee populations consequently pose significant challenges with respect to the accessibility and delivery of services that are culturally and linguistically appropriate. Moreover, as families with infants and young children continue to increase in number, their corresponding service needs will most likely exceed available resources.

The importance of achieving practical insights into working with Asian families is further reinforced by the earlier noted immigration trends. While Asia is home to more than half of the world's people, it is also the world's main source region for international immigrants (Fawcett & Carino, 1987). Asian immigration levels in the United States are projected to remain high for many years, given the unstable and often volatile political conditions in several Asian nations that lead to large numbers of immigrants and refugees as well as the desire on the part of many Asian immigrants to be reunited with their families (Bouvier & Agresta, 1987). Significant growth is also projected among Asian immigrant/refugee populations (particularly Southeast Asians) who have settled in the United States, due to high fertility rates. The birth rate of Southeast Asian women ages 14–40 years is nearly double the average national birth rate in the United States. Southeast Asian American women of childbearing age also constitute a larger proportion of Southeast Asian Americans than the proportion of all women of childbearing age in the United States (Keiter, 1990). A deeper understanding of Asian roots is thus necessary to serve effectively the growing needs of a once-invisible minority.

CHINESE AMERICANS

Geographic and Historical Origins

Chinese Americans reflect the extreme heterogeneity of the larger Asian American population. They are characterized by significant linguistic, social, and political differences. They also originate from many different provinces in the

People's Republic of China, Hong Kong, Taiwan, and numerous Southeast Asian countries. However, collectively, Chinese Americans join the "family" of well over 1 billion Chinese from these respective countries and constitute nearly one quarter of the total world population (Brigham Young University, 1986).

As the mother country, "China is as much an idea as it is a place; to be Chinese is to share a particular cultural identity" (Major, 1989, p. 1). This identity is tied to a common heritage in which every person of Chinese ancestry is a cultural heir to one of the world's oldest living civilizations—one that originated on the northern China plain over 4000 years ago and spread throughout the "Middle Kingdom"; it was viewed as the center of the world from which the influence of Chinese people and culture extended. The realm of the Middle Kingdom was called *tianxia* (all under heaven). Beyond precise geographical or political definition, *tianxia* represented the cultural and moral world of Chinese civilization—the essence of being Chinese (Porter, 1983).

Embodied in the spirit of Chinese foreign students, the realm of the Middle Kingdom was finally extended to the United States in 1820. The Chinese were the first of the early Asian immigrants and, in the late 1840s, began voluntarily departing China (primarily from Guangdong [Canton] province) by the tens of thousands. The discovery of gold in California served as the catalyst for emigration from a country plagued by widespread famine, economic depression, and ongoing civil wars. Chinese laborers, as sojourners, originally expected to amass their fortune in America or *Gam Saan* (Gold Mountain), then return home to their families in 3–5 years and retire in prosperity (Sung, 1971). Yet, the vast majority of them did not find gold and were forced to remain in America and struggle for survival.

Their survival was threatened as the labor market diminished and economic competition fueled anti-Chinese sentiment. Despite their profound contributions in constructing the transcontinental railroad and as service, factory, and farm laborers, the Chinese were forced to remain strangers through economic exploitation and racial antagonism. Escalating hostility toward the "Heathen Chinese" culminated in the passage of the Chinese Exclusion Act of 1882, which prohibited Chinese laborers from entering the United States and was later broadened to include all persons of the Chinese race. This was the first time in U.S. history that a federal law was enacted to ban a particular race from entering the country. The "Chinese invasion" and the "Chinese Problem" were thus addressed by legislating the disappearance of the Chinese presence in America. The experience of the Chinese in the 19th century signaled the beginning of a pattern to be repeated for subsequent Asian groups (Takaki, 1989). In fact, within 40 years of the Chinese Exclusion Act, *all* Asian immigration was banned.

The Chinese Exclusion Act was not repealed until 1943, when China became an American ally at the beginning of World War II. While the act had remained in force, more Chinese left than entered the United States. But the remaining Chinese immigrants survived in the face of institutional racism, persistent humiliation, racial violence, loss of property, loss of livelihood, and sometimes loss of life. Those who decided to stay or could not return to their homeland needed to change their status from laborers, who were targets of deportation, to businessmen, who were exempt. Chinatowns became the basis for this conversion, and drew upon traditional structures such as clans and family associations to organize an urban economic community built on the service industries (Chen, 1981; Huang & Ying, 1989). Chinatowns also emerged in many rural areas. Thus, the Chinese continued to create their own colonies or communities that served to perpetuate tradition and adherence to Chinese culture.

Despite the repeal of the Chinese Exclusion Act in 1943, a national origins quota system was imposed whereby only 105 Chinese (50% of whom were required to be professionals) were allowed into the United States each year. This system was abolished in 1965 by the Immigration and Nationality Act Amendments, which allowed 20,000 immigrants per country from the Eastern Hemisphere. Immediate family members were exempted from the quota, and preferred immigrant status was given to educated, professional, and skilled workers.

The 1965 immigrant law resulted in the second wave of Asian immigration, which produced a massive increase as well as changes in the Asian American population. Within 15 years, Chinese and Pilipinos surpassed Japanese as the largest Asian American populations, and nearly two thirds of all Asian Americans were foreign born. In contrast to the earlier immigrants who were primarily farmers and laborers with rural origins, the second-wave newcomers included significant numbers of professionals from the cities—who have been considered the most highly skilled of any immigrant group the United States has ever had. Unlike the first-wave immigrants, those in the second wave arrived as families rather than single men, and as settlers rather than sojourners (Doerner, 1985; Takaki, 1989).

The majority of second-wave Chinese immigrants have settled in two states, California and New York, where they have revitalized Chinatowns and transformed the Chinese American community into a predominantly immigrant community once again. As *San Yi Man* (new immigrants), they come primarily from urban areas and include Mandarin as well as Cantonese speakers. Most were initially refugees from the People's Republic of China, and usually emigrated from a second point of departure such as Hong Kong or Taiwan. After normalization of relations between China and the United States in 1979, the People's Republic of China was allowed to have its own quota; this was followed by dramatic increases in the number of family members reuniting with relatives in the United States (Takaki, 1989). During this same time period (between 1978 and 1980), ethnic Chinese who had constituted the business class in

Southeast Asia became targets for discrimination under the new Communist regimes; they thus joined the "third wave" of Southeast Asian refugees as "boat people" and came to the United States in large numbers.

The *San Yi Man* have thus dramatically contributed to the current diversity of the Chinese American immigrant population, which ranges from mono-lingual, less educated, and semi-skilled individuals to middle-class and afflu-ent, highly educated, city and suburban residents. They have immigrated to be reunited with families; to pursue their education as foreign students; to establish themselves in business, industry, and professions; and/or to seek refuge from political conflict and instability in China and Southeast Asia. For most new Chinese immigrants, "America is not *Gam Saan,* a place to work temporarily, but a new home where they hope to find greater economic opportunities for themselves and educational advantages for their children" (Takaki, 1989, p. 423).

Religious Origins

Throughout the past 2,000 years, Chinese as well as many other Asian cultures have been principally influenced by the doctrines and philosophies of Confu-cianism, Taoism, and Buddhism. Collectively referred to as the "three teach-ings" of Confucius, Lao Tzu, and Buddha Gautama, they serve as the religious-philosophical systems that undergird all facets of Asian life. Confucianism, Taoism, and Buddhism thus significantly contribute to the commonalities evi-dent in the world views, ethics, social norms, values, folk beliefs, and lifestyles of Chinese and Asian people. Each has its unique emphasis; however, together they have evolved into a complementary system of blended teachings that en-able Asians to integrate and be guided by complex mixes of corresponding thoughts and faiths (Leung, 1988).

Confucianism

Confucius (551–479 B.C.) expounded no systematic doctrine, but rather he ex-pressed a philosophy of humanity, spoke about man in society, and prescribed a way of life. He believed his mission was not to reform but to rectify his way-ward times by trying to restore the ethical, benevolent government of the past—the Way of the Ancients. "The origin of social harmony and good gov-ernment lay in the cultivation of individual virtues and the observance of re-ciprocal social obligations that were the moral fabric of society" (Porter, 1983, p. 96). Confucius's ideal was the "perfect gentleman" who behaved in a princely way and was characterized by the "five virtues":

Ren or *jen*: benevolence and humanism (the cardinal principle or primary virtue of Confucianism and the essential quality of humanity)
Yi: righteousness or morality
Li: proper conduct

Zhi or *chih*: wisdom or understanding
Xin: trustworthiness

The embodiment of these "five virtues" is *xiao* (filial piety), the duties owed to one's parents and ancestors (Major, 1989). Filial piety consists of unquestioning loyalty and obedience to parents and concern for and understanding of their needs and wishes. It also includes reverence for ancestors whose spirits must be appeased. Filial piety further extends to relations with all authority figures and defines a social hierarchy of allegiance and reciprocal moral obligations characterized by:

King/justice, subject/loyalty
Father/love, son/filiality
Elder brother/brotherly love, younger brother/reverence
Husband/initiative, wife/obedience
Friends/mutual faith

Confucius thus offered prescriptions for regulating "proper" human relationships, which served to maintain the social order. He believed human nature was at best neutral, but that anyone could be "made good" by cultivating virtues through study and self-discipline; such endeavor would, in turn, lead to proper conduct, both in personal and public life. His goal was not religious salvation, but rather the full realization *in this life* of the human potential for wisdom and virtue (Major, 1989).

Taoism

Unlike Confucianism, Taoism was not associated with any definitive historical figure, although Lao Tzu (604–? B.C.) is viewed as the legendary patriarch. He advocated the cultivation of inner strength, selflessness, spontaneity, and harmony with nature and man, rather than Confucius's group-oriented propriety and codes of conduct. In fact, society is the antithesis of *Tao,* which literally means the "way" or "path"—the ultimate reality that is eternal and enigmatic. Taoist philosophy stressed the need to transcend artificial man-made human culture (society) and to avoid worldly entanglements, since there is no valid way of making judgments in a world where everything is relative. Taoism thus encouraged the practice of training, asceticism, meditation, and discipline in the pursuit of good health and long life. Lao Tzu also explained natural and social phenomena by incorporating the ancient theory of the cyclical counterbalancing forces of yang (the creative, forward, dominating, and manifest force represented by the male and heaven) and yin (the receptive, recessive, submissive, and hidden background force represented by the female and earth). Everything in reality is not only regarded as generated from the interactions between these two forces, but everything is also composed of both yin and yang.

Taoism was ultimately transformed from an elite philosophy to an elaborate religion. Taoism further evolved into superstition, magic, divination, and sorcery. Its rituals and mystical practices were compatible with animism and, while also closely associated with the alchemical search for immortality, popular Taoism was widely accepted and perpetuated by the masses (C-Y. Cheng, 1987; E.K. Leung, 1988; Major, 1989; Porter, 1983).

Buddhism

Buddhism was founded by Prince Siddharta Gautama (560–480 B.C.) and entered China as an alien religion from India long after Confucianism and Taoism were already established as mature traditions. While Buddhism later profoundly influenced Confucianism, it was also radically transformed in the process (Porter, 1983).

Original Buddhist doctrine is summarized in the "four noble truths":

1. All life is suffering.
2. Suffering is caused by desire or attachment to the world.
3. Suffering can be extinguished and attachment to all things (including the self) can be overcome by eliminating desire.
4. To eliminate desire, one must live a virtuous life by following the eightfold path: right views, right thought, right speech, right conduct, right livelihood, right effort, right mindfulness, and right meditation.

Buddhism asks all of its adherents to follow this path, which is the basis for the monastic life of the bonzes (priests or monks).

Buddha Gautama taught his followers that the world has no reality; it is an illusion that only seems real because people want it to be so. Attachment to the illusion of reality inevitably produces suffering and leads to an endless cycle of rebirths governed by the law of karma (whereby an individual's fate in this existence is determined by what he or she did in the previous existence). The only escape from the cycle of birth, aging, sickness, and death is Buddhahood or enlightenment in dharma (the doctrine of the life of Buddha). The Buddhist's goal is to be released from the "wheel of life" or circle of reincarnation and reach nirvana, a state of complete redemption wherein the world and all sufferings are transcended, and one's soul is merged into the cosmic unity, the only true reality (Major, 1989; Te, 1989a).

Such beliefs obviously challenged the "Chinese attitude," which was much more instinctively down-to-earth and practical than the Indian view; whereas Buddhists denied the world, the Chinese affirmed it (Porter, 1983). Consequently, Chinese Buddhism had to accommodate itself to Chinese cultural imperatives by adopting the basic philosophy that filial piety is the highest morality; however, Buddhism was soon to influence a reinterpretation of Confucianism. Ultimately, Mahayana Buddhism became the dominant form in China. More specifically, the Chan (Zen in Japan) sect was most widely practiced and, with its emphasis on meditation and rigorous self-discipline, became almost indistinguishable from philosophical Taoism. Buddhism spread from China to Korea to Japan and has had a profound long-term influence on these cultures (Major, 1989).

Ancestor Worship

The "three teachings" are further complemented by ancestor worship, which is considered the universal religion of China and the foundation for popular religion. Ancestor worship serves as the central link between the Chinese world of man and the Chinese world of the spirits. Chinese ancestor worship, which should not be equated with simple adoration of the dead, is characterized by three basic assumptions:

1. All living persons owe their fortunes or misfortunes to their ancestors.
2. All departed ancestors, like other gods and spirits, have needs that are the same as the living.
3. Departed ancestors continue, as in life, to assist their relatives in this world, just as their descendants can assist them.

These assumptions contribute to corresponding beliefs and practices. Individual achievements and successes are viewed as evidence of one's ancestors' high moral worth and good deeds. Departed ancestors should be provided with offerings of food and various possessions (often in the form of life-size paper models of clothing, furniture, horses, servants, etc.). There remains a social tie between departed ancestors and living descendants; that is, one's condition may be improved by the spiritual efforts of departed ancestors, and the spiritual welfare of departed ancestors may likewise be enhanced by the worldly actions of living descendants. Belief in the mutual dependence and interaction between the living and the dead thus reinforces efforts (including a variety of traditional rituals) to maintain a positive and close relationship with one's departed ancestors as well as living kinsmen. The souls of ancestors stand apart from other spirits or gods who may be worshipped in a more neutral and distant fashion. Thus, "the worst imaginable plight for any Chinese is, while alive, to be without known parents and relatives, and when dead, to be without living descendants" (Hsu, 1981, p. 252).

Complementarity and Polytheism

Indigenous Chinese religion cannot be abstracted from its historical context. Although Neo-Confucianism, Christianity, and Islam have also been somewhat influential, the basic Chinese philosophical/religious orientation has remained rooted in the secular world and has been relatively consistent throughout the past 2,000 years. Adherence to the "three teachings" reflects a polytheistic orientation that stresses complementarity rather than conflict among Confucianism, Taoism, and Buddhism. Many Chinese temples, for example, were built expressly to house Confucius, Lao Tzu, and Buddha together; moreover, a person might typically pray at a Confucian temple before taking the civil service exams, call a Taoist doctor to cure an illness, and invite a Buddhist priest to chant at a funeral (Major, 1989).

Confucianism, Taoism, Buddhism, and ancestor worship have been embraced by a collectivistic Chinese society in which human relationships are inclusive, rather than exclusive. Polytheism encourages a belief in many gods and emphasizes the coexistence of all supernatural beings. Many Chinese will indicate that they have no *particular* religion or that, since all religions are essentially beneficial to man, they are all equally good. This orientation dramatically contrasts with the monotheistic orientation of most Western societies, with individualistic religions that emphasize a direct link between the one and only God and the individual human soul; the corresponding belief in individual self-reliance and an all-or-nothing attitude pervades nearly every aspect of life.

Thus, the American tendency to exclude and the Chinese tendency to include represent fundamental differences in religious orientations as well as many other values and belief systems (Hsu, 1981). These contrasts and more specific relationships between traditional religious/philosophical beliefs and disability and service utilization are subsequently discussed in this chapter.

Language/Linguistic Origins

The Chinese language contains a multiplicity of dialects. In contrast to regional American English dialects, the major Chinese dialects have evolved into distinctly different spoken languages that are mutually unintelligible. The national language or common speech of the People's Republic of China is *Putonghua* (Mandarin); it is spoken by more than 70% of the people. Mandarin includes various northern Chinese dialects and is spoken in the north, northwest, west, and southwest regions of China. The *Wu* dialects are spoken in the east. The most widely differentiated dialects (e.g., Cantonese, Min, Hakka) are spoken in the southeast. Among recent Chinese American immigrants, the greater number have been from Cantonese-speaking provinces of countries such as Hong Kong. Another popular dialect among immigrants is Toishanese, a Cantonese-related dialect from the Taishan province in the People's Republic of China. Taiwanese immigrants typically speak Fukienese and Mandarin. Cantonese is typically spoken among ethnic Chinese immigrants and refugees from Vietnam and other Southeast Asian countries (Tinloy, Tan, & Leung, 1986).

Chinese has many monosyllabic words. Each syllable of every monosyllabic word or a compound word has a distinctive pitch, referred to as a tone. In Mandarin, there are 4 basic tones; Cantonese has 10 tones. Tones do not refer to individual speaker expression, and have nothing to do with the mood or personality of the speaker. Instead, they convey different meanings for the syllables to which they are assigned. For example, depending upon which tones are used, the Cantonese word *mai* may mean either "buy" or "sell"; for the Mandarin word *ma,* there are at least four possible meanings (e.g., "mother," "hemp," "horse," "scold"), corresponding to four different tones. Moreover, there are many Chinese homonyms—that is, words that have the same sounds and tones, yet still have multiple meanings (Tinloy et al., 1986).

Apart from tonal pronunciation, the linguistic structure of Chinese differs significantly from English. Intonations tend to rise at the end of a sentence in the Chinese language, in contrast to English, where they tend to fall. There are no digraphs in Chinese (e.g., since there is no "th" sound, a word like "some-*th*ing" might be pronounced as "some*s*ing"). There are no gender pronouns, tenses, plural endings, or verb conjugations in Chinese; thus gender, time, and quantity are denoted by word additions rather than through the modification of words as in English (Chin, 1983). Words are thus very context bound wherein "the meaning of the whole determines the meaning of the parts" (L.L. Cheng, 1987, p. 33). Sequencing of sentence parts (subject, verb, object) is also different in the two languages.

Remarkably, all dialects of spoken Chinese share the same written language, which has been revered and respected for preserving Chinese culture and history while playing a critical role in binding the diverse peoples of China together. The Chinese written language has also served to cement ties betwen neighboring countries such as Korea and Vietnam—both of which used classical Chinese as their written language for official government documents and important works of literature (Major, 1989). The written language consists of approximately 40,000 ideographs, or characters, that represent an object or idea; there are also over 100,000 combined compounds (thousands of individual characters change meaning when used with other characters). A knowledge of 1,500 to 3,000 characters is adequate for basic literacy (Brigham Young University, 1986).

Contemporary Life

As previously noted, the number of Chinese immigrants/refugees from China (including Taiwan), Hong Kong, and various Southeast Asian countries dramatically increased throughout the late 1970s and 1980s and will likely remain high during the 1990s. A very significant future event that will continue to contribute to increased Chinese immigration is the formal conversion of Hong Kong (by agreement between Great Britain and China) to a Special Administrative Region (SAR) of China on July 1, 1997; Britain's 99-year lease of the New Territories (extending from Kowloon to the Chinese border) will expire at that time, and Hong Kong shall revert to Chinese sovereignty. To assure Hong Kong's smooth transition to its new status as an SAR, the agreement provides a guarantee from China that Hong Kong's unique political, legal, economic, and social systems will remain unchanged for another 50 years. Despite such an assurance, large numbers of Hong Kong immigrants (particularly businesspeople and professionals) are leaving to settle permanently in the United States and Canada (primarily in the provinces of Ontario and British Columbia). Fears of the ultimate "Communist takeover" by a potentially unstable and repressive Chinese government were greatly exacerbated following the brutal suppression of the prodemocracy movement in the People's Republic in June 1989.

Population distribution and immigrant settlement patterns in the United States indicate that the vast majority of Chinese are continuing to reside in the western and northeastern regions of the United States—particularly in the West and East Coast cities and metropolitan areas of San Francisco/Oakland, Los Angeles, and New York City (Bouvier & Agresta, 1987). Chinese, like other Asian populations, are generally electing to locate in communities where other Chinese reside and are thus accelerating the growth of urban as well as suburban Chinatowns. Throughout this process, "the different class backgrounds of the new immigrants has [sic] led to the formation of a bi-polar Chinese-American community—one divided between a colonized working class and an entrepreneurial-professional middle class" (Takaki, 1989, p. 425). Initial occupational downgrading and periods of underemployment and downward mobility are experienced by many recent immigrants; however, many eventually become successful and join the ranks of suburban Chinese professionals. In contrast, a great many Chinese immigrants with limited formal education and English language skills belong to a colonized labor force of low-wage laborers, employed as service workers and operatives in urban Chinatowns. Their condition is illustrated by the fact that, except for Southeast Asian refugees, the Chinese have the highest number of persons living below the poverty level of all Asian groups in the United States (U.S. Bureau of the Census, 1988).

KOREAN AMERICANS

Geographic and Historical Origins[1]

Traditionally known as *Choson* (Land of the Morning Calm), Korea is a peninsula stretching southward from the Asian mainland (Manchuria) for 600 miles. Historically, this location has had the advantage of providing easy access to adjacent cultures and the disadvantage of vulnerability as a target of invasion from neighboring countries. Thus, Korea served as a land bridge through which continental culture and religion were transmitted to Japan from China. However, for centuries, Korea was also plagued by attack from outside forces, foreign domination, and exploitation by China, Manchuria, and Japan.

The Korean peninsula was controlled by a series of powerful dynasties including the Silla Dynasty (57–935); the Koryo Dynasty (935–1392), from which the country's name *Korea* is derived; and the Yi Dynasty (1392–1910). These dynasties directed the political and cultural development of the region as well as the defense needed to protect against outside invasions. Toward this

---

[1]The historical overview provided in the first four paragraphs of this section has been adapted from Park and Song (1982).

end, Korea virtually closed itself off from the outside world during the later years of the Yi Dynasty, and thus became known to Westerners as the "Hermit Kingdom."

As the first step in its imperialistic expansionist movement, Japan overtook and formally annexed Korea in 1910. During the subsequent 35-year period of colonization, Japan attempted to eradicate Korean culture through educational, economic, and political means. However, in response to such domination, the Korean People adhered even more tenaciously to their own prevailing cultural values and traditions; they developed a fierce national pride and determination to seek independence.

Korea was finally liberated from Japan in 1945, at the end of World War II; but to disarm the Japanese, Soviet troops occupied the northern part of Korea and United Nations troops (predominantly U.S. forces) occupied the south. According to the Yalta agreement, the country was divided along the 38th parallel into "political zones" in which the respective governments of the Democratic People's Republic (North Korea) and the Republic of Korea (South Korea) were ultimatley established. The ensuing Korean War (1950–1953) was one of the bloodiest wars in history and brought total devastation to the entire country. Millions of Koreans died, and the majority of the population became homeless refugees within their own national boundaries. However, shaped by centuries of hardship and adversity, the Korean national character (pride, pragmatism, stubborn determination, endurance, and the will to survive and overcome) prevailed, and enabled the Korean people to rebuild their country. South Korea has since emerged as one of Asia's most influential nations, with a leading world economy.

Throughout their long history of both external and internal turmoil, Koreans have thus maintained remarkably homogeneous cultural traditions against great odds. The continuing need to unite for defensive purposes and strong adherence to traditional values were factors that promoted the development and maintenance of Korean cultural distinctiveness—particularly among the first generation of Korean immigrants to America. "The struggle of early Korean immigrants in the United States during the first half of the century reveals their immense pride in and dedication to the Korean people, Korean culture and the Korean Independence Movement" (K.H. Yu & Kim, 1983, p. 149).

Koreans have immigrated to the United States in three waves. The first wave consisted of farm laborers and their families (approximately 7,000) who were recruited to work in the sugar plantations of Hawaii to augment the dwindling labor force of Chinese and Japanese farm workers (Patterson & Kim, 1986). These first Korean immigrants arrived between 1903 and 1905. Unlike the original Chinese and Japanese immigrants, they had diverse occupational backgrounds and most were from urban rather than rural areas. Hawaii represented a haven from the Japanese imperial government that was controlling Korea at that time; it also provided opportunities for work for Korean immigrants who left conditions of poverty, famine, and drought in Korea. Hawaii, and later the U.S. mainland, also promised a better life for many Korean "picture brides" (about 1,000) who arrived between 1910 and 1924. During this period, approximately 900 additional Korean immigrants arrived; they consisted primarily of students, intellectuals, and political exiles who formed the core of Korean community leadership in America during the pre–World War II period (E-Y. Yu, 1983). The first wave of Korean immigrants were thus a relatively small and isolated minority, but retained a strong sense of ethnic identity and solidarity; as a people without a country who could not become American citizens, they organized their family life and communities around the nationalist movement for Korean independence from Japanese colonial rule (Takaki, 1989). These efforts continued from 1924 until the end of World War II, during which time there was no further immigration from Korea due to the 1924 Immigration Act.

The second wave consisted of Koreans who entered the United States between 1945 and 1964. Nearly a third of these new immigrants were students, many of whom became permanent residents. After the outbreak and ending of the Korean War (1950–1953), the majority of immigrants consisted of Korean wives of American servicemen (war brides) and war orphans (predominantly girls under 4 years of age) who were adopted. Thus, unlike the earlier first-wave arrivals, about three quarters of these interim immigrants were young women and children who were dependents of American citizens. They were dispersed throughout the country and remained isolated from the mainstream activities of the Korean community (Hurh & Kim, 1984; E-Y. Yu, 1983). During this postwar period, the larger Korean population was characterized by rapid dispersion and assimilation. Second-generation Korean Americans could not relate to their parents' nationalism and saw their future in America, not Korea. They thus left their parents' communities and intermarried at a rate higher than that of all other Asians until the mid-1960s. "With the loss of a unifying theme and the desertion of the second generation, the Korean community stagnated until revitalized in the 1970's by renewed immigration from Korea" (E-Y. Yu, 1983, p. 27).

The third wave of Korean immigration began after the landmark Immigration and Nationality Amendments Act of 1965 became effective. Prior to this time, the relatively small size of the Korean population and its widespread geographic dispersion contributed to Koreans' status as a hidden minority. The new wave of Korean immigration, however, led to a dramatic emergence of Koreans as a very visible group in America (Takaki, 1989). The phenomenal growth of the Korean population is reflected by the fact that since 1976, the number of Korean immigrants to the United States has exceeded 30,000 annually. Thus, Koreans in the United States have become one of the fastest growing ethnic minorities. Well over 80% are post-1965 immigrants (E-Y. Yu, 1983).

Religious Origins

One of the earliest religions of Korea was shamanism or spirit worship. As a system of beliefs about the supernatural world, shamanism originated in the tribal communities of ancient Korea and continues to be practiced in the rural areas as well as by many older Koreans. Shamanism is concerned with the relationship among people, spirits, and the universe. A great number of spirits are the objects of religious worship, and each has a specific function. Moreover, a person's life, death, happiness, misfortune, and all other events are dependent on the spirits. Spirits, which are immortal, must thus be worshipped and well served to prevent misfortune and to bring good fortune (Mun, 1979).

Animism, the basic principle of shamanism, is a belief that all forms of life and things in the universe maintain their existence by virtue of anima (soul). The universe is composed of the heavenly world, the earthly world, and the underworld, wherein everything is interrelated by shamanistic laws of cause and effect. Therefore, nothing is accidental (Mun, 1979). Shamans serve as intermediaries with the spirit world and are believed to have the power to prevent, diagnose, and treat (or cure) illness; to bring good luck and predict change in a person's fortune/misfortune; and to assure passage from this world to the next (Young-Kwon, 1978).

The previously described "three teachings" of Confucianism, Taoism, and Buddhism flowed into the peninsula from China in the first century A.D. and were also embraced by the Korean people. Taoism laid the groundwork for Korea's earliest belief systems and was later blended into Buddhist premises and teachings. While imported to Korea through China, Buddhism underwent profound transformation in ways suited to the Korean people. It served the people's spiritual needs and had the biggest impact on individual religious life and art. However, among the "three teachings," Confucianism exerted the principal influence.

Confucianism provided the foundation for the development of Korea's educational, social, and political systems. The initial impact of Confucianism in Korea was the establishment of higher learning. Confucianism then continued to strongly influence the ruling class and provided the state with capable government officials. During the Yi dynasty, Korea became the center of Confucian learning; Confucianism reached its theoretical and philosophical peak while becoming an integral part of the general public's daily lives (Yum, 1987). In having provided all-embracing values and an ideology for the Korean people, Confucianism thus serves as a key to understanding Korean culture (Mac-Mahon, 1977).

The introduction of Christianity to Korea marked the beginning of a major social and cultural transition period. The abolishment of laws forbidding Christian missionaries from entering Korea resulted in a rapid expansion of missionary activity in the late 1800s. The missionaries promoted modern education and the Western work ethic, and encouraged thousands of Koreans who converted to Christianity to emigrate to America. Significantly, 40% of all first-wave Korean immigrants were Christians (Takaki, 1989). As they established communities in the United States, their churches became forums for nationalistic education while also perpetuating traditional Korean values. Today, between 60%–70% of Korean Americans are affiliated with Christian churches, which continue to be the most important social and cultural institutions in the community. "Wherever there are Koreans there are churches, a pattern that clearly differentiates Koreans from other Asian immigrant groups" (E-Y. Yu, 1983, p. 39).

Language/Linguistic Origins

The Korean language reflects centuries of Chinese cultural influence. Approximately 50% of the Korean vocabulary is derived from Chinese. There are thus many words that have the same meaning in Chinese and Korean, but are pronounced differently. Furthermore, Korean, unlike Chinese, is not a tonal language. It consists of a single phonetic alphabet, *hangul,* with 24 phonetic symbols or characters representing different sounds that are combined to form words. Interestingly, the shapes of some *hangul* letters were originally designed to mirror the corresponding shapes of the tongue during articulation. Koreans take great pride in their languge, since it was invented in 1443, centuries before phonetics became a systematic discipline. In fact, Koreans celebrate the date when *hangul* was proclaimed the Korean vernacular script—probably the only linguistic holiday observed in the world (C.S. Lee, 1988; Wang, 1983).

There are several Korean dialects, but unlike the major Chinese dialects, they are mutually understandable. Korean morphemes or words are also predominantly polysyllabic (in contrast to generally monosyllabic Chinese words). Yet another distinction between the languages is the very elaborate Korean inflectional system (based on suffixes); Chinese has essentially no morphological inflections (Wang, 1983).

Thus, while the Korean vocabulary reflects significant Chinese influence, the language structure is uniquely different. However, given the additional historical influence of Japan, both the Korean and Japanese languages are genetically related and have many common grammatical features. The most important one is that they are "verb-final" languages—that is, for the vast majority of sentences, the verb always occurs at the sentence-final position (Li, 1983). This particular feature has great communicative significance wherein sentence-final verbs may indicate the attitude of the speaker in relation to the anticipated response of the listener. The speaker will typically state the subject and object while observing the listener's reaction, then adjust the verb to accommodate the listener. The speaker may also add a negative at the end, thereby reversing the entire meaning of the sentence, but preserving the human relationship (Weisz,

Rothbaum, & Blackburn, 1984). The language itself is thus designed to maximize interpersonal harmony and reinforce traditional values derived from the "three teachings." Confucian values, in particular, are also evident in the "honorific" system of the Korean language in which different verbs and nouns will be used in addressing or speaking with individuals of varying social status or rank, thus reflecting the hierarchical nature of the society (C.S. Lee, 1988).

Contemporary Life

The third wave of Korean immigration has been occurring within the context of rapid industrialization and economic modernization in South Korea. The concurrent population explosion has emerged as the most urgent domestic problem confronting South Korean society. In fact, South Korea's population density is the third highest in the world (Kim, 1987). Corresponding overurbanization in cities such as Seoul has created overcrowding, air pollution, unemployment, underemployment, and widespread exploitation of cheap labor; there is also extreme competition for college entrance and an oversupply of highly educated people as well as major human rights restrictions and curtailment of political freedoms. These conditions and the prospects for greater economic and educational opportunities in the United States are among the primary premigration push factors contributing to the current large-scale Korean emigration process (Kim, 1987).

The largest proportion of Korean immigrants have settled in California, particularly in the Los Angeles area. New York and Illinois, and the respective metropolitan areas of New York City and Chicago, have the second and third largest Korean populations. Within these and other population centers, Korean newcomers have shown a tendency toward rapid suburbanization and residential/geographic dispersal. In fact, relative to other recent Asian immigrants, Koreans are the most widely dispersed (E-Y. Yu, 1983).

This distinctive pattern of geographic mobility and dispersal reflects, in part, Korean adaptability to a new life setting and prior experience with the rapidly changing urban-industrial structure of Korea. But one of the most important contributing factors is the relatively high educational level and occupational preparation of Korean immigrants. A large percentage of college graduates and professionals embark on new ventures and are not bound to any particular locality once they overcome limitations of language and familiarity with American social customs. However, during the initial adjustment period, Korean immigrants typically suffer downward occupational mobility (E-Y. Yu, 1983).

Despite the fact that Koreans exhibit one of the highest levels of education among all ethnic groups in the United States, many recent immigrants are initially unable to practice within their profession or at their level of education. They thus frequently turn to self-employment. Korean Americans have the highest rate of self-employment relative to all other Asian American groups, and the most common source of income for Korean immigrants is the self-owned small business (E-Y. Yu, 1983). While Korean small businesses are penetrating white suburbs, shopping centers, and rural areas, a great many are located in inner-city sections of large metropolitan areas among predominantly African-American and Latino communities. As Korean green groceries, liquor stores, markets, and other small businesses have proliferated in such communities, they have also become targets of increasingly volatile conflict—thus eliciting a significant amount of recent media attention and a need for ongoing race relations and mediation resources (Siao, 1990).

In addition to occupational, economic, and interethnic struggles within the larger community, Korean immigrants are also faced with major family and generational conflicts. The vast majority (over 90%) of first-generation Korean parents list Korean as their major spoken language and actively encourage their children to learn it. However, despite these efforts, the children are mainly English speaking, and the differentiated language pattern between generations complicates family life (E-Y. Yu, 1983). Typical immigrant family parent–child conflicts thus arise from loss of parental authority and respect due to basic communication problems, acculturation clashes, unrealistic expectations, and limited availability of many parents and family members who work long hours and cannot provide adequate guidance and support for their children. The problems are more serious for school-age children who are Korean-born immigrants—the "1.5" generation. While requiring several years to attain English proficiency, these children gradually lose their Korean language skills and may also fail to develop a positive self-identity within either the Korean or American culture. Like other recent Asian immigrant youth experiencing similar identity crises, they have come to be referred to as a lost generation that adjusts by rejecting traditional values in favor of a peer subculture—which may include youth gangs (B-L.C. Kim, 1980).

Like their predecessors (or first-wave immigrants to America), the most recent adult Korean immigrants are profoundly proud of their natural heritage, rich culture, language, and distinctive history of nearly 5,000 years (K.H. Yu & Kim, 1983). They are also invested in teaching their children to become proud Koreans as well as successful Americans. However, in the process, many recent immigrants indicate that the first generation must be sacrificed in order to brighten the future of their children. Thus, propelled by the values of hard work and education, parents must struggle in order for their children to attend college and become professionals as they themselves had been in Korea (Takaki, 1989). Yet the resulting family stresses and persistent generational conflicts pose major challenges to family stability.

SOUTHEAST ASIAN AMERICANS

As previously indicated, the geographic region of Southeast Asia consists of several countries (a total of 10, including the new state of Bruni). The term

Southeast Asian has often been confused or used interchangeably with Indo-chinese. However, Indochina refers only to those countries situated on the In-dochinese Peninsula, located between China and India. It consists of Burma, Malaysia, and Singapore (former British colonies); Cambodia, Laos, and Viet-nam (former French colonies); and Thailand (the only Southeast Asian country that has never been colonized by Western powers) (Te, 1989a).

This section focuses specifically on the refugee populations from Cam-bodia, Laos, and Vietnam. They are designated by the geopolitical term "Southeast Asian refugee." Over 1 million Southeast Asian refugees have en-tered the United States since April 1975, as part of the aftermath of the Vietnam War and the civil wars in Cambodia and Laos (Huang, 1989; Keiter, 1990). Although people from other Southeast Asian countries have also been given refugee status since 1975, they constitute less than one half of 1% of the total; thus, the three nations of Cambodia, Laos,and Vietnam are the usual focus of discussion of Southeast Asian refugees (Gordon, 1987).

Although the focus is narrowed to refugees from these three countries, there are obviously significant historical, cultural, and linguistic differences as well as many distinct subcultural and ethnic minority groups among the peoples of Cambodia, Laos, and Vietnam. The following sections highlight the respec-tive backgrounds of these major Southeast Asian refugee populations and illus-trate their extreme diversity.

Geographic and Historical Origins

Cambodia

Bordered by Vietnam, Laos, Thailand, and the Gulf of Siam, Cambodia is a country of flat delta terrain with few plateaus and mountains. Cambodia is the European name for the country known as "Kambuja" or "Kampuchea." Its pre-dominant ethnic group is the Khmer people whose civilization dates back al-most 2,000 years to the Kingdom of Funan. Cambodia's long history has been punctuated by persistent political and military struggles, civil wars, and threats from neighboring states. However, the Angkor period (800–1430) was the "Golden Age" in which monuments were built in the city of Angkor Wat—the national symbol of an advanced and civilized Khmer empire that extended over a vast area, including much of present-day Thailand, Laos, and Vietnam. The post-Khmer period was marked by constant warfare with Thailand and Viet-nam and the decline of the empire. After years of Thai dominance, Cambodia became a French protectorate in 1863 and remained under French rule until 1954. At that time, then "King" Norodom Sihanouk negotiated Cambodia's complete independence from France; he subsequently established a monarchy, which he controlled for 16 "peaceful" years (Chhim, 1989).

During this period, Sihanouk played off Chinese, Soviet, and American interests. While brutally suppressing tiny groups of Communist Khmer Rouge in the countryside, he later (in 1965) allowed North Vietnamese Communist troops to establish sanctuaries and move supplies inside Cambodia's borders. Five years later, Sihanouk was deposed by General Lon Nol who established the Khmer Republic. While officially recognizing Lon Nol's new government, the United States then extended the Vietnam War into Cambodia by bombing North Vietnamese supply lines and storage facilities. However, backed and trained by the well-entrenched North Vietnamese Army, Khmer Rouge forces waged a full-scale war. By the end of 1971, an estimated 2 million of the country's 7 million population had been displaced and 20% of property had been destroyed (Chhim, 1989). Finally, in April 1975, while the North Vietnamese stormed Saigon, the Khmer Rouge forces led by Pol Pot marched into the capital of Phnom Penh and immediately started clearing the entire city of its 2.5 million inhabitants. The new regime officially renamed the country Kampuchea and initiated extreme measures to eradicate all Western influence. Pol Pot instituted a brutal program for the massive relocation of the urban population to the countryside and for the mass destruction of all Cambodians affiliated with the American-supported Lon Nol government (Takaki, 1989). The Khmer Rouge era (from mid-1975 to 1978) was thus infamous for unprecedented atrocities in which over half of Cambodia's population was decimated through torture, execution, disease, starvation, and exhaustion from forced marches and compulsory labor (Union of Pan Asian Communities [UPAC], 1980).

Pol Pot's army thus destroyed large segments of the middle and upper-middle classes, killing nearly all of the educated and professional people, while forcing the relocation and flight of the peasant classes as the bloodbath intensified with the Vietnamese invasion in 1978. Hundreds of thousands of "land refugees" fled on foot through the dense jungles infiltrated by guerrillas and Communist soldiers to the camps on the Thai/Cambodian border. They arrived malnourished, sick, diseased, weak, and depressed. Having been brutalized by the Khmer Rouge, at least half of these survivors had experienced the death of a family member (Huang, 1989). As victims of the most horrible genocidal war known to modern history, they left the "killing fields" behind, but the killing fields did not leave them (Takaki, 1989).

Laos

As the only "landlocked" country in Southeast Asia, Laos is wedged between Thailand and Vietnam and bordered by Burma and China to the north and Cambodia to the south. More than half of the country is covered by mountains and forests. Among the nearly 70 different ethnic groups in Laos, the majority are "lowland Lao"; other major ethnic groups include the Hmong (which means "free" and who are also known as Meo or Miao, the Lao of the mountain tops) and the Mien (which means "people"). The ancient Laotian kingdom of *Lan Xang* (Kingdom of a Million Elephants) was founded in 1353. After centuries of continued wars and conquests by neighboring countries such as Burma, Cambodia, and Thailand (then Siam), Laos was ultimately colonized by the French in 1893. After World War II (following a 4-year period of Japanese invasion and occupation), the French retook their French Indochinese territories (Cambodia, Laos, and Vietnam); however, Laotian nationalists led by the Pathet Lao began their struggle to overthrow French colonialism. The 1954 Geneva Accord finally established Laos as an independent state (Luangpraseut, 1989; Takaki, 1989).

Throughout the next 20 years, Laos's political history was one of prolonged civil strife and struggle among opposing forces seeking control of the country. This internal conflict merged with developments in Vietnam. By the 1960s, the Vietnam War had been extended into Laos. North Vietnam supported the Pathet Lao in order to protect the Ho Chi Minh Trail (which ran through Laos as a supply line to the south), while the United States gave assistance to the Royal Lao and the Hmong and Mien in the highlands to interrupt the movement of troops and military supplies. Shortly after Cambodia and South Vietnam "fell into Communist hands" in the spring of 1975, the Royal Lao Government also collapsed. As the Pathet Lao took power and established the Lao People's Democratic Republic, they began a campaign of bloody repression and reprisal—one in which the Mien and Hmong tribespeople (who had been recruited and trained as guerilla soldiers to conduct American military operations in Laos) were targeted for destruction as "tools of the CIA" or "lackeys of American imperialism" (Takaki, 1989). Thousands were killed in vicious military attacks, thousands more retreated further into the mountains to face starvation, and others were taken to "re-education centers" from which they never returned. No one knows how many more refugees died or were killed as they fled on foot across Laos to the MeKong River, where many more drowned trying to swim across to the Thai border. The long Indochinese war and subsequent brutal campaigns of retribution thus decimated the people of Laos. Almost all Hmong families, in particular, lost at least one or two members. In many cases, only the women and children survived (Tou-Fou, 1981). Ultimately, some 70,000 ethnic Lao, 10,000 Mien, and 60,000 Hmong sought sanctuary in America as refugees (Kourmarn, 1980; Takaki, 1989).

Vietnam

Because of its strategic location for trade and military activities, Vietnam has been called "a crossroads of the Asian world." It lies on the eastern coast of the Indochinese peninsula, and is bordered on the north by China, on the west by Cambodia and Laos, and on the south and east by the South China Sea (with 1,200 miles of coastline). The northern part of the country is a mountainous region surrounding the Red River Delta; the central region consists of a long series of small coastal plains and a range of high mountains; the southern part is a flat area formed by the MeKong Delta—the most productive agricultural area in Vietnam, where tropical monsoon conditions of heavy rainfall and a hot climate create ideal conditions for rice growing (Rutledge, 1987; Te, 1989a, 1989b; UPAC, 1980).

The Vietnamese people are most commonly thought to have originated from a mixture of the Viet tribes from southern China and the inhabitants of the Red River Delta, originally from Indonesia. While the Vietnamese represent approximately 85% of the total population, there are several different ethnic minorities in Vietnam; they include ethnic Chinese, over 30 mountain tribes (aboriginal people referred to by the French term *montagnards*), the Chams (who live primarily in the lowlands of the southern part of central Vietnam), the Cambodians or Khmers, and other smaller ethnic groups (Malays, Indians, Pakistanis, and French). Most of these ethnic groups left Vietnam in 1975 (Rutledge, 1987; Te, 1989a, 1989b).

Vietnam has a recorded history of over 2,000 years and 2,000 years of unrecorded history based on oral legends. The history of the Vietnamese people is characterized by a profound sense of national identity and long-term strength and resistance that have enabled them to survive as a nation despite centuries of foreign domination. China first ruled over Vietnam for about 1,000 years (from 111 B.C. to 938 A.D.). Numerous rebellions ultimately led to the overthrow of Chinese rule and a subsequent 900-year period of independence. This era of independence came to an end when the French conquered Vietnam and colonized the country from 1883 until 1954. During this period, French influence dominated Vietnamese culture; French became the second language of the Vietnamese, and the country experienced major changes and growth in medicine, architecture, government, and education. However, the Vietnamese people also suffered severe hardships (economic, social, changes in traditional cultural institutions, etc.) as well as the imposition of European social and economic systems on traditional lifestyles. They thus offered increasingly fierce resistance the longer the French remained in control.

As previously noted, the European colonial forces were driven out of Indochina by the Japanese during World War II. While the Japanese occupied Vietnam, Ho Chi Minh, a veteran Communist leader, organized an independence movement known as the Vietminh; their purpose was to fight the Japanese and to oppose French rule. When the war ended, the French, determined to resume their rule over Vietnam, reoccupied the South. However, the Vietminh seized power in the North and established the Democratic Republic of Vietnam. Vietnamese in both the northern and southern areas of the country were opposed to French rule. Thus, attempts to reinstate a French colonial regime by force resulted in open rebellion. In 1954, after 8 years of fighting, the Vietnamese defeated the French in the decisive battle of Dien Bien Phu. As a result of the ensuing Geneva Accord, Vietnam was divided into two separate states along the 17th parallel: North Vietnam with a Communist government based in Hanoi under Ho Chi Minh, and South Vietnam with a non-Communist regime based in Saigon headed by Premier Ngo Dinh Diem. The agreement called for a cessation of fighting, national elections, and reunification of the country by 1956.

However, both governments claimed exclusive right to rule Vietnam and civil war erupted. As hostilities between the North and the South escalated, China and the Soviet Union provided aid to North Vietnam, while the United States assisted the South Vietnamese government. By 1960, a full-scale war was underway within Vietnam. U.S. military involvement continued to expand and reached a peak in 1969 when the number of American troops in Vietnam had risen to over 500,000. The Vietnam War gave rise to increasingly widespread and sometimes violent domestic protest in the United States by those who viewed the war as immoral; they engaged in bitter debate with others who believed that America had a responsibility to combat the spread of Communism in Southeast Asia. Several years of peace talks culminated in 1973 with the Treaty of Paris, in which a cease-fire agreement was signed and stipulated the withdrawal of all U.S. troops from Vietnam. Two years later, North Vietnam launched a major offensive and, on April 30, 1975, the South Vietnamese government fell, the city of Saigon was overrun by northern troops, and the entire country was reunited under the Communist regime (Rutledge, 1987; Te, 1989b).

The cost of the prolonged, nearly 20-year conflict was high for all involved. Over 58,000 Americans died in Vietnam, and an estimated 2 million Vietnamese (both military personnel and civilians) were killed ("The Legacy of Vietnam," 1985). Many millions more were maimed and wounded, uprooted and homeless, and forced to flee as refugees within their own country. Ultimately, over 1 million Vietnamese would leave the country, seeking asylum in other Asian or Western countries. This was the first time in the 4,000-year history of Vietnam that an exodus of such magnitude had taken place (Te, 1989b). Tragically, hundreds of thousands of Vietnamese, particularly the "boat people," would endure countless horrors and die or be lost at sea in the process of escape. Many of those refugees who succeeded in making their way to displacement camps throughout Asia would further have to survive similar life-threatening conditions (starvation, disease, robbery, rape, extortion) on a daily basis for a great many years.

Waves of Refugees

"Black April" of 1975 was the beginning of mass evacuations of Vietnamese from Saigon. Well over 200,000 "first-wave" refugees were airlifted out of South Vietnam, resettling primarily in the United States and France. These Vietnamese were predominantly well-educated, urban, middle-class professionals who spoke English (and French) and had been closely associated with the Americans and the former South Vietnamese regime. In 1975, the United States resettled approximately 130,000 Vietnamese refugees, the majority of whom were initially placed in reception centers or processing camps located at Camp Pendleton in California, Fort Chafee in Arkansas, Elgin Air Force Base in Florida, and Fort Indiantown Gap in Pennsylvania. Basic adjustment to a new American lifestyle and "survival skills" training occurred within the camps. Sponsors were then found (a necessary condition of resettlement) and the refugees were dispersed throughout the country. The U.S. policy in 1975 was to disperse the Vietnamese geographically so that a sudden inpouring of refugees would not overwhelm a given local or state government; this dispersal policy was also predicated on the belief that more rapid adaptation to American society would occur if the Vietnamese were not concentrated in one place where they might form ethnic enclaves (Rutledge, 1987). However, within a few years, many Vietnamese began to relocate and gather in communities such as Orange County, California, where Mutual Assistance Associations (MAAs) were formed (Keiter, 1990; Takaki, 1989).

The second-wave refugees were typically the immediate families or other relatives of first-wave refugees and entered the United States between the fall of 1975 and fall of 1978. They included individuals who were at high risk in Vietnam because they had fought in the South Vietnamese army or, like their predecessors, had been associated with the U.S. or South Vietnamese government. Many had originally fled to other countries or were in refugee or displacement camps in Asia awaiting sponsorship and money to join their families in the United States. These second-wave refugees were relatively quickly resettled with their families (Keiter, 1990).

The third wave of refugees occurred between 1978 and 1980. This period saw the exodus of several hundred thousand "boat people" from Vietnam, consisting primarily of ethnic Chinese who faced persecution and were forced to leave the country. Other Vietnamese, in anticipation of being sent to "re-education centers" or "new economic zones" also began to flee. Moreover, many parents, resigned to the belief that their children had no future in Vietnam, arranged for their children's escape while they themselves remained behind (Huang, 1989). Together, these third-wave refugees "boarded crowded, leaky boats, risking their lives at sea where storms threatened to drown them and pirates waited to rob them and rape the women. Two thirds of the boats were attacked by pirates, each boat an average of more than two times" (Takaki, 1989, p. 452). Those boat people who survived typically landed in countries such as Thailand, Malaysia, and the Philippines where they were given temporary asylum in prison-like holding centers.

The third-wave refugees also included "land refugees" from Vietnam, Cambodia, and Laos who had languished in the desperate conditions of refugee camps for extended periods of time. Relative to earlier refugees, the conditions and methods of flight of the third-wave refugees were much harsher. They came to the United States as fishermen, farmers, and people from small coastal cities, rural areas, and villages, having had little prior contact with Americans. Their adjustment difficulties and culture shock were thus much greater (Huang, 1989). Moreover, although their stories of transition into urban American communities elicited sympathy and compassion among some, others viewed these "foreigners" with resentment, hostility, and contempt (Attorney General's Asian and Pacific Islander Advisory Committee, 1988). These negative attitudes were due, in part, to the refugees' relative cultural/linguistic insularity from the larger community, contrasting lifestyles, perceived dependence on welfare, and/or continuing threat to existing norms and practices among local workers (particularly fishermen).

Religious Origins

Among the religious or moral systems that have most profoundly influenced Southeast Asian cultures, Buddhism is predominant. There are two branches of Buddhism: Mahayana (Great Vehicle), which flourishes in Vietnam, as well as China, Japan, and Korea; and Hinayana (Little Vehicle) or Theravata, which flourishes in Cambodia and Laos, as well as Burma, Thailand, and Sri Lanka. Each branch is based on the same Buddhist doctrines that were previously described in this chapter and do not require a belief in a god, but insist upon the responsibility of each individual for his or her behavior. The ascetic life necessary to follow the doctrines of Buddhism is extremely strict, and most people are unable to adhere fully to it. Mahayana Buddhism thus offers nirvana to more people and is followed by the Vietnamese. Theravata Buddhism is stricter and followed by the Cambodians and Laotians; in fact, historically, nearly all young Cambodian and Lao males went to the local *wat* or temple for at least 3 months to spend time as a member of the *sangha* (monastic order) to learn to become a novice monk (Te, 1989a).

The religious life of Cambodia and Laos is given an added dimension by Brahmanism or Hinduism with its associated Indian philosophy, deities, and traditional worship of Brahma, the supreme being who is simultaneously the Creator, the Preserver, and the Destroyer (with a different wife for each different form he manifests). The Khmer and Lao have also been significantly influenced by animism and spirit worship. This is the belief that spiritual and supernatural powers are present throughout the universe, and all natural phenomena and things (animate and inanimate) possess an innate soul. It is further believed that these powers can and will change the destinies of human beings if the *Phi* (spirits, ghosts, demons, and other supernatural beings) are not satisifed (Chhim, 1989; Luangpraseut, 1989).

The various beliefs and rites of Brahmanism and animism are often mixed. They are at the core of the Lao *su-kwan* (*su* = "to invite," *kwan* = the "soul") ceremony or *Baci*. This ceremony is typically performed on important occasions (e.g., a wedding, pregnancy, birth of a child, recovery from a serious illness, death of a person, return home from a long journey, change of status or dwelling, reunion of family or friends). The purpose of the *Baci* is to contact the body spirits (or "thirty-two souls"), protect them, and bind them to the person who needs help since they are likely to leave his or her body on these occasions. Each of these mobile souls that preside over the body has its own organ of residence. The King soul is believed to "live" in our head (this is the main reason why some Southeast Asians do not wish their head to be touched or even pointed at by another person). A community elder is invited to perform the rite by chanting from a religious text to call the spirits or souls into the person receiving the *Baci*. Then the elder and all persons present will tie white pieces of yarn around the wrist of the person to bind the spirits to his or her body (the tied knot symbolizing the effective return of the absent soul). These are then worn for at least 3 days (Luangpraseut, 1989).

While the majority of Vietnamese are also Buddhists, their culture and lifestyle have been shaped by a mixture of Buddhism, Confucianism, and Taoism. Like the Chinese, many Vietnamese have adhered to the "three teachings" and practiced syncretism or a blending of beliefs. Animism has thus also been a strong influence on Vietnamese belief systems. The belief in spirits has led many Vietnamese to worship a host of deities such as the Earth god, the Luck and Fortune god, and so forth, and to observe astrology, fortune telling, omens, and natural signs. The calendar system is marked by a 12-year cycle of different animals that have natural and supernatural qualities. South Vietnam fell in the year of the Cat, which is considered an especially ill-fated year, whereas 1976 was the year of the Dragon and brought new hope. These beliefs are especially prevalent among rural populations of Vietnam, as well as among many urban people of all social classes—most of whom will not fail to consult a horoscope before an important event, transaction, or special occasion (Pan Asian Parent Education Project [PAPEP], 1982; Te, 1989a).

Ancestor worship is yet another very common practice among Vietnamese and underlies all other religions. An ancestral altar is typically placed in the main room of Vietnamese households where rites to honor the death of each ancestor can be performed on various occasions; this ceremony and form of worship serve to reinforce the enduring sense of respect and high esteem for the elderly.

Apart from other minor religions or religious sects unique to the Vietnamese, about 10% of the southern Vietnamese and many of those living in the United States are Catholic. European missionaries introduced Christianity in the form of Roman Catholicism to the Vietnamese people in the late 16th century. Catholicism subsequently flourished, was suppressed, then was reinstated and fostered during the period of French colonialism. Up to 1975, the Catholic church was a well-organized religious, educational, and political force in Vietnamese society. Although a relatively small percentage of the Vietnamese population was Roman Catholic, the religion significantly influenced the culture because many Vietnamese received their education in Catholic schools, and Catholics filled key positions in the government, the army, and the police. Almost one third of the first wave of Vietnamese refugees who came to America were practicing Roman Catholics (Rutledge, 1987; Te, 1989b).

Language/Linguistic Origins

Khmer or Cambodian is the official language of Cambodia and is the mother tongue of the Khmer people (approximately 85% of the country's population). Khmer is the major language of the Mon-Khmer family and includes multiple regional dialects that are spoken throughout the country; there are also minority languages such as Cham, Chinese, and hundreds of hill tribe languages (Chhim, 1989).

Khmer is a monosyllabic language in which there are many polysyllabic loan words and derivatives from Sanskrit (owing to historical ties to Indian culture); to a much lesser extent, Khmer also has words borrowed from Chinese, Thai, and Vietnamese. Unlike the Chinese, Lao, Thai, and Vietnamese languages, Khmer is a nontonal language (i.e., variations in pitch do not change the meaning of words). In fact, Khmer has a monotone but staccato quality, with a rising inflection at the end of each sentence. However, like Lao and Vietnamese, Cambodian is an uninflected language (i.e., there are no plural, possessive, or past-tense endings).

The Khmer written language consists of an alphabet that originated in southern India. It contains a total of 66 consonant and vowel symbols. Efforts to Romanize Khmer writing during French colonial rule were unsuccessful, largely because of resistance from religious circles. Moreover, exact transliteration of Khmer and English sounds is extremely difficult, if not impossible; thus, any Romanization of written Khmer by Westerners could only be an approximation. The Khmer script is written from left to right and from top to bottom. Like Lao writing, it has a decorative and artistic appearance (Chhim, 1989).

Lao is the national and official language of Laos, but is spoken by approximately 20 million people in Southeast Asia (this includes about 18 million Lao speakers in Northeast Thailand and other neighboring countries). There are also many minority languages in Laos such as Hmong, Mien, Thai-Dam, and other hill tribe languages. Lao is a monosyllabic, tonal language, but like Khmer, has a substantial number of polysyllabic words borrowed from Sanskrit.

Lao writing is also based on Sanskrit, but appears different from Cambodian script. It consists of 50 consonant and vowel symbols and four tone marks. The same consonant sound occurring in different words with different pitches will often be represented by different symbols. Lao script is also written from left to right (Te, 1989a). The appeal of the aesthetic Lao written language is complemented by the beauty and poetic quality of the spoken language. For example, the Lao equivalent of "thank you" literally means "from the heart" (Luangpraseut, 1989).

Vietnamese is the national language of more than 56 million speakers in Vietnam and over 1 million Vietnamese immigrants living overseas. It is not mutually intelligible with any other language spoken in Asia. Vietnamese is diversified into three main regional dialects (northern, central, and southern), which differ slightly in pronunciation and vocabulary, but not in grammar (they are thus intelligible across regions). The Vietnamese language is characterized by its tonal system, monosyllabic nature, and vocabulary that contains a great many loan words of Chinese origin. Moreover, like Chinese as well as Khmer and Lao, Vietnamese is an uninflected language; the concepts of plural, past tense, and so forth are expressed by context or by a separate word (Te, 1989a).

The current and only writing system used by the Vietnamese is based on the Roman alphabet. The Vietnamese alphabet was devised by European missionaries in the 16th century to translate the Bible into the vernacular, but it was rejected by the Vietnamese educated classes who continued to use the demotic writing system based on Chinese characters. It did not become the national writing system until after World War I. The alphabet consists of about 32 consonant (single and compound) and vowel letters and five tone marks. There is a highly consistent correlation between the sounds and the letters (Te, 1989a; Wei, 1983).

Southeast Asian refugees thus bring to the language-learning experience distinct linguistic variables that directly influence their ability to develop proficiency in English. The precise nature of various Southeast Asian languages and their effect on English language acquisition has been only recently examined; a few detailed treatments of specific Southeast Asian language systems (particularly Vietnamese) and their relationship to English have been published (e.g., Dien, Te, & Wei, 1986; Li, 1983; Te, 1989b; Walker, 1985). However, in addition to the unique characteristics of Southeast Asian languages, corresponding nonverbal communication patterns, relevant cultural characteristics, traditional values, and contemporary sociopolitical experiences further combine to exert strong influences on second-language acquisition and overall adaptation and adjustment to the dominant culture of the United States. These additional factors are addressed in subsequent sections of this chapter.

Contemporary Life

As previously noted, over 1 million Southest Asian refugees have entered the United States since April 1975. Although the outflow of refugees from Cambodia, Laos, and Vietnam has declined significantly in recent years (relative to the initial waves), hundreds of thousands of refugees remain in first asylum camps throughout Southeast Asia, awaiting resettlement. Since there continue to be no efforts to integrate them permanently into the areas of first asylum provided by neighboring countries, a great many of these refugees will ultimately resettle in the United States, which historically has taken more than half the refugees from the countries of first asylum. As relatives of refugees now in the United States, they are eligible for resettlement in this country under the family reunification provisions of the Refugee Act of 1980.

In addition to admission under the Refugee Act, other legal modes of entry such as the Orderly Departure Program (initiated in 1979) have allowed and will continue to allow many thousands of Vietnamese nationals (including significant numbers of former political prisoners and Amerasian children and youth to enter the country under nonrefugee immigrant status)(Gordon, 1987; Lin-Fu, 1987). Given the potential for substantial increases in "chain" migration of relatives and the continued flow of other Southeast Asian immigrants and refugees, as well as the exceptionally high birth rate of Southeast Asian American women (nearly double the U.S. national average), the Southeast Asian American population is projected to swell to 5 million by 1995 (Keiter, 1990).

Southeast Asians are located in every state in the United States, due primarily to initial resettlement efforts that were directed by federal policy toward widespread geographic dispersion. However, secondary migration, in combination with the tendency of the second- and third-wave refugees to locate in already-established ethnic communities, has led to greater concentrations of refugees in selected cities and states. More than half of the Southeast Asian American population resides in California (approximately 40%), Texas, and Washington State. Of the three major refugee nationality groups, residential concentration in California is most characteristic of the Vietnamese. Spurred by better training and employment opportunities, more desirable welfare benefits, reunification with relatives, the pull of established ethnic communities, and a more attractive climate, the Vietnamese have preferred to live in the larger urban communities throughout the state (Huang, 1989). Refugees from Cambodia and Laos have also settled in large numbers in California and in other areas of the West Coast, with particularly high concentrations of Mien people in Seattle, Portland, Sacramento, Oakland, San Jose, and Long Beach. Over half of the Hmong have congregated in California (especially in Fresno), but they are also located (along with large numbers of other Lao and Cambodian refugees) in urban centers in midwestern and eastern states such as Minnesota, Wisconsin, Massachusetts, and Rhode Island (Gordon, 1987; Takaki, 1989).

Of the total Southeast Asian refugee population in the United States, approximately 62% came from Vietnam, 21% from Laos, and 17% from Cambodia. It is estimated that about 30% of the refugees from Vietnam and 15% of those from Cambodia are ethnic Chinese (Lin-Fu, 1989). The age composition of the resident refugee population reveals a disproportionately large share of young people; nearly one third of the population consists of children who are school age or younger. Moreover, the percentage of young children will continue to increase given the extremely high fertility rate among recent Southeast Asian refugees and the relatively larger proportion of Southeast Asian women of childbearing age (14–40). For the Hmong and Cambodian populations, childbearing also tends to begin early in adolescence and continue into the upper end of a woman's reproductive life (often past 40 years). The corresponding dramatically higher percentages of births to Southeast Asian women under 17 and over 40 years (relative to the general population) further contribute to a greater incidence of high-risk pregnancies and low birth weight infants with special needs (Lin-Fu, 1989).

Continuing efforts to monitor and address the complex economic, psychological, and social adjustment of Southeast Asian refugees to the United States have yielded highly significant findings. The third-wave refugees, in particular, are characterized by very low levels of education, literacy, and extremely limited or no English language proficiency. Annual surveys conducted by the Office of Refugee Resettlement have consistently shown that, in their first few years of residence, Southeast Asian refugees manifest low labor force participation, high unemployment, low wages among those who are employed, and a high use of government cash assistance programs (U.S. Department of Health and Human Services, 1987). These characteristics are most dramatically illustrated by the Mien and Hmong, whose rate of unemployment reaches as high as 90%. In California, where nearly one third of refugee families have received public assistance for 4–10 years, the Hmong constitute what is becoming a permanent welfare class and most are barely surviving (Takaki, 1989). The additional factor of large family size and households contributes to overcrowded living conditions and extremely high rates of poverty. Relative to all other Asian groups in the United States, Southeast Asian refugees have the highest number of persons living below the poverty level (U.S. Bureau of the Census, 1988).

The significant economic difficulties of many Southeast Asian refugees are compounded by major health and mental health problems. Large numbers of Southeast Asians suffer from parasitism, anemia, malnutrition, growth retardation in children, tuberculosis, hepatitis, and selected genetic blood disorders such as thalassemia (Lin-Fu, 1989). Decades of war, trauma, torture, starvation, personal loss, and the profound psychological impact of the refugee experience have also contributed to the high incidence of acute and chronic mental disorders among Southeast Asian refugees (Cohon, 1981; Rumbaut, 1985). Among the more frequently encountered mental health problems are depression, anxiety, psychosomatic illnesses, and post-traumatic stress disorders (which may persist as long as 20 years after the refugee experience). Yet more severe, even fatal conditions and outcomes include reactive psychoses, hysterical conversion symptoms (e.g., psychosomatic blindness among Cambodian women), the "Hmong sudden unexpected nocturnal death syndrome," and suicide (Bliatout, 1982; DeAngelis, 1990; K-M. Lin & Masuda, 1981).

Southeast Asian refugees have also had to cope with the sheer need to survive and adapt to a host culture. They typically encounter barriers of poverty, prejudice and racism, pervasive uncertainty, and culture shock (K-M. Lin & Masuda, 1981). They must also respond to the severe disintegration of traditional family structures, role hierarchies, and social support systems as well as persistent cultural conflicts and challenges to long-held beliefs, values, and socialization practices. Consequently, the process of survival and Americanization often produces chronic family dysfunction (including domestic violence, divorce, and intergenerational alienation) and major youth adjustment problems, which may be expressed as self-destructive, antisocial, and acting-out behaviors (Huang, 1989; Le, 1983; Nguyen, 1988).

The economic, health, and psychosocial status indicators that have been highlighted tend to overshadow the relatively successful adjustments and achievements of many Southeast Asian Americans—particularly those among the earlier refugee populations. Impressive educational attainment, rapid movement into various professional fields, and aggressive growth in entrepreneurship have also been characteristic of the Southeast Asian American profile. Thus, as originally noted in the introduction to the section, Southeast Asians are extremely diverse peoples; they include "preliterate tribesmen from the mountains as well as college-educated professionals from the cities, welfare families as well as wealthy businessmen, and superachieving university students as well as members of youth gangs" (Takaki, 1989, p. 470). Between these stereotypical extremes is a very heterogeneous group of people who nonetheless share a common, overarching experience: As refugees unwillingly driven to America by the forces of war, they are truly the uprooted—who share memories of a painful past and a lost homeland.

VALUES

Cultural values are the core conceptions of what is desirable within the individual and the larger society of a given group of peoples (Gollnick & Chinn, 1990). They are thus a major factor in contributing to a sense of identity and characteristic ways of perceiving, thinking, feeling, and behaving. Central to an understanding of cultural values is a major dimension of cultural variation: individualism versus collectivism. Individualism is a cultural pattern found in most northern and western regions of Europe and in North America, while collectivism is most common in Africa, Asia, Latin America, and the Pacific (Triandis, Brislin, & Hui, 1988).

The traditional collectivist values of Chinese, Koreans, Cambodians, Laotians, and Vietnamese in particular are rooted in the "three teachings"—which were previously described in this chapter within the doctrines and philosophies of Confucianism, Taoism, and Buddhism. The corresponding predominant values pertaining to family, harmony, education, and selected virtues are detailed next.

Family

In accord with Confucian principles, the family is the basic unit or backbone of society. While guiding and protecting the individual, the family serves as the tie between the individual and society and is a model for society as a whole (Major,

1989; Te, 1989a). In fact, "all (traditional) values are determined by reference to the maintenance, continuity and functions of the family group" (UPAC, 1980, p. 10). As the central focus of the individual's life, the value of family engenders primary loyalty, obligation, cooperation, interdependence, and reciprocity. Ingrained with a profound sense of responsibility and duty to the family, individual members thus engage in sustained efforts to promote the welfare, harmony, and reputation of their family. Throughout this process, each individual views him- or herself as an integral part of the totality of the family and the larger social structure, and experiences a social/psychological dependence on others. This family-centered orientation and its attendant values contrast sharply with the more individualistic values of competition, autonomy, and self-reliance in the context of a society with significantly less well-defined, more highly varied, and often ambiguous social/familial roles and expectations (Chan, 1986).

The values of family and filial piety include reverence for elders, ancestors, and the past. An individual is viewed as the product of all generations of the family from the beginning of time. Individual behaviors therefore reflect upon one's ancestors as well as the entire "race." While striving to defend the family's honor and enhance its reputation, one must properly observe historical events and maintain family traditions. This orientation toward living with the past differs markedly from the individualistic cultural preoccupation with the future and living for tomorrow (Chan, 1986).

Harmony

Among Asian cultural groups, the practice of syncretism or blending of beliefs (e.g., those prescribed by the "three teachings") reflects a basic philosophical as well as pragmatic orientation: The keynote of existence is to reconcile divergent forces, principles, and points of view in an effort to maintain harmony. The individual must strive to achieve intrapsychic harmony, interpersonal harmony, and harmony with nature as well as time. This orientation is manifested in characteristic "situation centeredness." In interpersonal relationships, the individual thus mobilizes his or her thoughts and actions to conform to social reality (Chan, 1986). In accordance with Confucian and Taoist teachings, one avoids direct confrontation, conforms to the rules of propriety, and "gives face" or recognition and respect to others. These guiding principles translate into verbal, social, and emotional restraint and the consistent use of politeness, tact, and gentleness in interpersonal relations. Preservation of harmony is thus a primary value characteristic of "heart-oriented" (versus "mind-oriented") cultures and further reinforces a pervasive humanistic (versus materialistic) orientation among traditional Asian peoples (PAPEP, 1982).

Education

"The reverence and status conferred on teachers and the social significance of scholarship have firmly established the value of education in . . . Asian countries" (E.K. Leung, 1988, p. 91). Children are ingrained with a lifelong respect for knowledge, wisdom, intelligence, and love of learning. Confucian teachings emphasize the moral aspect of education as well as the belief that the development of the human character varies according to experience. Parents thus assume primary responsibility for ensuring that their children receive appropriate guidance. Throughout this process, securing a good education for their children becomes paramount. The children, in turn, fulfill their responsibility and obligation to the family primarily through successful academic achievement— the greatest tribute one can bestow upon one's parents and family (E.K. Leung, 1988). By excelling in school, the child brings honor to the family while preparing for future educational and occupational successes that will further enhance the family's social status and ensure its economic well being—as well as that of the individual and his or her own family, or the next generation (Serafica, 1990). These orientations and the principal value of education are embodied in the following Chinese proverb:

> If you are planning for a year, sow rice;
> If you are planning for a decade, plant trees;
> If you are planning for a lifetime, educate people.

Selected Virtues

The primary values of family, harmony, and education are further supported by highly valued virtues or character traits among Asian groups. The Vietnamese people, for example, place great value on the trait called *t'anh can cu,* which includes the combined characteristics of thrift, industriousness, patience, determination, endurance, tolerance, and accommodation. This quality has contributed to the profound strength and resiliency demonstrated by the Vietnamese and other Southeast Asian peoples throughout their respective histories of war, disruption, and loss (UPAC, 1980). When similarly expressed among Chinese, Korean, and other Asian groups, these characteristics translate into the ability to persevere without complaint, to "suffer in silence." Such character traits are reinforced within the context of a fatalistic orientation in which life is presumed to be essentially unalterable and unpredictable. There is thus a need for resignation to external conditions and events over which one presumably has little or no control. If human suffering is viewed as part of the natural order, then acceptance of one's fate, maintenance of inner strength, and emotional self-restraint are also considered to be necessary expressions of dignity (Chan, 1986).

Other major virtues include assumption of responsibility, hard work, self-sacrifice on all levels (spiritual, emotional, material, physical), modesty, and humility (which is often expressed through self-denigration). Again, these virtues are consistent with a collectivist orientation wherein individual achievements are valued in terms of their contribution to the group status and welfare, and needs for corresponding personal recognition are transcended.

As initially indicated, the above-described traditional cultural orientations and values derive from religious and philosophical foundations that are thousands of years old. They have thus been promoted throughout successive generations and continue to have a profound influence on the socialization of many Asian children (particularly among recent immigrant and refugee families). However, despite their enduring and historically adaptive nature, these values have undergone significant transformation within the contemporary Asian American experience. One can obviously anticipate wide individual variation in the extent to which traditional values are maintained or increasingly challenged, shifted, and diluted as alternative, contrasting values are adapted throughout the process of acculturation. The acculturation patterns of Asian immigrants and refugees are also complex and influenced by factors such as premigration experience, time of arrival, proximity to same-ethnic communities, age, gender, education, language proficiency, and socioeconomic status (E.K. Leung, 1988). Awareness and appreciation of such complexity is critical in determining the relative influence of traditional values among Asian families.

BELIEFS

Childrearing

The respective traditional childrearing beliefs and practices of Chinese, Korean, Cambodian, Lao, and Vietnamese families have been detailed in various publications (e.g., Ho, 1987; Morrow, 1989; PAPEP, 1982; K.H. Yu & Kim, 1983). Examination of this literature reveals obvious cultural variation among these ethnic groups—although there are few *formal* comparative cross-cultural studies of the different types of parental behaviors, beliefs, and values that influence childrearing (Sigel, 1988). However, as is the case with traditional cultural orientations and values, there are also many similarities among selected Asian groups with respect to family structure, dynamics, and socialization patterns. These shared characteristics as well as culture-specific practices are described in this section.

Family Structure

As previously indicated, the family and its structure and function serve as the most basic social institution among Asian peoples. Sustained throughout the centuries by the "three teachings," the primary reference groups are the immediate family (husband; wife; unmarried children; and, typically, sons' wives and children) and the extended family (immediate family and close relatives sharing the same family name as well as ancestors, and, in the case of the Hmong, all members of the "clan" living in the same community). The immediate family is characterized by well-defined, highly interdependent roles within a cohesive patriarchal vertical structure. This structure derives from the Confucian doctrine of filial piety that establishes a social hierarchy based on the "five relationships" and the "three obediences" (whereby a woman is instructed to obey: her father as a daughter, her husband as a wife, and her eldest son as a widow). Each family member has a particular designation and is referred to by corresponding honorific kinship terms, and forms of address that indicate his or her relative position and role within the family structure. Distinguished on the basis of generation, age, and gender, the hierarchy of authority and reverence begins at the highest level with grandparents (usually paternal), then proceeds to father, mother, oldest son ("big brother"), middle daughter, and youngest son. While this Confucian hierarchy is observed by the Chinese, Koreans, and Vietnamese, traditional practices among Lao families dictate that married couples initially live (for 2–3 years) in the bride's parental household, and the youngest son (or daughter) typically inherits the house site upon the parents' death (Luangpraseut, 1989).

Marital Roles

Within the immediate family, traditional marital roles have been characterized by the husband serving as the principal provider and family representative in the public domain—the "secretary of state" or "minister of foreign affairs." The wife serves as the "minister of the interior" and is primarily responsible for what happens inside the house, which includes raising and educating the children and taking care of financial matters (Dung, 1984). According to the Korean maxim, the woman's most important role is to be a wise wife and a good mother (PAPEP, 1982). She thus derives her status through her role as a wife, mother, or daughter-in-law. Moreover, within the ostensible power structure, the traditional Vietnamese saying applies—"the husband is king and his wife is his slave" (Thuy, 1980). In fact, a wife is almost considered a nonperson until she produces a son; she acquires increasingly greater power as she becomes a mother, then a mother-in-law (S.C. Kim, 1985). However, while the father is the acknowledged authority figure and head of the family, in the eyes of the children, the mother has the same status. She acquires profound psychological power over them and is seen as "the embodiment of love and the spirit of self-denial and sacrifice" (Te, 1989b, p. 69). She also has the power of the purse. Thus, "while the husband thinks he is the master of the house, the wife knows *she* is [italics added]" (S.C. Kim, 1985, p. 345).

Parental Roles/Responsibilities

The strongest family ties are between parent and child rather than between spouses. Parental roles and responsibilities supercede the marital relationship. Parents are thus readily prepared to sacrifice personal needs in serving the interests of their children and in providing for the welfare and security of the family as a whole. In turn, the parent assumes the right to demand unquestioning obedience and loyalty from the child. The role of the parent is to define the law, and the duty of the child is to listen and obey. Strict parental authority translates into personal accountability and responsibility for the child's behavior, which is considered a direct reflection of the parents' ability to provide proper guidance.

Infancy

Children are viewed as extensions of their parents. They continue the family lineage, bring status to the family name by virtue of their achievements, and literally give meaning to their parents' lives. The newborn child is thus treasured as a "gift from the gods." Given the infant's relative vulnerability, a number of corresponding traditional customs have been practiced. In ancient China, parents often dressed infant boys like girls and put silver dog collars on them in the belief that this would protect the child from evil spirits. Parents later continued to give children pets' names for nicknames because it was believed that animals had a better chance of surviving than human infants and would not be harmed by evil spirits. The Hmong tribespeople have traditionally guarded against malevolent spirits by not naming children until they are about 2 years of age and giving them numbers instead of first names when they are infants; children are also never called "number one" because the spirits might not look for "number two" until they have found "number one" (National Indochinese Clearinghouse, 1980; Olness, 1986). Vietnamese parents traditionally avoid praising the infant and may become anxious if complimentary comments regarding the infant's health or appearance are made by others for fear that a lurking evil spirit may overhear and attempt to steal the baby away. Similarly, infants are dressed in old clothes until their 1-month birthday celebration to avoid making the spirits jealous, thus causing the baby to become ill (PAPEP, 1982). If an infant does become ill, Cambodian parents may temporarily change his or her name to confuse the spirits (Hollingsworth, Brown, & Brooten, 1980).

Children are initially perceived as being relatively helpless and not responsible for their actions. Parents are thus very tolerant, permissive (by European American standards), and immediately gratify the infant's early dependency needs. Mother–infant interaction is characterized by an emphasis on close physical contact rather than active vocal stimulation; infants are carried much of the time, even during naps, or kept nearby and picked up immediately if they cry. Korean babies are customarily wrapped in a shawl or blanket, strapped around the mother's (or grandmother's) back and carried piggyback (K.H. Yu & Kim, 1983). Infants are rarely if ever left to sleep alone and, typically, sleep in the same room or bed with their parents and other siblings until school age or older. There is an absence of rigid schedules, and parents have later age expectations with respect to selected developmental milestones such as weaning; babies are usually breastfed on a demand basis and may continue to nurse up to 2 years of age or older.

In contrast, toilet training may be introduced when the infant is as young as 3–4 months old. It begins by placing the baby on the pot when the mother becomes sensitive to his or her schedule after selected feedings; she then recognizes how the baby typically signals elimination through facial expressions, behaviors, or noises, which she may imitate or initiate (PAPEP, 1982). However, despite this early onset of toilet training, no *strict* demands or pressures are placed on the child. In fact, although this practice is common among traditional Korean families, for example, there are no words for toilet training in the Korean language (K.H. Yu & Kim, 1983).

Throughout infancy and the toddler period, the child is thus provided with a very nurturant, indulgent, secure, and predictable environment by parents

(particularly the mother), older siblings, grandparents, and other members of the extended family, if available. Children are thus conditioned from infancy to respond to multiple caregivers and authority figures and learn to see the world in terms of a network of relationships. This experience serves as the foundation for the development of very strong family attachments and subsequent reciprocity.

Early Childhood and School Age

The preschool period represents a transitional phase wherein the child moves from a period of affection and indulgence (infancy to the late toddler stage— when he or she is not expected "to know any better") to a period of discipline and education as the child approaches school age and is expected to assume increasingly greater responsibility for his or her own behavior. Parental expectations for earlier acquisition of personal-social and self-help skills (e.g., grooming, dressing, completing chores) are evident.

Upon reaching school age, the child experiences accelerated movement toward independence training within the context of the family and home environment. The process is facilitated, in part, by inclusion of the child in adult affairs and activities such as weddings, funerals, and social and business functions. The child thus shares the same world with his or her parents and receives early exposure to socially appropriate patterns and proper codes of public behavior, which he or she quickly learns through participation, observation, and imitation. At this time, the father typically assumes a more active role in the child's social and moral development. The immediate parent–child relationship also becomes more formal, and adult demands are more rigidly enforced. In contrast to the repeated indulgence experienced during earlier years, the child is now subjected to markedly increased discipline.

As the child matures and acquires younger siblings, he or she must further assume selected childrearing responsibilities that augment those of his parents. Older siblings are routinely delegated the responsibility of caring for younger siblings and are thus expected to model adult-like behaviors, thereby setting good examples. The eldest son, in particular, is entrusted with the greatest responsibility as the leader among his siblings who must provide them with guidance and support. Like the parent, the older sibling is also periodically expected to sacrifice personal needs in favor of younger siblings. These roles are formalized to the extent that children in the family are addressed by kinship terms that indicate whether they are older or younger and that may further specify their ordinal position in the family. The "reciprocity" inherent in sibling relationships is clearly illustrated in the classic parental response to sibling arguments: the older sibling is generally scolded for not setting a good example, and the younger sibling is chastised for failing to respect his or her older brother or sister.

Conclusion

Children thus learn to view their role within the family and society in terms of relationships and obligations. They must readily acquire a sense of moral obligation and primary loyalty to the family. This translates into behaviors that serve to maintain and enhance the family name, honor, and face. Herein lies the "pride and shame" principle whereby individual behavior reflects on the entire family. On the one hand, highly valued individual achievements such as academic or occupational success serve to promote the family welfare and are a source of shared pride among family members. On the other hand, dysfunctional, antisocial, or otherwise negatively valued behavior exhibited by a family member contributes toward a collective family experience of profound shame.

Observance of specific roles, relationships, and codes of conduct results in a persistent awareness of the effects of one's behavior on others. In contrast to the more egocentric individualistic orientation, Asian children are socialized to think and act in proper relation to others and must learn to transcend their personal concerns. They are obliged to be sensitive to the social environment. The parent thus effectively controls the child by modeling appropriate behaviors by appealing to the child's sense of duty or obligation. Parents may thus periodically evoke fear of personal ridicule or the prospect of family shame as a consequence of misbehavior.

Behaviors that are punished include disobedience, aggression (particularly sibling directed), and failure to fulfill one's primary responsibilities. Typical forms of discipline include the use of verbal reprimands such as scolding and shaming, which result in disgrace. The child is reminded that his or her negative behaviors reflect poorly on the entire family and family name. The child can absolve him- or herself of this "loss of face" by actively displaying changes in behavior. It is not sufficient for children to ask for forgiveness and verbally promise to do better. Actions speak louder than words (Tinloy et al., 1986). Parents may respond to more serious transgressions by either threatening or actually engaging in temporary removal of the child from the family household and/or isolating the child from the family social life. On occasion, the use of physical punishment (e.g., spanking or paddling with a stick on the buttocks) is considered acceptable. While assuming primary responsibility for teaching the child to behave properly, the mother serves as the main disciplinarian for daily problems. The father assumes the role of implementing harsher punishment for more serious misbehavior.

Childrearing is based on the assumption of a child's inherent predilection for good. However, the development of positive character requires proper training during early childhood. Subsequent emphasis is placed on formal education and high standards of academic achievement—the child's primary means of fulfilling his or her family responsibility and obligation. While the family sacrifices and mobilizes its resources to provide an environment conducive to academic achievement, the child, in turn, is expected to work hard and do well; effort is viewed as more essential in contributing to success than is innate ability (Stevenson & Lee, 1990). Within this context, overt rewards and contingent praise are generally not given for positive achievements or behaviors, because they are expected. While parents may occasionally tell their children that they are proud of them, acknowledgment of accomplishments may be more often manifested in the form of exhortations to "do better," to strive for even higher levels of achievement. Family pride may also be expressed by the mother preparing a special meal or by the father asking the child to take on a special task that shows the family's confidence in his or her abilities. These indirect forms of acknowledgment extend to extrafamilial relationships whereby public discussion of the child's accomplishments with others outside the family is considered arrogant and inappropriate. In fact, unsolicited recognition and compliments are often politely dismissed, may cause silent embarrassment, or are negated by immediate counter-discussion of the child's other faults and by self-deprecating remarks. The virtues of humility and modesty are thus modeled in such behaviors (Chan, 1986; Tinloy et al., 1986).

In general, Asian parents who adhere to more traditional childrearing values and practices are relatively controlling, restrictive, and protective of their children. Children are taught to suppress aggressive behavior, overt expressions of negative emotions, and personal grievances; they must inhibit strong feelings and exercise self-control in order to maintain family harmony. There is a typical avoidance of frank discussion or highly verbal communication between parent and child—particularly in the area of sexuality, which is suppressed in cultures where physical contact between members of the opposite sex is minimized and public displays of affection are rare and embarrassing. The communication pattern is also one way: parent to child (the parent speaks, and the child listens). The father is particularly distant in this respect and generally neither invites confidences nor initiates "talks" with his children. The mother–child relationship is closer and more verbal. Father–mother interaction is often characterized by indirect communications, inferences, and unstated feelings.

The protective and controlling orientation of Asian parents may also be manifested in a basic distrust of outsiders. In an attempt to control outside influences, parents often restrict the child's social interaction by allowing access to only selected role models (e.g., family and close friends)—this may include the child's peer group and playmates. Independent peer interaction and autonomous social behavior (including ultimately leaving the family to reside outside the home) typically occur at much later ages relative to European American norms. However, although Asian parents tend to promote family interdependence, they may simultaneously encourage the development of individual independence *outside* the family. While the primary collectivist value system reinforces deference to the group, it also supports personal control and self-improvement in the accomplishment of internal goals. This is the element of independence that is conducive to success and achievement in the larger so-ciety, which, in turn, enhances the family welfare and fulfills filial obligations. Thus, while traditional values continue to influence childrearing practices significantly, immigrant/refugee families may adopt bicultural socialization strategies that enable children to function effectively in their respective ethnic subcultures and the mainstream culture of the society at large (Harrison, Wilson, Pine, Chan, & Buriel, 1990; C.C. Lin & Fu, 1990).

Medical Care

There is considerable variation among Chinese and Korean immigrants and Southeast Asian refugee groups with regard to health beliefs and health care practices. Many families utilize a pluralistic system of care that includes a blending of traditional Chinese medicine and various folk medicine practices with Western medicine. An examination of the more common traditional health orientations and healing cultures of the respective ethnic groups is thus warranted.

Health Beliefs

Throughout centuries of isolation from the rest of the world, ancient Chinese scholars developed a distinctive and extremely well-organized system of medicine that continues to dominate medical thinking in China up to the present time. This unique system has further influenced the medical concepts adopted by the peoples of Korea, Japan, and Southeast Asia.

Fundamental to traditional Chinese medicine is the philosophy of Taoism, the cosmic forces of yin and yang, and the "five elements." Tao signifies "the way" or the harmony between heaven and earth; following the Tao enables one to be in accord with the fundamental laws of nature and the universe. The basic dualism of the universe is represented by the interaction of yin and yang, which can be used to classify everything, whether it is concrete or abstract, physical or moral. Yin is the passive or negative female force that includes the moon, earth, water, evil, poverty, and sadness, and produces cold, darkness, and emptiness. In contrast, yang is the active or positive male force that includes the sun, heaven, fire, goodness, wealth, and joy, and produces warmth, light, and fullness (Lee, 1989; Tom, 1989). Yin and yang are not regarded as conflicting principles, but as mutually necessary complementary forces, as indicated in the symbol of the Tao,

> Each penetrates the other's hemisphere and together they are resolved in an all-embracing circle. Intimately associated with yin and yang are the Five Elements. It was believed that all things are composed of five elements: metal, wood, water, fire, and earth. The proportions of these elements are determined by the mutual influence of yin and yang. (Tom, 1989, pp. 71–72)

Chinese concepts of health and disease are thus closely related to these principles.

> Since man and the universe have been created by the same elements, man is subject to the same forces that govern the universe. If man remains in harmony with the Tao, and yin and yang and the Five Elements are in proper balance he can enjoy good health and longevity. Imbalance, however, results in illness and death. (Tom, 1989, p. 72)

More specifically, diseases are thought to be caused by both internal and external factors. The traditional classification system divides body parts between the yang-related surface organs and the yin-related internal organs. Chinese physiology considers the five viscera (heart, spleen, lungs, liver, and kidneys) to be the main organs corresponding to the "five elements," which when out of balance result in illness. Other diseases are thought to be caused by external climatic elements such as wind, cold, heat, dampness, and dryness (Tom, 1989).

The hot/cold classification of various diseases provides a means of both diagnosing and treating selected illnesses and medical conditions. For example, excessive "heat" or yang illnesses are generated from within the body itself and include such conditions as skin eruptions, cold sores, fevers, and ear infections. "Cold" or yin maladies are caused by intrusion of cold or "bad wind" into any part of the body and may contribute to symptoms such as coughing, headaches, muscle aches, diarrhea (from a "cold" stomach), and infectious airborne diseases such as measles, as well as other diseases such as cancer (R.V. Lee, 1989; Lew, 1989; Muecke, 1983a). Wind is presumed to enter the body during periods of vulnerability such as during surgery and during and after childbirth. Yin illnesses may also be produced by loss of blood (which has the quality of heat and yang). Improper diet is yet another cause of imbalance. It is believed that most foods have hot or cold properties and, when digested, turn into air that is either yin or yang. Thus, intake of selected cold foods (e.g., fruits/ vegetables such as melon, bean sprouts, seawood and cold juices, rice water) or hot foods (e.g., chicken, beef, pork, fried food, coffee, ginger and other spices) is prescribed for hot or cold illnesses. For women, the traditional prenatal as well as restorative postpartum diets include selected hot/cold foods and exclude others. During pregnancy, explicit taboos and dietary restrictions dictate exclusion of foods such as shellfish, rabbit, and lamb, and avoidance of hot foods and medications such as iron supplements during the third trimester or "hot" period. During the "cold" period (1 month postpartum), women may abstain from vegetables, fruits, and juices, and selected hot foods such as beef; pork and chicken are considered benign and are encouraged along with salty foods (R.V. Lee, 1989; Wong, 1985).

Among internal factors believed to contribute to illness are excessive emotions, which include joy, anger, hate, jealousy, sorrow, worry, and fear. As previously indicated, among most Asian cultures, there is great value placed upon the ability to control emotions and subjugate them to reason. However, when selected emotions are not openly expressed and accumulate in intensity within the body, they are manifested in the form of physical illness. A related Korean folk illness is called *Hwa-Byung*: *Hwa* refers to "anger" and "fire," while *Byung* means "sickness." Thus, individuals suffering from repressed or suppressed anger of long duration may manifest somatic symptoms such as loss of appetite, indigestion, epigastric pain, alternating diarrhea and constipation, dyspnea, hypertension, palpitation, headaches, dizziness, and fatigue. Interestingly, similar kinds of multiple somatic symptoms have been found among Chinese with "frigophobia" (or morbid fear of cold weather) who believed that their problems stemmed from a disturbance of yin–yang balance and the element of fire. However, most persons with frigophobia have been men, in contrast to *Hwa-Byung,* which is primarily a condition of women (K-M. Lin, 1983).

These beliefs reflect an orientation in which there is often no clear differentiation between psychological and physical problems. Psychological stresses are seen as capable of producing both, and psychological disturbance is often expressed through somatic symptoms (K-M. Lin & Masuda, 1981). This tendency toward somatization corresponds to the holistic philosophy of Chinese medicine that does not separate mental illness from physical illness. Health maintenance thus entails ensuring harmony between the yin and yang forces of the body, mind, and emotions. Illness is an affliction of the *whole* person—a generalized lack of well-being.

In addition to the more metaphysical causes of illness associated with traditional Chinese medicine, Asian folk medicine may further attribute illness to supernatural causes such as soul loss. As described in a previous section, many Southeast Asian groups believe that the body is inhabited by more than one soul (the numbers vary according to different ethnic groups). These souls inhabit various organs and parts of the body, the primary one being the head. Good health requires that all souls be present within the body and in harmony. When one or more souls are lost from the body, a wide range of symptoms from physical illness to emotional and mental problems may occur. The earlier-described Lao soul-calling ceremony (*Baci*) is a means by which illness can be prevented or health restored. Apart from soul loss, illness is also believed to be caused by a malevolent spirit or from an offense against good spirits or deities (Lew, 1989).

Health Practices

Among Southeast Asians, beliefs in the supernatural etiology of illness (particularly mental illness) are among the most widespread. Corresponding treatment can include soul calling, exorcism, ritualistic offerings, chanting or recitation of sacred prayers, and other spiritual healing ceremonies such as sprinkling the person with holy water. The treatment is typically performed by or in consultation with priests, shamans, spiritual masters (e.g., the *Kru* [he who knows] Khmer among Cambodians), or sorcerers (Bliatout, Ben, Bliatout, & Lee, 1985; Egawa & Tashima, 1982; Kemp, 1985).

A variety of diagnostic and treatment methods exist for illnesses resulting from perceived metaphysical causes within the context of traditional Chinese medical theory as well as Ayurvedic medicine, which followed Indian cultural influences into Cambodia and Laos. With respect to diagnostic procedures, the best physician is viewed as one who intrudes on the body the least (Muecke, 1983b). The physician or healer typically employs four methods of making a medical diagnosis: looking, listening, inquiring, and feeling the pulse. Pulse diagnosis is considered the best method and is used to indicate the condition of the humors and vital organs (Egawa & Tashima, 1982; Tom, 1989). Abdominal palpation may also be used. In contrast, Western medical practice often relies upon patient histories and extensive laboratory tests, as well as symptomatology for the diagnosis of illness and disease. Many traditionally oriented Asians may thus perceive American physicians as too dependent upon ostensibly irrelevant questions, unnecessary physical exams, and excessive and invasive tests such as X rays and blood sampling, the latter being particularly problematic for those who believe venipuncture will upset the "hot–cold" balance of the body, result in soul loss, and/or that the body cannot reproduce lost blood (Muecke, 1983b).

Among the more widely used traditional treatment methods are herbal medications, a great many of which are based on sound pharmacological principles. Some of these same medications were also discovered in Western medicine, including iodine from seaweed, ephedrine from a native herb, calcium from the velvet of deer horn, and a fine clay used in diarrhea drugs. However, some of the more popular exotic remedies such as ginseng and angelica root or dried sea horse, snake, and rhinoceros horn appear to have questionable if any pharmacologial properties (Tom, 1989). Aside from the specific effects and relative efficacy of various herbs and medications, the way in which they are obtained and ingested significantly contrasts with Western prescription medication. Moreover, in terms of "hot–cold" therapy, Western medications are generally classified as "hot" and, with their many chemical agents, are perceived as very potent compared to the more natural herbal medicines, most of which are "cool." Concern about side effects may lead some Asian patients to adjust the dosage of various prescriptions downward or stop taking them altogether if there has been no quick relief of symptoms (which is expected). They may also have difficulty understanding or appreciating why it is necessary to continue using selected prescription medications (e.g., antibiotics) well after specific symptoms have abated. Such expectations and orientations reflect a traditional focus on disease symptoms rather than underlying causes. Thus, there is a tendency to self-medicate and independently manage both prescribed and over-the-counter medication as well as to utilize more traditional herbal medication simultaneously or alternatively (Muecke, 1983a, 1983b).

Additional treatment methods for a variety of illnesses and conditions include therapeutic massage, acupressure, acupuncture (practiced for 4,000 years), and moxibustion (a technique of burning mugwort leaves on the skin at the site of the acupuncture after the needle has been withdrawn) (Tom, 1989). Yet another traditional practice that is self-care in nature and derives from "hot–cold" therapy is dermabrasion. Considered a massage treatment, various dermabrasive techniques entail abrading the skin in selected areas of the face (forehead and bridge of the nose), neck, thorax, chest (over the ribs), and back (over the spine). It is generally done to treat "wind illnesses" such as fever, muscle ache, headache, coughing, sore throat, and respiratory symptoms. The most popular form of dermabrasion is coining or *cao gio* (scratch wind). The practice involves first covering the affected area with a medicated ointment such as tiger balm, then gently rubbing the area with the edge of a coin (or spoon) until dark spots that look like bruises can be seen. This procedure allows the "toxic wind" to be brought to the body surface and released; supposedly, the sicker the affected person is, the darker the spots will be (Dien et al., 1986). Other dermabrasive techniques include pinching, cupping (or pressure massage), burning, and steam treatment. These practices all typically produce welts and superficial bruises that may last a few days and can easily be mistaken as signs of physical abuse (Masterson, 1988; Nguyen, Nguyen, & Nguyen, 1987). As indicated by various health professionals, these "treatment bruises" may mimic the lesions of inflicted trauma, but are *not* harmful procedures. There is no medical reason to discourage what are considered to be well-intended, emotionally nurturant folk practices (Muecke, 1983b; Yeatman & Dang, 1980). However, to the extent that they are stigmatized by the host society, the opportunity for cross-cultural education and awareness should be made available.

Disability

Among the various Asian ethnic groups, the most severe disabling conditions (e.g., those associated with developmental disabilities, physical/sensory impairments, and serious emotional disturbance) are traditionally viewed with considerable stigma. Such stigma is created, in part, by traditional attributions linking specific disabilities to various causes.

Causation

Many of the traditional beliefs and attributions regarding the etiology of disabilities mirror the previously described health beliefs about varying causes of illness. The more naturalistic or metaphysical explanations often focus on the mother's presumed failure to follow prescribed dietary and other health care practices during pregnancy and/or the postpartum period. These are illustrated by various case examples of families who have sought assistance for their children with developmental special needs. One mother, a recent Chinese immi-

Case Example #1

At about 18 months of age, Tuyet, a Vietnamese child, had become increasingly withdrawn, stopped talking, and began demonstrating spontaneous and severe tantrums. She was ultimately referred to an early intervention program for children with special needs when she was 2½ years old. Throughout the initial months of the program, Hoa, Tuyet's mother (who spoke little English), was consistently reluctant to participate actively in on-site program activities that encouraged parents to engage in verbal and sensorimotor stimulation of their children, with staff guidance. She was also unable to implement successfully a behavioral intervention program at home designed to promote prosocial behaviors and speech development as well as reduce Tuyet's problem behaviors such as tantruming. In a subsequent contact with Tuyet's Vietnamese-speaking regional center counselor (case manager), Hoa appeared distressed and indicated ambivalence about continuing to participate in the early intervention program. Shortly thereafter, Tuyet was absent from the program for several days, reportedly due to illness. When Tuyet returned, her primary therapist noticed that she had visible long red marks and welted areas on her neck and chest. When asked about the marks, Hoa was embarrassed and avoided offering any explanation.

Hoa had, in fact, used coining to alleviate Tuyet's earlier cold and flu symptoms. However, as she later disclosed to Tuyet's regional center counselor, she was fearful of telling the therapist at the program about this practice; she felt that the therapist would neither understand nor accept this explanation. Moreover, she had heard of other parents in the community being reported by school authorities for suspected child abuse after coining their children.

Hoa also shared her distress associated with Tuyet's condition. Tuyet had been recently diagnosed as "autistic" by the program assessment team. Hoa was unable to understand adequately the various explanations and verbal information she was provided about this disorder, and no literature on autism in the Vietnamese language was available to her at this time. Given that the professionals could offer no definite facts regarding the etiology of autism, Hoa presumed that Tuyet's disability was the result of the traumatic experiences she and her family had undergone while escaping from Vietnam by boat. More specifically, she had witnessed the drowning death of her sister during her initial month of pregnancy with Tuyet. Hoa, as well as her husband Hũng, suspected that this incident contributed directly to Tuyet's ill-fated condition.

Hoa also had been hesitant to verbalize her feelings of discomfort related to continued participation in the early intervention program. While not wishing to appear critical of the program staff or to offend the Vietnamese counselor who made the original referral, Hoa questioned the value of the various activities in which she and Tuyet were expected to engage. She had assumed a somewhat fatalistic orientation toward Tuyet's condition, and could not appreciate the benefit of systematic efforts to enhance Tuyet's speech development and social interaction; moreover, from a more traditional childrearing perspective, Hoa felt that intense verbal and social stimulation of such a young child was unnatural and inappropriate relative to Tuyet's level of understanding and developmental status. Hoa also was very self-conscious about her limited English skills and was reluctant to "perform" various parent–child interaction activities in front of other parents and the program staff. She was thus inhibited from full participation by her sense of modesty, inadequacy, and loss of face or embarrassment in having to be taught publicly how to parent her own child. The behavioral home intervention program further challenged Hoa's need to indulge Tuyet and respond relatively unconditionally to her demands; Hoa was similarly resistant to using contingent verbal praise and social rewards for "good" behavior—an uncommon practice for more traditionally oriented Vietnamese parents.

Fortunately, Hoa later had the opportunity to participate in a unique parent education program for Vietnamese-speaking families. She was able to obtain various written materials (translated into the Vietnamese language) pertaining to autism, child development, and behavior management. Hoa also profoundly benefited from personal contact with other Vietnamese parents of children with special needs. Her long-standing sense of isolation and confusion about her daughter's condition was greatly diminished as she continued to attend successive parent education sessions. Upon completion of the program, Hoa actively participated in the subsequent development of the Vietnamese Parents with Disabled Childrens Association, a family support, education, and advocacy organization. She thus emerged as a parent leader in her community and remained committed to assisting other families as part of a debt of gratitude for the program benefits she had received.

grant and parent of a child with Down syndrome, attributed her daughter's hypotonia to her failure to drink adequate amounts of beef bone soup during pregnancy. Another Chinese mother believed that her son's epilepsy was due to her having eaten lamb (a forbidden meat) during pregnancy; in fact, one of the Chinese colloquialisms for epilepsy is synonymous with a disease in lambs that results in seizures (Lim-Yee, 1983). A Vietnamese mother was concerned about having eaten shellfish during her pregnancy with her son as a possible cause of his mental retardation and hyperactivity.

Aside from these individual attributions, it is noteworthy that some traditional beliefs regarding dietary and nutritional practices may actually contribute to increased perinatal risk. For example, some expectant mothers may believe or be warned that prenatal vitamins and supplements can result in excessive iron intake and a fetus with hard bones, thus contributing to a potentially difficult labor and delivery (Lim-Yee, 1983). A related belief (particularly among the Hmong and Mien women) is that weight gain must be restricted to produce a small infant and an easy delivery (Doutrich & Metje, 1988); this belief, however, may be related to the practical consideration that a large baby can pose a serious threat to a pregnant woman with a small pelvis when, in remote rural areas, adequate obstetrical care is not available during delivery. In addition to prenatal dietary practices, mothers ascribing to the "hot–cold" principles of health care must exercise caution because of their body's vulnerability to cold wind and the need to protect against postpartum illness—referred to as *sanhoobyung* by the Koreans (Do, 1988). They thus are encouraged to have only sponge baths and avoid shampooing their hair for up to a month after delivery so that they do not become ill and the new baby does not "fall apart" (Stringfellow, 1978, as cited in Hollingsworth et al., 1980). One mother of a developmentally delayed and multiply disabled child, for example, attributed his condition to her having fallen overboard into the sea and her subsequent exposure to cold and the elements shortly after his birth, while escaping from Vietnam as a "boat person."

Mothers may also believe that they contributed to their children's disabilities by violating certain taboos during pregnancy. One mother, for example (who was ethnic Chinese-Vietnamese), worked throughout her pregnancy as a seamstress and thus frequently used scissors; she felt that this caused her daughter's unique congenital hand anomaly, characterized by fused fingers and a split thumb. This attribution is consistent with the traditional belief that women should avoid using scissors, knives, and other sharp objects during pregnancy for fear of causing a miscarriage or birth defects such as cleft lip; ironically, although this belief is widely held among the hill tribeswomen of Cambodia and Laos, the incidence of congenital anomalies (e.g., cleft lip) among their children is exceptionally high because of "inbreeding" (R.V. Lee, 1989). Another mother (Chinese from Hong Kong) of a child with a cleft palate and other congenital facial anomalies assumed that these were related to her having seen horror films and pictures of evil gods during the initial stages of her pregnancy. Yet another mother (Korean) of a child with autism attributed his inconsolable crying to her having attended a funeral when she was pregnant; she also indicated that his condition was compounded by her frequent mood swings and temper outbursts during pregnancy. This latter belief reflects an expectation among many Asian cultures that the prospective mother must engage in "prenatal education" of her growing fetus, or "womb rearing" as it is referred to by the Chinese. More specifically, the expectant mother must counsel her unborn child in physical, intellectual, and moral principles and must speak and act at all times as a proper role model—as if the child were listening, observing, and learning (Hollingsworth et al., 1980; Masterson, 1990).

Among other types of causal explanations for disability in a child is the more popular belief that it represents a divine punishment for sins or moral transgressions committed by the parents or their ancestors. For example, a Chinese father reported that his persistent gambling and involvement in an extra-marital affair at the time of his wife's pregnancy caused his son to experience neonatal distress and subsequent cerebral palsy. A Cambodian father attributed his daughter's "club" foot to an incident when he and his pregnant wife were escaping as refugees through the jungles of Thailand; in an attempt to hunt and kill a bird with a rock, he instead only wounded its claw and leg. In yet another case, a Korean mother of an emotionally disturbed boy believed her son's problems were linked to his grandfather who was an alcoholic (Chan, 1986). Such attributions often contribute to a prolonged sense of guilt, self-blame (the "What-did-I-do-wrong?" syndrome), and a fatalistic orientation toward accepting one's karma. Parents may consequently fail to seek formal assistance and intervention actively for their child and/or employ religious practices to amend their personal or family member's past wrongdoing.

Spiritual attributions are also employed when demons, ghosts, or evil spirits are believed to be involved in causing disability. For example, a Korean mother of two boys with mental retardation claimed that their sickness was caused by the "spirit of a dead horse" that had entered their bodies during her respective pregnancies. She, in turn, sought the cure for their affliction by resorting to daily prayer and meditation. Another mother (Chinese) insisted that her daughter with severe delays was possessed by a ghost and would regularly bring her to a monk who sang chants, gave offerings to appease the spirits, and provided her with a "lucky charm" made from special herbs to hang around the child's neck. In cases of children with epilepsy, family members are known to seek the help of shamans, priests, or spiritual masters to perform healing rituals and exorcisms (Chan, 1986). Beliefs in the threat of errant spirits roaming the household will lead to the practice (particularly among Southeast Asians) whereby expectant mothers must avoid standing/sitting near doorways (Lee, 1989).

Nature and Meaning of a Disability

Traditional assumptions regarding the etiology of various disabilities are typically accompanied by corresponding views concerning their respective nature and meaning. Among many Asian languages, a number of different terms are used to describe characteristics associated with conditions such as mental retardation or mental illness. These terms are often highly varied, possibly inconsistent, and do not necessarily connote the same meaning or refer to more precise clinical descriptions and definitions characteristic of Western terminology. For instance, mental retardation may be equated with learning disabilities or emotional disturbance, which, in turn, may be narrowly defined in terms of extreme deviance involving overtly aggressive, antisocial, acting-out behavior.

Parents, however, may be highly tolerant of deviant behavior in young children and reluctant to admit their perceived inability to cope with problems by seeking professional help. A sense of parental inadequacy is particularly acute if their school-age children are exhibiting persistent learning and/or psy-

Case Example #2 (adapted from Lim-Yee, 1983)

Sandy, a Chinese girl with Down syndrome, was referred at 2 weeks of age to the Chinatown Child Development Center (CCDC) Infant Program. The referring physician wished to have CCDC staff provide information to Sandy's family about her condition and to consider providing follow-up developmental and family support services.

Sandy's parents, Lily and Chia-wei, were non—English speaking and had recently immigrated to the United States from Hong Kong. Her paternal grandmother lived with the family. Chia-wei had very limited contact with Sandy due to his working two jobs, 6 days a week. At the time of the referral, Lily was having difficulty bottle feeding Sandy and was feeling increasingly isolated and depressed.

During the initial visit, CCDC staff attempted to explain the condition of Down syndrome, about which neither Lily nor the grandmother knew anything. The staff was cautious about using the term "mental retardation" because of the many different Chinese language equivalents and the tendency for Chinese to associate it with "mental illness." Moreover, when told that developmental delay was characteristic of children with Down syndrome, the grandmother asked how it was possible to make such a prediction when the child was only 2 weeks old. In this initial session, the staff further avoided more technical explanations of Down syndrome with respect to genetic etiology, chromosomes, and association with increasing maternal age. In fact, such information may have served to further "implicate" Lily as the one who caused Sandy's condition. She was already concerned that she was being punished by ancestors or the gods for having used scissors (while working as a seamstress) throughout her pregnancy; this, in turn, presumably contributed to Sandy's disability and was believed to be specifically linked to her right-hand anomaly (characterized by fusion of her fingers into two large digits—giving a scissor-like appearance). Moreover, Lily's mother-in-law also blamed her for not drinking enough beef bone soup during pregnancy, thereby causing Sandy's "floppiness" or poor muscle tone (hypotonia). The grandmother had also wanted this second grandchild (Sandy had an older sister) to be a boy. She herself had given birth to three sons, but only one had survived. She was thus very concerned about having a grandson to carry on the family name. Instead, another granddaughter had been born and she was also "abnormal."

Although Lily continued to bring Sandy for developmental activities and group sessions at CCDC, she was chronically depressed and complained of the overwhelming burden of caring for Sandy while facing a blaming mother-in-law and a nonsupportive husband. She chose not to participate in a Chinese American parent support group, and individual counseling provided by a bilingual-bicultural Chinese American therapist was only minimally effective. This situation persisted, even after the birth of her third child, a son, 2 years later. Lily continued to remain emotionally detached from and rejecting of Sandy.

When Sandy was about 4 years old, Lily made a trip to Hong Kong, during which time she consulted a fortune teller to ask about Sandy. He told Lily that Sandy was a "lucky charm" and explained that Sandy was responsible for bringing about the long-awaited son. He also pointed out that Sandy had brought additional good fortune by helping the family financially (in the form of Supplemental Security Income [SSI] checks). He thus convinced Lily that Sandy should be treasured.

After the trip, there were dramatic positive changes in Lily's (and even the grandmother's) attitude toward and relationship with Sandy. The quality and quantity of care for Sandy improved significantly, and Lily's chronic depression lifted. What could not be accomplished in months of supportive counseling was done in a half-hour consultation with a fortune teller in Hong Kong.

chosocial difficulties at school. Such problems are traditionally attributed to laziness and oppositional behavior on the part of the affected child as well as the presumed inability or failure of the parents to provide proper training. Given such training and sufficient parental resolve, these children may be ultimately expected to outgrow their difficulties.

Each of these traditional views pertaining to the causes and nature of various disabilities typically create family embarrassment, shame, and stigma. Even if provided with objective information about the child's disability, parents must still cope with the prospect that their affected child will be unable to fulfill expectations of academic or occupational achievement that give the family a "good name." The subsequent reactions experienced by parents may vary considerably and are influenced by a number of unique family and child characteristics as well as relative experience in receiving information/assistance from professionals (Chan, 1986).

ISSUES OF LANGUAGE

Culture is communication and vice versa. Effective intercultural interactions are primarily a function of the success of the communication process between culturally different persons. Cultural competence is defined as the ability to establish interpersonal relationships with persons from a different culture by developing understanding through effective exchange of both verbal and non-verbal levels of behavior (Hall, 1976). The primary challenge of this goal is to address the fact that "the message perceived is not always the message intended" (Te, 1989a).

Intercultural communication difficulties are not simply a matter of different languages, but of different thought patterns, different values, and different communication styles. The previously detailed "language/linguistic origins" of Chinese, Korean, Cambodian, Lao, and Vietnamese revealed considerable diversity among these respective languages as well as contrast with the English language. Moreover, the psycholinguistic characteristics of these languages (how they influence thought) and the corresponding verbal/nonverbal communication patterns serve to reinforce the earlier-described traditional cultural values. Consistent with a primary orientation toward situation centeredness, each of these Asian languages is very context bound. In fact, Asian cultures are among the highest context cultures in the world; that is, within these cultures, most of the meaningful information is either in the physical context or internalized in the person who receives the information, while relatively little is contained in the verbally transmitted part of the message (Hall, 1976). The speaker or sender's true intent is thus often camouflaged in the context of the situation. The receiver must thus have knowledge of shaded meanings, nonverbal cues, and subtle affect in order to interpret correctly the speaker's intent, without specific reference to what he or she means. This style contrasts dramatically with the low-context Eurocentric cultures where information is conveyed primarily through the verbal code and communication is more precise, explicit, and straightforward.

The languages of high-context Asian cultures also reflect a collectivist orientation, which places the highest value on human relationships and the preservation of harmony and face. This value takes precedence over pure task efficiency and getting to the "business" end of goal attainment; the more important aim is to achieve *mutually* satisfactory and face-saving outcomes. Thus, the principal goal of communication is to promote unity and harmony. This is facilitated, in part, by characteristic communication patterns and styles that employ formality and honorific language systems that convey proper respect for authority, status, and position by special terms of address and polite behaviors. More specifically, personal characteristics such as age, sex, education, occupation, social status, family background, and marital or parental status may each serve to dictate what is communicated between individuals and in what manner. Respective individual attributes and the nature of a given relationship may traditionally determine language style/structure and behaviors such as who will bow the lowest, initiate communication, change subjects, speak more loudly or softly (or not at all), look away when eyes meet, and be most accommodating (Shon, 1980). Individuals from low-context cultures may perceive such formalism as excessive and unnecessary. However, observing the rules of propriety is considered an essential aspect of harmonious social interaction.

Preservation of group harmony is also enhanced by indirect communication styles that are significantly more intuitive and contemplative than low-context, direct, open communication styles. In the interest of preserving face, there is a characteristic reluctance to contradict, criticize, disappoint, or otherwise cause unease or discomfort in another. An indirect style of responding is thus adopted whereby the use of the word "yes" and ostensibly affirmative head nodding can actually mean "no"; that is, the listener may tell the speaker what he or she thinks the speaker wants to hear, rather than giving an absolutely truthful answer that might offend him or her. The listener may also be noncommittal or hesitant in response to a direct question when reluctant to do something that is not fully understood, is disagreeable, and/or when saying "no" is to be avoided. Unfortunately, such behavior is frequently misinterpreted or evaluated by low-context cultures as evasive, devious, and dishonest. Individuals who are socialized to be sensitive to subtle culture-specific cues and nuances thus take pride in their ability to "know" intuitively (without benefit of words) what others are thinking and feeling through a kind of mental telepathy (Crystal, 1989). Koreans refer to this ability as *nun-chi* (reading the eyes)—an affective sense by which one can quickly and accurately assess another's genuine attitudes and emotional reactions to a given topic, proposal, or situation that arises in an ongoing dialogue. This process enables the parties engaged in conversation to understand what is going on without being told and to detect whether others are really pleased or satisfied (Gudykunst & Ting-Toomey, 1988; Yum, 1987). Early on, children are thus taught to observe nonverbal cues that guide behaviors in social interactions; moreover, they are scolded (e.g., "Have you no eyes!") and feel ashamed if they lack ability to meet someone's needs without them being articulated.

Nonverbal communicaton thus conveys significantly more information in high-context Asian cultures, wherein silence is particularly valued. Again, the signficant contrast between communication styles (Asian versus European American) is illustrated by the perception of a recent Southeast Asian refugee: "In America, you value freedom of speech; in Vietnam, we value freedom of silence" (Chu, 1990). Others have noted that "in most cultures throughout the world, individuals start talking when they have to; Americans, instead, tend to stop talking when they have to." The relative importance of silence among Asian cultures is further evidenced by proverbs such as: "Keep your mouth shut, your eyes open." "He who knows, talks not; he who talks, knows not." Silence, as opposed to verbal behavior, is perceived by native-born Chinese, for example, as a primary control strategy in conversation (Wiemann, Chen, & Giles, 1986). On the one hand, maintaining silence in a conversation may serve as an expression of interest and respect. On the other hand, if silence follows consistent verbal responses and affective acknowledgment on the part of a listener, it may indicate disagreement or negative reactions such as anger (the "silent treatment"). In fact, a typical practice among many Asian peoples is to refuse to speak any further in conversation if they cannot personally accept the speaker's attitude, opinion, or way of thinking about particular issues or subjects. A related aspect of silence is the state of mind referred to by the Chinese as *wu-wei*. It describes one who is alert but not tense, deliberately nonactive without being passive, relaxed but concentrated. In this state, one continues to "express" thoughts without words. Thus, as suggested in the proverb, "Think three times before you act," doing or saying nothing at the right time can be an appropriate action.

Eye contact and facial expressions serve as yet additional examples of contrasting styles. Direct and/or sustained eye-to-eye contact with relative strangers may be interpreted as a sign of hostility or considered impolite and even shameful (between male and female, it may have sexual connotations). Similarly, direct eye contact with an elder or person in authority or a family member of higher status is considered disrespectful. Affective expressions also have differing connotations. In general, the value placed upon control of emotional expression contributes to a demeanor among selected Asian groups that is often interpreted by Eurocentric individuals as "flat," "stoic," "enigmatic," even "inscrutable." Koreans, for example, in keeping with the national character of the "Land of the Morning Calm," may present with a demeanor referred to as *myu-po-jung* (lack of facial expression). Casual smiling and direct eye contact when greeting or interacting with strangers is considered inappropriate. In fact, Koreans as well as many Southeast Asian groups, may smile when embarrassed. Smiling, rather than verbal comments (e.g., "I'm sorry"), serves as an expression of apology for minor offenses. Smiling can also be an expression of deference to an authority figure who scolds a child or criticizes an adult; it indicates sincere acknowledgment of fault or the mistake committed and that one is neither offended nor harbors any ill feeling or resentment toward the interlocutor (as opposed to an expression of disrespect or nonverbal challenge to authority). Smiling (or blushing) is also considered a proper nonverbal response to a compliment. The person who delivers the compliment should not expect a "thank you" in return. A verbal response of gratitude on the part of the recipient would suggest a lack of modesty. If a verbal response is needed, the recipient may deny the compliment, saying that they do not deserve it (Te, 1989a). Smiling may further be used to mask other emotions (e.g., pain or discomfort) or to avoid conflict.

Various gestures and body language also have differing meanings. The American gesture for waving "good-bye" (particularly to a child) actually approximates the gesture for "come here" used by Southeast Asians (i.e., slowly waving all fingers, closed and in unison with the palm down, facing inward). Furthermore, the American gesture for "come here" (using the pointing finger with hand raised and palm inward) is a hostile, aggressive gesture among Southeast Asians or is the manner in which one beckons dogs, lower animals, or an "inferior" person. The crossing of the index and middle fingers as a gesture for "good luck" is actually an obscene gesture with sexual connotations for Southeast Asians.

With regard to acceptable interpersonal space, Asians typically prefer to maintain greater distance from those they are talking to than the average American comfort zone of 12 inches to an arm's length. Physical touching or body contact between men and women is also avoided in public; however, public handholding between same-sex members (both men and women) is commonly practiced and considered socially acceptable among many Asian cultures. In general, the significant contrasts in nonverbal behaviors and patterns of communication serve as a constant reminder that "not all people smile in the same language" (Te, 1989a, p. 54).

SUMMARY AND RECOMMENDATIONS

Summary

The dramatically accelerated growth of the Asian American population is largely attributable to the continuing waves of Asian immigrants and refugees throughout the past 25 years. In contrast to the earliest Asian immigrants who were primarily farmers and laborers, the relative newcomers (following the landmark Immigration and Nationality Act Amendments of 1965) include significant numbers of Chinese and Korean professionals and people considered to be the most highly educated and skilled of any immigrant group in the country's history. The withdrawal of the United States from Vietnam in 1975 further led to the mass exodus of hundreds of thousands of Southeast Asian refugees (Cambodians, Laotians, Vietnamese) seeking sanctuary in America. Over time, this population has become increasingly diverse, including preliterate rural tribespeople as well as college-educated urban professionals.

Such diversity among the more recent Asian immigrants and refugees has contributed to the formation of bipolar, ethnic communities—divided between the two extremes of unskilled, working or "welfare" classes (with the highest rates of poverty) and successful professional, entrepreneurial upper-middle classes. Moreover, apart from the varying educational and social class backgrounds, the heterogeneity of the Asian American population is further reflected in diverse ethnic, cultural, and linguistic characteristics and unique historical, sociopolitical, and economic conditions in the respective countries of origin. However, despite such diversity as well as rapid growth and increasing visibility, the new Asian immigrants and refugees have been persistently confronted with stereotypic, undifferentiated, and often hostile perceptions. They still find themselves viewed and treated as "strangers from a different shore" (Takaki, 1989, p. 18).

This perception serves to disguise the reality of distinct lifestyles, customs, traditions, world views, ethics, social norms, values, and folk beliefs with ancient religious and philosophical origins. In particular, the Chinese, Korean, and Vietnamese cultures are rooted in some of the world's oldest civilizations (over 4,000 years) and have been principally influenced by the doctrines and philosophies of Confucianism, Taoism, and Buddhism—the "three teachings." Together with ancestor worship, shamanism (including animism and spirit worship), and Christianity, the "three teachings" have evolved into a complementary system of blended beliefs. The practice of syncretism or polytheism has thus enabled Asians to integrate complex mixes of corresponding thoughts and faiths that provide both practical and spiritual guidance. These beliefs have further shaped the traditional collectivist values that are common to the various Asian cultures and that have been preserved with pride and dedication throughout the centuries.

The predominant Asian values pertaining to family, harmony, education, and selected virtues offer fundamental guidelines for living. The family, for example, is the basic unit of society and the central focus of the individual's life. Harmony is the keynote of existence. Successful academic achievement is the greatest tribute one can bestow upon one's parents and family. Virtues such as patience, perseverance, self-sacrifice, maintenance of inner strength, self-restraint, modesty, and humility are each considered necessary expressions of dignity that promote the group welfare. These values have contributed to the profound strength and resiliency demonstrated by Asian peoples throughout their respective histories of severe hardship, war, disruption, and loss. They have been maintained for many generations and continue to influence the contemporary socialization experiences of Asian American children. However, despite their enduring and historically adaptive nature, these collectivist values contrast sharply with the more Eurocentric individualistic values and have been transformed in the process of acculturation. The relative influence of traditional values among Asian immigrant/refugee families must thus be considered in the context of complex economic, psychological, and social adjustment patterns and factors such as premigration/migration experiences, time of arrival, proximity to same-ethnic communities, age, gender, education, language proficiency, and socioeconomic status.

Although traditional values have indeed been transformed, the extent to which they have historically influenced childrearing beliefs and practices among Asian cultures is readily apparent. As the most basic social institution, the family is characterized by well-defined, highly interdependent roles within a cohesive patriarchal vertical structure—one that derives from the Confucian doctrine of filial piety. The respective marital and parental roles/responsibilities typically entail significant personal sacrifice and accountability in return for the right to assume strict authority over and unquestioning obedience and loyalty from the child. Children, in turn, are viewed as extensions of their parents. They are treasured, protected, and readily indulged within a very nurturant, secure,and predictable social environment (involving both immediate and extended family members) throughout infancy and the toddler period. As they approach and enter school age, children experience accelerated movement toward independence training and direct participation in the adult world. The child thus assumes increasingly greater responsibilities as an older sibling and learns to view his or her role in the family and society in terms of specific relationships, obligations, and codes of conduct. In general, more traditional childrearing beliefs and practices promote family interdependence and deference to the needs of the group. However, they also support personal control, self-improvement, and the development of individual independence *outside* the family—all of which are conducive to successful achievement in the larger society, thereby enhancing the family welfare and fulfilling filial obligations.

Traditional childrearing beliefs and practices are complemented by various health beliefs and health care practices that have endured for many centuries. Among Chinese and Korean immigrants and Southeast Asian refugees, the more common traditional health orientations include a blending of traditional Chinese medicine and folk medicine practices. Related fundamental concepts include maintaining balance between the cosmic forces of yin and yang, the "five elements," and internal body organs. Lack of clear differentiation between mental illness (or psychological problems) and physical illness is yet another aspect of the holistic philosophy of Chinese medicine. In addition to natural or metaphysical explanations of health/illness, supernatural beliefs and spiritual healing practices are also prevalent—particularly among the Southeast Asian refugee populations. The contrasts between traditional Asian health care practices and those of Western medicine include significantly less invasive diagnostic and treatment procedures, use of herbal medications versus prescription medications, and the use of therapeutic massage, acupressure, acupuncture and moxibustion, and dermabrasion. The importance of understanding these traditional health care practices is underscored by the fact that many Asian families utilize a "pluralistic" system of care that blends folk medicine with Western medicine. Thus, the relative compatibility of various health orientations often becomes a central issue in the care of infants and children with disabilities and developmental special needs. Further, many of the traditional beliefs and attributions regarding the etiology of various disabilities directly reflect traditional health beliefs about the varying causes of illness.

A final area of focus encompasses issues regarding language characteristics and communication styles among the various Asian ethnic groups. The previously detailed "language/linguistic origins" of Chinese, Korean, Cambodian, Lao, and Vietnamese revealed considerable diversity among these respective languages as well as contrast with the English language. Moreover, corresponding psycholinguistic characteristics and verbal/nonverbal communication patterns serve to reinforce traditional cultural orientations and values. Asian languages, for example, are situation centered or context bound; they are thus often dependent upon the receiver's ability to interpret correctly the speaker's intent without specific reference to what he or she means. Consistent with the primary value of preserving harmony and face in human relationships, Asian languages employ relatively formal rules of propriety and communication that promote harmonious social interaction. Indirect communication styles; reluctance to criticize or contradict overtly; and ability to "read" others' genuine attitudes, opinions, or feelings through nonverbal cues also serve to preserve group harmony. A significant amount of information is thus conveyed through nonverbal forms of communication, including silence (and the timing of verbal exchanges), facial expressions (e.g., smiling), eye contact, body movements and gestures, posture and positioning, and interpersonal space. Relative to more Eurocentric cultures, the subtle and often distinctly different (if not entirely opposite) meaning of such nonverbal communication may create significant communication barriers and conflicts—well beyond basic language differences. Thus, the primary challenge in achieving the goal of successful intercultural communication is to address the fact that the message perceived is not always the message intended.

Recommendations for Interventionists

The effectiveness of programs and providers serving multicultural populations "rests heavily upon the sensitivity, understanding, and respect paid to the specific cultural, [linguistic], familial, and individual diversity involved" (Anderson & Schrag-Fenichel, 1989, p. 18). Early interventionists must thus develop ethnic competence. This process requires several tasks, which include: 1) clarification and awareness of one's own values, assumptions, and biases; 2) gathering and analyzing ethnographic information regarding the cultural community within which each family resides; 3) determining the degree to which the family operates transculturally; and 4) examining each family's orientation to specific childrearing issues (Hanson, Lynch, & Wayman, 1990). Understanding recent immigrant/refugee families further entails acquisition of culture-specific knowledge of traditional values, beliefs, and practices pertaining to family, religion, childrearing, education, health, mental health, and disability, as well as language characteristics and communication styles. These topics have been addressed throughout this chapter in relation to selected Asian ethnic groups. Ethnic or cultural competence, however, also requires learning and refining skills necessary to engage in successful cross-cultural interactions and corresponding behavioral (as well as attitudinal) changes on the part of individual service providers. Culturally competent programs for young children and their families must similarly incorporate administrative strategies, policies, program designs, and services that are increasingly responsive to culturally diverse client populations (Roberts, 1990). The following recommendations therefore address practical considerations in responding to various cultural orientations and behaviors related to service utilization by Asian families.

Outreach

Critical to the process of gaining initial access to selected Asian families and clients is a recognition of the "trust" factor and the degree to which traditional family-centered and ethnic community orientations contribute toward a tendency to view "outsiders" with a degree of suspicion (D. Sue, 1981). Helping professionals and various human services agencies must be aware of the "proper" entry points to Asian communities. More specifically, certain formal and informal communication networks and established social relationships within selected Asian communities play a major role in determining how a family in need will initially view an available public service. Trust typically begins when contact with a particular agency or helping professional has been initiated or affirmed by friends, relatives, or respected authorities (Leung, 1988). In some Asian communities (e.g., the Hmong), identified community leaders are usually consulted in relation to health or other matters involving external resources; their counsel, approval, and recommendations are often sought *first* (Keiter, 1990).

Thus, third parties or indigenous intermediaries who have credibility within the family or ethnic community may assume a major role in providing initial support, reassurance, and needed information about available services and their value, thereby facilitating the family's successful entry into a system. Providers and agencies need to identify such community gatekeepers, acknowledge their potential liaison role, and establish working relationships with them. The information source through which a family learns about a particular service, the nature of corresponding word-of-mouth communications, and initial encounters or first experiences all profoundly contribute to the agency's reputation within the community and its ultimate acceptability (Chan, 1985).

Working with Interpreters

To the extent that the previously described intermediaries are bilingual, they may be relied upon as interpreters (and/or translators) for non– or limited–English speaking families during initial contacts as well as for subsequent client/family interactions. In many instances, families may prefer or assume that English-speaking family members, relatives, friends, advocates, indigenous community representatives, or bilingual staff from other agencies will accompany them on the first visit and continue to be available to serve as interpreters; issues of trust, moral support, dependency, personal relationships, and a collectivist or group orientation may reinforce this preference. Lack of available and appropriate bilingual/bicultural personnel or access to "outside" interpreters may also be a practical agency constraint that further reinforces this arrangement.

However, whether utilizing intermediaries as interpreters or selecting others, a number of important considerations warrant attention (see Chapter 3, this volume). Further guidelines for selecting, preparing, and training interpreters (particularly for parent meetings and developmental/psychoeducational assessments) have been offered elsewhere in relation to selected Asian groups (e.g., Dien et al. [1986] for Vietnamese-speaking children/families; Tinloy et al. [1986] for Chinese-speaking children/families).

Initial Expectations/Orientations

Once contact has been established with agencies/providers, more traditionally oriented Asian American families will likely expect an initial formality characterized by well-defined roles and clear communication regarding what is being requested of them and what specific services can be offered. Professionals are viewed as authority figures who are directive; who employ structured, practical problem-solving approaches; and who provide specific advice, "answers," and recommendations. (Providers who are relatively nondirective and who fail to offer practical assistance promptly may be perceived as indifferent or uncaring.) The professional thus is assumed to have expertise and the ability to offer assistance that uniquely supplements family resources; moreover, such assistance may relate to more immediate areas of need that are not typically addressed by a given provider's discipline or specialty knowledge/skills. The establishment of credibility and the provision (or "giving") of services that yield direct benefits from the outset are thus likely to facilitate client follow through and maintenance of the professional–client relationship (S. Sue & Zane, 1987). These considerations are especially significant for those recent immigrant/ refugee families who may have very high expectations of "American" services and who have been referred for formal assistance after having exclusively drawn upon, and possibly exhausted, family resources and coping strategies in response to the child's problems and needs.

Throughout the initial process of developing client/family relationships, providers also should be cognizant of traditional parental orientations toward schools and professionals entrusted with the education and related care of children with special needs. Filial piety defines a social hierarchy of allegiance that proceeds downward from "king" to "teacher" to "father." Parents thus are expected to respect and honor teachers and professional specialists by assuming a corresponding "dependent" orientation of deference, noninterference, and delegation of authority and responsibility (Chan, 1986; L.L. Cheng, 1987). They are predictably unfamiliar with and likely confused by mainstream philosophical movements and legislative mandates that have legitimized parent rights/ responsibilities and dictated parent/family involvement. In fact, these concepts and expectations may be both alien and threatening—particularly if formal requests for parent participation are interpreted as indications that the child's difficulties have exceeded the professionals' teaching or intervention capabilities, and the parents thus are being held accountable.

Face Saving and the Counseling Process

Whether parents are requested to meet with professionals or have initiated efforts to obtain assistance, their ultimate public disclosure of child- or family-related problems is often extremely difficult. Such disclosure could be considered a betrayal of family loyalty or trust, an act of weakness, and/or a form of disgracing the family's honor and reputation. This belief is reinforced by a more general reticence to burden others with problems that the parent or family should presumably be able to resolve internally. Moreover, sharing personal problems and concerns with an authority figure (even though such an individual is an identified helping professional) may be construed as an act of disrespect. This perception particularly affects counseling transactions with mental health professionals whose roles and expectations are conceptually foreign to many traditionally oriented Asian families (Chan, 1986).

Sensitivity to an individual's or family's need to save face can be demonstrated in various ways. The helping professional is cautioned against venturing into a frank discussion of specific problem areas too quickly. Although the family may expect initial formality, the professional is encouraged to spend time establishing personal rapport and to allow for discussion of information that may be tangential or even unrelated to the referring problems or perceived needs. Asian American parents place great value on professional sensitivity to the family's face-saving needs and positive regard for indirect approaches to typically stigmatic problem areas. Thus, there is often a need to reframe problems and approach them in a more circular fashion while establishing mutual trust, respect, and movement toward a more personalized relationship. This may be manifested in the professional's continued expression of interest and concern for the family's general health and well-being and flexibility and accommodation in relation to "when, where, and what;" that is, willingness to meet at variable times, in more informal, culturally familiar surroundings (including the home), and provision of direct assistance or accompaniment in contacts with other agencies/professionals while assuming multiple provider roles, including that as an active child and family advocate (Chan, 1986).

Unfortunately, agency fiscal constraints and/or the professional's designated roles and responsibilities may prohibit or limit such involvement. Nonetheless, the professional can still effectively communicate genuine regard for the family's welfare and cultivate personalized relationships while observing agency guidelines/policies and recognizing reasonable boundaries in satisfying the family's dependency needs. The counseling process can thus be conceptualized within a "cultural-developmental" framework involving various phases and appropriate timing of selected interventions (Serafica, 1990).

Communication Styles and Assertiveness

Mainstream providers and agencies are often frustrated by the subtleties and slower paced process that typically accompany successful relationship building with many Asian immigrant/refugee families. More ethnocentric providers may further interpret culturally appropriate behavior patterns as indicative of passivity, submissiveness, excessive dependency, or even resistance. Such value judgments can then accelerate efforts to prompt aggressively the parents or family members into greater self-disclosure, independent decision making, and definitive action. The resulting provider–family conflicts and alienation often enhance provider preferences for clients who are ostensibly more sophisticated and cooperative, and who demonstrate initiative.

Service providers may thus directly contribute to deteriorating relationships by failing to acknowledge certain behavior patterns as manifestations of deference to authority. When interacting with professionals, Asian American clients may convey respect for authority by engaging in prescribed behaviors such as repeated head nodding, avoidance of direct eye contact and affective expression, refraining from asking questions, interrupting for clarification, or making their needs/desires explicit, and withholding critical comments. The primary importance of conveying respect and adhering to traditional virtues such as patience, reserve, and "holding back" can result in a persistent reluctance to seek explanations of services and policies or to clarify specific verbal communications and agency/provider expectations. Moreover, limited— or non–English speaking Asian American clients who are unfamiliar with the system are most likely to demonstrate such reluctance while remaining in a great need of relevant information. This tendency is particularly apparent in the area of self-advocacy and Asian American parents' orientation toward pursuing their legal rights and service entitlements for their children with special needs. In contrast to the belief that "the squeaky wheel gets the grease," Asian Americans may be more inclined to abide by the proverb "the nail that raises its head is hammered down."

Traditional Asian American parents may further postpone indicating their choice of alternatives or following through on multiple recommendations that are presented to them. The perceived ambiguity of the professional–client relationship exacerbates parental anxiety and fear of committing a social error in behavior or speech that will invoke a "loss of face." When given options, parents may be primarily concerned about selecting those that are presumed to be most valued by the professional. If unsure, parents will conservatively avoid "second guessing" the professional and the possibility of selecting the "wrong" choice or course of action—thereby preventing potential loss of face. The previously described traditional value placed on private preparation before public action may translate into "doing or saying nothing at the right time" as an appropriate action. The professional therefore must be patient and allow for sufficient time and input to facilitate client decision making. Throughout this process, he or she must recognize the family as the primary social unit, observe protocols, and respect the traditional hierarchical roles of senior family members in collectively providing input, making decisions, and addressing problems as they relate to the child or other family members.

Reciprocity

Successful professional–client relationships are often characterized by the traditional Asian American parent's ensuing sense of obligation and reciprocity. As particulary embodied in the Korean concept of *unhae,* such reciprocity applies to "favors" that are graciously given and willingly returned. A twofold obligation thus arises from interchanges in which those in "superior" positions grant assistance to those who require and depend upon their services; the recipients, in turn, owe a debt of gratitude that can be repaid when a fitting occasion arises. In the absence of opportunities to respond reciprocally to the professional's own needs for assistance or to provide direct monetary repayment, family members may display their gratitude through personalized gift giving, invitations to attend significant family events (e.g., weddings, graduations) or social occasions, and other expressions of appreciation. Such reciprocity is the basis of a longer term relationship or bond of friendship that persists well after the initial "debt" has been paid. Thus, a professional's refusal to accept a client's offer of gifts, favors, or invitations to participate in more personal social interactions may be construed as rejection and failure to give face. Considerable tact, forethought, and sensitivity must be employed in such situations.

ALTERNATIVE SERVICE DELIVERY AND TRAINING MODELS

The previously detailed cultural orientations and behaviors may have a significant impact on service utilization by many Asian American families. Among the most frequently cited service utilization barriers in the literature are: difficulty communicating with professionals and lack of practical information about needed services and sufficient awareness/understanding of how to access the "system" (Chan, 1978; Rogow, 1985; Shu, 1989; Smith & Ryan, 1987; Yao, 1988; Yee, 1988, cited in E.K. Leung, 1988). Such barriers are often experienced by a great many parents/families of children with disabilities irrespective of ethnic background. However, they are exacerbated by the cultural/linguistic characteristics of recent immigrant and refugee families.

Throughout continuing efforts to promote greater client/family access to needed services within selected Asian American communities, a number of alternative service delivery models have been developed. While delivering culturally and linguistically appropriate services, many related programs have further linked Asian American clients to more comprehensive service networks. Such programs have promoted interagency service coordination; resource sharing; effective utilization of indigenous community-based providers; and establishment of sufficient numbers of visible and well-respected bilingual, bicultural, multidisciplinary professionals and staff who can serve each of the major Asian ethnic groups in a given community. Specific examples of such programs (most of which have been located in urban areas with high concentrations of various Asian American populations) are further described by Chan (1981, 1987), Cleveland (1987), and Murase, Egawa, and Tashima (1985).

Each of these alternative service delivery models and approaches are integrally related to issues of training. As Asian American communities continue to undergo accelerated growth, the number of available bilingual, bicultural providers to serve their respective needs has become increasingly inadequate. Given critically deficient resources and the acute shortages of personnel, education and training programs for non– or limited–English speaking parents have been an essential means of promoting access to needed services as well as increased parental involvement and advocacy in the formulation of policies and development of programs for infants and young children with disabilities. A series of model parent education and training projects serving Chinese, Korean, and Vietnamese populations have been successfully developed and implemented (Chan, 1990). They have incorporated training of trainers and parent–professional collaboration strategies designed to enhance the impact of relatively short-term "demonstration" projects. The hallmark of the projects' success has been the subsequent organization of formal parent groups among the various Asian American parent participants.

> Selected parent trainers have assumed instrumental leadership roles in guiding the establishment and incorporation of parent organizations serving Chinese, Korean, and Vietnamese families with children with disabilities. These organizations are engaged in pioneering efforts to provide mutual support, education/training, and advocacy for their respective members and communities. (Chan, 1990, p. 86)

Parent leaders have also emerged as representatives who serve on various local and statewide advisory and policymaking bodies charged with prioritizing needs and developing corresponding plans and services.

Related efforts to augment resources for Asian American and other culturally diverse populations include systematic student recruitment and preservice training initiatives (e.g., Keiter, 1990) and comprehensive multicultural education and training programs designed to promote cultural competence among advocates, early interventionists, and providers of services for children with disabilities (Chan, 1990). The commitment of resources to effective service delivery and training models thus entails sustained collective endeavor on multiple fronts. Throughout this complex and challenging process, all who serve Asian American clients and families are called upon to demonstrate flexibility, versatility, and sensitivity in responding to their diverse nationalities, immigrant histories, cultural orientations, language characteristics, life experiences, and unique personal circumstances. As we continue to cultivate our knowledge and understanding, we are cautioned against "judging the tree before seeing the fruit." While investing significant energy and time to dig deeper into an awareness of ourselves as well as others, "we should not call it a well until we see the water."

REFERENCES

Anderson, P.P., & Schrag-Fenichel, R. (1989). *Serving culturally diverse families of infants and toddlers with disabilities.* Washington, DC: National Center for Clinical Infant Programs.

Arnold, F., Minocha, U., & Fawcett, J.T. (1987). The changing face of Asian immigration to the United States. In J.T. Fawcett & B.V. Carino (Eds.), *Pacific bridges: The new immigration from Asia and the Pacific Islands* (pp. 105–152). New York: Center for Migration Studies.

Asians in America: 1990 census. (1991, August). *Asian Week.* San Francisco: Great Printing House.

Attorney General's Asian and Pacific Islander Advisory Committee. (1988). *Final report.* Sacramento, CA: Office of the Attorney General.

Benhamida, L. (1988). *Interpreting in mental health settings for refugees and others: A guide for the professional interpreter.* Minneapolis: University of Minnesota, Refugee Assistance Program–Mental Health Technical Assistance Center.

Bliatout, B.T. (1981). *Hmong sudden unexpected nocturnal death syndrome: A cultural study.* Portland, OR: Sparkle Publishing Enterprises.

Bliatout, B.T., Ben, R., Bliatout, H.Y., & Lee, D. T-T. (1985). Mental health and prevention activities targeted to Southeast Asian refugees. In T.C. Owan (Ed.), *Southeast Asian mental health: Treatment, prevention, services, training, and research* (pp. 183–207). Washington, DC: National Institute of Mental Health.

Bouvier, L.F., & Agresta, A.J. (1985, May). The fastest growing minority. *American Demographics, 7,* 31–33, 46.

Bouvier, L.F., & Agresta, A.J. (1987). The future Asian population of the United States. In J.T. Fawcett & B.V. Carino (Eds.), *Pacific bridges: The new immigration from Asia and the Pacific Islands* (pp. 285–301). New York: Center for Migration Studies.

Brigham Young University. (1986). *Culturegram.* Provo, UT: Brigham Young University, David M. Kennedy Center for International Studies, Publication Services.

Chan, S. (1978). *Services for the developmentally disabled: A study of Asian families within a Regional Center system.* Unpublished doctoral dissertation, University of California, Los Angeles.

Chan, S. (1981). Serving Pacific Asians with developmental disabilities. *Journal of the Asian American Psychological Association, 6,* 3–8.

Chan, S. (1985, April). *Reaching out to Asian parents.* Paper presented at the Annual Convention of the Council for Exceptional Children, Anaheim, CA.

Chan, S. (1986). Parents of exceptional Asian children. In M.K. Kitano & P.C. Chinn (Eds.), *Exceptional Asian children and youth* (pp. 36–53). Reston, VA: Council for Exceptional Children.

Chan, S. (1987). Something old, something new, something borrowed and something whatever. In J.O. Cleveland (Ed.), *Service delivery models for outreach/prevention/intervention for Southeast Asian refugee infants, children and their families— Conference proceedings* (pp. 22–30). San Diego: San Diego–Imperial Counties Developmental Services.

Chan, S. (1990). Early intervention with culturally diverse families of infants and toddlers with disabilities. *Infants and Young Children, 3,* 78–87.

Chen, J. (1981). *The Chinese of America: From the beginnings to the present.* New York: Harper & Row.

Cheng, C-Y. (1987). Chinese philosophy and contemporary human communication theory. In D.L. Kincaid (Ed.), *Communication theory: Eastern and Western perspectives* (pp. 23–43). San Diego: Academic Press.

Cheng, L.L. (1987). *Assessing Asian language performance: Guidelines for evaluating limited English-proficient students.* Rockville, MD: Aspen.

Chhim, S-H. (1989). *Introduction to Cambodian culture.* San Diego: San Diego State University, Multifunctional Resource Center.

Chin, J.L. (1983). Diagnostic considerations in working with Asian-Americans. *American Journal of Orthopsychiatry, 53,* 100–109.

Chu, T.L. (1990, April). *Working with Vietnamese families*. Paper presented at the Harbor Regional Center Conference, Towards Competence in Intercultural Interaction, Torrance, CA.

Cleveland, J.O. (Ed.). (1987). *Service delivery models for outreach/prevention/ intervention for Southeast Asian refugee infants, children, and their families— Conference proceedings*. San Diego: San Diego–Imperial Counties Developmental Services.

Cohon, D. (1981). Psychological adaptation and dysfunction among refugees. *International Migration Review, 15*, 255–275.

Crystal, D. (1989, September). Asian Americans and the myth of the model minority. *Social Casework*, pp. 405–413.

DeAngelis, T. (1990, July). Cambodians' sight loss tied to seeing atrocities. *APA [American Psychological Association] Monitor, 21*, 36–37.

Devine, E., & Braganti, N.L. (1986). *The traveler's guide to Asian customs and manners*. New York: St. Martin's Press.

Dien, T.T., Te, H.D., & Wei, T.T.D. (1986). *Assessment of Vietnamese speaking limited English proficient students with special needs*. Sacramento: California State Department of Education, Office of Special Education, Personnel Development Unit.

Do, H.K. (1988). *Health and illness beliefs and practices of Korean Americans*. Unpublished doctoral dissertation, Boston University, School of Nursing.

Doerner, W. (1985, July 8). Asians: To America with skills. *Time*, p. 5.

Doutrich, D., & Metje, L. (1988). *Cultural factors and components of prenatal care for the Hmong and Yiu-Mien*. Unpublished master's thesis, Oregon Health Sciences University, Portland.

Dung, T.N. (1984). Understanding Asian families: A Vietnamese perspective. *Children Today, 13*, 10–12.

Egawa, J., & Tashima, N. (1982). *Indigenous healers in Southeast Asian refugee communities*. San Francisco: Pacific Asian Mental Health Research Project.

Fawcett, J.T., & Arnold, F. (1987). Explaining diversity: Asian and Pacific immigration systems. In J.T. Fawcett & B.V. Carino (Eds.), *Pacific bridges: The new immigration from Asia and the Pacific Islands* (pp. 453–473). New York: Center for Migration Studies.

Fawcett, J.T., & Carino, B.V. (1987). International migration and Pacific Basin development. In J.T. Fawcett & B.V. Carino (Eds.), *Pacific bridges: The new immigration from Asia and the Pacific Islands* (pp. 3–25). New York: Center for Migration Studies.

Gardner, R.W., Robey, B., & Smith, P.C. (1985). Asian Americans: Growth, change, and diversity. *Population Bulletin, 40*, 2–8.

Gollnick, D.M., & Chinn, P.C. (1990). *Multicultural education in a pluralistic society*. Columbus, OH: Charles E. Merrill.

Gordon, L.W. (1987). Southeast Asian refugee migration to the United States. In J.T. Fawcett & B.V. Carino (Eds.), *Pacific bridges: The new immigration from Asia and the Pacific Islands* (pp. 153–173). New York: Center for Migration Studies.

Gudykunst, W.B., & Ting-Toomey, S. (1988). *Culture and interpersonal communication*. Newberry Park, CA: Sage.

Hall, E. (1976). *Beyond culture*. Garden City, NY: Anchor.

Hanson, M.J., Lynch, E.W., & Wayman, K.I (1990). Honoring the cultural diversity of families when gathering data. *Topics in Early Childhood Special Education, 10*, 112–131.

Harrison, A.O., Wilson, M.N., Pine, C.J., Chan, S.Q., & Buriel, R. (1990). Family ecologies of ethnic minority children. *Child Development, 61*, 347–362.

Ho, D.Y.F. (1987). Chinese pattern of socialization: A critical review. In M.H. Bond (Ed.), *The psychology of Chinese people* (pp. 1–37). Hong Kong: Oxford Press.

Hollingsworth, A.O., Brown, L.P., & Brooten, D.A. (1980, November). The refugees and childbearing: What to expect. *RN*, pp. 45–48.

Hsu, F.L.K. (1981). *Americans and Chinese: Passages to differences*. Honolulu: University of Hawaii Press.

Huang, L.N. (1989). Southeast Asian refugee children and adolescents. In J.T. Gibbs & L.N. Huang (Eds.), *Children of color: Psychological interventions with minority youth* (pp. 278–321). San Francisco: Jossey-Bass.

Huang, L.N., & Ying, Y-W. (1989). Chinese American children and adolescents. In J.T. Gibbs & L.N. Huang (Eds.), *Children of color: Psychological interventions with minority youth* (pp. 30–66). San Francisco: Jossey-Bass.

Hurh, W.M., & Kim,K.C. (1984). *Korean immigrants in America*. NJ: Associated University Press.

Keiter, J. (1990). *The recruitment and retention of minority trainees in University Affiliated Programs—Asian-Americans* (M.L. Kuehn, Ed.). Madison: University of Wisconsin–Madison.

Kemp, C. (1985). Cambodian refugee health care beliefs and practices. *Journal of Community Mental Health Nursing, 2*, 41–52.

Kim, B-L.C. (1980). *The Korean American child at school and at home, project report*. Urbana: University of Illinois.

Kim, I. (1987). Korea and East Asia: Premigration factors and U.S. immigration policy. In J.T. Fawcett & B.V. Carino (Eds.), *Pacific bridges: The new immigration from Asia and the Pacific Islands* (pp. 327–345). New York: Center for Migration Studies.

Kim, S.C. (1985). Family therapy for Asian Americans: A strategic-structural framework. *Psychotherapy, 22*, 342–348.

Kourmarn, Y.S. (1980). *The Hmongs of Laos: 1896–1978* (Indochinese Refugee Education Guides, General Information Series #16—"Glimpses of Hmong History and Culture"). Washington, DC: National Indochinese Clearinghouse.

Le, D.D. (1983). Mental health and Vietnamese children. In G.J. Powell (Ed.), *The psychosocial development of minority group children* (pp. 373–384). New York: Brunner/Mazel.

Lee, C.S. (1988). *Korea—Land of the morning calm*. New York: Universe Press.

Lee, R.V. (1989). Understanding Southeast Asian mothers-to-be. *Childbirth Educator (American Baby), 8*, 32–39.

The legacy of Vietnam. (1985, April 15). *Newsweek*, pp. 32–71.

Leung, E.K. (1988). Cultural and acculturational commonalities and diversities among Asian Americans: Identification and programming considerations. In A.A. Oritz & B.A. Ramiriz (Eds.), *Schools and the culturally diverse exceptional student: Promising practices and future directions* (pp. 86–95). Reston, VA: Council for Exceptional Children.

Leung, P., & Sakata, R. (1988). Asian Americans and rehabilitation: Some important variables. *Journal of Applied Rehabilitation Counseling, 19*, 16–20.

Lew, L.S. (1989, May). *Understanding the Southeast Asian health care consumer: Bridges and barriers*. Paper presented at the National Symposium on Genetic Services for the Medically Underserved, Washington, DC.

Li, C. (1983). The basic grammatical structures of selected Asian languages and English. In M. Chu-Chang (Ed.), *Asian- and Pacific-American perspectives in bilingual education: Comparative research* (pp. 3–30). New York: Teachers College Press.

Lim-Yee, N. (1983, April). *Parental reactions to a special needs child: Cultural differences and Chinese families*. Paper presented at the Annual Convention of the Western Psychological Association, San Francisco.

Lin, C.C., & Fu, V.R. (1990). A comparison of child-rearing practices among Chinese, immigrant Chinese, and Caucasian-American parents. *Child Development, 61*, 429–433.

Lin, K-M. (1983). Hwa-Byung: A Korean culture-based syndrome? *American Journal of Psychiatry, 140,* 105–107.

Lin, K-M., & Masuda, M. (1981). Impact of the refugee experience: Mental health issues of the Southeast Asians. In Special Service for Groups (Ed.), *Bridging cultures: Southeast Asian refugees in America* (pp. 32–52). Los Angeles: Asian American Mental Health Training Center.

Lin-Fu, J.S. (1987). Meeting the needs of Southeast Asian refugees in maternal and child health and primary care programs. In J.O. Cleveland (Ed.), *Service delivery models for outreach/prevention/intervention for Southeast Asian refugee infants, children, and their families—Conference proceedings* (app. E). San Diego: San Diego–Imperial Counties Developmental Services.

Luangpraseut,K. (1989). *Laos culturally speaking.* San Diego: San Diego State University, Multifunctional Resource Center.

MacMahon, H. (1977). *"Confucianism" the Korean way.* Seoul: Samsung.

Major, J.S. (1989). *The land and people of China.* New York: J.B. Lippincott.

Masterson, L. C-C. (1988, Summer). Chinese folk medicine and child abuse. *California Regional Centers Journal,* pp. 23–26.

Masterson, L. C-C. (1990, May). *Working with Chinese families.* Paper presented at the Lanterman Regional Center Conference, Enhancing Multicultural Awareness: Serving Immigrant Families, Los Angeles.

Morrow, R.D. (1989). Southeast Asian child rearing practices: Implications for child and youth care workers. *Child & Youth Care Quarterly, 18,* 273–287.

Muecke, M.A. (1983a). Caring for the Southeast Asian refugee. *American Journal of Public Health, 73,* 431–438.

Muecke, M.A. (1983b). In search of healers—Southeast Asian refugees in the American health care system. *Western Journal of Medicine, 139,* 835–840.

Mun, S.H. (1979). Shamanism in Korea. In Y.C. Shin (Ed.), *Korean thoughts* (pp. 17–36). Seoul: International Cultural Foundation.

Murase, K., Egawa, J., & Tashima, N. (1985). Alternative mental health services models in Asian/Pacific communities. In T.C. Owan (Ed.), *Southeast Asian mental health: Treatment, prevention, services, training, and research* (pp. 229–259). Washington, DC: National Institute of Mental Health.

National Indochinese Clearinghouse. (1980). *Glimpses of Hmong history and culture* (Indochinese Refugee Education Guides, General Information Series #16). Washington, DC: Author.

Nguyen, N.T. (1988, June 17). Perspective on the Southeast Asians in the United States. *Asian Week,* pp. 2, 19.

Nguyen, N., Nguyen, P.H., & Nguyen, L.H. (1987). *Coin treatment in Vietnamese families: Traditional medical practice vs. child abuse.* Unpublished paper.

Olness, K.N. (1986). On "Reflections on caring for Indochinese children and youths." *Developmental and Behavioral Pediatrics, 7,* 129–130.

Pan Asian Parent Education Project. (1982). *Pan Asian child rearing practices: Filipino, Japanese, Korean, Samoan, Vietnamese.* San Diego: Union of Pan Asian Communities.

Park, S.J., & Song, K.S. (1982). The Korean community. In Pan Asian Parent Education Project, *Pan Asian child rearing practices: Filipino, Japanese, Korean, Samoan, Vietnamese* (pp. 51–76). San Diego: Union of Pan Asian Communities.

Patterson, W., & Kim, H-C. (1986). *The Koreans in America.* Minneapolis: Lerner Publications.

Porter, J. (1983). *All under heaven: The Chinese world.* New York: Pantheon Books.

Randall-David, E. (1989). *Strategies for working with culturally diverse communities and clients.* Washington, DC: Association for the Care of Children's Health.

Roberts, R.N. (1990). *Workbook for: Developing culturally competent programs for children with special needs.* Washington, DC: Georgetown University Child Development Center.

Rogow, S.M. (1985, April). *Where service begins: Working with parents to provide early intervention, considerations for the culturally different.* Paper presented at the annual convention of the Council for Exceptional Children, Anaheim, CA.

Rumbaut, R.G. (1985). Mental health and the refugee experience: A comparative study of Southeast Asian refugees. In T.C. Owan (Ed.), *Southeast Asian mental health: Treatment, prevention, services, training, and research* (pp. 433–486). Washington, DC: National Institute of Mental Health.

Rutledge, P. (1987). *The Vietnamese in America.* Minneapolis: Lerner Publication Co.

Serafica, F.C. (1990). Counseling Asian American parents: A cultural-developmental framework. In F.C. Serafica, A.I. Schwebel, R.K. Russel, P.D. Isaac, & L.J. Meyers (Eds.), *Mental health of ethnic minorities.* New York: Praeger.

Shon, S. (1980). *Some aspects of psychotherapy with Asian and Pacific people.* Unpublished manuscript.

Shon, S.P., & Ja, D.Y. (1983). Asian families. In M. McGoldrick, J.K. Pearce, & J. Giordono (Eds.), *Ethnicity and family therapy* (pp. 208–228). New York: Guilford Press.

Shu, K.E. (1989). *Professional perceptions of differences in parental attitudes and behaviors and the behavioral manifestations of autism in Chinese and American children.* Unpublished doctoral dissertation, Teachers College, Columbia University, New York.

Siao, G.W-T. (1990, August 10). L.A. Koreans, blacks try to work out differences. *Asian Week,* pp. 14–15.

Sigel, I.E. (1988). Commentary: Cross-cultural studies of parental influence on children's achievement. *Human Development, 31,* 384–390.

Smith, M.J., & Ryan, A.S. (1987). Chinese-American families of children with developmental disabilities: An exploratory study of reactions to service providers. *Mental Retardation, 25,* 345–350.

Stevenson, H.W., & Lee, S. (1990). Contexts of achievement: A study of American, Chinese, and Japanese children. *Monographs of the Society for Research in Child Development, 55* (1–2, Serial No. 221).

Sue, D. (1981). Cultural and historical perspectives in counseling Asian Americans. In D. Sue (Ed.), *Counseling the culturally different: Theory and practice* (pp. 113–140). New York: John Wiley & Sons.

Sue, S., & Zane, N. (1987). The role of culture and cultural techniques in psychotherapy. *American Psychologist, 42,* 37–45.

Sung, B.L. (1971). *The story of the Chinese in America.* New York: Collier.

Takaki, R. (1989). *Strangers from a different shore: A history of Asian Americans.* Boston: Little, Brown.

Te, H.D. (1989a). *The Indochinese and their cultures.* San Diego: San Diego State University, Multifunctional Resource Center.

Te, H.D. (1989b). *Introduction to Vietnamese culture.* San Diego: San Diego State University, Multifunctional Resource Center.

Thuy, V.G. (1980). *Getting to know the Vietnamese and their culture.* New York: Frederick Unser Publishing Co.

Tinloy, M.T., Tan, A., & Leung, B. (1986). *Assessment of Chinese speaking limited English proficient students with special needs.* Sacramento, CA: Special Education Resource Network, Resource Service Center.

Tom, K.S. (1989). *Echoes from old China.* Honolulu: University of Hawaii Press.

Tou-Fou, V. (1981). The Hmong of Laos. In Special Service for Groups (Ed.), *Bridging cultures: Southeast Asian refugees in America* (pp. 73–82). Los Angeles: Asian American Mental Health Training Center.

Triandis, H.C., Brislin, R., & Hui, C.H. (1988). Cross-cultural training across the individualism-collectivism divide. *International Journal of Intercultural Relations, 12*, 269–289.

Union of Pan Asian Communities. (1980). *Understanding the Pan Asian client: Book II.* San Diego: Author.

U.S. Bureau of the Census. (1988). *Asian and Pacific Islander population in the United States: 1980.* Washington, DC: U.S. Government Printing Office.

U.S. Department of Health and Human Services. (1987). *Report to Congress: Refugee Resettlement Program.* Washington, DC: Office of Refugee Resettlement.

U.S. General Accounting Office. (1990). *Asian Americans: A status report.* Washington, DC: Author, Human Resources Division.

Walker, C.L. (1985). Learning English: The Southeast Asian refugee experience. *Topics in Language Disorders, 5*, 53–65.

Wang, W.S-Y. (1983). Speech and script relations in some Asian languages. In M. Chu-Chang (Ed.), *Asian- and Pacific-American perspectives in bilingual education: Comparative research* (pp. 56–72). New York: Teachers College Press.

Wei, T.T.D. (1983). The Vietnamese refugee child: Understanding cultural differences. In D.R. Omark & J.G. Erickson (Eds.), *The bilingual exceptional child* (pp. 197–212). San Diego: College-Hill Press.

Weisz, J.R., Rothbaum, F.M., & Blackburn, T.C. (1984). Standing out and standing in: The psychology of control in America and Japan. *American Psychologist, 39*, 955–969.

Wiemann, J., Chen, V., & Giles, H. (1986, November). *Beliefs about talk and silence in a cultural context.* Paper presented at the Speech Communication Association Convention, Chicago.

Wong, C. (1985, April–June). Yin and yang of nutrition. *Perinatal Nutrition Newsletter, California Department of Health Services*, p. 1.

Yao, E.L. (1988). Working effectively with Asian immigrant parents. *Phi Delta Kappan, 70*, 223–225.

Yeatman, G.W., & Dang, V.V. (1980). *Cao Gio* (coin rubbing) Vietnamese attitudes toward health care. *Journal of the American Medical Association, 244*, 2748–2749.

Young-Kwon, K. (1978). *A handbook of Korea.* Seoul: Korean Overseas Information Services.

Yu, E-Y. (1983). Korean communities in America: Past, present, and future. *Amerasia Journal, 10*, 23–51.

Yu, K.H., & Kim, L.I.C. (1983). The growth and development of Korean-American children. In G.J. Powell (Ed.), *The psychosocial development of minority group children* (pp. 147–158). New York: Brunner/Mazel.

Yum, J-O. (1987). Korean philosophy and communication. In D.L. Kincaid (Ed.), *Communication theory: Eastern and Western perspectives* (pp. 71–86). San Diego: Academic Press.

APPENDIX A
CONTRASTING BELIEFS, VALUES, AND PRACTICES

Traditional Asian	Dominant culture
<u>Civilization</u>: Agriculture	Industrial
• Harmony with nature	• Mastery over nature
<u>Religion</u>: Polytheistic, Spiritualistic, Humanistic	Monotheistic, Christian
<u>Philosophy</u>: Heart-oriented	Mind-oriented
• Comtemplative, circular thinking	• Analytic linear thinking
• Fatalism	• Personal control over environment and one's fate
• Stoicism, patience	• Optimism, eagerness to take action
• Tradition, living with the past	• Change, future orientation
• Being (person orientation)	• Doing (task orientation)
• Self-denial, self-discipline	• Self-assertiveness, self-gratification
• Spiritualism, detachment	• Materialism
<u>Social Orientation</u>: Collectivist (we)	Individual (I)
• Group welfare, public consciousness	• Self-actualization, privacy
• Mutual interdependence, collective responsibility, obligation, reciprocity	• Individual autonomy, independence, self-reliance
• Hierarchy, role rigidity, status defined by ascription (birthright inheritance, family name, age, sex)	• Equality, role flexibility, status defined by achievement
• Conformity	• Challenge or question authority
• Cooperation, nonconfrontation, and reconciliation	• Competition, aggressiveness
<u>Family</u>:	
• Family as primary unit	• Individual as primary unit
• Family solidarity, responsibility, and harmony	• Individual pursuit of happiness, fulfillment, and self-expression
• Continued dependence on family is fostered	• Early independence is encouraged

(continued)

251

Traditional Asian	Dominant culture
• Hierarchical family roles, ascribed status	• Variable roles, achieved status
• Parent–child (parental) bond is stressed	• Husband–wife (marital) bond is stressed
• Parent provides authority and expects unquestioning obedience, submission to structure	• Parent provides guidance, support, explanations, and encourages curiosity, critical/independent thinking
• Family makes decisions for the child	• Child is given many choices
• Children are extension of parents	• Children are individuals
• Parents ask: "What can you do to help me?"	• Parents ask: "What can I do to help you?"
• Older children are responsible for the siblings' actions	• Each child is responsible for his or her own actions
Expression: Indirect	Direct
• Implicit, nonverbal	• Explicit, verbal
• Formal	• Informal
• Goal oriented	• Spontaneous
• Emotionally controlled	• Emotionally expressive
• Self-effacing, modest	• Self-promoting, egocentric

APPENDIX B
CULTURAL COURTESIES AND CUSTOMS

The following behaviors and expectations should be considered when interacting with selected Asian American populations. Failure to recognize and respect culturally appropriate customs, gestures, and so forth, and/or acting in a contrary manner may risk offending clients and families who adhere to traditional social practices.

GREETINGS

- Greet family members in order of age, beginning with the oldest and typically the male members first.
- Use Mr., Mrs., Miss, or other appropriate title with the *family* name (surname) for Chinese and Koreans and with the individual's *first* (given) name for Cambodians, Lao, and Vietnamese.

Order

	1	2	3	Example	Formal greeting
Chinese	LAST		FIRST	Tien Chang-Lin	Dr. Tien
Korean	LAST		FIRST	Kim Bok-Lim	Mrs. Kim
Cambodian	LAST		FIRST	Pok Than	Mr. Than
Lao	FIRST		LAST	Kamchong Luangpraseut	Mr. Kamchong
Vietnamese	LAST	MIDDLE	FIRST	Nguyen Van Hai	Mr. Hai

After marriage, Chinese, Korean, and Vietnamese women typically keep their own family name and do not combine it with their husbands' family name (e.g., if a Miss Lee marries a Mr. Chen, she may be referred to as Mrs. Lee).

- Women typically do not shake hands with men. Younger people do not shake hands with an elder or significantly older person. While a handshake between men is often acceptable, an initial slight bow before shaking hands or waiting for the other man to extend his hand first may be more appropriate. (The traditional Lao greeting or *wai* consists of bowing one's head slightly, joining hands and raising them from the chest to the head—depending upon the degree of respect one wishes to express).
- Kissing, hugging, slapping a person on the back, or putting one's arm around another's shoulders is considered inappropriate. In general, direct physical contact (particularly between men and women) should be avoided.

(continued)

NONVERBAL COMMUNICATION

- Avoid prolonged gazing or expecting direct/sustained eye-to-eye contact with individuals who are relative stangers and in formal interactions.
- Touching the head (including a child's) is often considered threatening or offensive by Cambodians, Lao, and selected Buddhists because of the spiritual belief that it is the most sacred part of the body.
- Waving arms to elicit attention, and pointing or beckoning with an index finger are considered to be signs of contempt. Instead, point with an open hand and indicate "come here" by waving the fingers of one hand closed together with the palm down, facing inward.
- Winking or batting one's eyes at another is impolite.
- When sitting, if one's legs are crossed, the soles and toes of the feet should point downward or away from the other person. In very formal situations, keep both feet on the floor and place hands in the lap or keep them visible.
- Emotional restraint, formality, reserve, tact, and politeness are essential. Avoid engaging in demonstrative behavior and talking or laughing loudly.

CONVERSATION

- In an initial encounter or first meeting, refrain from asking personal questions of the other party too quickly, but be prepared for people to ask personal questions of you (e.g., "Where are you from?" "How old are you?" "Are you married?" "How many children do you have?").
- Avoid talking about what people think of the government and current foreign policy issues or internal political events/affairs pertaining to their native country.

PRIVATE HOMES

- Removing one's shoes before entering a house is considered appropriate for many Asian groups.
- Expect to be offered food or drinks, and partake of such hospitality.
- If a guest comments or offers compliments about a particular household object, the host may feel compelled to give it to him or her as a gift.

GIFT GIVING

- Gifts are offered and received with both hands (as is the case with politely handing something to another person or receiving other objects).
- Gifts are typically not opened in the presence of the giver(s).

HOLIDAYS

The principal holiday for most Asian countries is the Lunar New Year. New Year's Day is the first day of the first month of the lunar calendar; it usually falls between January 19th and February 20th (Cambodians and Lao celebrate their New Year's Day in the fifth month of the lunar calendar—usually falling in mid-April, just after harvest time). The Vietnamese New Year's Day is known as "Tet" and is celebrated throughout the country for a period of several days.

More detailed information regarding specific customs and practices associated with the Lunar New Year as well as other native holidays celebrated by Chinese, Koreans, and Southeast Asians is provided by Brigham Young University (1988), Devine and Braganti (1986), Te (1989a), and Tom (1989).

AGES, BIRTHDATES, BIRTHDAYS

Among the Chinese and Vietnamese, age is traditionally counted from the time of conception and thereafter according to the lunar calendar. A child is thus considered 1 year old at birth. He or she then becomes 2 years old on New Year's Day of the lunar calendar, even if born as late as the last day of the preceding lunar year. New Year's Day is thus especially meaningful because it serves as the common birthday for the entire nation; everyone becomes one year older at that time.

Personal birthdays are typically not celebrated except one month after the birth of an infant son, and on the first anniversary of his birth. The Chinese celebrate these two birthday occasions by hosting a "red egg and ginger" party for relatives and friends. At this time, red-tinted hard-boiled eggs and sliced pickled ginger (symbols of a new birth) are served with a feast or dinner. In the initial celebration at age 1 month, the infant son was traditionally given a first name at that time and his head was shaved by an elder, grandparent, or his mother. He was then dressed in a red gown (red is the color of good luck) and carried to the temple by his father wherein the gods and spirits of ancestors were notified of the birth of a son. Special offerings of foods, including red eggs and ginger, were also made at that time.

OTHER CUSTOMS/BELIEFS

While red is the color of good luck, white is the color of mourning and represents death; it is the color typically worn at funerals. Thus, when entering a

(continued)

255

hospital for the first time, seeing white sheets and doctors and nurses in white may suggest that those who stay there are going to die.

Another belief among Chinese and Koreans is that the number four is unlucky; when translated, it sounds like the word "death." The number four in combination with other numbers also translate into threatening phrases and may lead to avoidance of various homes/businesses with corresponding addresses. The number eight is synonymous with "prosperity" and is believed to bring good luck and fortune.

APPENDIX D
VOCABULARY

| English | Chinese | | Korean | Vietnamese |
	Cantonese	Mandarin		
Hello	Nay-ho	Nee-how	Ahn-nyong-ha-say-yo (In person)	Chao qui ong (Mr.)/ba (Mrs.)
Goodbye	Joy-geen	Jai-jen	Ahn-nyong-hee-ga-say-yo (Person leaving) Ahn-nyong-hee-gye-say-yo (Person staying)	Xing Chao
Yes	Heigh	Suhr	Yeh	Vang
No	Mm-heigh	Boo-suhr	Ah-nee yo	Khong
Please	Ching-nay	Ching-nee	Jeh-song hahm-nee-dah	Xing
Thank you	Doh-jeh	Sheh-sheh	Kahm-sah hahm-nee dah	Kam on
Father	Ba-ba	Fu-cheen	Ah buh ji	Cha
Mother	Ma-ma	Mu-cheen	Un muh ni	Meh
Family	Gah-ting	Ja-ting	Gah jok	Gia-dinh

chapter 9 ⎯⎯⎯⎯⎯⎯⎯⎯⎯⎯⎯⎯

FAMILIES WITH
PILIPINO ROOTS

Sam Chan

He who does not know where he came from will not get to where he is going.

Financial indebtedness is easily paid but not a debt of kindness.

Gentle speech will soften a hard heart.

If they throw stones at you, throw them bread.

Silent water is deep. Noisy water is shallow.

Clean your own yard before you clean another's.

The hardest person to awaken is the one who is already awake.

While averaging about 40,000 admissions per year, Pilipinos are the largest Asian immigrant group to the United States and the second largest (after Mexicans) of all legal immigrant groups (Cariño, Fawcett, Gardner, & Arnold, 1990).

> To understand why, among all countries in Southeast Asia, the Philippines is the largest contributor to U.S. immigration, it is important to take into account the country's long colonial experience with the United States. Although decolonization occurred several decades ago, the formal severing of political ties does not sunder overnight the social, cultural, and economic links that bind former colonies and mother countries and generate population movements between them. The Americanization of Filipino culture is pervasive and a major factor in the integration of Filipinos to the United States. (Cariño, 1987, pp. 308, 310)

⎯⎯⎯⎯⎯⎯⎯⎯

The reader will note the spelling "Pilipino" throughout this chapter. The term "Pilipino" came into use during the ethnic consciousness movement of the late 1960s. It was argued that "Filipino" was a remnant of the colonized mentality because the pre-Hispanic Tagalog language did not contain an "F" sound. More recently, others have argued that some languages in the Philippine Islands do have "F" sounds, making the use of "F" or "P" a matter of individual preference (Attorney General's Asian and Pacific Islander Advisory Committee [Attorney General], 1988).

BACKGROUND

While Pilipinos may have a decidedly Western orientation and share a heritage of many significant ideas and values rooted in Euro-Christian ethics, their traditional social and cultural characteristics contrast sharply with those of mainstream America. The Pilipino "national character" and sense of identity is thus complex. Although the Philippines is located geographically in Asia. "There is a general sense of being neither this nor that, of sharing something of the Pacific islands, of being heavily influenced by Spanish and American cultures, and of perceiving only a remote historical relationship with the major cultures of Asia" (Gochenour, 1990, p. 42). Further examination of the unique history of the Philippines and of Pilipino immigration to the United States serves to illustrate how this country has been a "Pacific Bridge" between many cultures.

Geographic and Historical Origins

The Republic of the Philippines is a rugged 1,000-mile-long archipelago bounded on the north by Taiwan and on the south by Indonesia. It is a nation of 7,100 islands and islets with a tropical climate and mountainous terrain. Most of the people live on the coastal plains of the 11 largest islands (out of approximately 500 islands that are inhabited). These islands are divided into three major geographic groups: 1) Luzon, the largest and one of the most northern islands (where Manila and the new capital, Quezon City, are located), Mindoro, and Palawan; 2) the Visayas or central islands, which include Cebu, Negros, Leyte, Panay, Samar, Masbate, and Bohol; and 3) Mindanao, the southernmost island (Gochenour, 1990; Pan Asian Parent Education Project [PAPEP], 1982; Winter, 1988).

Pilipinos have developed certain stereotypic perceptions about people from these respective island groups. Ilocanos (who inhabit a barren region called Illocos in northern Luzon) are people who have endured many hardships throughout history and are perceived as being spartan, industrious, thrifty, and proud of their culture. Tagalogs (who live in the central plains and southern area of Luzon) are viewed as more cosmopolitan, urbane, nationalistic, and Western-oriented. The people of the Visayan or central islands have been described as a cross between Ilocanos and Tagalogs. The people of Mindanao have been highly influenced by Islam and Muslim cultures (PAPEP, 1982).

The Philippines is the most ethnically diverse country in Asia, and native Pilipinos are descendants of many racial groups. The three major indigenous groups include the Negritos, the Malays, and the Indonesians. Among the original migrants to the Philippines (about 25,000 to 30,000 years ago) were pygmy people, ancestors of the Negritos, who today inhabit the remote rain forests of northern Luzon. The Negritos were ultimately displaced by successive waves of Malays who began arriving in about 1500 B.C. The Malays constructed the astounding irrigated rice terraces along the mountain slopes in northern Luzon—"one of the wonders of the world" (Winter, 1988, p. 10).

They also introduced many elements of a more advanced civilization, including a written language. In fact, much of Pilipino culture, including the Tagalog language, has Malay roots. Moreover, about one third of present-day Pilipinos are descendants of the Malays (Gochenour, 1990; Winter, 1988). Subsequent invasions by Indonesians and the entry of Arab and Chinese traders and settlers further contributed to enduring Hindu, Confucian, and Islamic influences that have profoundly affected Pilipino culture. Chinese, in fact, are now the second largest ethnic group in the Philippines (PAPEP, 1982).

History of Colonialism

In 1521, Magellan led a Spanish expedition to make the official European discovery of the archipelago that was later named the "Filipinas," in honor of the Spanish prince who became Philip II, King of Spain (Winter, 1988). As the first white people to come to the Philippines, the Europeans imported "colonialism"— the idea of owning a territory thousands of miles from home, inhabited by people culturally and racially different from themselves. Spain's conquest of the Philippines was followed by 400 years of Spanish rule in which the missionaries, government officials, and representatives of the Spanish empire imprinted upon the Pilipino culture and consciousness some of its most enduring characteristics. Most of the population was converted to Hispanic Catholicism, and the visible aspects of culture (e.g., fine arts, dress, cuisine, customs) were heavily influenced or modified. Centuries of Spanish rule also left Pilipinos with "a legacy of attitudes that are firmly embedded in society: an equation of light skin with status, the identification of foreign with authority and indigenous with inferiority, and a conception of officialdom as a system serving its own ends, not those of the people" (Gochenour, 1990, p. 6).

The development of an emerging national consciousness eventually led to the Philippine Revolution toward the close of the 19th century. In the context of the Spanish–American War, American military forces arrived in Manila in 1898 as allies of the Pilipinos against the Spanish. Although the rebels were promised Philippine independence in return for their support in land battles against the Spanish, they were ultimately betrayed. Following the Spanish defeat, the Philippines were ceded to the United States. American leaders claimed that while they had not entered the war to gain territory, they did not believe that the Philippines were yet ready for independence (Winter, 1988). In later explaining how he had made the decision to approve the annexation of the Philippines, President William McKinley said he had gone down on his knees to pray for "light and guidance" from the "ruler of nations" and had been told by God that it was America's duty to "educate" and "uplift" the Pilipinos. He echoed the sentiments of American Protestant clergy leaders who sought to fulfill the "manifest destiny" of the Christian Republic through the conquest of Asia; in fact, McKinley rhetorically asked, "Do we need their consent to perform a great act for humanity?" (Takaki, 1989, p. 324).

The people of this new American possession were seen by their guardians as backward natives to be "civilized" by Americans seeking to carry the "white man's burden" (Takaki, 1989). The goal of annexation thus was based on an ideology of racial and religious supremacy while being further justified in terms of corresponding commercial and military gains. In response to this betrayal and seizure, Pilipinos continued their struggle for independence—this time against the United States. The ensuing bitter and bloody 3-year campaign (1898–1901) waged by the United States to overcome the "Philippine Insurrection" resulted in the deaths of nearly 1 million Pilipinos (Gochenour, 1990; Winter, 1988).

One form of colonialism thus was replaced with another. Americans, in the presumed spirit of white paternalism and benevolence, saw themselves as bestowers of education, religion, public health, development, and democracy to their "little brown brothers" (Gochenour, 1990). Thirty years later, the Pilipinos became self-governing, and the Tydings-McDuffie Act of 1934 promised complete independence by 1946. However, the country remained a territorial possession of the United States, which retained control over its economy and military forces.

World War II came abruptly to the Philippines. The Japanese attacked Manila within a few hours after Pearl Harbor and took over the country 5 months later. The ultimate Japanese surrender and close of World War II brought the return of the exiled Philippine government to Manila. Moreover, the United States kept its promise and, on July 4, 1946, the Philippines was finally granted its long-sought independence and proclaimed the Republic of the Philippines (Winter, 1988).

A long history of external domination and influence remains potent in Pilipino life and thought. None of the attitudinal legacies of the Spanish were removed by 4 decades of U.S. rule. Yet, the pervasive Americanization of Pilipino culture also occurred—as evidenced by the fact that years after independence, Pilipino schoolchildren were still learning the American Pledge of Allegiance, and their education focused more on the United States than on neighboring countries in the Pacific. Two successive colonial eras led to the saying: "The Filipino is a product of four centuries of the convent and two generations of Hollywood" (Gochenour, 1990, p. 32). Contemporary Pilipino culture is thus a composite of foreign and indigenous elements. "Neither history nor geography permitted the Filipinos time to consolidate their parochial and isolated strands into a culture integrated enough to repel outside pressures and influence" (Gochenour, 1990, p. 5). Nevertheless, despite centuries of colonialism, Pilipinos never allowed themselves to become "carbon copies" of their rulers. They have pursued a dual historical path of understanding, accommodating to, placating, or opposing the overwhelming power foreigners have exercised in their lives while simultaneously preserving what is essentially Pilipino in themselves (Gochenour, 1990).

Waves of Immigration

Similar to other Asian immigrants, Pilipinos have come to the United States in successive waves. However, unlike the Chinese, Japanese, and Koreans, Pilipino migrants came from a territory of the United States. Thus, despite the restrictions placed on the immigration of workers from other parts of Asia, Pilipinos migrated freely to the United States, protected by their colonial status as U.S. "nationals." Although they were preceded by relatively small groups of *pensionados* (students), the "first wave" of Pilipino immigrants were brought into the United States in response to massive recruiting campaigns in the early 1900s by agricultural interests (particularly the sugar industry) in Hawaii and California. These immigrants consisted mainly of young, single, male contract laborers "Sakadas" from the Ilocos region. Between 1906 and 1934, about 120,000 Pilipinos came to Hawaii and the West Coast. Pilipinos were hired in large numbers to fill the void of cheap labor when Oriental exclusion policies and the passage of the Immigration Act of 1924 completely halted Chinese, Japanese, Korean, and Asian Indian immigration. While the Sakadas worked in Hawaiian plantations, the West Coast "Pinoys" were concentrated in three general types of work; agricultural "stoop" labor (particularly on large California farms), domestic and personal services, and the fishing and canning industries that extended from California to the Pacific Northwest and Alaska (Okamura & Agbayani, 1991; Takaki, 1989; Winter, 1988).

While enjoying protected status as U.S. nationals, Pilipinos were not immune from the racial discrimination that other Asian groups had traditionally experienced. Anti-Pilipino sentiment grew in proportion to their increasing numbers and, as the Great Depression engulfed the nation, fear and hatred mounted. White-nativist reactions against Pilipinos were fueled by intensifying economic competition between white workers and Pilipino laborers. This ethnic hostility erupted into racial violence, including vigilante activity and a series of widely publicized race riots in California farming towns in 1929 and 1930. The extreme anti-Pilipino violence was further rooted in fears of Pilipino sexuality. The refusal of Pilipino men to accept the color bar in their frequent relationships with white women triggered resentment, anxieties, and underlying fear of their "threat to white racial purity." California's antimiscegenation law that prohibited marriage between whites and "Negroes, mulattoes, or Mongolians" thus was amended in 1933 to add persons of the Malay race to the restricted category (12 other states had similar laws). Increasingly viewed as social "undesirables" with "offensive personality traits and behavior" (Okamura & Agbayani, 1991), Pilipinos nonetheless competed (sometimes all too successfully) for jobs and for white women (Posadas, 1986–87). The exclusionist movement, led by organized labor, claimed that Pilipinos were biologically unassimilable, did not "belong," and should not be permitted to immigrate to the United States. However, the Pilipino "problem" had no easy solution. A repatriation scheme at the height of the Depression failed, and national immigration restriction and West Coast antimiscegenation laws promised only limited control.

Finally, in 1934, the Tydings-McDuffie Act closed the door to Pilipino immigration by reclassifying all Philippine-born Pilipinos as aliens and limiting their immigration to 50 persons a year (Attorney General, 1988). Although ostensibly passed in order to establish the Philippines as a commonwealth and to provide independence in 10 years, the real purpose of the act was Pilipino exclusion. A year later, Congress responded to the demands of exclusionists and passed the Repatriation Act; this law offered Pilipinos free one-way transportation to the Philippines on the condition that they forfeit their right of reentry to the United States. Thus, originally allowed to enter the United States as "cheap labor," Pilipino migrants had completed their "period of service to American capital" and were no longer wanted because of their labor militancy or needed because of the availability of Mexican labor (Takaki, 1989, p. 333). But most of the Pilipino sojourners (who originally did not see America as a place to bring families and to settle) did not return to the Philippines. Racial prejudices, social isolation, and persecution minimized the "old-timers' " (or first-generation "Manongs") chances for acculturation, and resulted in their retention of traditional Pilipino culture as they struggled for survival in America (Santos, 1983). Their "real" story was later chronicled with great detail and sensitivity in the writings of Carlos Bulosan (1946), who drew deeply from his own experiences and those of fellow Pilipinos to give his compatriots their voices.

Following the passage of the Tydings-McDuffie Act in 1934, emigration from the Philippines dropped to a mere trickle. The "second wave" of Pilipino immigrants occurred between 1946 and 1964. During World War II, thousands of Pilipino nationals were "permitted" to serve in the armed forces or to work in defense factories. Through their often-heroic deeds, profound contributions, and sacrifices to the war effort (more than half of the 200,000 Pilipinos who served in World War II were killed), Pilipinos dramatically proved their loyalty to the United States, despite years of discrimination and violence. A corresponding positive change in American attitudes toward Pilipinos resulted in new policies, laws, and rulings that gave resident Pilipinos the right to own property and to become citizens, and declared antimiscegenation laws unconstitutional. The passage of the War Brides Act of 1946 further allowed resident Pilipinos who had served in the U.S. armed forces in the Philippines and who had married there, to bring their wives, children, and dependents to the United States. As military "push" and "pull" forces contributed to this second wave of Pilipino immigration, new employment opportunities opened up in areas such as aircraft, electronics, and chemical industries; the newer immigrants (unlike the first-wave "old-timer" Pinoys of the pre–World War II era who were largely agricultural laborers) were also able to find jobs as clerks and accountants, and in many other fields formerly closed to them (Winter, 1988). Nonetheless, it has taken over 40 years to fulfill the promise of citizenship to the Pilipino veterans of World War II. The recent passage of the Immigration Act of 1990 finally enables the estimated 50,000 surviving Pilipino veterans (most of whom are still living in the Philippines) to be eligible for U.S. citizenship (Meinert, 1990).

The "third wave" of Pilipino immigrants has occurred since the 1965 U.S. immigration reform, which eliminated the restrictive national-origins quota system and dramatically increased the number of immigrants admitted from Asia as a whole. The new law favored the entry of relatives of people already living in the United States and of professionals. With regard to the latter group, one major consequence of the 1965 amendments has been the "brain drain" from the Philippines: the immigration of persons with professional and technical qualifications. In 1970, for example, nearly one half of all Pilipino immigrants were professionals (including scientists, engineers, attorneys, accountants, teachers, physicians, nurses, and pharmacists). Facilitated by an educational system that reflects American modes of learning, programs, practices, and priorities, the country was producing college graduates much faster than a primarily agriculturally based economy could absorb them (Morales, 1974; Pernia, 1976). Some have argued that this professional emigration represents lost educational investment in that the Philippines bears the cost of educating this highly skilled labor but does not directly benefit from it (Cariño, 1987). While the "brain drain" from the Philippines has been considerably reduced since the 1970s, large numbers of highly educated young adults and professionals have continued to immigrate to the United States in search of better employment opportunities.

The "third wave" or post-1965 "newcomer" immigrants include those immigrating to the present time; however, a "fourth wave" of immigrants were those who fled the Philippines as political exiles and refugees during the martial law era, beginning in 1972 and continuing for nearly 10 years. This was a period in which Ferdinand Marcos (originally elected president of the Philippines in 1965) began to rule by decree after the Congress was dissolved, the Constitution was revoked, and opposition leaders were arrested. Under a new constitution, Marcos retained absolute power to act as both president and prime minister for an unlimited time. Among those who ultimately left the Philippines to live in self-imposed exile in the United States was former senator Benigno Aquino, Jr., leader of the increasingly popular "People's Power" party and Marcos's most important political opponent (Winter, 1988). Aquino's momentous return to the Philippines on August 21, 1983 and his immediate assassination upon deplaning at the Manila airport triggered an accelerated anti-Marcos movement—one that had long been supported and promoted by Pilipino American activists and fourth-wave political exiles/refugees, who were instrumental in alerting the American public to the mounting atrocities committed by the Marcos regime and years of dictatorial abuse and misrule. Thus, when Corazon

(Cory) Aquino, the slain senator's widow, announced her candidacy for president in a "snap election" (which Marcos had hastily called to appease U.S. supporters), she effectively unleashed the "People Power" movement (Bello & Reyes, 1986–87). Marcos's subsequent "official" victory was the result of massive election fraud, which resulted in the United States switching its support to Corazon Aquino. A relatively immediate, but remarkably peaceful revolution and transition of power followed. After 20 years of Marcos rule, he was finally ousted, and Cory Aquino was installed as the first woman president of the Philippines in March 1986.

The "people's victory" and Corazon Aquino's new leadership offered the promise of democratic reform and touched the hearts of many Americans— whose understanding of the Philippines unfortunately often begins and ends with a "woman dressed in yellow" (Gochenour, 1989). Within recent years, the news media have also focused on coup attempts by Marcos loyalists, Communist insurgency attacks, and growing anti-American sentiment related to the giant U.S. military bases, the most visible symbol of America's long-standing military presence in the Philippines (Drogin, 1990, September 25). Internal political unrest and instability have been fueled by severe and persistent social and economic problems: rapid population growth and increasing density and scarcity of land; rampant inflation, unemployment, and widespread poverty; and huge foreign debt and domination by foreign capital (Cariño, 1987). These "push" conditions contribute to the daily exodus of over 1,000 skilled and unskilled workers, who leave Manila to seek their fortunes abroad, and the more than 300,000 Pilipinos who apply for visas to the United States each year (Drogin, 1990, September 14, September 25). Thus, while the future of the Philippines remains very uncertain, continued mass immigration to the United States and other countries is inevitable.

Religious Origins

The Philippines is the only nation in Asia that is predominantly Christian. Due to over 400 years of rule by Spain, about 85% of the population is Roman Catholic (Winter, 1988). "During centuries of Spanish colonialism, Catholicism was the only acceptable faith, and its teachings, vocabulary, and practices left an indelible stamp upon Filipino consciousness" (Gochenour, 1990, p. 34). The American occupation also brought Protestantism to the Philippines. Today, Pilipinos exhibit a growing interest in various evangelical and charismatic movements. Thus, while 3% of the population is Protestant, 6% belong to indigenous Christian cults, including the Philippine Independent (or Aglipayan) Church, and *Iglesia ni Kristo* (Church of Christ), an independent offshoot of the Catholic church (Brigham Young University [BYU], 1986; Gochenour, 1990).

As a result of contact with Arab and other Muslim traders who frequented the southern part of the archipelagos during the 14th and 15th centuries, Islam was already a presence in the Philippines before the arrival of the Spanish.

Today, Islam is a significant minority religion that is predominant in much of the southern island of Mindanao. About 5% of the Pilipinos are Muslims (called Moros). The historical tension between Christians and Muslims continues, and the fiercely independent Moros have maintained a separatist movement that has challenged the Philippine government and spilled over into direct confrontation and violence (BYU, 1986; Gochenour, 1990). Finally, a small percentage of the Philippine population is Buddhist, and, in remote areas, rural peoples are still influenced by traditional folk beliefs and practices that preceded Spanish colonial rule.

A great many Pilipinos may be followers of Roman Catholicism, but they may still practice ancient rituals. In fact, Pilipino people are known to blend more "primitive" beliefs with Christian practices imposed on them through a history of conquest and colonialism. This, like many other Asian ethnic groups, Pilipinos may assume a polytheistic orientation (PAPER, 1982).

Language/Linguistic Origins

Throughout the 7,100-island archipelagos, Pilipinos speak 87 languages and dialects. The three major dialects are Ilocano (northern Luzon), Tagalog (central and southern Luzon), and Cebuano (southern islands) (BYU, 1986). Linguistically, these three dialects and all major Pilipino languages are historically related as a subfamily of the Austronesian languages and share most of their basic grammatical features (Li, 1983). Despite their similarities, centuries of isolation have produced distinct and mutually unintelligible languages (Gochenour, 1990). Regional divisions and linguistic differences and barriers have thus endured to the present; they have created major difficulties in promoting educational and cultural development (PAPEP, 1980).

For a period of time during the Marcos regime, there was a popular movement to establish and mandate the use of a national language called "Pilipino." Pilipino is primarily Tagalog, the language spoken by a minority of people in the Manila region, with a few words invented or borrowed from other Pilipino dialects. Because of its main basis in Tagalog, Pilipino has never gained full acceptance by speakers of other dialects, although it is a required subject of study in the public schools throughout the islands (BYU, 1986; Gochenour, 1990).

With so many dialects, English has been and continues to be the unifying language. In fact, the Philippines has the third-largest English-speaking population in the world (BYU, 1986). English is the language of the public schools (from fourth grade through college) and is the de facto national language of commerce, law, government, and often popular entertainment. It is the language of status, wealth, and authority. The power of English and its selective usage is exemplified in the Pilipino home environment. Members of a Pilipino family will typically speak to one another in their particular regional dialect, with an added sprinkling of English words. Yet is is very possible for the father, when admonishing a child, to summon up a tone of authority by employing a few English words or shifting entirely into English if he can. Similarly, educated Pilipino friends may normally converse in their local dialect, but gradually shift into English if the subject becomes technical or especially serious. This shifting may be related to vocabulary, but it often reflects the way Pilipinos feel about the language. "Things may be easier to say in English, or the use of English may serve to emphasize the importance of the topic. The speakers may feel that they can be more precise in English or that English is less personal and not as potentially threatening" (Gochenour, 1990, p. 38).

The use of English can also affect sensitivities. If, for example, in an ordinary transaction between two Pilipinos, one of them addresses the other in English, it may be viewed as an attempt to show off and to "put down" the other. Moreover, the Pilipino tendency to equate facility in English with social class and intelligence may foster self-consciousness and insecurity in dialogues with native English-speaking Americans. Many Pilipino immigrants pride themselves on being English speakers and may have demeaned those in the Philippines who speak *carabao* (water buffalo) or "bamboo English." However, once in the United States, they may find their own version of English to be unacceptable and a cause for embarrassment (Santos, 1983). Furthermore, when speaking to Pilipino immigrants who appear to be fluent in English, Americans usually presume that their English language comprehension is extensive, while often it is not. This expectation obviously contributes strain in Pilipino–American interactions, "tension which the American is certain to feel much less than the Filipino," who is typically his or her own harshest critic (Gochenour, 1990, p. 40).

English in the Philippines often contains an admixture of indigenous language elements. A Pilipino's first language or native dialect significantly influences his or her accent, intonation, vocabulary, syntax, and idiomatic expressions when he or she speaks English (Santos, 1983). The phonological systems of the various languages are also a factor. For example, because Tagalog distinguishes more vowel sounds than do other dialects, a Pilipino from Manila finds it naturally easier to make the distinction in English between, say, "bit" and "bet" than would someone from Cebu. As previously noted, the sound of "f" does not occur in most of the indigenous languages of the islands; thus, Pilipinos commonly substitute the "p" sound for "f." The native English speaker hearing the sentence, "I *prepered* this report," could easily be uncertain whether the Pilipino speaker meant "I preferred this report" or "I prepared this report" (Gochenour, 1990, p. 39).

Indigenous Philippine languages are prepositional, verb-initial (i.e., basic sentences have their verbs in the sentence-initial position), and regularly stress the next-to-last syllable in most words (Li, 1983). Like many other Asian languages, they also have a single word for the gender pronouns, "he" and "she." Apart from grammatical and phonological characteristics, it is noteworthy that one particular dialect called "Chabacano" (a local language spoken in the area around the city of Zamboanga in Mindanao) is heavily mixed with Spanish. Other Pilipinos know a fair number of Spanish words that have entered their particular regional dialects, and many Pilipino people and places have Spanish names. However, as a functional language, Spanish is clearly peripheral, and a relatively small number of Pilipinos speak it fluently (particularly because it was used exclusively by the upper classes during the period of Spanish rule) (Gochenour, 1990; Winter, 1988).

The Philippines is regarded as the only nation in Asia that is predominantly English speaking, and Pilipinos are often assumed to be fully proficient in the English language. The preceding discussion, however, serves to illustrate the reality of an extremely multilingual country where English is a second language. It also offers cautions and considerations regarding the dynamics of communication with English-speaking Pilipinos.

CONTEMPORARY LIFE

The 1990 Census population count indicated that there are 1.4 million Pilipinos living in the United States, the second largest Asian American group (next to the Chinese). Pilipinos are among the fastest growing groups and constitute nearly 20% of the Asian and Pacific Islander population in the United States (U.S. Bureau of the Census [USBC], 1991). Well over two thirds of the Pilipino American population is concentrated in the West with over 50% of their total in California and another 12% in Hawaii. The next largest numbers of Pilipinos are found in Illinois, New York, New Jersey, and Washington. The Pilipino American population is primarily urban, with the greatest concentrations in cities and metropolitan areas such as Los Angeles–Long Beach; San Francisco–Oakland; Honolulu; New York; Chicago; Washington, D.C.; Seattle; San Diego; and Stockton and San Jose, California (USBC, 1988a).

Due to prior and ongoing Pilipino immigration to the United States, nearly two thirds of the Pilipino American population is foreign born. However, the vast majority of Pilipinos age 15 years and over are American citizens. Further reflecting their substantial immigrant numbers is the fact that about two thirds of Pilipinos (age 5 years and older) speak a language other than English at home (USBC, 1988b).

With regard to employment and socioeconomic status, Pilipinos are among the highest ranked Asian American groups. A majority of Pilipinos are employed in technical, sales, and administrative support work, and as managers and professionals. Pilipinos' reputation as a "hardworking" people is supported by the following facts: Among Asian Americans, Pilipinos have the highest percentage of their population (age 16 years and over) in the labor force, the highest percentage of employed women, and the highest proportion of families with three or more workers (USBC, 1988b). With regard to median family income, Pilipinos rank third behind Japanese and Asian Indians. However, Pilipino female individual income is foremost among Asian Americans and considerably above the national median (USBC, 1988b). (More recent demographic data for specific Asian American groups based upon the 1990 census were not available at the time of the writing of this chapter.)

The educational attainment of Pilipino Americans is relatively high. Pilipinos are also unique among Asian Americans in having a greater proportion of female than male high school and college graduates. These characteristics are consistent with the fact that the Pilipino immigrant population includes more women and more people with generally superior educational qualifications and occupational experience than the population of the Philippines (Cariño et al., 1990).

The preceding review of social, economic, and educational characteristics of the Pilipino American population indicates that they compare very favorably to other Asian American groups as well as to national medians and rates. However, if adjustments are made for nonethnic factors such as years of work experience, education, and generation, Pilipinos may be shown to earn considerably less than their white counterparts and must confront persistent conditions of underemployment and "glass ceilings" (Suzuki, 1989). A particularly well-known and well-documented aspect of this phenomenon is that many Pilipino medical and health care professionals remain unlicensed and working in jobs that are either totally unrelated to their training and education or considerably below their former positions in the Philippines (Takaki, 1989). In addition to this pattern of occupational downgrading, there are also substantial differences in the socioeconomic status among Pilipinos in the various states. Pilipinos in Hawaii, for example, are one of the most economically disadvantaged and have the lowest educational attainment of any of the major ethnic groups (Okamura & Agbayani, 1991).

Third- or fourth-wave, post-1965 Pilipino immigrants are thus vulnerable to related social and psychological problems. The experience of downward occupational mobility, for example, results in considerable loss of self-esteem, disappointment, frustration, and possible depression. Many Pilipino professionals who came to the United States in search of better economic opportunities are often shocked to learn that their previous education and employment experiences are not legitimately valued or even recognized; they must confront the failure experience of being rejected for positions they thought they were qualified to hold (Okamura & Agbayani, 1991). Many miss the psychological benefits of higher status, social privileges, and greater respect and recognition that they enjoyed in the Philippines—even though the financial compensation for their work was inadequate. Those Pilipino immigrants from the upper echelons of Philippine society must confront the American reality that family names associated with high social status in their native country are now common Spanish surnames that may translate into "second-class" citizenship (Santos, 1983).

The problems associated with loss of ascribed status, social dislocation, and employment discrimination are often compounded by family stresses and generational conflicts. The cultural discontinuities experienced by most immigrant families contribute to a weakening of extended-family ties, loss of parental authority and credibility, and increasing youth alienation—characterized in part by Pilipino youth gang activity and disproportionate numbers of Pilipino American school dropouts. Young people are likely to reject their parents' and other elders' advice to be patient and hope that the next generation fares better. The young may accuse their elders of colonial mentality while the elders accuse the young of being shameless and ungrateful (Santos, 1983). The continuing clashes between traditional Pilipino values and those of the "host" society are discussed in detail in the following section.

VALUES

Family

To understand Filipinos is to accept the complete centrality of the family—and that means the extended family, including several generations. No other single aspect of life is likely to be as important, lasting or influential on choices and decisions from childhood to old age. . . . [The typical Pilipino individual] exists first and foremost as a member of a family and looks to the family as the only reliable protection against the uncertainties of life. (Gochenour, 1990, p. 18)

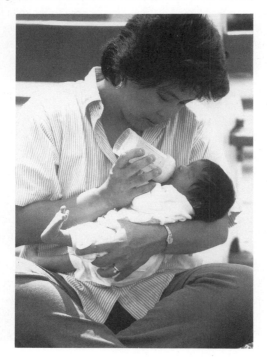

Reliance upon the family for love, support, and refuge has historically been as much an economic necessity as it is a cultural tradition. However, the Pilipino relationship to family is not just a practical trade-off of autonomy for social security. It transcends socioeconomic, educational, and regional differences and is part of a collectivistic cultural orientation or way of perceiving the place of the individual in the social context (Gochenour, 1990; Santos, 1983). Thus, for Pilipinos, the family is the source of one's personal identity and of emotional and material support; it is also the focus of one's primary duty and commitment (Okamura & Agbayani, 1991).

Concern for the welfare of the family is expressed in the honor and respect bestowed on parents and older relatives, the care provided to children, and the individual sacrifices that are made on behalf of family members (Okamura & Agbayani, 1991). A primary focus on the needs of immediate as well as extended family members may translate into behaviors such as considerable sharing of material things. A Pilipina, for example, can walk into a store to buy a blouse for herself and come out with one for her sister instead (Gochenour, 1990). Pilipinos living in the United States will routinely send money, clothes, household goods, and other items as well as bring many gifts on personal visits to extended family members "left behind" in the Philippines. Examples of individual sacrifices on the part of various family members might include postponing marriage or passing up a job promotion that would entail transferring to another location away from the family. However, family loyalty might also dictate that a young parent temporarily leave his or her family and children in order to pursue better educational, training, or employment opportunities in the United States or other countries (Santos, 1983). This sense of family obligation begins early on when children are conditioned to be grateful to their parents for their birth. A lifelong debt of gratitutde or *utang na loob* (debt that is inside) thereby creates binding relationships of love, respect, and obedience (PAPEP, 1982).

Authority

"Traditional Pilipino families and other social systems are highly authoritarian. Age, power, prestige, and wealth are the chief sources of authority" (Santos, 1983, p. 140). Within the family, age determines a hierarchical system of authority that flows downward from oldest to youngest. Outside the family, other factors such as social class, professional status or official government affiliation, and ecclesiastical positions may supersede age as determining factors in the locus of authority.

The relationship between those in authority and those subject to it is further permeated by *utang na loob*. Authority figures enjoy many privileges and prerogatives such as obedience; respect; adulation; and gifts in the form of money, material items, and personal services. These gifts are given to seek or return favors or to acknowledge a person's position of authority (Santos, 1983).

Those in authority must, in turn, assure that this reciprocity is created in a socially acceptable manner; one that conveys mutual respect and achieves the overall objective (for both the authority figure and subordinates) of maintaining group harmony.

Throughout this ongoing exchange process, the accent is on the personalized aspect of the relationship. The authority that allows some avenue of communication is presumably more trustworthy. Moreover, Pilipinos perceive authority to be ultimately *personal* and thus subject to influence and affiliation. The corresponding presumption is that whatever the law or the rules might say, someone in authority is making decisions based on personal motivations. The arbitrary use of authority and privilege is thus expected. In essence, within the larger social context, authority may be typically viewed as something to be dealt with personally as best one can by alternately placating it, keeping it at a distance, or using it to one's advantage when possible (Gochenour, 1990).

Among family and friends, Pilipinos tend to find authority for action in group consensus. The preference is for decision making within the group or for solicitation of advice from someone senior. When individual, personal decisions must be made, there is often a need to have further confirmation. The Pilipinos' tendency to enlist the opinions of others is again consistent with a more collectivist orientation and primary affiliation with the groups or contexts in which they live; these include family, neighbors, the *barkada* (peers), work associates, and other larger loyalties and identifications. Pilipinos are defined by, and linked to, the identity of groups to which they belong (Gochenour, 1990).

Harmony

Group identity is reinforced through the creation and maintenance of sustained, secure interpersonal relationships. The goal of preserving harmony between individuals, among family members, and among the groups and divisions of society is supported by basic Pilipino values that have continued to be reported in the literature since the 1960s. Several well-known studies conducted at that time focused on the concepts of *pakikisama, hiya, amor propio,* and *utang na loob*.

Pakikisama represents both a value and a goal that consists of maintaining good feelings and getting along with others. Achieving "smooth interpersonal relationship" (S.I.R.) may take precedence over clear communication and accomplishing a particular task. In order to avoid stressful confrontations, Pilipinos may lavish extravagant praise on one another, use metaphorical language rather than frank terms, hide negative feelings or depressed spirits, smile when things go wrong, and refrain from expressing anger or losing their temper (Guthrie, 1968). *Pakikisama* is also pursued by showing sensitivity to *hiya* and *amor propio*.

Hiya, although commonly translated as "shame," has been further described as a feeling of "inferiority, embarrassment, shyness, and alienation which is experienced as acutely distressing" (Guthrie, 1968, p. 62). It is integrally related to the concept of "face" and a preoccupation with how one appears in the eyes of others. *Hiya* is inculcated as a necessary part of a child's development and used as a means to shape approved or desired behaviors. Thus, an individual's capacity for appropriate behavior with authority figures is a reflection of one's family and upbringing and the fear of "losing face" (PAPEP, 1982).

This profound concern for "face" further derives from the value of *amor propio*. While literally translated as "self-respect" or "self-esteem," *amor propio* has been characterized as "the high degree of sensitivity that makes a person intolerant to criticism and causes him to have an easily wounded pride" (Union of Pan Asian Communities [UPAC], 1980). Pilipinos learn to withstand a "loss of face" in some situations; particularly when they perceive themselves to be at fault. But it is devastating to be publicly criticized, insulted, belittled, or humiliated, or to lose one's self-respect. It thus becomes essential to behave in ways that will ensure that everyone's "face" and *amor propio* are not threatened (Gochenour, 1990).

The previously described value of *utang na loob* is also an integral aspect of maintaining group harmony and relationships that require the balancing of obligations and debts. *Utang na loob* binds the persons involved more closely—in contrast to the typically "American" orientation in which the discharge of a personal obligation tends to liberate or release the individual to go on being him- or herself (Gochenour, 1990). As one of the most important facets of Philippine life, group acceptance is contingent on loyalty and devotion. The services of friendship are thus always reciprocal and safeguarded by these value systems (UPAC, 1980).

Alternative Concepts and Other Values

Critics of the 1960s values studies maintain that concepts such as *pakikisama, hiya, amor propio,* and *utang na loob* have been inappropriately generalized from vernacular terms associated with specific behaviors and situations into all-pervading, organizing values and trait complexes (Lawless, 1969). They have been perceived as a central core of fundamental cultural traits that create and define an almost stereotypic Pilipino character and have further been accepted as valid by scholars, foreigners, and Pilipinos in general (Okamura & Agbayani, 1991).

As one of the most outspoken critics of studies presented in English of Philippine values, Enriquez (1987, p. 30) argued that most of these studies employ "the colonizer's perspective and colonial language" rather than making use of indigenous concepts available in native Philippine languages. Thus "the organization and logic of the value system" from a Pilipino perspective is lacking. He further contended that *pakikisama, hiya,* and so on represent only "surface values" that derive their significance from the "core" value of *kapwa* (shared identity).

Recent studies on Pilipino values have focused on siginificantly less abstract concepts. One of the most comprehensive studies of Pilipino character traits and values was conducted by a Philippine Senate–commissioned task force in 1988. The study identified the following major strengths of the Pilipino character: *pakikipagkapwa-tao* (having a regard to the dignity and being of others), family orientation, joy and humor, flexibility, adaptability and creativity, hard work and industry, faith and religiosity, and ability to survive (Licuanan, 1988). Each of these characteristics is summarized by Okamura and Agbayani (1991) and has been consistently identified by Church (1986) in a review of other studies on Pilipino personality values or ideals.

Pakikipagkapwa-tao is manifested among Pilipinos in their basic sense of justice and fairness and concern for others' well-being. Pilipinos recognize the essential humanity of all people and regard others with respect and empathy. This orientation instills a heightened sensitivity to the nature and quality of interpersonal relationships, which are the principal source of security and happiness. The related family orientation and interdependence among Pilipinos was previously detailed.

Pilipinos' sense of joy and humor is evident in their optimistic approach to life and its travails. The ability to laugh at themselves and their predicament is an important coping mechanism that contributes to emotional balance and a capacity to survive. This characteristic is complemented by Pilipino flexibility, adaptability, and creativity that are manifested in the ability to adjust to often-difficult circumstances and prevailing physical and social environments. Pilipinos have a high tolerance for ambiguity that enables them to respond calmly to uncertainty or lack of information. As resourceful, creative, fast learners, Pilipinos often improvise and make productive and innovative use of whatever is available. These qualities have been repeatedly demonstrated in their capacity to adapt to living in any part of the world and in their ability to accept change (Okamura & Agbayani, 1991).

The related capacity for hard work and industry among Pilipinos is widely recognized. Pilipinos are universally regarded as excellent workers who perform well whether the job involves physical labor and tasks or highly sophisticated technical functions. This propensity for hard work, which often includes a highly competitive spirit, is driven by the desire for economic security and advancement for oneself and one's family. This achievement orientation is further accompanied by typically high aspirations and great personal sacrifices.

Each of the above characteristics strengthens the Pilipino's ability to survive and endure despite difficult times and often little resources. Moreover, these characteristics cluster around distinctly religious beliefs and a deep faith in God. This faith is evident in Pilipinos' ability to accept reality (including failure and defeat) in terms of God's will and to adopt a philosophical/religious attitude that cushions them from disappointments. Pilipino faith is related to the concept of *bahala na* ("It's up to God" or "Leave it to God"), which has tended to be incorrectly equated with an expression of fatalism and a passive acceptance or resignation to fate. *Bahala na* can instead be viewed more positively as determination in the face of uncertainty or stressful, problematic conditions. While it is an indication of an acceptance of the nature of things, including one's own inherent limitations, *bahala na* operates psychologically to elevate one's courage and conviction to persist in the face of adversity and to improve one's situation (Enriquez, 1987; Okamura & Agbayani, 1991).

Apart from the more fundamental Pilipino personality characteristics and values are those related to physical appearance. As briefly noted at the outset of the chapter, centuries of Spanish and American colonial rule reinforced the Pilipino tendency to equate light complexion with high social status. "White" meant everything associated with the ruling classes: worth, beauty, desirability, and power. While the lighter-skinned Pilipino usually has either Chinese or Spanish blood in the family line, having *Spanish* ancestors is likely to be a point of pride (Gochenour, 1990). Similarly, for many Pilipino Americans, white Americans constitute a very powerful reference group. Many may not only equate being light complected with being beautiful or handsome, but also think that to be American is to be white. This perception or value is often unfortunately transmitted to the children and may contribute to feelings of inferiority and second-class status. Corresponding negative self-concepts based on skin color are further reinforced by the growing realization that other "brown" ethnic groups and people of color do not enjoy the same social and economic status as their white counterparts (Santos, 1983).

Status is further integrally linked to education. Pilipinos view education as a "passport to good jobs, economic security, social acceptance, and as a way out of a cycle of poverty and lower-class status, not only for their children, but for the whole family" (Santos, 1983, p. 146). Education, then, is not an individual but a family concern and considered to be an economic investment toward which family members must contribute significant effort and often personal sacrifice. Once successfully graduated and employed, the individual must assume the responsibility of helping his or her parents finance the education of the next child. The next child is then responsible for the next, and so on. This practice reflects the value of *utang na loob* in which the debt of gratitude incurred to the whole family ensures the graduate's contribution to family welfare—which takes precedence over individual economic and social mobility (Santos, 1983). Thus, degrees, diplomas, certificates, good grades, and academic honors are much-sought-after symbols. Such achievements are typically recognized with great pride and significant attention by extended family, friends, and the larger community. Moreover, if one is well educated, Pilipinos expect that person to talk, act, and dress the part (Gochenour, 1990).

The preceding review of traditional Pilipino values reveals complexity as well as contrast between such values and those corresponding to more individualistic, Eurocentric cultural orientations. There are also apparent contrasts between various Pilipino values and observed behaviors among Pilipinos. These contrasts can be expected between immigrant and American-born Pilipinos and among those of varying social class, generation, and degree of acculturation. Thus, as is the case with other Asian ethnic groups, awareness and appreciation of such contrasts and complexity are critical in determining the relative influence of traditional values among Pilipino families.

BELIEFS

Childrearing

Formal studies of Pilipino childrearing beliefs and practices have shown considerable consistency in their findings (Church, 1986). Moreover, the specific socialization patterns and "training" for desirable childhood traits and behaviors (particularly during infancy/toddlerhood and early childhood) are highly consistent with other Asian cultural groups. However, Pilipino childrearing beliefs and practices are reinforced within a traditional family structure and extended family system with characteristic similarities and differences relative to other Asian cultures.

Family Structure

The complete centrality of family life and the importance of family loyalty, obligation, and interdependence were previously described. These values are supported by a family structure and kinship ties that reflect the multicultural Pilipino heritage. Having withstood Hispanic Catholic influence, the ancient Malay tradition of equality between men and women translates into a bilateral extended kinship system. Both the mother's and father's lineages are of equal importance. Thus, for example, names may be inherited through the male line or both the father's and mother's family name. Inheritance patterns further call for equal division between daughters and sons (UPAC, 1980).

While expanded through bilateral lineage, the extended family system is further enlarged by the *compadre* (godparent) system. In addition to relatives by blood and marriage, each Pilipino gains relatives through godparent rituals and ceremonies. Typically a close friend or neighbor of the natural parent is called upon to serve as a godparent (known as *ninong* or *ninang* to the child) and assumes a modified parental relationship to the child by virtue of acting as a sponsor at the religious rights of baptism, confirmation, and, later, marriage. *Compadres* also assume roles as benefactors who may be expected to oversee their godchild's religious education, aid the child in times of financial need, and contribute to the cost of the child's education. In addition to *compadres*, landlords and employers may further be viewed as surrogate parents to adult family members; thus, other social institutions and relationships also become incorporated into the extended family system. Through this expanded network of kin-

Case Example #1

Tony, a 5-year-old Pilipino boy with autism, was receiving in-home intensive tutoring, speech therapy, and behavior intervention through a well-known program based at the University of California–Los Angeles (UCLA). At the time of his referral to the regional center for case management services, the immediate need and priority was to identify and place Tony in an appropriate preschool program.

In presenting Tony's early developmental history to the counselor, Tony's mother, Cora (who had separated from her husband, Roy, when Tony was about 3 years old), described how difficult Tony was to care for. Her oldest daughter (15 years of age) was very helpful and assumed a major caregiving role whenever Cora (a nurse) needed to work the late-afternoon early-evening shifts. Tony's *comadre* or godmother was also available to care for him regularly in her home. However, despite the availability of such family supports and resources, Cora was often overwhelmed by Tony's persistent attention deficits, behavior problems, tantrums, and hyperactivity. Prior to having learned of the UCLA program for autistic children, Cora had been unable to find any professional resources that were effective in helping her to better manage Tony's problems. In fact, his *comadre* suggested that Cora consider taking Tony to a faith healer after a psychologist was unsuccessful in remediating his tantrums and oppositional behavior. Tony's *comadre* recalled a young child she had known in the Philippines who cried inconsolably and seemed to live in his own world. She was convinced that a faith healer succeeded in driving the evil spirit (which was presumably contributing to the child's condition) from his body. Cora was reluctant to act upon this suggestion, and felt that her personal spiritual faith would ultimately enable her to find help. Moreover, Tony's isolated special talents (e.g., ability to write his name and nearly every major auto company/make/model) were a sign that he also had a "gift from God."

Thus, when Cora was finally able to find the UCLA project and witness the immediate benefits of the home intervention program she became very attached to the staff and was profoundly grateful for their help. However, her loyalty and debt of gratitude to the UCLA team contributed toward a major decision-making dilemma. The team felt that despite Tony's significant deficits in social skills and pragmatic language, he should be placed in a regular kindergarten program and that all efforts should be made to prepare him for a mainstreaming experience. In a subsequent individualized education program (IEP) meeting, Tony was declared eligible for public preschool services, but the district's school psychologist insisted that Tony's level of functioning warranted special education placement.

After visiting and observing several public school programs (with the regional center counselor and the UCLA team leader), Cora continued to be caught in the middle between UCLA (who maintained that the special education classes were inappropriate) and the school district personnel (who continued to challenge the mainstreaming recommendation). Cora was unsure as to the regional center counselor's position and neither wished to offend the UCLA team nor to disagree with the school district. Consequently, she enrolled Tony in her own church summer preschool program. She was told by the director after Tony's first day that he was just not "fitting in." He was allowed to continue attending 2 days per week, but received a minimum of individualized attention from an untrained aide. The counselor was disturbed by this turn of events and felt that Tony "lost out" on a full summer's educational programming, while Cora had to cover personally the expense of an inadequate preschool program. She realized that Cora's need to avoid conflict with authority figures was sufficiently compelling to make financial sacrifices as well as to select an undesirable alternative for her son. Thus, Tony's and Cora's needs were subjugated to the greater value placed upon maintaining smooth working relationships with professionals and those to whom Cora was indebted.

ship relationships, a Pilipino is likely to consider 100 or more individuals as "relatives" (PAPEP, 1982; Santos, 1983; Yap, 1982).

The extended family is, in effect, the basic unit of Philippine society. Within given households, nuclear families average six to eight members in size. Unmarried adult daughters and sons typically remain in their parents' home. Additional extended family members such as grandparents, aunts, uncles, or cousins may also live in the same house and assume vital roles (PAPEP, 1982; Santos, 1983).

Marital and Parental Roles/Expectations

It is believed that young people should not marry before they have completed some kind of educational preparation for a career so that they will be economically self-sufficient. They should also be sufficiently mature to assume the responsibilities of raising a family. The typical age for marriage is thus 20–25 years for Pilipino women and 25–30 years for men. Once married, Pilipinos are expected to start their families within a year or so. The birth of a child fixes the ties between the married couple's respective families. The bond of marriage is also considered permanent; Catholicism and Philippine law prohibit divorce, except among Muslims and some unassimilated groups (PAPEP, 1982).

Although the father may be ostensibly perceived as the main authority figure in the Pilipino nuclear family, the mother has considerable authority and influence. She generally controls the finances, may work full time (even with many children at home), and earn as much or more than half the family income. Women enjoy high status in the family and in the Pilipino society at large. Bilateral lineage attests to this higher status of Pilipinas compared to women in other Asian countries. The long-accepted phenomenon of the "working mother" in the Philippines thus does not pose a drastic role change as it does for other recent Asian immigrant families in the United States (PAPEP, 1982).

Egalitarian roles and relationships between Pilipino men and women are further reflected in family decision-making processes. Family authority is based on respect for age, regardless of sex. Family decisions are made only after a consensus has been reached to ensure that the ultimate decision will be representative of and acted upon by all family members. Family disagreements are avoided, if possible; when disagreements do occur, they are kept strictly within the family (PAPEP, 1982).

Children are the center of the parents' concerns. They are viewed as an extension of the family and recipients of the family's good fortune. Many adults may assume responsibility for a child within a family, but do not strictly adhere to the Confucian expectation of *unquestioning* child obedience. Parents are expected to *persuade* a child to accept their point of view, rather than impose their authority on the child without consideration for the child's preferences or wishes. The child, in turn, is expected to show proper respect and obedience, to compromise, and to maintain good relationships with all other family members (PAPEP, 1982).

Infancy/Toddlerhood

In the Pilipino culture, the birth of children is an expected and desired outcome of marriage. Most couples prefer to have children of both sexes, and there is

typically no special preference for males over females. Children are considered a special "gift from God," and a large family is proof of God's favor and blessing (Guthrie & Jacobs, 1966). The newborn child's vulnerability contributes to the use of folk practices by many Pilipina mothers, such as keeping garlic and salt near the baby to protect him or her from evil spirits, wrapping a 50¢ coin on the baby's umbilicus with a belly band to make it heal faster, and pinning religious medals on a baby's clothing to offer the protection of angels. A baby's clothes are loose and comfortable and preferably white in color to symbolize the purity God gives to every newborn (Affonso, 1978).

Most Pilipina women do not take their newborns out of the house until 3 or 4 weeks of age; the first trip is usually to the doctor and the second to the priest for a blessing or conditional baptism. Many Pilipino families postpone formal baptism until the baby is 1–3 months old, when the parents have raised enough money for a baptismal party, which is second in importance only to the marriage feast. Before a baptism, parents choose a Christian name for the infant and select godparents (who help pay for the baptism and give the child gifts). Children are almost always named for the saint on whose feast day they were either born or baptized; babies can also be named by combining or contracting parents' names and the names of favorite relatives or friends (PAPEP, 1982).

Infancy is characterized by indulgence, constant attention, and few, if any, demands on the child. The child is frequently cuddled and carried, and crying (even the tiniest whimper) is attended to quickly by feeding, holding, and other consoling tactics. This practice is made possible or easier by the presence of extended family (who can assume significant caregiving roles) and/or the availability of inexpensive domestic help in the Philippines (Church, 1986; Yap, 1982). The Pilipino infant/toddler is thus the center of household attention and constantly cared for by a family member or maid. Since the young child is never alone, he or she may be several years old before having a first experience of being temporarily unsupervised (Guthrie & Jacobs, 1966).

The emphasis on dependency and physical closeness is further manifested in breastfeeding on demand until a child is as old as 2–2½ years of age, and sleeping with parents and, later, siblings for an extended period of time. The process of toilet training is yet another occasion for helpfulness and closeness for the Pilipino child. It involves imitation of and assistance from other family members. Because of this assistance, very few children are fully toilet trained before the age of 2 or 2½ years (PAPEP, 1982). Thus, throughout infancy and the toddler period, childrearing is characterized by significant indulgence, protectiveness, gradual training for responsibility, and minimal adult anxiety about early performance (Church, 1986).

Early Childhood

A shift from a highly indulgent to a more authoritarian stance occurs as the child approaches school age. Particularly after the Pilipino child is weaned, older brothers, sisters, relatives, and neighborhood children become substitutes for the mother's constant attention. Older children, regardless of their sex, are expected to help with household chores and to care for younger siblings. The younger child, in turn, must learn to conform to family expectations of respect for authority and obedience to adults, parents, older siblings, and other substitute caregivers. The child is further expect to know the difference between good and bad behavior and is subject to various discipline practices (PAPEP, 1982).

> Discipline in traditional Pilipino homes depends a great deal on appeals to duties and obligations of family members based on their respective roles . . . .Children are disciplined by spanking, hitting, scolding, embarrassment through teasing, or reprimanding for being *walang hiya* (shameless), *bastos* (crude), *walang utang na loob* (ungrateful), or for being a source of shame to the family. (Santos, 1983, p. 141)

Traditionally, the mother is the chief disciplinarian; because she typically spends more time with the children, she finds more occasions calling for punishment. The father tends to punish the children less frequently—in part, because of their recognition of his absolute authority (Santos, 1983).

Among those behaviors that are more severely punished or condemned are sibling-directed aggression as well as hostility toward kinship group members. Teasing serves as a means of limit setting and controlling or suppressing anger and hostility; it is also an outlet for anger and an acceptable substitute for overt aggression and direct criticism. Children are encouraged to subordinate their personal interests and competitive behaviors for the sake of cooperation and maintaining family harmony and smooth interpersonal relationships. Modesty, politeness, respect, and patience are consistently encouraged in daily behavior (PAPEP, 1982).

Stricter parental authority and guidance thus foster mutual dependency and loyalty throughout the Pilipino child's transitional socialization experiences during the preschool period. In fact, earlier surveys conducted in the Philippines have indicated that "obedience to parents" is one of the highest ranked childrearing values, second only to "trust in God" (Church, 1986). Such expectations and corresponding practices condition the child to abide by the previously described traditional values. As the child attains school age, he or she has typically developed a strong sense of family responsibility while further understanding the traditional rules and values governing interpersonal relationships.

Medical Care

As is the case among other Asian immigrant groups, there is considerable intracultural diversity among Pilipinos with regard to health beliefs and health practices. Centuries of colonialism and the Americanization of Pilipino culture have obviously infused the science of Western medicine and contributed to the training of thousands of Pilipino health care professionals. However, just as the larger contemporary Pilipino culture is a composite of foreign and indigenous elements, health orientations and healing practices may also incorporate traditional Pilipino folk medicine. The various aspects of such folk medicine warrant review.

Health Beliefs

"Diseases are traditionally conceptualized as either natural or supernatural in origin. In practice, however, people seem to make no clear-cut distinction between the two (Montepio, 1986–87, p. 152). Explanations of illness (particularly chronic, debilitating illnesses) are typically multicausal.

> Among the natural forces believed to affect health are overwork, overexposure to natural elements, overeating, insufficient nutrition, lack of sleep, too much worry, unsanitary environment, and imbalance of hot and cold elements. Supernatural ailments are those that result from the displeasure of environmental spirits, souls of the dead and evil people, or from punishment for transgression against God, against fellow human beings, or against nature. (Montepio, 1986–87, p. 152)

The particular belief in *usog* or *tuyaw* is widespread in the Philippines. Individuals afflicted with various illnesses or conditions that are not readily treated by conventional medicines may have had contact with a person who possessed a power similar to the Spanish *mal de ojo* (evil eye). The Pilipino counterpart appears more powerful because "it can be transmitted through the eyes and also the hands, fingers, words (as through a greeting), or in extreme cases, through physical proximity to a possessed person who had been exposed to the sun's heat" (Montepio, 1986–87, p. 155).

Health Practices

Studies of health practices among Pilipino Americans suggest that people originally from rural areas in the Philippines are more knowledgeable regarding home remedies, traditional healing techniques, and supernatural ailments, while those from urban areas rely more on Western medical intervention and over-the-counter drugs. However, in both rural and urban areas, indigenous and modern health care systems are utilized simultaneously (Montepio, 1986–87).

Among the more traditional forms of self-medication are certain Chinese oils or ointments, which serve as "cure-alls" in relaxing, heating, and comforting the muscles or providing relief for dizziness, colds, headaches, sore throats, and so forth. Other self-medication may include the use of folk healing techniques consistent with the Chinese hot/cold classification system of diseases and concept of wind illnesses (cf. Chapter 8, this volume). For example, a technique called *ventosa* is used for treating joint pains believed to be caused by the presence of "bad air." This technique consists of wrapping a coin with cotton, wetting the tip with alcohol, lighting it, and placing the coin on the aching joint area, then immediately covering it with a small glass or cup. The fire is extinguished as soon as it is covered, creating a vacuum that will suck the "bad" air out of the joint (Montepio, 1986–87). Beyond such home remedies, more serious illnesses typically warrant seeking the help of a local "healer" who may utilize a variety of treatments including the use of herbs and roots (McKenzie & Chrisman, 1977).

While healers are presumed to possess a God-given gift, their relative popularity and prestige in the community depends a great deal upon their interpersonal relationships with their patients. People in rural areas are accustomed to friendly and accommodating folk healers and expect the same treatment from physicians. If these expectations are not met, they avoid Western health centers or switch doctors. Moreover, when healers are viewed with trust and respect, they are often expected to perform "instantaneous" healing. If there is no immediate improvement in an illness or related symptoms, patients may change doctors (Montepio, 1986–87).

The various types of healers common throughout the Philippines include midwives, masseurs, and specialists for supernaturally caused ailments. While these types of healers each have native labels, there is no traditional word for "faith healers," the newest and increasingly popular genre of Philippine folk healers. Faith healers do not attempt to identify or diagnose a disease, in contrast to the traditional concern for identifying the cause of illness (which could presumably be supernatural). Their orientation is holistic and uniform and incorporates the belief in concurrent physical, emotional, and spiritual healing. Regardless of the patient's specific affliction, the same techniques are employed (Montepio, 1986–87).

In a regular session, the faith healer's techniques include blessing the body with holy water, laying on of the hands, and anointing with oil. The technique of laying on of the hands is a very important aspect of faith healing and is practiced by several other groups such as the Pentecostal-Charismatics and the Cuban-American *santeros*. In laying on hands, it appears as though the healer is attempting to transfer the healing energy from her hands to the patient's body through the forehead. The healer also anoints the patient by wetting his or her fingers with consecrated oil and making the sign of the cross on the forehead, on each eye, and on the chin of the patient. If certain body parts need healing, they will be directly anointed. The patient, in turn, typically attests to the sense of warmth or flow of energy that seems to enter his or her body and provides instant well-being (Montepio, 1986–87).

These healing techniques are enhanced by ritualized prayer, chanting, and the creation of an "atmosphere" that reinforces the patient's faith. During healing sessions, the faith healer, for example, typically wears a white dress of soft, flowing material, creating an ephemeral quality; white (worn by the Virgin Mary) is the symbol of purity, but is also associated with environmental ghosts and spirits (Montepio, 1986–87).

Whether in the Philippines or the United States, faith healing and more traditional folk healing practices are typically utilized simultaneously with modern medicine. In fact,

> the healer never advises against going to doctors or hospitals. In several cases, spiritual healing is used only after these doctors have diagnosed a disease as incurable. Even after a patient feels that he has been healed by [traditional healers], he still goes back to his doctor to establish that he actually is cured. Western medicine is thus used to validate the efficacy of spiritual healing. (Montepio, 1986–87, pp. 159–160)

Folk healers may serve as indigenous allies whose work can complement modern health practitioners and who can provide the psychological, emotional, and spiritual well-being necessary to the healing process.

Disability

Similar to many other Asian ethnic groups, Pilipinos traditionally view the more severely disabling conditions with considerable stigma. In fact, according to selected Pilipino American professionals working in the field of developmental disabilities, this profound stigma partially explains the paucity of Pilipino literature pertaining to disability issues (Fuentes, 1990; Soldevilla, 1989). Such stigma derives, in part, from traditional attributions linking specific disabilities to various causes.

Causation

Many of the traditional beliefs regarding the etiology of disabilities (particularly physical conditions) are consistent with the previously described health beliefs about varying causes of illness. Naturalistic explanations might focus on the mother's failure to follow prescribed dietary practices during pregnancy. For example, excessive intake of sweet foods is believed to contribute to an obese baby. There are also foods that should be excluded from the prenatal diet: squid (because it might get tangled in the women's body and cause the umbilical cord to wrap around the fetus's neck), crab (because it might cause clubbed fingers and toes), dark foods (because they might result in a dark-skinned baby), and taro (because it is believed to cause the baby to have eczema or skin problems) (PAPEP, 1982).

Religious beliefs are also employed to account for various disabilities. The traditional Pilipino's deep faith in God and belief in *bahala na* may reinforce a fatalistic orientation whereby a disabling condition is accepted as God's will. Disability in a child, however, may also represent a divine punishment for sins or moral transgressions against God that were committed by the parents or their ancestors. This spiritual attribution contributes to a shared sense of *hiya* (shame) that affects the entire family; it may further negatively affect the chances of siblings to find desirable marital partners because of presumed hereditary "taint" (Fuentes, 1990).

Case Example #2

Rebecca (Becky), a 5-year-old Pilipino girl with moderate mental retardation, was referred for regional center case management services when she began attending kindergarten. Becky had been diagnosed at 1 year of age as having a genetic disorder (Prader Willi syndrome). However, she had not received any subsequent early intervention or special education services, nor had she been seen by any medical specialists.

This history was surprising to the regional center counselor when she conducted her initial interview with Becky's parents, in light of their professional backgrounds. Becky's father, Macario, was a physician and her mother, Lorenza, a teacher in the Philippines. Since having immigrated to the United States about 10 years ago, Macario had worked as a lab assistant and Lorenza as a travel agent. They had two older children who were excelling in school and whom they were very proud of. Becky, however, was a source of constant stress and shame for the family. They had attempted to cope with her overeating, extreme obesity, behavior problems, and mental retardation throughout the past 4 years without any outside assistance. Macario was described as a "very proud man" who seemed humbled by his loss of job status, persistent modest income, and family living situation, and the public stigma associated with caring for Becky.

The counselor was sensitive to the emotional impact of Becky on the family as well as her parents' adjustment experiences and need to preserve their dignity and "face." She thus did not dwell on why they had not sought services for Becky prior to this time. She instead discussed resources such as respite care and behavioral intervention programs that could be made available to assist them. Macario and Lorenza indicated their appreciation and said they would consider utilizing such help. Lorenza, however, noted that her mother and older sister would soon be arriving from the Philippines to live with them for an indefinite period. She felt that the responsibility of caring for Becky could thus be shared with other family members, and outside resources would not have to be utilized.

Further inquiry, however, revealed that Lorenza's mother and sister would probably not be arriving for another 6 months. They also had not seen Becky since she was an infant and were relatively unaware of the severity of her condition. Moreover, Macario indicated that he had considered placing Becky outside the home. He was told by a Pilipino co-worker that her sister-in-law owned a group home and cared for children with mental retardation. He seemed encouraged by the fact that there were Pilipino care providers in the community, but was reluctant to pursue such resources and make contact with them on his own. The counselor suspected that Macario was concerned about his reputation and sense of pride and shame in dealing directly with fellow Pilipinos to seek help for his daughter. She felt that he was willing to have her act on his behalf as an intermediary to explore out-of-home placement. However, although Lorenza would not directly offer her opinion or concerns about placing Becky, she seemed interested in continuing to keep Becky at home. This situation posed a major dilemma for the counselor with regard to her next course of action and how best to counsel Becky's parents.

Disabilities also may be associated with supernatural ailments that are attributed to other spiritual causes. Infants who are chronically irritable and engage in prolonged, inconsolable crying are presumed to be troubled by evil spirits (PAPEP, 1982). Similarly, children with serious emotional disturbances or disabilities such as autism as well as epilepsy are often traditionally described as being "possessed," the victims of angry or evil spirits (Church, 1986).

Nature and Meaning of a Disability

As indicated in Chapter 8, the respective terms related to specific disabilities are highly varied among Asian ethnic groups. Similarly, traditional Pilipino conceptions of selected disabling conditions vary according to their expression (e.g., mental, emotional, physical) and presumed etiology. These differing conceptions further suggest corresponding treatment modalities such as previously described under traditional health practices.

While the types of "outside" assistance and treatment/intervention resources that are sought may vary considerably, the family typically remains centrally involved in the primary care of the child with a disability. As the most reliable source of protection and support for the child with a disability, the family is also the focus of siblings' primary duty and commitment. Parents thus expect their older sons and daughters to continue to provide the primary care for a family member with a disability. In fact, the long-standing tradition of family and small-group orientation has contributed to a proliferation of Pilipino care providers who have established small group homes or community-based residential facilities serving clients with developmental disabilities. These providers caring for children may naturally view their "clients" as family members and fully include them in daily living activities and socialization experiences that incorporate many aspects of Pilipino culture and traditional lifestyle (Marquez, 1991; Soldevilla, 1989).

ISSUES OF LANGUAGE

The receiver-oriented and relatively indirect style of most Asian languages is also characteristic of Pilipino communication patterns. These patterns are integrally related to primary Pilipino values such as family, authority, interpersonal harmony, concern for others' well-being, and the importance of "face." Similar to other Asian ethnic groups, Pilipinos typically employ formality and honorific language that conveys proper respect for authority, status, and position by terms of address and titles. For example, a physician or lawyer will continue to be addressed as Dr. Cruz or Attorney Ramos by clients, friends, and colleagues well after more personalized and informal relationships have been established (in contrast to the American tendency to move more rapidly toward a first-name basis) (Santos, 1983).

Respect for authority and concern for "face-saving" further reinforce the frequent use of euphemisms, third parties, and saying "yes" when the opposite is meant (Santos, 1983). Pilipinos will often go to great lengths to avoid making a direct appeal when they have encountered a problem or wish to convey an important request. They instead prefer to introduce a go-between "to cushion the transaction and escape the embarrassment that might result from presenting the matter face-to-face with the other person" (Gochenour, 1990, p. 50). In their wish to be accommodating, Pilipinos may also find it impolite or embarrassing to decline social invitations or to respond directly to other requests that might elicit a negative answer or contrary opinion. While apparently concurring in some manner (through failure to express or defend an alternative point of view) or ostensibly indicating agreement, Pilipinos may actually be privately opposed to the issue or question at hand. Thus, due to values such as *pakakisama* and *amor propio,* mistakes will go unmentioned, questions unasked, and issues unsettled (PAPEP, 1982). This communication style may obviously challenge a more Eurocentric orientation that values frankness, directness, honesty, and sincerity, and potentially contributes to a perception of Pilipinos as being two-faced (Gochenour, 1990).

Consistent with other high-context cultures, Pilipinos have a highly developed sensitivity to the nonverbal aspects of communication (Gochenour, 1990). While considerably less dependent upon spoken words than are European Americans, Pilipinos watch their listeners carefully and identify body language cues to assess what the person is feeling. The essence of this more intuitive and affective sense that guides nonverbal communication is captured in the phrase "talking with one's eyes" (PAPEP, 1982). Pilipino sensitivity to context thus "extends from a keen awareness of appropriate speech and behavior in a given situation to a well-developed instinct for what is implied and not stated" (Gochenour, 1990, p. 61). This sensitivity is further complemented by a high tolerance for ambiguity that enables Pilipinos to respond calmly to uncertainty or lack of information. Again, however, this orientation may conflict with the characteristically Eurocentric utilitarian emphasis on forthrightness and achieving results in the least amount of time (Gochenour, 1990).

SUMMARY AND RECOMMENDATIONS

Summary

Pilipinos constitute the largest Asian immigrant group to the United States (nearly two-thirds of the Pilipino American population is foreign born). Originating from a nation of over 7,000 islands and the most ethnically diverse country in Asia, Pilipinos have immigrated to the United States in successive waves since the early 1900s. The more recent waves of Pilipino immigrants (post-1965 and 1972) have included large numbers of highly educated young adults and professionals in search of better employment and economic opportunities. However they must typically confront persistent conditions of occupational downgrading and underemployment. The problems associated with loss of ascribed status, social dislocation, and employment discrimination are often compounded by family stresses and generational conflicts. Alienated Pilipino youth increasingly challenge their elders' "colonial mentality" and traditional values.

Four hundred years of Spanish colonial rule have indeed stamped upon the Pilipino culture and consciousness some of its most enduring characteristics. One form of colonialism was replaced by another, and 40 years of U.S. rule further contributed to the pervasive Americanization of Pilipino culture. Native Pilipinos thus may have a decidedly Western orientation and share a heritage heavily influenced by Hispanic Catholicism and Euro-Christian ethics. However, their indigenous Malay roots and historical Hindu, Confucian, and Islam influences have further shaped a sense of identity and traditional values that reflect other Asian cultures but are also uniquely Pilipino.

Among the principal traditional Pilipino values are the centrality of the family (and the importance of family interdependence, loyalty, and obligation), hierarchical and highly authoritarian social systems, and preservation of interpersonal harmony. The associated concepts of *pakakisama* (achieving smooth interpersonal relationships), *hiya* (shame), *amor propio* (self-respect), and *utang na loob* (debt of gratitude) have been variously perceived as fundamental cultural traits versus surface values that derive their significance from the core value of *kapwa* (shared identity). The Pilipino character has further been defined in terms of basic strengths: regard for the dignity of others, family orientation, joy and humor, flexibility, adaptability and creativity, hard work and industry, faith and religiosity, and ability to survive—which is reinforced by the concept of *bahala na*. Education is also highly valued as a means of upward mobility; it is integrally linked to status and enhancement of family welfare and reputation.

The traditional Pilipino family structure and extended family system serve as the vehicle for transmitting basic values through specific socialization practices and childrearing beliefs. A bilateral extended kinship system (including *compadres* and many other surrogate parents and "relatives" from various social institutions) forms the basic unit of Philippine society. Within the immediate nuclear family, the respective traditional marital and parental roles are characterized by: a commitment to marriage as a permanent bond, relatively egalitarian roles, status, a balance of power between men and women (although the father may be formally recognized as the main authority figure), and the expectation of reciprocity between parent and child in meeting mutual needs and maintaining good relationships. The specific Pilipino childrearing practices employed from infancy throughout early childhood are highly consistent with the more traditional childrearing practices and orientations of many Asian cultural groups (cf. Chapter 8, this volume).

While Pilipino culture has been infused with the science of Western medicine, popular health beliefs and practices have incorporated traditional Pilipino folk medicine as well. Folk orientations conceptualize disease (as well as disabilities) in terms of either natural or supernatural origins. Diseases or illnesses originating from natural causes are typically treated through the use of self-medication or other techniques derived from the hot/cold classification and wind illness concepts of Chinese medicine. "Faith healers" are the newest and increasing popular genre of folk healers who may be utilized regardless of the presumed etiology of various illnesses. Folk health beliefs and practices further extend to conceptualizations of the cause as well as nature and meaning of specific disabilities (whether mental, physical, or emotional). An important consideration for early interventionists and those providing services for children with special needs is that families may simultaneously utilize traditional folk healing practices in conjunction with modern medicine and health care resources. In fact, Western medicine is often used to validate the efficacy of spiritual healing. The profound impact of a child with a disability on the family must also be considered in terms of potential shame and stigma. This shared experience will typically result in coping strategies that draw heavily upon spiritual faith and parental expectations that all family members will make personal sacrifices to participate in the primary care and support of the child with a disability.

Characteristic Pilipino communication patterns are a final area of focus. They are integrally related to primary values such as family, authority, interpersonal harmony, concern for others' well-being, and the importance of "face." Thus, similar to other Asian groups, Pilipinos traditionally employ formality and honorific language (in conveying respect for authority, status, and position), indirect communication styles, and further have a highly developed sensitivity to the nonverbal aspects of communication.

The preceding summary serves to highlight the complexity of the Pilipino American population. This includes contrasting cultural orientations relative to the blending of Eurocentric and more indigenous collectivist values as well as contrasts between immigrant and American-born Pilipinos and among those of varying social class, generation, and degree of acculturation. Thus, as is the case with other Asian ethnic groups, awareness and appreciation of such contrasts are essential in determining the relative influence of traditional culture factors among Pilipino families.

Recommendations for Interventionists

The following recommendations correspond to selected elements of service utilization that were highlighted in Chapter 8. They address practical considerations in responding to more traditional cultural orientations, values, and behaviors that may be demonstrated by Pilipino families.

Outreach

The previously described "trust" factor and importance of "proper" entry points to Asian communities similarly applies to many Pilipino families. Pilipinos traditionally operate within a "circle of loyalty" that begins with the immediate family, proceeds to the extended family kinship system (including *compadres*), and finally reaches authority figures (Morales, 1990). Thus, in seeking direct services or assistance for a child with a disability, the family may typically utilize intermediaries or third parties (who are often extended family members) to make initial contact with appropriate providers or agencies. This practice serves to convey respect for the providers who are viewed as authority figures and as such, are not directly approached to request assistance. It also enables a family to filter information and learn more about the personal/professional qualities of the provider(s) through the perspectives of a trusted go-between. Early interventionists should be receptive to this practice and avoid rigid insistence on initial direct contact with the identified child and his or her family members, to the exclusion of designated intermediaries. Restrictive agency policies and relevant client/family confidentiality issues must be examined in this light.

Initial Expectations/Orientations

The ascribed credibility of professionals is based upon their presumed expertise and ability to offer practical assistance in the form of direct benefits or services. In the context of the traditional Pilipino value system, they are expected to assume an authoritarian and directive role. Professionals would give explanations and advice and recommend specific courses of action. While assuming an authoritarian and somewhat paternalistic role, the interventionist is also expected to be personable and subject to influence and affiliation. He or she must be sensitive to the family's desire for acceptance and an appropriate level of emotional closeness (Okamura & Agbayani, 1991). This type of relationship allows for the ultimate expression of *utang na loob* and reciprocity that preserves the family's "face" and dignity.

"Face Saving" and the Counseling Process

While typically demonstrating a heightened sensitivity to the nature and quality of interpersonal relationships, Pilipinos are particularly concerned about "face" and how one appears in the eyes of others. The profound stigma associated with various disabilities and the corresponding sense of family shame or *hiya* may create significant apprehension about public "loss of face"—particularly when seeking special services. Yet, at the same time, traditional families will maintain a deep religious faith and the *bahala na* spirit; this orientation promotes a high tolerance for ambiguity that enables them to respond calmly to uncertainty or lack of information and to remain determined in the face of stressful, problematic conditions.

Early interventionists must be sensitive to the "face-saving" needs of families by using caution in frankly discussing specific problem areas too prematurely. They must also respect and incorporate the family's religious, spiritual, and philosophical beliefs as adaptive coping strategies, rather than dismiss them as defenses, denial, fatalism, and/or lack of initiative and motivation to pursue prescribed courses of action actively. Respect for the family's need to engage in collective decision-making processes is also necessary. Sufficient time must be allowed for the family to seek advice, confirmation, and group consensus before making important decisions.

Communication Styles

Consistent with the value of *pakakisama*, achieving smooth interpersonal relationships often takes precedence over clear and forthright communication. Characteristic Pilipino communication patterns thus include formality and honorific language, indirectness, and heightened sensitivity to the nonverbal aspects of communication. Concern for interpersonal harmony may reinforce verbal and nonverbal behaviors that serve to mask, if not contradict, genuine intent, thoughts, opinions, or feelings that could threaten another's "face" and *amor propio*.

Early interventionists are advised to exercise significant patience and tolerance in responding to such communication styles. They should also suspend culturally biased judgments regarding the presumed honesty and integrity of Pilipinos who seem to avoid frank and direct modes of expression. While some degree of frustration is expected, responding with sardonic questions such as, "Am I supposed to be a mind-reader?" is equally ethnocentric. Learning the subtleties of Pilipino communication styles is facilitated by fully appreciating the core values that support them.

REFERENCES

Affonso, D. (1978). The Filipino American. In A.L. Clark (Ed.), *Culture, childbearing, health professionals* (pp. 128–153). Philadelphia: F.A. Davis.

Attorney General's Asian and Pacific Islander Advisory Committee. (1988). *Final report.* Sacramento: Office of the Attorney General.

Bello, M., & Reyes, V. (1986–87). Filipino Americans and the Marcos overthrow: The transformation of political consciousness. *Amerasia Journal, 13,* 73–83.

Brigham Young University. (1986). *Culturegram: Republic of the Philippines.* Provo, UT: Author, David M. Kennedy Center for International Studies, Publication Services.

Bulosan, C. (1946). *America is in the heart: A personal history.* Seattle: Author.

Cariño, B.V. (1987). The Philippines and Southeast Asia: Historical roots and contemporary linkages. In J.T. Fawcett & B.V. Cariño (Eds.), *Pacific bridges: The new immigration from Asia and the Pacific Islands* (pp. 305–325). New York: Center for Migration Studies.

Cariño, B.V., Fawcett, J.T., Gardner, R.W., & Arnold, F. (1990). *The new Pilipino im-*

migrants to the United States: Increasing diversity and change. Honolulu: East-West Population Institute, East-West Center.

Church, A.T. (1986). *Filipino personality: A review of research and writings.* Manila: De La Salle University Press.

Devine, E., & Braganti, N.L. (1986). *The traveler's guide to Asian customs and manners.* New York: St. Martin's Press.

Drogin, B. (1990, September 14). Paychecks full of pain and profit. *Los Angeles Times,* pp. A1, 28.

Drogin, B. (1990, September 25). Filipinos love the U.S. but hate the bases, *Los Angeles Times,* p. H7.

Enriquez, V.G. (1987, November). Filipino values: Toward a new interpretation, *Tagsibol.* pp. 29–34.

Fuentes, N. (1990, May). *Working with Pilipino families.* Paper presented at the Lanterman Regional Center Conference, Enhancing Multicultural Awareness: Serving Immigrant Families, Los Angeles.

Gochenour, T. (1990). *Considering Filipinos.* Yarmouth, ME: Intercultural Press.

Guthrie, G.M. (1968). *The Philippine temperament: Six perspectives on the Philippines.* Manila: Bookmark.

Guthrie, G.M., & Jacobs, P.J. (1966). *Child rearing and personality development in the Philippines.* University Park: Pennsylvania State University Press.

Lawless, R. (1969). *An evaluation of Philippine culture—Personality research.* Quezon City: University of the Philippines Press.

Li, C. (1983). The basic grammatical structures of selected Asian languages and English. In M. Chu-Chang (Ed.), *Asian- and Pacific-American perspectives in bilingual education: Comparative research* (pp. 3–30). New York: Teachers College Press.

Licuanan, P.B. (1988, April 27). *A moral recovery program: Building a people— Building a nation.* Report submitted to Senator Letician Romas-Shahani.

Marquez, E. (1991, April). *Pilipino care providers.* Paper presented at the San Gabriel/ Pomona Regional Center Conference, Enhancing Multicultural Awareness, Baldwin Park, CA.

McKenzie, J.L., & Chrisman, N.J. (1977). Healing, herbs, gods, and magic: Folk health beliefs among Filipino-Americans. *Nursing Outlook, 25,* 326–329.

Meinert, D. (1990, November 27). Filipino vets get citizenship. *Daily Breeze.*

Montepio, S.N. (1986–87). Folk medicine in the Filipino American experience. *Amerasia Journal, 13,* 151–162.

Morales, R. (1990, April). *Considerations in serving Pilipino clients.* Paper presented at the Harbor Regional Center Conference, Toward Competence in Intercultural Interaction, Torrance, CA.

Morales, R.F. (1974). *Makibaka: The Pilipino-American struggle.* Mountain View, CA: Mountain View Press.

Okamura, J.Y., & Agbayani, A. (1991). Filipino Americans. In N. Mokuau (Ed.), *Handbook of social services for Asians and Pacific Islanders* (pp. 97–115). Westport, CT: Greenwood Publishing Group.

Pan Asian Parent Education Project. (1982). *Pan Asian childrearing practices: Filipino Japanese, Korean, Samoan, Vietnamese.* San Diego: Union of Pan Asian Communities.

Pernia, E.M. (1976). The question of the brain drain from the Philippines. *International Migration Review, 10,* 63–72.

Posadas, B.M. (1986–87). At a crossroad: Filipino American history and the old-timers' generation. *Amerasia Journal, 13,* 85–97.

Roces, A., & Roces, G. (1985). *Culture shock! Philippines.* Singapore: Time Books International.

Santos, R.A. (1983). The social and emotional development of Filipino-American children. In G.J. Powell (Ed.), *The psychosocial development of minority group children* (pp. 131–146). New York: Brunner/Mazel.

Soldevilla, E. (1989, September). *Serving Pilipino clients*. Paper presented at the North Los Angeles County Regional Center Conference, Cross-cultural Issues in a Multicultural Society—Personal and Professional Aspects, Los Angeles.

Suzuki, B.H. (1989, November/December). Asian Americans as the "model minority"—Outdoing whites or media hype? *Change*, pp. 13–19.

Takaki, R. (1989). *Strangers from a different shore: A history of Asian Americans*. Boston: Little, Brown.

Union of Pan Asian Communities. (1980). *Understanding the Pan Asian client: Book II*. San Diego: Author.

U.S. Bureau of the Census. (1988a). *Asian and Pacific Islander population in the United States; 1980*. Washington, DC: U.S. Government Printing Office.

U.S. Bureau of the Census. (1988b). *We, the Asian and Pacific Islander Americans*. Washington, DC: U.S. Government Printing Office.

U.S. Bureau of the Census. (1991, June 12). 1990 census counts on specific racial groups. *U.S. Department of Commerce News* (not paginated).

Winter, F.H. (1988). *The Filipinos in America*. Minneapolis: Lerner Publications.

Yap, J. (1982, May). The Filipino American Family, *The Asian American Journey, 5*, 15–17.

APPENDIX A
CONTRASTING BELIEFS, VALUES, AND PRACTICES

As previously indicated, many native Pilipinos have a decidedly Western orientation and share a heritage heavily influenced by Hispanic Catholicism and Euro-Christian ethics. However, their sense of identity is uniquely Pilipino. Moreover, while Pilipinos may be ambivalent about their "Asian-ness," many of their traditional beliefs, values, and practices reflect the collectivist orientation of many Asian cultures.

Thus, Appendix A (presented in Chapter 8) is applicable to traditional Pilipinos with the following exceptions regarding religion and family:

- Pilipinos are predominantly monotheistic (i.e., Christian–Roman Catholic).
- The kinship system is bilateral (versus patrilineal, as in the Confucian tradition) and the roles between men and women are relatively more egalitarian.
- While child obedience is highly valued, parents are expected to use persuasion and to model the concepts of compromise, mutual respect, and maintaining smooth interpersonal relationships—as opposed to demanding unquestioning obedience and absolute submission to authority.

APPENDIX B
CULTURAL COURTESIES AND CUSTOMS

The following behaviors and expectations are representative of customs in the Philippines. Although Pilipino Americans constitute a highly diverse population characterized by many levels of acculturation, there remains a need to demonstrate sensitivity to the families and clients who value traditional social practices. (Much of the information provided in this section was obtained from Devine and Braganti [1986]. Another publication that provides a survey of contemporary Pilipino culture, with particular focus on practical "dos" and "don'ts" is *Culture Shock! Philippines* [Roces & Roces, 1985].)

GREETINGS

On first and subsequent meetings, the appropriate greeting is a handshake between both same-sex adults and between men and women. "Foreign" men should wait for Pilipino women to extend their hands. Pilipinos may also greet each other by making eye contact, then raising and lowering their eyebrows.

Special terms such as *lolo* and *lola* are used (particularly among relatives) when greeting older persons. Even greater honor is shown by placing their hand on your forehead—a time-honored gesture of respect.

- Always make a special point of greeting and saying goodbye to older people.
- When visiting a family's home, expect children to leave shortly after they greet you. They do not remain when a guest is visiting.

NONVERBAL BEHAVIOR AND COMMUNICATION

- Beckoning someone with an index finger is a sign of contempt. Instead, indicate "come here" by waving the fingers of one hand closed together with the palm down, facing inward.
- Raising the eyebrows means "No."
- Men or boys (as well as women or girls) may hold hands in public; this gesture has no sexual implications. However, physical contact with members of the opposite sex is to be avoided in public.
- Never show anger in public. People are expected to control their emotions and must avoid direct confrontation.
- Pilipinos often smile when upset or embarrassed.
- Pilipinos may laugh at a crucial point in a meeting as an indication that they are giving their most important message(s).

(continued)

CONVERSATION

- In an initial encounter, be prepared for people to ask personal questions of you (e.g., the price of clothing you're wearing, whether you're married, your profession and how much money you make, where you are going). Such questions are typically intended to be an expression of interest in the person and a way of showing concern or pleasure at seeing a person or of sharing in the other's condition or good fortune (as opposed to simply being inappropriately nosey or intrusive). In fact, the question "Where are you going?" is a direct translation of a common Pilipino greeting, meaning in effect no more than "Hi." A typical response that is given might be, "Just there" or "Just walking." The importance of the interaction is the exchange of friendly responses rather than the exchange of content and information per se (Gochenour, 1990).
- Avoid discussing the political situation in the Philippines and religion.
- Do not immediately assume that Pilipino immigrants who appear to be fluent in English have extensive English language comprehension. You may need to speak somewhat more slowly and carefully to avoid misundertandings. However, you should also be wary of offending truly English-proficient Pilipinos who speak with an "accent" by speaking to them in an overly simplistic manner. You should further refrain from correcting certain word pronunciations, grammar, and so on and/or fixating on selected English words or phrases that may be initially difficult to understand. As noted earlier, there is typically a high degree of self-consciousness among English-speaking Pilipino immigrants as to their relative English language proficiency. The importance of preserving their "face" should outweigh the need to comprehend literally all of their speech during an initial encounter.
- In conversation or meetings with a family, questions are typically first directed to the father. If elders are participating, it is very important not to disagree publicly with them.

PRIVATE HOMES

- Removing your shoes before entering a house is considered appropriate for some Pilipinos—particularly those from rural areas.
- Expect to be offered food or drinks, and partake of such hospitality.
- If served a meal, you will typically be given a fork and spoon, but not a knife. The spoon is to be held in your right hand and the fork in your left. Push food onto the spoon with the fork, and eat from the spoon.

(continued)

GIFT GIVING

- Apart from food and other personal gifts that serve as small tokens of appreciation, Pilipinos may also select material gifts of significant value. The Philippines is a very stratified society, and people are thus very oriented to status symbols such as designer clothes, belts, handbags, watches, and so on. Such gifts may pose significant dilemmas for interventionists employed by agencies that enforce policies prohibiting the acceptance of gifts of this nature.
- Gifts, when appropriate to accept, are not opened in the presence of the giver(s).

APPENDIX C
SIGNIFICANT CULTURAL EVENTS/HOLIDAYS/PRACTICES

HOLIDAYS

Publicly celebrated holidays in the Philippines include Labor Day (May 1), Philippine Independence Day (June 12), Philippine-American Friendship Day (July 4), National Heroes' Day (November 30), and Rizal Day (December 30), the anniversary of the death of Dr. Jose P. Rizal, a Philippine national hero. There are also several religious holidays that are observed; these include Maundy Thursday (3 days before Easter), Good Friday (2 days before Easter), Thanksgiving Day (September 21), and All Saints' Day (November 1). During Holy Week (the week before Easter), people do not eat meat or attend parties or sporting events. They stay at home, going out only to church every day (Devine & Braganti, 1986).

The major holidays of New Year's Day (January 1) and Christmas (December 25) are usually celebrated privately in the home, as are special occasions that call for special celebrations (described next).

SPECIAL HOUSEHOLD CELEBRATIONS

Birthdays, anniversaries, baptisms, confirmations, graduations, and departures of guests and relatives are among the special occasions that are typically celebrated at home. The celebrants customarily spare no expense in setting a lavish display of food and drink for their guests and friends.

> These celebrations provide opportunities to display one's hospitality and showcase one's material success. Meals for company are seldom sit-down affairs. Tables are loaded with several entrees, desserts, and other delicacies served buffet style. Usually an extraordinary amount of food is prepared . . . . This is not viewed as extravagance, but as a gesture of generosity. Extreme care is taken not to be criticized for being *kuripot* (stingy) in preparing only enough, or worse, insufficient food or drink for guests. Extra food is usually given to guests to take home with them. Care is also taken to avoid being criticized as *mayabang* (show-off). The hosts usually apologize to guests for not having prepared more . . . .
>
> These celebrations tend to be very adult centered. Even children's birthdays become occasions for parents to invite their adult relatives and friends, with children, to the festivities. The birthday celebrant is not the "star of the show" as is customary at American birthday parties. Traditionally, presents are not opened during the parties. This custom ensures the avoidance of appearing too anxious or greedy on the part of the birthday celebrant and possibly embarrassing some guests who may not have brought gifts or who may think their gifts are not as good as those of others . . . . There are no special games or activities planned for the children. They eat and play by themselves while the adults visit or help in the kitchen. [With increasing acculturation,] many Filipino-American families are now incorporating some of the more child-centered aspects of birthdays and other celebrations. (Santos, 1983, p. 137)

Note: The traditional rituals and practices associated with newborns and baptisms were described in the "Beliefs, Childrearing," section of this chapter.

APPENDIX D
VOCABULARY

English	Tagalog	Pronunciation
Hello (How are you?)	Kumusta po kayo	koo-moos-ta pó kī-yo
Goodbye	Paalam na po	pa-ah-lahm na pó
Yes	Oo po	oh pó
No	Hindi po	heen-dée po
Please	Paki	pay-key
Thank you	Salamat po	sah-lah̃-maht po
Father	Tatay	tah-tī
Mother	Nanay	nah-nī
Family	Familya	fah-méel-ya

chapter 10

FAMILIES WITH NATIVE HAWAIIAN AND PACIFIC ISLAND ROOTS

Noreen Mokuau and Pemerika Tauili'ili

Native Hawaiian

He lei poina 'ole ke keiki. (A lei never forgotten is the beloved child.)
—Pukui, 1983, p. 82)

Ua mau ke ea o ka 'aina i ka pono. (The life of the land is perpetuated in righteousness.)
—(state of Hawai'i motto)

Samoan

E iloa tama a tagata o fafaga i upu, ao tama a manu e fafaga i fuga o laau. (Human children are fed with words [wisdom], but animal offspring are fed with fruits.)

O le ala i le pule ole tautua. (The way to the family title is through loyal and faithful service to the family.)
—Betham, 1972, p. 18

The Pacific Ocean encompasses approximately 64 million square miles (Quigg, 1987), with the central area being divided into three major geographic areas known as Melanesia, Micronesia, and Polynesia. Fiji, New Hebrides, New Caledonia, and the Solomon Islands make up the major land areas of Melanesia; the Mariana, Marshall, Caroline, Gilbert, and Ellice Islands form Micronesia; and New Zealand, Tonga, Tahiti, Samoa, and Hawai'i make up the major island geography of Polynesia. This chapter describes the two Pacific Island groups with the highest population census in the United States, native Hawaiians and Samoans. The descriptive information on background origins, contemporary life situation, values, beliefs, and language provides the context from which to examine appropriate and effective intervention with these populations.

BACKGROUND

Geographic Origins

The origin and migration of native Hawaiians and Samoans to the islands of Hawai'i and Samoa is subject to varied accounts (Nordyke, 1989) because there is no written information to document the geographical movements. However, data from archeological, botanical, and linguistic studies trace the probable origin of Polynesians to southern Asia (Nordyke, 1989). Buck (1965) suggested that the ancestors of the Polynesian people came from the Himalayas, moved through the Malay archipelago and then migrated east into the Pacific. The Polynesians, strong seafaring voyagers, hypothetically traveled through either the Micronesian chain or the Melanesian islands to eventually reach the Polynesian islands of Hawai'i and Samoa. Native Hawaiians settled in Hawai'i about 2,000 years ago (Blaisdell, 1989) and Samoans settled in Samoa about 1,000 years before that (Nordyke, 1989). In the years considered "precontact," or before Western contact, native Hawaiians and Samoans developed unique cultural systems that flourished.

Historical Origins

The robust cultural systems that native Hawaiians and Samoans developed underwent significant change with the advent of Western influence. The introduction of Western culture to Samoa occurred in 1722, with the arrival of the Dutch navigator Jacob Roggeveen. Soon thereafter, in the 1830s, Christian missionaries and the London Missionary Society converted the Samoan peoples to their teachings (Brigham Young University, 1977). The United States, England, and Germany asserted their influence over Samoan culture through administration and occupation throughout the major portion of the 20th century. In 1900, Samoa was divided into two parts; American Samoa, which was administered by the United States; and Western Samoa, which was administered by a German and then a New Zealand administration. These countries wrought major changes in cultural subsystems such as religion, education, economics, and politics. In 1990, American Samoa is still affiliated with the United States as a territory and Western Samoa, while now an independent nation, still maintains ties with New Zealand as well as with the United States.

Native Hawaiians were introduced to Western culture with the arrival of the English ships led by Captain James Cook in 1778. By 1820, missionaries began the conversion of these islands to Christianity and "raising the heathen of Owhyhee" (Young, 1980, p. 7). Throughout the 19th century, visitors from the United States, England, Germany, Spain, Portugal, and other countries influenced massive changes not only in the religious practices, but also in the political and socioeconomic practices of native Hawaiian people. Nordyke's (1989) statement that "the coming of Westerners had a fatal impact on the Hawaiians" (p. 18) is most dramatically characterized by the tragic decline of the pure-blooded native Hawaiian population by the 20th century. This depopulation is primarily attributed to diseases to which the native Hawaiians had no immunity such as chicken pox, measles, and venereal diseases (Young, 1980). The decline in the pure-blood population is still evident in the 20th century, partially through high infant mortality rates, but also because of intermarriage. In the early part of this century, laborers were brought over from China, Japan, and the Phillipines to work on the plantations; these groups experienced interracial marriages. Hawai'i assumed statehood in 1959, and with it, attendant privileges and problems.

Religious Origins

The prevailing religious systems in both Hawai'i and Samoa are Christian. The historical association of these islands with the United States implies that the

Case Example #1

Alisi was born in Western Samoa and immigrated to Hawai'i 5 years ago with her first husband, a Samoan pastor. Shortly after their move to Hawai'i, Alisi's husband died prematurely; she relied heavily on the church network for support for her and her 2-year-old son. Alisi, now 38 years old, is remarried and has a second child.

Despite having lived in Hawai'i for 5 years, Alisi is limited in her awareness and knowledge of Western ideas. The information that she does have has been gained primarily from watching television and is therefore quite biased and distorted. She lives in a predominantly Samoan community, associates almost exclusively with other Samoans who attend her church, and participates actively in Samoan cultural events such as weddings and funerals.

One of the conflicts between Alisi's Samoan culture and Western ideas has brought her to Family Court, where she has been accused of physically abusing both of her children. When the children have not responded quickly to her demands, she has used rulers and belts as a method of discipline. When asked to explain such harsh treatment, Alisi has said that "when you spare the rod, you spoil the child."

To be successful, the Family Court workers who are working with Alisi will have to intervene in a culturally appropriate way. Because Alisi is relatively traditional in her values and views of the world, it would be helpful to emphasize the family, the pastor, and the church network. Some of the following intervention strategies might be useful: 1) involve the entire family when exploring alternative ways of childrearing and discipline, 2) invite the family's pastor to participate in some of the sessions, and 3) schedule group discussions with others from the Samoan community who have temporarily had their children removed from their homes because of child abuse.

general picture of religion throughout the nation exists for the state of Hawai'i and the territory of American Samoa. In Hawai'i, in addition to Catholic and Protestant denominations, there are sects with origins in Eastern religions. In American Samoa, the principal denominations are the Christian Congregational Church, the Roman Catholic Church, the Methodist Church, and the Church of Jesus Christ of Latter-Day Saints (Mormon) (Brigham Young University, 1977). The church assumes a very powerful role in the lives of the Samoan people, with each village having a church, strict observation of the Sabbath, and the practice of prayer hours.

Precontact religions for native Hawaiians and Samoans were similar in terms of the beliefs in natural environment and ancestral worship. There is appreciation of these precontact religions in both cultures, but in Samoan culture, the dominance of Christian teachings is still prevalent. In native Hawaiian culture, the appreciation has manifested itself in a resurgence of concepts and practices such as those associated with the expression of dance in the hula. The mixing of Christian ways with precontact religious beliefs is seen in the practice of a Christian minister who preaches Christ, yet still invokes the help of his ancestral guardian spirit (Kanahele, 1986). It is further manifested in the increased willingness among native Hawaiians to "relearn" and practice religious beliefs associated with the individual's relationships with nature and gods.

Language Origins

Native Hawaiian and Samoan cultures are predicated on oral traditions and languages that come from a common stock and are linguistically similar. However, with the influence of foreign colonization came changes requiring a written language and the learning of English. Native Hawaiians had their language displaced; since the arrival of Westerners, they have predominantly written and spoken English. Few native Hawaiians are bilingual. Samoans, however, have retained their spoken language while resorting to writing in the English language; the overwhelming majority of Samoans are bilingual. Samoans in American Samoa speak Samoan both in the workplace and home whereas Samoans in the United States speak Samoan primarily in the home.

CONTEMPORARY LIFE IN THE UNITED STATES

The 1980 census showed that the two largest Pacific Islander groups in the United States were native Hawaiians (172,000) and Samoans (40,000), and that these groups lived primarily in the states of Hawai'i and California (United States Bureau of the Census, 1988). Specifically, native Hawaiians tend to reside in the islands to which they are indigenous, Hawai'i, and the majority of Samoans have settled in California.

However, the 1980 census calculations of population size appear to represent an undercounting of both native Hawaiians and Samoans. The Hawai'i Department of Health conducts an ongoing survey, which in 1986 revealed that there were more than 200,000 persons of mixed Hawaiian blood, and approximately 8,000 persons of pure-blood in the state of Hawai'i alone (Nordyke, 1989). The California Department of Mental Health estimated the Samoan population in California in 1981 to be approximately 90,000 (State of California, Department of Mental Health, 1981).

The migration of Samoans to California and Hawai'i has occurred as recently as the 1950s (Mokuau & Chang, 1991). Three major reasons for the migration include: 1) the transfer of naval base personnel with the closing of the United States Naval Base in American Samoa in 1951, 2) increased opportunities for education and employment in the United States, and 3) the increase in population and the concomitant lack of employment and economic opportunities in American Samoa (State of California, Department of Mental Health, 1981). As is true of other newly arriving immigrant populations, Samoans have tended to settle in communities in which there are established ethnic enclaves.

VALUES

Values represent what is deemed to be important in life and thereby serve as an index and guide to the way people define themselves and the world in which they live. Any exploration of values must take into account two key considerations: 1) values may change in definition and form over time, and 2) persons may vary in their perception of and adherence to the same set of values. The values of precontact native Hawaiian and Samoan cultures were altered significantly and, to a large extent, caused to deteriorate with the infusion of Western languages, religions, lifestyle practices, and behavioral norms over 200 years ago. For example, Kanahele (1986), in his hypothesis that native Hawaiians lack ethnic identity and pride, stated that it is only through rediscovery and reassertion of primal values and achievements that native Hawaiians can recover their identity and self-esteem.

The values that exist today have relative worth for different persons. For native Hawaiians and Samoans, the degree of acculturation to the majority American culture influences their profile of values. For Samoans who have a relatively short history of residence in the United States, there have been fewer opportunities for acculturation than for native Hawaiians. Thus, their maintenance of cultural values will be stronger. Within each of these Pacific Islander groups, there is also intragroup variation in the promotion of values because of differences in geographical residence, age, gender, socioeconomic status, and so on. The following section highlights major values of both native Hawaiian and Samoan cultures; however, the usefulness of this information is contingent on the interventionist's emphasizing an understanding of the uniqueness of the individual in the context of these cultural values.

Case Example #2

Kehau was born and raised in Honolulu but moved to California with her mother after her parents divorced 7 years ago. Kehau is now 17 and living with her mother in a small apartment complex in an urban area in southern California. Kehau is of part Hawaiian ancestry and comfortably identifies with native Hawaiian cultural values and traditions. In fact, her initial adjustment to California was tumultuous. She frequently got into trouble in school and was difficult for her mother to control at home. In family counseling sessions at that time, Kehau talked of missing her extended family and friends in Hawai'i and felt that her mother's need to work so many hours left little opportunity for mother–daughter contact.

Kehau has just been referred to a family counseling clinic by her school advisor because she is pregnant and unsure of what to do about the pregnancy. She is inclined to have and raise the child, but her boyfriend is unwilling to get married or to participate in the counseling sessions. Kehau's mother is actively involved in the counseling sessions and is supportive of Kehau's inclinations to have the child.

For the counselor, there are several cultural issues that must be considered. Kehau's background suggests that there are unresolved issues related to her leaving her family and friends in Hawai'i and the possibility of an identity conflict in regard to her own cultural origins. In addition to providing educational information on pregnancy and informing both Kehau and her mother of possible options and their consequences, the counselor may want to consider the following strategies for emotional support that may be culturally distinctive if directed toward the family unit. These strategies include: 1) strengthening the mother–daughter relationship by recommending ways that they can build time together; 2) exploring opportunities for Kehau, and possibly her mother, to visit family and friends in Hawai'i; and 3) seeking opportunities in their community, which is a densely populated native Hawaiian neighborhood, to develop networks of support.

Native Hawaiian Values

Most major values of native Hawaiian culture appear to be derivatives of values associated with relationships, particularly as they reflect the relationship of the individual to the family, the community, the land, and the spiritual world. The fundamental unit in native Hawaiian culture is the *'ohana* (family), or relatives by blood, marriage, and adoption (Handy & Pukui, 1977). Emphasis is placed on the needs of the family unit rather than on the needs of any individual family member. In traditional times, the family unit functioned as part of a larger geographical region, and the importance of relationships within the general community was acknowledged. Handy and Pukui (1977) also suggested that implicit in the value of familial relationships is the recognition of the value of the *'aina* (land) as a source of food and nourishment. However, the relationship of the family and the land is more than just a physical linkage; it is perceived as a spiritual bond between family members and nature. This spiritual bond is amplified as living family members recognize and interact with deceased ancestors who are represented in nature.

> One . . . hears that old Hawaiians are sometimes observed talking to plants and trees before picking their flowers—asking before taking—and that they often leave offerings when they take something of significance. . . . Many Hawaiians also believe that they have ancestral spirits (*'aumakua*) who dwell in animal or other nature forms. . . . And they think of their ancestral spirits, and the nature forms they inhabit, as family members. (Dudley, 1990, pp. 1–2)

There are several implications that might be drawn for interventionis ɜ working with native Hawaiian people who maintain these values. First and foremost, the interventionist should focus on the family system, rather than just the individual, as the client. For example, the goals or objectives identified as part of the intervention should advance the needs and desires of the family over the aspirations of one family member. Second, the high value placed on relationships suggests that interventionists must define and address culturally appropriate ways of interpersonal interactions among native Hawaiian peoples. For example, Howard (1974), in a behavioral study of a native Hawaiian community, suggested that native Hawaiians favor interpersonal styles that emphasize cooperation over confrontation. Howard stated that native Hawaiians tend "to avoid situations that had a potential for conflict, shame, or any other form of social disruption" (p. 101). Finally, interventionists must consider the native Hawaiian valuing of spiritual relationships. Communion with the land and with spiritual ancestors is critical for many native Hawaiians, and the interventionist must be sensitive to such values and not impose Western clinical judgments of "bizzare" or "crazy." In fact, in a proactive way, values of spirtual relationships might even be incorporated into the intervention plan (Mokuau, 1990).

Samoan Values

In a broad way, there is some similarity between the major values of native Hawaiian culture and Samoan culture. "Dominant values . . . in Samoan culture focus on the family, communal relationships, and the church" (Mokuau & Chang, 1991). The Samoan way of life is organized around the *aiga* (family), which is a hierarchical system comprising nuclear and extended families. The structure is determined by rank or chiefly status, as well as by age and gender. For example, a *matai* (village chief) has responsibilities for the welfare of all related families in a village, and each household may have their own chief. The females are subordinate to the males and the young always defer to the old (State of California, Department of Mental Health, 1981). The family works toward the goal of well-being for the entire family, which may be as large as an entire village. The values inherent in such a system include reciprocity, cooperation, and interdependence.

The church is a highly valued institution in Samoan culture with direct interface with the family system. The structure and responsibilities of the family are affirmed by the church; the church, in turn, is supported by contributions from the families. Religious practices are strictly adhered to and include participation in prayer hours in the morning and the evening, attending church on the Sabbath day (Brigham Young University, 1977), and observance of rituals. For example, children learn from a very early age to respond to simple religious questions such as: 1) Who made you? (God), 2) Who struck the rock? (Moses).

There are several implications for intervention that emerge from a discussion of values. Similar to the situation with native Hawaiians, the client focus for the Samoan population should be on the family unit rather than the individual. Due to the emphasis on the extended family system, it would be extremely difficult for the interventionist to deal with such a large group of people. However, conferring with and involving persons in the extended family system who have authority, such as the chiefs, may be appropriate and helpful to the resolution of family problems. Another implication relates to the hierarchical nature of the family system and the appropriate ways to initiate and maintain discussions in the process of intervention. It is important to have a knowledge of the family lineage, to recognize the members who exercise family authority, and to thereby acknowledge through appropriate greetings these persons of authority. In order to further any discussion, it is also important for interventionists to recognize the rituals of culturally appropriate behavior such as: 1) presenting a posture of interest and concern for the welfare of the family, 2) not delving into personal issues or difficulties too soon in the intervention process, and 3) maintaining all conversations from a sitting position, never standing. Finally, as the status of the church and the pastor is recognized by Samoans, the involvement of this religious person as part of the intervention process would seem to be culturally appropriate.

BELIEFS

Beliefs, a body of ideas held by a group to be true, share the same characteristics as values. They may change over time, and the perceptions and strength of these beliefs among individuals may be different. Beliefs involving children, disability, causation, and medical care are in some ways manifested in the behavioral norms of native Hawaiians and Samoans. The following section highlights beliefs and behavioral norms that may be especially relevant to interventionists.

Native Hawaiian Beliefs

The worth of children in native Hawaiian culture is captured in the saying, a "house without children is a house without life" (Young, 1980, p. 12). Young further described the Hawaiians' commitment to their children: "In any Hawaiian community children are everywhere. In virtually every home children are coddled, showered with attention, and fondled. Seldom is an infant left alone when crying. There is much contact, touching, and caressing" (p. 12).

The care of children is promoted in the strongly interdependent family system, and many persons have childrearing responsibilities. While parents have primary charge of their children, grandparents and other native Hawaiian elders also contribute to the physical, emotional, and spiritual care of the children. In traditional times, the *hiapo* (first born child) was permanently given to the grandparents, and on other occasions, infants who were not the first born were sometimes given to other relatives who asked for them (Pukui, Haertig, Lee, & McDermott, 1972). Due to the closeness of the family unit, the giving of the child did not necessarily mean parent–child separation. Rather, it meant that the child grew up in a household in which he or she could count on the support of the grandparents, parents, and other family seniors. While the process of giving the child away is not observed today, it is not uncommon for the child to have a strong relationship with grandparents and to have many family members taking care of his or her welfare.

There is very little information on children's disabilities in traditional native Hawaiian culture. It is not clear whether the unavailability of information is due to the low numbers of disability in historical times, or to the preference to

emphasize only the healthy children. A noted authority on native Hawaiian culture, Mary Kawena Pukui, when discussing infants born with congenital abnormalities, recalled that children with club feet were accepted and that massage efforts were used to correct the malformed foot (Pukui et al., 1972). Pukui also recalled that abnormal infants or miscarried fetuses that resembled things of nature such as fishes or lizards were returned to the ocean or the pool. The pre-Christian belief was that the child looked like and was a form of the family ancestral spirits and must be returned to these ancestor gods. This type of historical belief assumes importance for intervention today because it affirms the value of spirtualism, and the need to consider spiritual variables when working with native Hawaiians. There is a sense that life events are directly related to the working of the spiritual world, and while individuals are not totally helpless to these events, some things are beyond the control of the individual. It is known that congenital abnormalities and infant mortality rates are higher for native Hawaiians than for other ethnic groups in Hawai'i today (Bell, Nordyke, & O'Hagan, 1989), and thus, an understanding of the historical importance of spiritualism may play an important role in intervention.

Medical care, in historical times, was often left to *kahuna lapa'au* (medical experts) who used prayers, physical massage, and medicinal plants and herbs (Blaisdell, 1989). In contemporary times, there is still much credibility attributed to persons of such status, and it would behoove the interventionist to maintain a respectful position toward such persons. Pukui et al. (1972) suggested that to denigrate the client's belief in the "*kahuna* man" or "prayer lady" may only reinforce resistance to accepting treatment at a medical clinic or hospital (p. 165). Wegner (1989) further stated that "Although systematic evidence about the utililization of health care services is lacking, the limited evidence reviewed . . . suggests that native Hawaiians receive fewer health care services [than other ethnic groups in Hawai'i] . . . and appear to participate less in health education, health promotion, and screening and referral programs . . ." (p. 150), even though they experience substantially higher rates of health problems (Johnson, 1989). Underutilization of services might be attributed to many reasons, including lack of geographical accessibility, high cost of services, cultural encapsulation of the health care worker, and cultural inappropriateness of the programs. Attention to these areas will facilitate native Hawaiians' use of medical clinics and hospitals in the future.

Samoan Beliefs

"Samoan culture views children as an asset and source of pride" (Brigham Young University, 1977, p. 6). Biological parents are responsible for the discipline and training of their children. Oftentimes, however, the chief of the family may function in a parental role and may exercise as much authority as the biological parents (Markoff & Bond, 1980). The day-to-day care of young children is handled by older siblings.

In line with the highly interdependent nature of the family structure, chil-

dren are taught the importance of mutual sharing. Thus, this belief in sharing may be manifested in children leaving the home for indefinite lengths of time to visit with uncles and aunts or married brothers or sisters (State of California, Department of Mental Health, 1981). Children are also taught to behave properly and to respect their elders. Illustrations of proper and respectful behavior include sitting down while addressing an older person and not interrupting an adult conversation. The emphasis on interdependence and proper behavior in the family system encourages the use of social control as a form of childrearing. In Samoan culture, social control and discipline tend to be overt and direct, and often involve physical punishment. "Punitive measures are regularly employed by age three, when children first begin to be involved in the work of the household, and continues through mid-adolescence" (Markoff & Bond, 1980, p. 187).

Information on children's disabilities is not documented in the literature, and is not a subject discussed in everyday conversation. However, considering the value of children in Samoan culture and the Samoan family's commitment to the church, the belief that emerges is that the child with a disability is the result of a poor relationship with God. Newborns are viewed as special gifts from God. In the case of a child with a disability, it is believed that God must be displeased with the family. Samoans are a very religious people with a strong faith in their Christian God and other native supernatural powers. They believe that they personally exercise very little control over their own destinies, and that it is the supernatural powers that cause life events. With disabilities, sometimes parents will blame themselves or their partner for the child's condition. Interventionists must deal with such feelings of guilt and blame among the parents as well as other members of the family and examine the religious connotations of having a child with a developmental disability.

The use of Western medical facilities is linked with Samoans' religious beliefs. In general, they believe that God works through hospital care or medication and if they do right before God, healing will occur. Their preference, however, is to use traditional healing persons or advice from relatives or their pastors. "Samoans have an iron-clad faith in their local or herbal remedies and their bush doctors" (Fiatoa & Palafox, 1980, p. 254). In particular, there is the *fofo* (Samoan massage), which is administered with leaves, roots, and fruits. This massage is used for every conceivable childhood illness, from rashes to defective spines (Fiatoa & Palafox, 1980).

ISSUES OF LANGUAGE

As noted earlier, few native Hawaiians are adept at speaking the Hawaiian language, whereas the majority of Samoans are bilingual. Interventionists must practice caution when working with these bilingual Samoan clients since language can prove to be a barrier to assessment and intervention. Some possible difficulties include: 1) Samoan words that have multiple English meanings, and 2) English words for which there is no equivalent Samoan word (Fiatoa & Palafox, 1980). The use of interpreters may be helpful, but as is typical in any translation of language, there is the possibility of meanings being interpreted inaccurately.

Nonverbal communication is important to both Pacific Island cultures. Traditionally, both cultures have relied on oral traditions, particularly through chants and songs, to document their lineage, values, and beliefs. While the "spoken word" could have various levels of power, so could the "unspoken word." In native Hawaiian culture, for example, paralinguistics is reflected in guttural sounds indicating agreement or musical sounds indicating greetings. Examples in Samoan culture include the biting of one's teeth, which indicates anger and frustration, or the movement of the shoulders, which indicates confusion or ambivalence. As the specific nuances of nonverbal language are sometimes difficult to ascertain, the interventionist must thoughtfully consider the combined messages of verbal and nonverbal communication.

SUMMARY AND RECOMMENDATIONS

Summary

Broadly examined, culturally sensitive intervention refers to a helping transaction that is predicated on an understanding of the individual in the context of his or her culture. For native Hawaiians and Samoans, culturally sensitive intervention specifically refers to a knowledge of the influence of historical variables on the current-day values, beliefs, and lifestyle practices of these peoples. Native Hawaiians have experienced over 200 years of dramatic social changes, which have raised questions about the survival of this population as a distinctive people (Wegner, 1989). In a similar time period, Samoans have also been exposed to Western influence but not to as devastating a degree as native Hawaiians. In the Samoan islands, the majority of the population is still Samoan; in Hawai'i, the majority of the population is non–native Hawaiian. Samoan culture today is in a great state of transition; however, the comfort for Samoans is the awareness that *fa'a Samoa* (the Samoan way) still predominates in the Samoan islands. For native Hawaiians, that comfort is less tangible.

Recommendations for Interventionists

A few recommendations are offered to facilitate culturally sensitive practice with native Hawaiians and Samoans. These recommendations are appropriate for those persons maintaining a close connection with traditional values and beliefs, and may be less appropriate for more acculturated individuals.

- Focus attention on the family system rather than the individual as the vehicle for intervention. Inherent in this focus on the family is the acknowledgment of the status and responsibilities of different members, and a knowledge of the interpersonal dynamics of family members. Furthermore, the goals and processes of intervention should address the needs of the collective unit.
- Give consideration to traditional values and beliefs about spiritualism, particularly as it relates to healing. These values and beliefs should be respected and worked with rather than rejected (Territory of American Samoa, 1990). Traditional healers may provide consultative information, work directly in collaboration with Western interventionists, or, on some occasions, may be used as referrals.
- Promote the utilization of bicultural and bilingual workers with these populations. Encourage the training and development of native Hawaiian and Samoan individuals to work with their peoples, as well as the training and development of other culturally diverse peoples to work with them. Content for training may include knowledge of historical variables, general values and beliefs, problem areas, coping patterns, and healing styles.

The effectiveness of intervention can only be brought about when there is an awareness of the richness of cultural diversity and a commitment to enhance the quality of life through an understanding and a promotion of that richness. The usefulness of these recommendations for native Hawaiians and Samoans will only be apparent when interventionists refuse to "impose" Western values and beliefs, and instead start to "infuse" culturally appropriate values and beliefs into the practice situation.

REFERENCES

Bell, B., Nordyke, E., & O'Hagan, P. (1989). Fertility and maternal and child health. *Social Process in Hawai'i, 32,* 87–103.

Betham, M. (1972). The family, the heart of Samoana. In *Samoan Heritage Series proceedings* (pp. 15–19). Honolulu: University of Hawai'i, College of Continuing Education and Community Service.

Blaisdell, K. (1989). Historical and cultural aspects of native Hawaiian health. *Social Process in Hawai'i, 32,* 1–21.

Brigham Young University. (1977). *People of Samoa.* Provo, UT: Brigham Young University, Language and Intercultural Research Center.

Buck, P. (1965). Polynesian migrations. In E.S. Handy, K. Emory, E. Bryan, P. Buck, & J. Wise (Eds.), *Ancient Hawaiian civilizations* (pp. 23–34). Tokyo: Charles E. Tuttle Company.

Dudley, M. (1990). *Man, gods, and nature.* Honolulu: Na Kane O Ka Malo Press.

Fiatoa, L., & Palafox, N. (1980). The Samoans. In N. Palafox & A. Warren (Eds.), *Cross-cultural caring* (pp. 250–271). Honolulu: University of Hawai'i, School of Medicine.

Handy, E.S., & Pukui, M.K. (1977). *The Polynesian family system in Ka'u, Hawai'i.* Tokyo: Charles E. Tuttle.

Howard, A. (1974). *Ain't no big thing, coping strategies in a Hawaiian-American community.* Honolulu: University Press of Hawai'i.

Johnson, D. (1989). An overview of ethnicity and health in Hawai'i. *Social Process in Hawai'i, 32,* 67–86.

Kanahele, G. (1986). *Ku kanaka, stand tall.* Honolulu: University of Hawai'i Press and Waiaha Foundation.

Markoff, R., & Bond, J. (1980). The Samoans. In J. McDermott, Jr., W.-S. Tseng, & T. Maretzki (Eds.), *People and cultures of Hawai'i* (pp. 184–199). Honolulu: University of Hawai'i, School of Medicine and University Press of Hawai'i.

Mokuau, N. (1990). A family-centered approach in native Hawaiian culture. *Families in Society: The Journal of Contemporary Human Services, 7,* 607–613.

Mokuau, N., & Chang, N. (1991). Samoans. In N. Mokuau (Ed.), *Handbook of social services for Asian and Pacific Islander Americans* (pp. 155–170). Westport, CT: Greenwood Publishing.

Nordyke, E. (1989). *The peopling of Hawai'i.* Honolulu: University of Hawai'i Press.

Pukui, M.K. (1983). *'Olelo no'eau, Hawaiian proverbs and poetical sayings.* Honolulu: Bishop Museum Press.

Pukui, M.K., Haertig, E.W., Lee, C., & McDermott, J. (1972). *Nana I ke kumu* (Vol. II). Honolulu: Hui Hanai.

Quigg, A. (1987). *History of the Pacific Islands Studies Program at the University of Hawai'i: 1950–1986.* Honolulu: University of Hawai'i, Pacific Island Studies Program.

State of California, Department of Mental Health. (1981). *Samoans in America.* Oakland: Author.

Territory of American Samoa. (1990). *Mental health plan 1989–1991.* Pago Pago, AS: Author.

United States Bureau of the Census. (1988). *We, the Asian and Pacific Islander Americans.* Washington, DC: U.S. Government Printing Office.

Wegner, E. (1989). Recommendations for more effective health care. *Social Process in Hawai'i, 32,* 149–167.

Young, B. (1980). The Hawaiians. In J. McDermott, Jr., W-S. Tseng, & T. Maretzki (Eds.), *People and cultures of Hawai'i* (pp. 5–24). Honolulu: University of Hawai'i, School of Medicine and University Press of Hawai'i.

APPENDIX A
CONTRASTING BELIEFS, VALUES, AND PRACTICES

Beliefs, values, and practices	Western	Native Hawaiian	Samoan
Unit of focus	Individual	Extended family	Extended family
Family system	Egalitarian	Hierarchical	Hierarchical
Religious/spiritual	Christianity	Combination of traditional and Christianity	Christianity
Language	English	English	Combination of Samoan and English
Interpersonal styles	Competitive	Cooperative	Cooperative
Childrearing	Verbal discipline	Verbal and physical discipline	Physical discipline
Healing styles	Western medicine	Combination of Western and traditional medicine	Combination of Western and traditional medicine

APPENDIX B
CULTURAL COURTESIES AND CUSTOMS

NATIVE HAWAIIAN

- It is inappropriate to touch a child on the top of the head because this area is considered sacred.
- It is taboo to name one's child after persons who were specifically blessed with their own names unless permission is given.

SAMOAN

- It is inappropriate to walk past an elder or a person with status (e.g., pastor) without a show of physical deference such as the bowing of the head and body and downcast eyes.
- It is inappropriate for a child or adult to stretch his or her legs toward others when sitting in a *fale* (traditional Samoan home).
- It is inappropriate to eat or drink while standing or walking.

APPENDIX C
SIGNIFICANT CULTURAL EVENTS/HOLIDAYS/PRACTICES

Event/holiday/practices	Date	Description
Native Hawaiian		
King Kamehameha Day	June 11	Celebrates the birthday of the first king of Hawai'i.
Prince Kuhio Day	March 26	Honors the Hawaiian monarch Prince Kuhio.
Aloha Week	September	A week of festivities including Hawaiian pageantry, canoe races, parades, hula dances, and a variety of other forms of entertainment.
Samoan		
Flag Day	April 17	Celebrates the date when American Samoa became a territory of the United States.
White Sunday	3rd Sunday of October	A religious celebration for children when they perform before the congregation and are accorded special rights and privileges.
Funerals	Throughout the year	Funerals are significant events in Samoan culture and are recognized with the exchange of gifts and the presentation of fine meals.

APPENDIX D
VOCABULARY

English	Hawaiian	Pronunciation	Samoan	Pronunciation
Family	'ohana	o-HA-nuh	Aiga	eye-ing-a
Father	Makua kane	mah-khuah khah-neh	Tama	tah-mah
Mother	Makuahine	mah-khuah hee-neh	Tina	ti-NAA
Child	Keiki	keh-kee	Tamaititi	tah-mah-ee-ti-ti
Hello	Aloha	ahh-loh-ha	Talofa	tah-LOH-fah
Goodbye	Aloha	ahh-loh-ha	Tofa soifua	toh-FAH soh-ee-FU-ah
Please	'Olu'olu	o-lu o-lu	Fa'amolemole	FAH-a-mohlay-MOH-lay
Thank you	Mahalo	ma-HAA-lo	Fa'afetai tele lava	FAH-a-fay-tai te-le lah-vah

chapter 11 _____

FAMILIES WITH
MIDDLE EASTERN ROOTS

Virginia-Shirin Sharifzadeh

Arabic
Patience is the key to freedom from grief and sorrow.

الصَّبْرُ مِفْتَاحُ الفَرَجِ .

The beginning of wisdom is the fear of god.

رَأْسُ الحِكْمَةِ مَخَافَةُ اللَّهِ

Iranian
A whisper of love in the teacher's instruction can bring to
school the reluctant student on a holiday.

درس معلم اَر بود زمزمه محبتی جمعه به مكتب آورد طفل گريزپای را

Prophet Mohammed
Heaven lies beneath the mothers' feet.

Iranian, Arabic, Kurdish, and Turkish
You shall receive with the same hand with which you
give.

(Kurdish script)   لەوەدەس دأَكرى لە دەس نە رّى

The Middle East is a region with a rich diversity of cultures, languages, and
religions. Since the 1980s, there has been a large increase in the number of
immigrants to the United States from different countries in this region. Interventionists developing programs for young children and their families can profit
by understanding the cultural patterns that shape the behavior of their clients
from the Middle East. Interventionists can be more effective if they can anticipate the perspectives and behaviors of the families with whom they are working
and plan accordingly. This chapter addresses some general beliefs and practices
shared by a majority of people in the Middle East.

BACKGROUND

Geographic Origins

There are different opinions as to what are the boundaries of the Middle East. Generally, however, the Middle East refers to the area in Asia and Africa comprising the political states of Lebanon, Syria, Israel and the Occupied Territories, Jordan, Iraq, Saudi Arabia, Kuwait, Bahrain, Qatar, the United Arab Emirates, Oman, Yemen, Egypt, Sudan, Turkey, and Iran. In addition, the "Middle East" is used as a cultural designation for a society and civilization found not only in that region but also to some degree in a number of adjacent countries such as Afghanistan, Pakistan, Libya, Tunisia, Algeria, Morocco, and Cyprus (Fisher, 1969).

The geographic location of the Middle East has made it one of the world's greatest human junctions, with exposure to cultural influences from several directions. The Middle East is a convenient landbridge between Africa and Eurasia, and between the Mediterranean world and the Asia of India and the Far East, and as such has hosted nations, tribes, traders, armies, and pilgrims—who along the way discovered the wealth of the area and the civilization of its people.

With the exception of the tropical climate, the Middle East represents all varieties of climates and physical environments—ranging from the severely cold Alpine climate in the mountainous regions of Northwest Iran, to the hot and arid deserts in the central regions of Iran and Saudi Arabia. In between these two extreme climates, countries in the Middle East enjoy a wide range of subtropical and semitropical environments, which enable them to produce almost any kind of agricultural crops and products. There is, therefore, a wide variation in the food tradition of the Middle Eastern countries.

In countries to the east of the region such as Iran and Afghanistan, rice is the staple food and tea is the predominant drink of the people. In most other countries of the Middle East, however, bread is the staple food and people generally drink coffee.

Among the countries in the Middle East, Iran and Lebanon have almost unique situations. Although the two countries are very different in size, they represent the largest variations in climates, physical features, languages, and religions existing in the region.

Historical Origins

The Middle East is the seat of mankind's earliest civilizations. The valleys of the Indus, the Tigris-Euphrates, and the Nile—blessed with a warm climate, a fertile soil, native animals and plants, waters available for controlled irrigation, and varied mineral resources—were most favorable for the propagation of human life, and for the growth of an organized society (Fisher, 1969).

The Sumerian people, an Asiatic type of Mediterranean race, arrived at one of the mouths of Tigris-Euphratis before 4000 B.C. Hence evolved the Sumerian city-states with society divided into technological-social classes, nobility, priests, traders, farmers, and artisans—divisions that have persisted as constant factors in all of the Middle Eastern civilizations (Fisher, 1969). Similar civilizations were established at the same time by the Semites (probably coming from the desert, and the Hamites (coming from East and North Africa) along the Nile and the Tigris-Euphratis. During the second millennium B.C., Indo-Europeans from eastern Europe and western Asia began a wave of southward movement. In their transition to an organized life on the Middle Eastern pattern of greater specialization and division of labor, these migrants added something in religion, the art of writing, metallurgical skills, political organization, transportation, irrigation, and astronomy (Fisher, 1969).

From the beginning of the first millennium B.C., significant empires began to rise and fall in the Middle East, each trying to unite the area under one cultural and political system. The most significant of these empires, before the rise of Islam, were the Assyrian, the Babylonian, the Egyptian, the Persian, the Greek, and the Roman Empires. The vision of cultural unity, however, may have been more closely achieved with the spread of Islam.

Religious Origins

The Middle East is the birthplace of several major monotheistic religions in the world. Religion has always played, and continues to play, an important role in the formation of cultural, social, and political structures in this region. In the tradition of Middle Eastern societies, religious identity serves as a point around which historical memories, social customs, and political loyalties tend to cluster. People from the Middle East do not consider religion to be a strictly private and personal matter, and hence, are not usually offended by questions such as: "What is your religion?" The same people, however, would be perplexed if asked the question, "What is your race?" Because of the significance of religion in the Middle East, one must be especially sensitive to the role that religion has played in shaping the values and customs of the people in the region.

The earliest known system of belief among different people in the Middle East was to honor a hierarchy or a multiplicity of gods associated with natural forces. The first monotheistic religions in the Middle East emerged during the first millennium B.C. in Iran and Palestine. In Iran, Ahura Mazda (the "Wise Lord") came to be worshipped as the supreme god under the guidance of the religious teacher, Zoroaster. In Palestine, the Jews or Hebrews came to believe in Yahweh as the creator of the universe.

The conquests of Alexander the Great in the first millennium and the establishment of the Greek cities spread Greek polytheism in the Middle East. Monotheism thus remained limited and contained for many centuries until the emergence of Christianity during the Roman Empire.

The Roman Empire adopted Christianity as the official religion in the fourth century A.D. Problems arose over the nature of Christ and his relationship with God. The earliest Christians, hence, branched off into the Melkites, the Monophysites, and the Nestorians.

The Coming of Islam

The rise of Islam in the seventh century and the formation of the Empire of Caliphs, stretching from Spain and Morocco to central Asia, marked a new period in the religious history of the Middle East. Muslims (Moslems) believed that God had given His final revelation to the Prophet Mohammed, whom they believed to be the last in a succession of prophets including Moses and Jesus. The Qur'an (Koran), the holy book containing Mohammed's revelations, was believed to be the full expression of the divine will for human life. The main body of Muslims, who were later called Sunnis, believed that the Prophet had transmitted his temporal authority to a line of caliphs.

The major split in Islam took place over the position of the fourth caliph, Ali, the cousin and son-in-law of Mohammed, who was murdered and succeeded by Muawiya, the governor of Syria. Ali's supporters, known as "Partisans of Ali" (Shi'a 'Ali), developed the doctrine that Ali was not only the temporal ruler of the community, he was also the Imam, the only authoritative interpreter of the Qur'an. They also held that the office of Imam could be designated only to members of his and the Prophet's family. The Shi'as, however, differed among themselves over the issue of the line of transmission. Hence developed the branches known as the "Twelvers" or simply the Shi'as, the Zaidis, and the Seveners (also known as Isma'ilis).

Judaism, Christianity, and Islam all underwent new kinds of divisions from the 16th century onward. The opening to the modern Western world in the 19th century may have also played a role in such developments.

The Present Situation

With few exceptions, all the religious beliefs just mentioned continue to have adherents in the Middle East. The most widespread of all the religions in the Middle East is Islam in its Sunni form. Its followers number in the majority in Egypt, Turkey, Syria, Jordan, Saudi Arabia, South Yemen, most of the Persian Gulf States, as well as Afghanistan, Pakistan, and countries in North Africa. It is also present in all the other countries of the region.

Shi'a'ism in its "Twelvers" form is followed by most Iranians and a majority of people in Iraq. It is also widespread in the Persian Gulf, Saudi Arabia, eastern Turkey, and southern and eastern Lebanon. Zaydis Shi'a'ism is followed in northern Yemen. Other Shi'a branches have followers in small communities in Syria, Yemen, Lebanon, Israel, and western Iran.

Followers of the Eastern Orthodox Church are to be found mostly in Lebanon, Syria, Jordan, Israel, Cyprus, and some other countries. The Nestorian Church has its followers among Assyrians in northern Iraq and western Iran and some other countries. Armenian monophysites are found mainly in Syria, Lebanon, and Iran. There are also Coptic Catholics in Egypt; Maronite Christians in Lebanon; Greek Catholics in Lebanon, Syria, Jordan, and Israel; Chaldean Catholics in Iraq and Iran; Syrian Catholics in Syria and elsewhere; and Armenian Catholics in Lebanon and elsewhere.

The Jewish population of the Middle East is mostly concentrated in Israel. Many Israeli Jews, however, have immigrated to Israel from western, central, and eastern Europe and are referred to as Ashkenazis. The Jewish people from the Mediterranean or the Middle East are known as Sephardis. Of the latter Jewish communities in the Middle East that still exist, the communities in Turkey and Iran are the largest.

Iran also has the world's largest, albeit shrinking, communities of Zoroastrians and Bahais. (For more information on religions in the Middle East, the reader is referred to *The Cambridge Encyclopedia of the Middle East and North Africa* [Mostyn & Hourani, 1988].)

Language Origins

Unlike Europe, where almost all languages derive from the common Indo-European language family, Middle Eastern languages are divided among three very different language families: the Hamito-Semitic, the Indo-European, and the Altic. Language is one of the primary ways by which the peoples from the Middle East differentiate themselves and define their national identities or political allegiances.

The most widely spoken language in the Middle East is Arabic. A sister language to Hebrew, it belongs to the Semitic subdivision of the Hamito-Semitic language family. There is a distinction between written and colloquial Arabic. Written Arabic, which is the religious and literary language throughout the Arab world, does not vary and serves as a bond between all Arabs. It is a spoken form of standard Arabic that is used as a *lingua franca*. At the regional level, however, Arabic has a number of dialects that may be so different as to preclude communication unless standard Arabic is used.

Globally, Arabic ranks as the sixth most common first language. It is the chief language in 18 countries in the Middle East and North Africa (with the exception of Iran, Turkey, and Israel). The significance of the Arabic language, however, far surpasses its rank, because it is also revered by most non-Arab Muslims as the language of Revelation, not subject to substitution or translation. The Arabic alphabet consists of 29 letters, all of which, except the first, are consonants. They are written from right to left. The most approved word order in Arabic grammar is verb + subject + object. However, one may also find the subject put first.

Turkish, Persian (Farsi), and Kurdish are three other widely spoken languages in the Middle East. The Turkish group of languages belongs to the Altic language family. Turkey is the sole country in which Turkish is the predominant language. In the Middle East, Turkish is also spoken by almost one third of Iranians (mostly called Azeri Turks from the Iranian province of Azerbaijan), as well as by groups in Afghanistan and Cyprus. Modern Turkish used in Turkey employs a modified form of the Roman alphabet, consisting of 29 letters. The most frequent word order in modern Turkish is subject + object + verb.

Persian (also known as Farsi) belongs to the Indo-European language family. It is the third most widely spoken language in the Middle East. The overwhelming majority of all Persian speakers are in Iran, where Persian is also the official language. Persian is also spoken in western Afghanistan and Bahrain and in small communities around the Persian Gulf. The Persian language (along with Shi'a'ism) is a major component of Iran's distinctive national identity and helps to differentiate the country from its neighbors. Modern Persian is also written from right to left and uses a modified Arabic script, which makes it appear as one with Arabic. The two languages, however, are completely different. There are, nevertheless, many Arabic words used in Farsi. The word order in Persian is subject + object + verb.

Related to Persian and also widely spoken is Kurdish, which is the language of large Kurdish populations of Iran, Iraq, Turkey, and Syria. Hebrew (the official language of Israel), Armenian, Assyrian, and Greek are other major languages spoken by large groups in the Middle East region. (For more information on Middle Eastern languages, the reader is referred to *The Cambridge Encyclopedia of the Middle East and North Africa* [Mostyn & Hourani, 1988].)

CONTEMPORARY LIFE

Immigration to the United States

The history of large-scale immigration to the United States by people from the Middle East goes as far back as the late 19th and early 20th centuries. Christian tradesmen from the Syrian province of the Ottoman Empire were probably the first Arabs who, in 1875, came to the United States seeking opportunities (Thernstrom, Orlov, & Handlin, 1980). In the period between 1890 and 1930, large groups of Armenians fled the persecution of the Turkish government, and some sought refuge in the United States.

During the 20 years that followed the Armenian exodus, there were no large-scale immigrations to the United States from any country in the Middle East. However, with new developments in transportation technology and new possibilities in cultural and educational exchanges, more and more people from different countries in the Middle East arrived in the United States as visitors or students, and some remained.

Political Events and Recent Immigration Patterns

The establishment of the State of Israel in 1948 led to the development of new conflicts and hence, a new exodus from the Middle East. Palestinians whose lands were taken by the newly established Jewish state became refugees in different countries and account for much of the post–World War II Arab immigration to the United States (Thernstrom et al., 1980). Besides Palestinians, many Jewish people also migrated from Israel to the United States. Among them were also some Middle Eastern Jews who had first resided in Israel but then moved westward.

The two major Arab–Israel wars of 1967 and 1973, the continued Arab–Israeli conflict, the Lebanese Civil War (which started in 1975 and still continues), and the political instability of many regimes in the region have resulted in a continuous flow of Arab immigrants of different ethnic and religious backgrounds from the Middle East to the United States.

Political events that began in the mid-1970s have also led to the migration of large groups of Iranians, Afghans, and Iraqis to the United States. The largest number of Kurdish refugees in the United States arrived from Iraq in 1975, following a failed uprising that resulted in their severe persecution.

Two events in 1978 led to additional migrations: the beginning of the Iranian Revolution and the occupation of Afghanistan by the Soviet Union. The Iranian Revolution brought dramatic changes in the political and social structure of Iran. These changes led large groups of Iranians, among them many religious minorities, to immigrate to the United States. Also, many Iranian students and visitors acquired U.S. residency status and remained. The occupation of Afghanistan by the Soviet Union led to the migration of large groups of rural, nomadic as well as urban Afghans from Afghanistan. Many Afghans who had higher education or better economic means moved westward and a relatively large number took refuge in the United States.

The Iran–Iraq war, which began in 1980 and lasted until 1988, resulted in a continuous flow of Iranian immigrants to the United States, making the Iranians the largest group of immigrants from the Middle East since the late 1970s. The Iran–Iraq war also encouraged large groups of Iraqis of Arab and Kurdish origin to flee the repressive conditions of war.

Most recently, the occupation of Kuwait by Iraq in 1990 and the subsequent Persian Gulf War in 1991 can be expected to result in a new surge of emigration from the region. The tragic plight of the Kurds, in particular, in the aftermath of the Persian Gulf War suggests that the flow of Kurdish emigration from the region will continue and some Kurds may arrive in the United States.

Most of the immigrants from the Middle East are concentrated in a few cosmopolitan regions in the United States. The report by the Immigration and Naturalization Service (1987) indicated that immigrants from the Middle Eastern countries are mostly concentrated in California, New York, Michigan, New Jersey, Illinois, Massachusetts, Texas, Florida, and Ohio. California has been

---

Case Example #1

An Iranian couple whose first and newly born child, Moin, was diagnosed in Iran as having serious health problems immigrated to the United States in the hope that their son's situation could be dramatically improved by advanced medical intervention. The couple spent a great deal of time and money going to different doctors and hospitals. However, as time went on, it became clear that the child would have severe mental and physical disabilities for the rest of his life.

As Haleh, Moin's mother, struggled to confront the reality of her son's disabilities, overwhelming feelings of responsibility and guilt overtook her. Her reaction to those feelings was to become overprotective of her son and to devote all of her time to his care. The reaction of Moin's father, Farhad, was to pull away and become disengaged from his wife and son. This reaction was reinforced by Haleh's total preoccupation with Moin and her neglect of Farhad, and Farhad's need to work long hours in his business to earn enough money to cover the high costs of Moin's health care.

The relationship between Moin's parents continued to deteriorate, and Farhad left his wife and son. Haleh and Moin moved into her male cousin's home, who took it upon himself to take full care of his relatives. During this time, Haleh learned about early intervention and enrolled Moin in a program. Through the support of her cousin, the interventionists, and another Iranian parent whom she met in the program, Haleh began to regain her own equilibrium; Moin made small but significant gains. Farhad continued to maintain contact with Haleh's cousin and agreed to meet the father of the other Iranian child in the early intervention program. After Farhad had many long talks with the other father, and observed the other child, he also began seeing Moin and Haleh again—ultimately, Farhad and Haleh were reunited.

Throughout this process, the interventionists listened carefully to Haleh and her cousin. They recognized the cultural issues that made acceptance of a son with a disability especially difficult, and introduced Haleh to another Iranian parent when she indicated that she was interested. They worked with her to identify goals for Moin and worked diligently with her to accomplish them. When Farhad returned to the family, the interventionists welcomed him to the program and acknowledged his role as the head of the household.

---

the most preferred state since 1976; this preference may be related to the location of family members who had immigrated earlier as well as to the opportunities available in a growing state.

VALUES AND BELIEFS

In spite of the great variation in language, religion, and social and political systems, most Middle Eastern societies share many similar values pertaining to family interactions and childrearing practices. However, it is important to recognize that there are considerable differences across groups within any culture. This is certainly true among Middle Eastern people. Educated people who have come from urban areas often do not share many of the values and practices of those from more traditional rural areas. Factors such as the type of work, availability of time and space, degree of religious faith, level of education, and degree of exposure to a Western way of life are important determinants in shaping the family values and childrearing practices among many Middle Eastern families.

Most Middle Eastern families in the United States come from educated backgrounds, and almost all of the Middle Eastern people who came to live in the United States before the 1980s can speak English (Sabagh & Bozorgmehr, 1987; Thernstrom et al. 1980). Although the knowledge of English and the educational level of the more recent immigrants have been lower than their predecessors, a great majority of them have at least a high school degree (Bozorgmehr & Sabagh, 1988; Thernstrom et al. 1980). While a knowledge of English and higher educational background can facilitate better communication between Middle Eastern families and non–Middle Eastern interventionists, overt and subtle cultural differences continue to interfere with the clarity and efficiency of intervention in many instances.

Role of the Family

Family in its extended form is the most important institution in the Middle East. It is very common for three generations of a family to live together in the same house. Other family members may live as close as a few blocks away or as far away as in another city. The physical remoteness, however, rarely affects the loyalty to the extended family.

In most cultures in the Middle East, the individual's first and foremost loyalty is primarily to his or her family, clan, or kin. Family interactions and dynamics, in turn, are shaped by the religious rules and a patriarchal family structure. Religious rules provide the strongest guidelines in shaping the relations within the family. This contrasts with many industrialized, Western societies where secular rules coming from formal institutions often govern the nature of interaction even within the family.

The extended family performs important functions in the Middle Eastern societies. It provides many of the services that are currently performed by formal organizations in the West. It is within the network of the extended family that the children, the elders, and those with disabilities are often nurtured and protected. In addition to being a source of guidance and support, the family is also where most of the recreational and entertaining activities take place.

In most Middle Eastern cultures, the collective achievement of the family is often cited by its members as a source of pride and identity. It is very common to cite the achievements of ancestors, uncles, aunts, or even distant

cousins and take extreme pride in them. Identification with the family achieve-ments is generally as important and sometimes even more important than iden-tification with one's personal achievements. This interconnectedness of achievement and pride within the family contrast sharply with the mainstream American values of individual achievement and independence.

Strong family ties and the need to interact with family members often per-sist among Middle Eastern individuals and families who immigrate to the United States. Whenever possible, Middle Eastern families or individuals in the United States try to bring relatives from their homelands to stay with them over long periods of time. The emphasis, in much of the West, on the nuclear family is not easily understood or appreciated by the newly arrived immigrants. It is often hard for many Middle Eastern families to relate to the multitude of social organizations that are devised to replace the functions of the extended family. Even when they understand the purpose and function of these support organizations, some may still view them as unfamiliar or impersonal. In their preference for familial and informal networks, many may try to establish quasi-extended families around themselves. The clustering together of people of the same religion, language, or nationalities from the Middle East, in addition to other purposes, may also have the function of filling the psychological vacuum created by the absence of the extended family.

In sum, Middle Eastern families in the United States bring with them a deep-rooted and strong belief in the informal support system provided by the extended family in their homelands. This contrasts with the emphasis placed on the role of formal organizations as sources of support to the family in the United States. While time may be a factor in bridging this gap, differences in attitude and values are likely to persist for a long time. An interventionist dealing with a Middle Eastern family may greatly facilitate communication by trying to establish a more informal relationship with the family.

Family Size

In the tradition of most Middle Eastern societies, all men and women must have children, and not having children is a reason for great unhappiness. The motive for having children is often as strong, and many times even stronger, than that for love and intimacy in many marriages in the Middle East. The desire for many children and a strong preference for male children have been observed among followers of Judeo-Christian faiths in the Middle East, but most particularly among Muslims. Islam strongly endorses procreation. "Wealth and children are the ornaments of this life," says the Qur'an (Sura 18). In Egypt, for example, prior to the modern age, a wife's worth in the eyes of her husband and even her acquaintances depended upon her fruitfulness and upon the preservation of her children (Lane, 1963). This attitude was not limited to Egypt and has not completely vanished in the Middle East. Part of the great desire for large families, however, was due to a high infant mortality rate, which often left parents with few or no children in spite of many births (Prothro & Diab, 1974).

The birth of a boy has always been a reason for great celebration in a traditional Middle Eastern family. The reasons for this preference are of course not any different from those that make boys more prized in many traditional Western families. Professional and lay midwives in villages all over the Middle East can tell stories of occasions when they have received gold jewelry for helping deliver a boy and sour faces for delivering a girl!

In addition to the joy of having children, in most Middle Eastern cultures, children are needed to support the parents in their old age. Many Iranians believe that children are like canes in the hands of the old parents. In the eyes of Middle Eastern cultures, once children arrive, parents must put aside their individual interests and fully attend to the needs of their offspring. Negligence and lack of love and care toward children is severely scorned in these societies. Yet, among many traditional or uneducated families, a good part of the responsibilities for childrearing may also be placed on God's shoulders. Thus, the definition of care and attention varies greatly from society to society in the Middle East. Many lower income families or traditional families have more children than they can possibly attend to by modern or middle-class definitions of childrearing. Having many children, however, is usually justified by a strong belief that God will protect them and will provide for them. One commonly hears the idiom "that who gave teeth will also give bread" from Muslims in Iran.

Most Middle Eastern societies have strict laws against abortion and only tolerate birth control. However, birth control and abortion are available in large cities. Abortion is generally performed illegally by physicians in their private clinics and is mostly used by affluent women in less religious families.

BELIEFS

Pregnancy and Childbirth

Pregnancy and childbirth are generally regarded as a strictly women's affair in most Middle Eastern cultures. Men view themselves as responsible to provide the material necessities and to make major arrangements but do not engage in day-to-day caregiving procedures during pregnancy or following the birth of the child. This attitude, however, is manifested in different degrees depending on the family's educational background and degree of traditional beliefs.

Women in many rural areas in the Middle East often go through pregnancy without being seen by a doctor. This is in great part because in most rural areas in many Middle Eastern countries, medical care and facilities are not readily available. However, frequent visits to a doctor by pregnant women may also be hindered by religious beliefs. For example, in many traditional Muslim families, men do not like their wives to be seen by a male obstetrician/gynecologist. Women themselves usually prefer to be seen by a female obstetrician/gynecologist.

For most women in rural areas who do not have easy access to medical services, a natural system of care is provided by older, experienced women. These women, who could be regarded as equivalents of midwives, often use external signs such as changes in the expression of the eyes, the paling of the skin, the shape of and changes in the navel, or the location and kinds of pains to assess the condition of the pregnant woman. To reduce pain or discomfort, they usually use herbal medicine. The same women often help with the delivery of children in rural houses. In instances when they face abnormal situations such as unfamiliar signs or sequences, they often urge the pregnant woman to seek the help of a medical doctor.

In many rural areas around the Middle East, children are born in the houses with the help of midwives or experienced women. Childbirth at home, however, is not limited to women in rural regions. A study on the health status of some immigrants in the United States shows that childbirth at home among Iraqi women is a rule rather than an exception. This was found to be independent of economic factors (Young, 1987). While the study did not indicate the reasons, one reason could well be the unwillingness of traditional Muslim women to be exposed to strange environments.

Among urban, middle-class people, the procedures for childbirth are very similar to what goes on in the West. Deliveries take place in the hospitals. Men, however, are not generally present in the labor room during delivery. In the tradition of most Middle Eastern cultures, it is not socially acceptable for men to watch women during delivery.

Once at home, the mother usually becomes the primary caregiver of the baby. During this period, the father may take more responsibilities for the older siblings; however, there are usually members of the extended family who come to the rescue of the mother. The extended family usually provides the Middle Eastern woman with a network of support and relieves the mother from the burden of attending to every aspect of infant care or childrearing all by herself.

In most Muslim cultures, these social norms have been strongly influenced by the religious belief that assigns separate roles for men and women. For example, women's roles are generally perceived as childbearing, childrearing, and homemaking. Men perceive themselves as bread-winners and moral authorities who are charged with dealing with the affairs of the outside world. While separation of men and women is much more emphasized in the Muslim religion, the pattern of pre- and postnatal care mentioned above is not limited to Muslim groups. Most societies from the Middle East, regardless of religious background, follow similar patterns. For example, practices such as Lamaze that engage both men and women in the process of pregnancy and childbirth are not common. Many traditional Middle Eastern men living in the United States may resist taking part in activities that they regard as belonging to women.

Feeding and Health Care

Whenever possible, Middle Eastern women prefer to breastfeed their babies. Although Islam allows women to refrain from breastfeeding their babies if they wish, they rarely choose to exercise this right. Weaning from the breast may vary depending on the child's readiness to accept solid food, or on the mother's circumstances. Powdered formulas are regularly used to substitute for the mother's milk. Middle Eastern mothers, in general, feed their babies on a very flexible schedule. Feeding is usually in response to the infant's demand. The child may be eating solid food (rice puree) or even drinking water or light tea from a cup before weaning occurs. The strict feeding schedules once advocated in the United States are not common in the Middle East.

Traditional approaches to medicine are keys to solving most minor health problems of babies from Middle Eastern families. In Iran, for example, a mother may calm a baby's stomach pain by using fig syrup or mint essence. Light tea sweetened by rock sugar is also commonly used for stomach pain. Many Iranian women use rice water instead of milk when their babies have diarrhea. Herbal mixtures are commonly used to soothe a baby's rashes. For young children, fruit juices such as sweet lemon juice may be used to get rid of the flu. Cooked turnips, starch, or quince seeds are regularly used to relieve congested lungs, and pediatricians in Iran put children with chickenpox or smallpox on a strict diet of watermelon.

The use of traditional medicine is different from region to region and is often rooted in the experiential knowledge that passes across generations. Iranians, for example, believe that food can be classified into "hot" and "cold" categories, and that people too can have hot and cold natures. *Garmi* (hot) food, they believe, thickens the blood and speeds the metabolism while *sardi* (cold) food dilutes the blood and slows the metabolism. Dates, figs, and grapes are examples of hot fruits; plums, peaches, and oranges are among cold fruits (Batmanglij, 1986). A dietary balance of hot and cold food is believed essential for health. This firm belief in hot and cold character and the healing qualities of different foods is shared by all groups of people in Iran, including many Iranian pediatricians. An Iranian mother who lives in the United States and who is the author of an Iranian cookbook wrote:

> My son, like many other five-year-olds, sometimes eats too many dates or chocolates. Because he has a hot nature—something I learned very early in this life!—too much of this hot food does not agree with him at all. Drinking watermelon or grapefruit juice, or nectar from other cold fruits quickly helps restore his balance—and his smile. (Batmanglij, 1986, p. 2)

Middle Eastern parents, especially in the colder climates, like to have their young children well covered and warmly dressed. Many mothers believe that children can catch cold even with a breeze. They are particularly careful to cover their baby's heads and ears. This may seem to be overdressing in the eyes of an American interventionist. However, it is good to know that overdressing may be perceived as a way of preventing problems that may put the parents in need of medical care. One Iranian mother in the United States firmly believed that there were more ear infections among children here than in Iran, and she attributed it to the common use of hats for children in Iran. While this is merely an opinion, it attests to the rationale behind many practices that may seem strange to the Western interventionist.

Proximity and Physical Contact

Proximity to and physical contact with babies are very prevalent among Middle Eastern families. In general, Middle Eastern mothers stay closer to their babies, have more physical contact with their babies, and are less concerned than Western mothers about the individuation process.

Babies may have a separate bed, although not usually a separate room. Babies' beds in many rural areas in the Middle East are also small wooden cradles. Babies may share a room with other siblings or even be tended on the mother's bed. Cradling is very common and, accompanied by a lullaby, is often used to put a baby to sleep or to comfort a crying baby. Iranian mothers, for example, often cradle their babies on their legs, outstretched on the floor or on the bed; with their hands free, they usually perform other tasks. As with their feeding, Middle Eastern mothers generally do not follow a fixed schedule to put their babies to sleep. This contrasts with the common practice in many Western societies where babies are put to bed at regular times and are expected to go to sleep without much cradling or assistance from the mother.

Middle Eastern mothers are also much more permissive than their Western

counterparts in allowing their babies and young children to be kissed, held, or hugged. Babies are generally included in social activities of the family; they are regularly picked up, talked to, and played with in these family circles.

Attachment versus Individuation

A major difference in the childrearing practices between Middle Eastern families and Western families is in the nature of parent–child attachment and separation/individuation. In the United States, a great emphasis is usually placed on early individuation and independence of the child from the parents. Among Middle Eastern families, the emphasis is often on attachment and parent–child bonding.

Kagan (1984) suggested that there is a general tendency to attribute to infants characteristics that are opposite to those valued in adults in the culture. Americans, he argued, valuing independence and individuality, tend to view the baby as dependent and undifferentiated from others. In contrast, many Eastern cultures, valuing a close interdependence between people, see the infant as potentially too autonomous and needing to be developed into a dependent role in order to encourage the mutual bonding necessary for adult life.

These differences, however, can be a source of confusion and misunderstanding between the Middle Eastern parent and the Western interventionist.

Independent achievement, privacy, and physical distance from others are generally valued by most adult Anglo-European Americans and seem to be the norms. This is reflected in the appropriation of separate rooms for the children, emphasis on early toilet training, self-feeding, bathing, regular schedules for sleeping, and less physical contact. Middle Eastern mothers are less concerned about early toilet training of their children. They do not press for their children to eat, bathe, or put on their clothes independently at an early age. Thus, Middle Eastern children may differ from American children in the chronology of self-help skills. This should not be interpreted as a deficiency in the child but as a difference in parental attitude toward the child's independence. However, many Middle Eastern parents may wrongly view an emphasis on early separation and individuation as lack of adequate love, and neglect in parental duty.

Likewise, there are different attitudes toward the need for privacy. In most Middle Eastern cultures, social interaction and connectedness take precedence over the need for privacy. This, however, does not mean that people from the Middle East do not value their privacy. While for many Americans privacy requires actual physical distance, many Arabs, for example, achieve it by becoming silent and temporarily tuning out in a crowd (Safadi & Valentine, 1985). Such a silence or tuning out may be interpreted as rude or as daydreaming by many Americans. On the one hand, a long period of silence or pause in an American family may create uneasiness and may be a sign of tension. In many Middle Eastern families, on the other hand, talking too much, talking aloud, and talking while eating is discouraged among children.

In sum, Middle Eastern parents would generally prefer to see their children grow as an interdependent member of the family rather than as an independent individual. This perspective requires a different pattern of child care from that normally emphasized in the United States. In general, Middle Eastern children have strong and relatively secure emotional bonds with their parents. They are also generally dependent on their parents for a longer period of time than are most American children.

THE CHILD IN THE CONTEXT OF THE FAMILY

The emphasis on relations and interdependence as opposed to separation and independence is also evident in the Middle Eastern family's pattern of social interaction. Middle Eastern parents, particularly mothers, rarely have social and recreational activities separate from their children. Family gatherings, picnics, cinemas, and, to a lesser extent, sports events are among the most common social events in the Middle East; children are usually included in all of them. Most Middle Eastern boys do not start to have activities of their own until after puberty; for unmarried girls, this may come even later. Many American parents, in contrast, have social, recreational, and leisure activities independent of their children.

Entertainment

Family get-togethers are the most important and common form of entertainment in the Middle East. Marriages, national and religious feasts, or even mournings are all occasions for family members and friends to get together and socialize. On many of these occasions, food is the central theme of the festivity or gathering, and music and dance usually abound, depending on the kind of ceremony. Family gatherings, however, need not be justified by particular occasions. In most Middle Eastern countries, family members and friends tend to visit one another on a regular basis. In these gatherings, children are not usually given a particular place or realm separate from the adults. They are, in general, expected to find other children and entertain themselves in any way they can.

Middle Eastern families in the United States observe their religious and national events very closely. The most significant feast among Muslims is *Eid-Ghorban*, which marks the termination of the *Hajj* or pilgrimage to Mecca, the Muslim house of God. *Fetr* is the second important Muslim feast, which terminates the fasting month of *Ramadan*. These events, however, fall on variable dates of the year as the Muslim calendar is a lunar calendar. The most significant feast for most Iranians in the United States is the Iranian New Year on March 21. *Norooz*, originally a Zoroastrian tradition celebrating spring, is observed by all Iranians, Afghans, and some Lebanese regardless of religious faith or ethnic origin. An interventionist's knowledge and participation in some of these events can help bridge the cultural difference and improve mutual respect and cooperation during the course of intervention.

Young Children and Guests

In the tradition of most Middle Eastern cultures, guests are to be honored and respected. A Middle Eastern family always has time for a guest or a visitor. A guest is usually given the best place, is offered the best food, and is treated with much respect. Many Middle Eastern cultures have proverbs and idioms emphasizing the importance of guests. Muslims especially believe that guests are "endeared by the God" and must be well treated. Middle Eastern hospitality, however, goes beyond differences in religion or social class. A poor Middle Eastern family may go as far as offering to the guests the only food available in order to maintain its dignity in so important a matter.

Children, like their parents, must try to accommodate a guest. If the guest is staying overnight, they may have to give up their regular bed or room. They are expected to interact with the guest and not to retreat into their separate quarter or corner.

In general, a Middle Eastern child spends more time with the parents and other adults than the average American child; and on the average, an American child spends more time alone than the average Middle Eastern child. Less space, however, is not the only reason for more adult–child contact in the Middle Eastern family. Many Middle Eastern parents, coming home from work, prefer to spend more time with their children rather than putting them to bed early. Young children, particularly before school age, can stay up as long as they can keep up with their parents. When they do go to bed early, an adult, usually the mother, grandmother, or an older sibling, accompanies them until they go to sleep. They are allowed to fall asleep on the parents' bed or in a gathering and are then transferred to their beds. Middle Eastern children rarely express the need to take a teddy bear or a toy to bed, a need that is commonly observed among American children.

In sum, the sleeping and waking patterns of young children in Middle Eastern families generally follows that of their parents very closely. This pattern may allow greater contact and bonding between parents and children. Unfortunately, very often it persists even after the children start school. A Middle Eastern child not performing well in school on a particular day may well have been socializing the night before! Afternoon naps, however, are very common for children and adults in the Middle East, and young children are encouraged to take naps in the afternoons.

Children's Responsibilities and Work

Children are usually encouraged to take up responsibilities within the family at an early age. The degree and types of responsibilities expected from children, however, differ according to social class and the degree of traditionality of the family. Children from rural or poor urban sectors often have to learn various tasks necessary for survival as early as 4 or 5 years of age. In many rural areas, little boys are expected to help with the farming tasks or help with family subsistence. They may work for other people outside of the house to earn extra money. Little girls as young as 5 or 6 years may do a variety of household activities such as taking care of younger siblings, cleaning the house, or even cooking. This, however, is generally true for poor, overburdened families all over the world.

The Middle Eastern families who reside in the United States usually come from economically advantaged backgrounds. Children in such families are primarily expected to study and to succeed in school. This expectation, however, is very uneven for boys and girls. Highest achievement is usually expected for boys, while girls are expected to get only a modest education. In general, girls are expected to learn household activities around the age of 5 or 6 years. Boys are usually exempt from doing household chores. Attitudes toward girls' education differ according to the family's educational standards and values. On the one hand, in some very traditional Muslim families, a girl's education may not extend beyond elementary school or just before puberty. Among other reasons for this differential treatment is a concern for girls' modesty, a fear that a girl attending school may be unguarded or exposed. On the other hand, many nontraditional Middle Eastern families who value education highly may have similar aspirations for both girls and boys. Having higher aspirations for girls, however, does not usually change the division of labor in the family; girls continue to have more household responsibilities than do boys.

Role of the Father

The father is usually the head of the family. He is looked upon as the breadwinner, the parent who controls the family finances, the agent of socialization with the world outside the family, the moral authority, and the final disciplinary agent in the family. All of these titles help put the father at a much higher level than the mother and the children and separate him from much of the day-to-day activities that bind the mother with the children.

Patriarchy is dominant in almost all religions and cultures in the Middle East. It is present in varying degrees depending on the level of education and traditionality of the family. Some of the most extreme forms of patriarchy are prevalent among traditional Muslim families in the Persian Gulf region. In these families, women and children are often put into the same category and live under the authoritarian rule of the father. Women in these families have minimal economic power. Their roles are strictly limited to childbearing and childrearing, and they have very little contact with the outside world. They look to their husbands for major and even minor decisions. The fathers in these families are primarily disciplinary agents in their contact with their children. Although fathers often enjoy playing and spending time with their infants and toddlers, they rarely engage in caregiving activities and have very little awareness of the intellectual and psychological development of their children.

Many Middle Eastern families in urban and rural regions, however, fall outside of this most extreme category. This is particularly true in families in which women have economic productivity. In many parts of the Middle East, women work along with men and have substantial authority in minor and major decisions. However, in most instances, the power of these women is invisible, and the title of "all-powerful" remains with the father. The power of women is further limited by their lower level of education and lesser contact with the outside world.

Many interventionists visiting the Middle Eastern family in the United States may find themselves talking with the father rather than the mother even though the real authority over the children's lives may be the mother. One reason, of course, is that among recent immigrants from the Middle East, there are many mothers who do not speak English. The other reason, however, is that many Middle Eastern men, particularly those from traditional Muslim families, see themselves as the sole agents of communication between the family and the "stranger." This allows the Middle Eastern father to control the type and the amount of information that leaves the family territory and to define the family ideology. Concern for family honor, dignity, and integrity is so great among some Middle Eastern men that they commonly forbid their wives and children to talk to strangers. Survey researchers, for example, have found it particularly difficult to collect information on Middle Eastern families through formal channels (Bozorgmehr & Sabagh, 1988). These researchers have emphasized the use of informal channels such as contacting the religious and community leaders and requesting that they endorse a certain survey.

The father's level of education and his level of belief in the intervention may interfere with the effectiveness of communication if he is acting as a mediator between the interventionist and the mother. For instance, an early interventionist complained that during a visit, the father kept summarizing her lengthy instructions into one or two brief sentences. Even though she did not speak the language, she believed that her message was not effectively translated to the mother. Although this is an isolated example, it is also a reminder that, in some cases, using an English-speaking friend or relative who is trusted by the family may be a reasonable alternative to direct communication between the interventionist and the mother.

Discipline

American parenting styles have been alternately described as authoritative, permissive, or authoritarian (Baumrind, 1971; Satir, 1972). The most commendable parenting, or the authoritative form, is said to be characterized by high demands, low control, and high warmth. The permissive parents are usually low in both demand and control and are high in warmth. The authoritarian parents are high in demand, high in control, and low in warmth. While Middle Eastern parenting may represent all these forms, the general pattern among Middle Eastern families falls outside of the three categories. Middle Eastern parents are, in general, high in demand, high in control, and high in warmth.

The first signs of discipline appear with toddlers' exploration around the house. Before this time, a very permissive atmosphere prevails. There are no rules or rigid schedules requiring disciplinary action. Children are toilet trained when they demonstrate readiness. The mother usually places them on the toilet, but there is no punishment for lapses in toilet training before the age of 3. Similarly, children are not subject to much discipline regarding their eating, dress, or sleeping.

During these early years, fathers have very little influence in shaping the behavior of the child. When the child cries, or wets, or disrupts, the father usually calls on the mother to correct the situation. Toddlers may be scolded or spanked for touching breakable objects, putting things in their mouth, or moving toward a dangerous area in the house. Iranian mothers commonly use phrases like "Don't touch that!", "Don't do it!", or "Spit it out!" for their toddlers.

The father takes a more direct responsibility, especially for boys, around the age of 4 or 5 years. Discipline and punishment vary depending on the father's belief system and level of education. Before the turn of the century, physical punishment was believed to be a viable way of disciplining boys and was commonly used in religious schools and even by regular teachers. Today, however, physical punishment is an exception rather than the rule, particularly among the educated families. Parents who use it, however, are not usually subjected to legal or social scrutiny. The general attitude in the Middle East is that children "belong" to the parents and all parental behavior is motivated by love.

In families governed by strict tradition, rules are often to be obeyed without much explanation. In less traditional families, however, children have much more freedom and rules are subject to revision by parents. Generally, Middle Eastern children learn what is expected from them by watching the interaction among family members. Some of the major disciplinary rules among Iranian families are:

- Older family members should be respected.
- Children must not disobey the parents or talk back to them.
- Children should not interrupt when adults are talking.
- In the presence of a guest or during a visit, children should not make a lot of noise or touch the food without permission.
- Children should take very good care of their toys, clothes, and school materials.
- Children should not touch objects that do not belong to them.
- When siblings fight, the older sibling usually has to give in.
- Children should cooperate with the parents and other family members.
- Parents must know and approve of their children's friends and acquaintances.
- Girls in particular are not allowed to spend time outside of the house unsupervised.

In sum, prior to age 3, there are few rules in the life of a Middle Eastern child. Rules, in general, have more to do with the nature of interaction with others than with the young child's personal projects. Middle Eastern children start learning the rules by watching parental reactions. Generally, rules are not explained to the child through intimate parent–child talk. Such rules as respect and obedience are not to be questioned or explained. Parents normally expect the children to learn about rules by watching the pattern of interaction in the larger family. Children are often reminded of a good or bad behavior of a certain child in the family. Other members of the family also act as disciplinary agents.

The absence of an extended family poses serious disciplinary problems for Middle Eastern parents in the United States. Without the support of the extended family, parents have a hard time controlling their children, or setting examples of desired behavior. Many may have a hard time sharing their power with a school or a teacher they barely know. In general, however, Middle Eastern parents have less concern about the acculturation of their sons than their daughters. One of the greatest fears of most Middle Eastern families in the

United States is what they regard as peer pressure in the schools for early sexual activities among girls. The author of this chapter knows a number of families with daughters who have decided on a reverse immigration solely on the basis of this concern.

Intellectual Development

The Middle Eastern infant normally comes in contact with a great deal of natural stimulation in the environment. Surrounded by adults, the infant is constantly touched, moved, and talked to within the first 2 years of life. Toddlerhood, however, brings a number of restrictions in the infant's world. Independent explorative behavior may become limited for parents' convenience or fear of injury. Children are generally discouraged from touching objects that belong to adults. Availability of toys depends on the family's economic status. During toddlerhood, verbal stimulation comes frequently from adults other than the parents. The Middle East is rich with history, legends, literature, and poetry. Storytelling is particularly common in the Middle East. In most parts of the Middle East, there are usually rhymed poems about everything, and children learn to recite them from an early age. Sharing picture books and reading from books are usually seen in the middle class and among more educated parents.

It is the assumption of most Middle Eastern parents that their children should do well in school. When children do well, there is generally less overt praise or material reward than is common in the United States; children are doing what is expected of them. However, when children do not do well, parents may present a variety of attitudes, including denial, blaming the school, blaming the child, and/or feeling ashamed.

Atittudes Toward Disability

Guilt and shame are two common feelings when a child with a disability is born to a Middle Eastern family. Guilt is felt by the mother who is usually held responsible for the birth of a child with a disability. Shame is felt by the father who often views his child's disability as a personal defeat and a scar on the family's pride. The results of guilt and shame are usually overprotection, continuous denial, isolation or even total abandonment of the child in many Middle Eastern families. These attitudes, however, take different degrees depending on the family's familiarity with the field of special education.

Uneducated mothers may feel that they are being punished for some wrongdoings during the pregnancy or even before. A previous abortion, for example, may be linked to the birth of a child with a disability. Lifting heavy objects, unsuccessful attempts for abortion, eating special types of food, or even thinking about certain taboos during pregnancy may be associated with birth defects among less educated women.

Social attitudes vary depending on the kind and degree of disability. Blindness, deafness, or plegia may arouse pity for the individual and sympathy

Case Example #2

Six-year-old Yusef, the second child of a young couple from the Middle East, has very little functional language and manifests some behaviors associated with autisim. However, he has shown that he can learn certain things quite fast. For example, he recognizes musical notes and can write his name. Yusef receives special education services and speech therapy.

Yusef's parents are both educated. However, they spend very little time, if any, promoting Yusef's intellectual growth at home. Yusef's father works all day; at home, he rarely spends time on a planned, purposeful activity with his son. The family has just had a new baby, who keeps the mother busy for a good part of the day. Besides, Yusef's mother, who believes in traditional roles for women, says that cooking, washing, and organizing the house leave little time for her to work with Yusef.

These parents have put their trust in the school to take full responsibility for Yusef's education and training, and do not believe that it is part of their role to encourage the intellectual growth of a child with Yusef's problems at home. They are also busy with work and other family members and cannot see how they could take on additional responsibility for teaching Yusef. One of their friends, who observed Yusef's eagerness to learn tasks at home and has seen how much his behavior improves when he is engaged in "helping," suggested that his mother ask the teacher for some suggestions on "homework" for Yusef. At her friend's urging, Yusef's mother agreed.

Yusef's teacher was excited by the opportunity to blend school and family goals, and asked if she could talk with them about family expectations and routines and if she could make a home visit. The parents agreed, and the teacher gathered information about their expectations for Yusef and their other children in the home, their current routines, and the time constraints that each parent feels. She then worked with them to decide on several activities that they could work on with Yusef as they carried out their normal, daily routine. For example, after Yusef's mother set out placemats, Yusef could be taught to add the place settings to get ready for dinner; as his father raked the yard, Yusef could be responsible for removing dead blossoms from the flower beds.

In this case, a friend and teacher were able to help Yusef's parents find ways to supplement his school experience with activities at home. Even though the parents did not want to assume the role of teachers or tutors, they were very comfortable having Yusef participate in the family's normal routines.

for the family; an overprotective, charitable, but nonetheless cooperative attitude may be directed toward these individuals.

Children with mild mental and/or learning disabilities but without apparent physical signs can usually lead a near typical life under the strong protection of the family. If the family does not stress education, many may even go un-noticed. Girls may marry and form a family; boys may learn a trade and earn a living under the supervision of a family member. Boys with mental handicaps, however, have much higher chances to be part of a typical life than do girls. Severe mental disability, however, often provokes pity for both the child and the family and may lead to alienation.

Strong negative stereotypes against severe mental disability often results in families with such children to isolating themselves from many social activi-ties. Parents hesitate to take their child to public places for fear that the child and the family may become objects of pity. For example, talking to a stranger, an Iranian father may leave out mention of his child with severe disabilities and talk instead only about his other children. The isolation and limited contact with other adults makes caregiving particularly difficult and stressful for the mother. The child with a disability often gets used to one or two persons, usu-ally the mother and female siblings. Members of the extended family may be less eager to take responsibility for fear they may not know how to respond to the child's special needs.

The social isolation is also motivated by the common assumption that chil-dren with severe disabilities do not understand their situation and do not care. There is little faith among many Middle Eastern families that children with mental disabilities can become relatively self-sufficient. Thus, little attempt is made to train or educate such children at home.

The idea of special schools for children with disabilities, however, is not new in the Middle East. Middle Eastern countries were among the first to re-ceive the concept of special education. In Iran, for example, the first center for children with disabilities was established during the late 1950s by Shahnaz Shahnavaz, a pioneer Iranian female child psychologist. In spite of parental support and social appreciation, the center had to battle against a multitude of obstacles often created by a nonsupportive government. In 1991, there are many schools and centers for children with special needs all over the Middle East. However, widespread services for children with disabilities continue to be among low priorities in the agenda of many Middle Eastern governments.

Social acceptance and widespread support for children with disabilities in the United States relieves immigrant Middle Eastern parents of many of the tensions at home. Blame, guilt, shame, and denial, however, may still be ob-served in many such families, depending on their level of education and tradi-tional beliefs. Parents may be reluctant to talk about their child who is disabled, particularly with other Middle Easterners. There is a possibility that some fam-ilies may even prefer an American interventionist for fear they may "lose face" with a Middle Eastern interventionist. This, however, is open to speculation. Language continues to be a major barrier to adequate services to such families. This is particularly true about Middle Eastern children with speech problems who are caught between the language spoken at home and that used by the therapists at school.

In sum, Middle Eastern parents accept the reality of having a child with a disability less readily than most American parents. Denial, guilt, and shame persist for a long time and may interfere with an effective and positive intervention. Societal acceptance and support can help change this attitude among many immigrants—particularly those with less traditional concerns and a longer history in the United States.

ISSUES OF LANGUAGE AND COMMUNICATION

The Middle East is rich in language diversity, and many Middle Easterners are bi- or multilingual. Arabic, Turkish, Farsi, Kurdish, Armenian, Hebrew, and Assyrian are commonly spoken as are dialects of each of these languages. Because schools in some Middle Eastern countries include English instruction in their curriculum, many educated Middle Easterners come to the United States fluent in English.

Cultures of the Middle East are high-context cultures in which what is left unsaid is as important as what is said. Individuals rely heavily on shared experience, the situation, and nonverbal cues in communicative interactions. Although no generalization applies to all individuals, there are several things to keep in mind when interacting with families with Middle Eastern roots. A direct "no" is considered to be impolite for it could result in confrontation or hurt feelings. A weak "yes," "maybe," or "perhaps" may commonly replace a direct "no." However, a weak "yes" may also indicate agreement; therefore, individuals communicate their preferences very indirectly, relying upon the listener to understand the intended meaning. This may be further complicated by the formality of the cultures, which demands that all of the behavioral codes be followed. For example, in interactions with professionals, respect requires that the family give the impression that they are not in conflict with the professional's recommendations. Therefore, instead of saying "no" or "that won't work in our family," families may give the impression that they are in agreement, but may not act on the suggested interventions.

Indirect communication also applies to saying "yes." When offered something, individuals from Middle Eastern cultures may verbally deny that they want it. For example, if a hostess offers tea, instead of saying "yes, please" a Middle Eastern guest may say "thank you," or "it's fine" expecting the hostess to understand that such a response is a polite assent. The confusion that direct communicators may experience as they try to sort out what is really being said, may require a cultural mediator's skills—until the interventionists are familiar enough with the families and the culture to understand their communication style and intent.

Case Example #3

Mona, a 2-year-old girl from a Middle Eastern family, showed signs of delay in speech. For some time, both the parents and the day-care provider attributed the speech delay to the child's confusion between the language spoken at home and that spoken at the center, each thinking that the child could speak the other language better. When the parents and day-care provider learned of each others' concern, they arranged to have Mona tested by a speech and language therapist. The testing, which was conducted in English, resulted in a recommendation that Mona receive special services and a suggestion that speaking to her in English at home might help her. Both the diagnosis and the recommendations were unacceptable to Mona's family. They did not think that their daughter was retarded (the only reason that they were aware of that necessitated receiving special services), and speaking in their native language at home was a strong and important value that they held.

After hearing the parents' objections, the therapist suggested that she find another speech and language therapist who could evaluate Mona's language skills in her native language. This bilingual therapist confirmed the need for speech therapy; however, in talking with Mona's parents in their native language, she discovered that one of them also had a speech problem. The therapist was able to explain Mona's problem to the family, assure them that Mona was not mentally retarded, and affirm the importance of continuing to use their native language in the home. Therapy was provided and Mona began to show improvement in both languages.

In this example, the importance of bilingual testing and a bilingual-bicultural interpreter is highlighted. The language (and cognitive) skills of children in multiple language environments can only be accurately determined when they are assessed in both languages. In addition, the importance of maintaining one's native language in the home is a value that many families from other countries hold, and it is one that should be supported.

Unlike the United States, where long pauses in conversation or silence in groups typically indicates tension, periodic silence in a group in Arab cultures provides individuals with personal privacy; and being quiet in a group or "tuning out" of the conversation for periods of time are quite accepted and valued. Filling the silence is neither expected nor desired at such times.

Social distance, or the distance between speakers in conversation, is less than the distance maintained by Anglo-European Americans or those socialized in the United States. Middle Easterners may stand much closer in face-to-face interactions, and this proximity is not viewed as threatening or aggressive.

Greetings and touch among Middle Easterners also differ from those of mainstream culture in the United States. It is common for men to kiss each other on both cheeks in greeting and for women to exchange hugs and kisses; but such a public show of affection between men and women would be uncommon unless they were close family members. It is also common for male friends to hold hands and for female friends to hold hands. This does not indicate sexual preference, but rather is a way of showing friendship and support.

The guidelines for translators and interpreters presented in Chapter 3 are relevant to working with families from Middle Eastern cultures. In addition, it is important to recognize the importance of gender roles in these cultures. A traditional Middle Eastern woman would find it extremely difficult to discuss issues that are considered private to women, such as details of her pregnancy or child's birth, with a male translator. Likewise, traditional men, particularly young men, would find it difficult to speak with a female interpreter about personal information that is considered to be private to men. In arranging for interpreting and translation, these gender roles must be honored.

Language, both verbal and nonverbal, is one of the most important features of any culture. Through learning and understanding the communication style and preferences of families from the Middle East, interventionists can gain additional insights into the various cultures of the Middle Eastern families whom they serve.

SUMMARY AND RECOMMENDATIONS

Summary

The Middle East is both a geographic and cultural designation that is rich in diversity. Differences in language, religion, and social and political systems have shaped groups of people who hold widely varying world views. There is also considerable diversity within each of the groups. Educated, urban individuals may be quite different in their beliefs and practices than those from more traditional, rural areas. However, despite the differences within and across groups, there are also bonds that link people of Middle Eastern heritage. Of particular importance are the values and beliefs pertaining to family interactions and childrearing practices that are shared among many Middle Eastern societies.

The extended family is the most important institution in the Middle East, and the foremost loyalty among many Mideasterners is the family, clan, or kin. The rules of family interaction are, in turn, shaped by religion, with Islam being the primary religious influence among many from the Middle East. Children are highly valued, and mothers have primary responsibility for nurturing and caring for them. Fathers are usually the head of the family and the primary agent of socialization with the outside world. Although fathers typically enjoy playing with and spending time with their young children, they rarely engage in the day-to-day chores of caregiving. Sons are more valued than daughters. The birth of a child with a disability is cause for guilt and shame within the family of very traditional Middle Easterners.

The importance of family interactions and the high value placed upon caring and providing for young children are strengths that families with Middle Eastern roots bring to intervention. As interventionists become familiar with general beliefs and practices common to families from the Middle East and the ways in which those are expressed or not expressed among the individual families with whom they work, effective partnerships can be developed.

Recommendations for Interventionists

The Middle Eastern population of the United States is increasing in number. They represent a multitude of nationalities, languages, religions, and cultures. This chapter has been written to promote an understanding of some of the values and practices shared by a majority of people in the Middle East. The following recommendations provide some specific suggestions to assist interventionists in their interaction and relationships with their clients from the Middle East:

- Try to learn the family's history of immigration. Is the family newly arrived to the United States? If not, what generation are they? Are the parents American born, and, if so, how close are the family ties? Middle Eastern parents born in the United States are more likely to be Westernized. Do not assume, however, that newly arrived or first-generation Middle Easterners are homogeneous. They are different in their level of education, traditional background, religious beliefs, and attitudes toward adopting Western values. Some may have fresh roots in the rural regions in the Middle East, while others may have received an education in the West even before immigrating to the United States. Higher education, however, does not always equate with adoption of Western values. Certain traditional values may persist even among highly educated people from the Middle East.
- Establish relationships with the families and observe the family's patterns of interaction to help understand the family's position and orientation.
- Gather information about the extent of the family's support system. Are members of the extended family present? Is there a grandmother or aunt on her way to the United States? Are there any fellow countrymen in the neighborhood who can or do help? What are some of the role divisions in the family? What is the relative status of the father and the mother in the family?
- Try to establish a direct contact with the mother, but never discount the father or his role. Whenever possible, use a nonbiased interpreter to communicate information to the mother so that the information that she receives related to the child and the intervention program are not filtered through the father.

- Use informal, personalized forms of communication with Middle Eastern families rather than direct, assertive communication. Establish rapport and confidence before moving ahead with the intervention, keeping in mind that it is far more effective to come into the family as a friend who wants to help rather than as an authority figure.
- Use tactful inquiry to be sure that the family has clearly understood the message and to learn whether or not they accept it. Politeness requires that they show agreement even though they may disagree; but once the interventionist departs, the parents may continue their preferred practice. The inquiry should be gentle and carefully worded to avoid putting family members on the spot or pointing out disagreement within the family.

REFERENCES

Batmanglij, N. (1986). *Food of life: A book of ancient Persian and modern Iranian cooking and ceremonies*. Washington, DC: Mage.

Baumrind, D. (1971). Current patterns of parental authority. *Developmental Psychology Monograph, 1*, 1–103.

Bozorgmehr, M., & Sabagh, G. (1988). High status immigrants: A statistical profile of Iranians in the United States. *Iranian Studies, 21*(3,4), 5–37.

Bozorgmehr, M., & Sabagh, G. (1989). Survey research among Middle Eastern immigrant groups in the United States: Iranians in Los Angeles. *Middle East Studies Association Bulletin, 23*(1), 23–34.

Fisher, S.N. (1969). *The Middle East*. New York: Alfred A. Knopf.

Immigration and Naturalization Service. (1987). *Annual report: Statistical yearbook*. Washington, DC: U.S. Government Printing Office.

Kagan, J. (1984). *The nature of the child*. New York: Basic Books.

Lane, E.W. (1963). *The manners and customs of the modern Egyptians*. London: Dent and Sons.

Mostyn, T., & Hourani, A. (1988). *The Cambridge encyclopedia of the Middle East and North Africa*. New York: Cambridge University Press.

Prothro, E.T., & Diab, L.N. (1974). *Changing family patterns in the Arab East*. Beirut, Lebanon: American University of Beirut.

Sabagh, G., & Bozorgmehr M. (1987). Are the characteristics of exile different from immigrants? The case of Iranians in Los Angeles. *Sociology and Social Research, 71*(2), 77–84.

Safadi, M., & Valentine, C.A. (1985). *Contrastive analysis of American and Arab nonverbal and paralinguistic communication* (Position paper). (ERIC Document Reproduction Service No. ED 272 935)

Satir, V. (1972). *Peoplemaking*. Palo Alto, CA: Science & Behavior Books.

Thernstrom, S., Orlov, A., & Handlin, O. (Eds.). (1980). *The Harvard encyclopedia of American ethnic groups*. Cambridge, MA: Belknap Press.

Young, R.F. (1987). Health status, health problems, and practices among refugees from the Middle East, eastern Europe and Southeast Asia. *International Migration Review, 21*(3), 760–782.

APPENDIX A
CONTRASTING BELIEFS, VALUES, AND PRACTICES

Middle Eastern	Anglo-European American
Informal support system	Formal support system
Children are brought up to live interdependently	Children are brought up to live independently
Identity is defined more by family achievement	Identity is defined more by individual achievement
Mothers are more willing in allowing children to be picked up, kissed, or hugged	Mothers are more reluctant in allowing children to be picked up, kissed, or hugged
More flexible time schedule for eating, sleeping, and toilet training	More regulated time schedule for eating, sleeping, and toilet training
Less freedom for independent learning and exploration	More freedom for independent learning and exploration
Respect for old age, spiritual maturity, and wisdom	Respect for youth, physical fitness, and intelligence
Children not permitted to make many independent decisions	Children make more independent decisions

APPENDIX B
CULTURAL COURTESIES AND CUSTOMS

In a Middle Eastern house, it is *not* appropriate to:

- Walk in with shoes on, unless family members do the same
- Sit with your back to an adult who is present
- Sit with your feet up or legs crossed in front of elders

Appendix C
Significant Cultural Events/Holidays/Practices

ALL THE MUSLIM WORLD

Eid-al-Adha (the feast of sacrifice also known as *Ghorban*) is the "big feast" of all Muslim believers. It marks the end of the *Hajj* or the pilgrimage to Mecca.

Eid-al-Feter marks the end of the month of *Ramadan* during which Muslim believers observe fasting every day from sunrise to sunset.

Eid-al-Moled-e-Nabi (the birth of the Prophet) is a national holiday in all Muslim countries. Arab Muslims use a lunar calendar. The dates of these holidays, therefore, vary each year on a solar or a Christian calendar.

IRAN, AFGHANISTAN, PARTS OF IRAQ AND LEBANON

Norooz (The new day) begins on March 21 and lasts 13 days. A spring festival and originally a Zoroastrian tradition, it is the major feast for Iranians and Afghans and marks the beginning of the solar calendar used in these two countries. *Norooz* is a national feast celebrated by all ethnic and religious groups in Iran.

MIDDLE EASTERN CHRISTIANS

Easter is the major celebration of all Christians in the Middle East.

APPENDIX D
VOCABULARY

English	Arabic	Farsi	Turkish	Kurdish
Mother	Ŏomm	Mädar	Änne	Däy'k
Father	Abb	Pedar	Bäbä	Bäo'k
Brother	Akh	Barädar	Kärdes	Brrä
Sister	Ŏokht	Khähar	KizKärdes	Khoishak
Family	Äēlå	Fämēl	Aēlä	Mäll
Hello	Marhabä	Saläm	Merhabä	Chōni
Goodbye	Maa, salami	Khōdä, häfez	Güle Güle	Sar chäo
Thank you	Shōkran	Mōtshakeram	Sagōl	Sepäset Däkäm
Please	Rejä, an	Khähesh Mikōnam	Lutfen	Shäyanineya
How are you?	Kif Hälak?	Häl-e-shōma-chetoreh?	Nasilsiniz?	Chōni Chäki?

PART III

SUMMARY AND IMPLICATIONS

Part III synthesizes the information presented in Parts I and II and provides recommendations for interventionists working in service delivery systems. Implications for working with families from diverse cultural groups and strategies are outlined as the reader is led through the intervention process from the beginning contact with families to the implementation and evaluation of services. It is the intent of the recommendations in this section to enhance the sensitivity and awareness of service providers to issues of variability across families in childrearing, health care, and communication. It is also the intent of the recommendations to increase the skills of interventionists in their interactions with families from diverse cultures.

chapter 12

STEPS IN
THE RIGHT DIRECTION
IMPLICATIONS FOR INTERVENTIONISTS

Eleanor W. Lynch and Marci J. Hanson

On a deeper level the process of coming to know another culture allows us to gradually become ourselves again. Many of us, not knowing which of our behaviors may be culturally acceptable (or neutral) and which may not, err on the side of caution and move through intercultural situations in a state of semiparalysis, earnestly practicing the greatest possible self-restraint; we do and, in particular, we say nothing that may reflect badly on us. We are, quite literally, not ourselves.
—Craig Storti (1989), p. 93

The American landscape is now a kaleidoscope of cultures, and the changing patterns of color, customs, and language have introduced new energy, new concepts, and new concerns. One of the greatest concerns associated with increasing diversity is how human services agencies and programs can respond sensitively and effectively to families whose language, experience, and needs differ from those of the dominant culture in the United States. Defining, creating, and maintaining caring, responsive services is one of the most challenging tasks that face agencies and interventionists at the threshold of the 21st century.

Much of what is needed to develop and implement high-quality services that are cross-culturally appropriate and effective must be accomplished at the systems level. To encourage the entrance of persons of color into the human services professions, training and support must begin early. Young adults need to be mentored throughout their school years, supported to stay in school, and encouraged to enter university training programs in the human services. At the same time, comprehensive educational, health, and social programs that prevent failure, illness, and the hopelessness of poverty need to be put into place. Organizational policies that support the recruitment and hiring of individuals from diverse cultural and ethnic backgrounds, staff development that increases intercultural competence throughout the organization, and a commitment to changing practices that compromise or discriminate against those from diverse backgrounds must be incorporated into each agency's way of thinking and way of doing business. A great deal remains to be done to help systems embrace diversity. However, this book is about diversity at the interpersonal level—the face-to-face level of an interventionist and a family. Therefore, this final chapter reviews basic themes of the book and recommends steps that interventionists can take to make the intervention process more appropriate for families from diverse cultures.

REVIEWING THE THEMES

Cross-Cultural Competence: What It Is and What It Is Not

Throughout this book, several phrases have been used interchangeably— cultural sensitivity, cross-cultural competence, intercultural effectiveness, and ethnic competence. All refer to ways of thinking and behaving that enable members of one cultural, ethnic, or linguistic group to work effectively with members of another. Green (1982) defined ethnic competence as being "able to conduct one's professional work in a way that is congruent with the behavior and expectations that members of a distinctive culture recognize as appropriate among themselves" (p. 52). It includes: 1) an awareness of one's own cultural limitations; 2) openness, appreciation, and respect for cultural differences; 3) a view of intercultural interactions as learning opportunities; 4) the ability to use cultural resources in interventions; and 5) an acknowledgment of the integrity and value of all cultures (Green, 1982).

There are several things that cultural competence is not. It is not becoming a member of another culture by a wholesale adoption of another group's values; attitudes; beliefs; customs; or manners of speaking, dress, or behavior. In fact, such overidentification would "be manipulative and patronizing" (Green, 1982, p. 52). Abandoning one's own cultural identity and substituting another is not a form of respect, but rather a statement that culture can be easily shed. Further, cultural competence does not imply that individuals can be categorized into groups and that little variability within cultural groups exists. Rather, cultural identification is viewed as one variable that guides an individual's lifeways— not a total prescription for a way of life. Finally, being culturally competent does not mean knowing everything about every culture. It is, instead, respect for difference, eagerness to learn, and a willingness to accept that there are many ways of viewing the world.

Transactional and Situational Nature of Cultural Identity

Over 25 years ago, Barth (1969) suggested that ethnic identity is transactional and situational. Instead of being a category to which one automatically does or does not belong, ethnic or cultural identity is defined by the boundaries that group members use in their interactions with the larger society. Characteristics, traits, ceremonies, and so forth are important only insofar as they are markers of inclusion or exclusion used by the group to define itself from others.

As interventionists work with families, the influence of the family members' cultural identity may change based upon a given situation. For instance, a family of an infant may be eager for early educational intervention for their child and so they actively participate in the education program. In this situation, the family chooses a practice that is consistent with the view generally held in the dominant culture of valuing early intervention. Families whose cultural background is different regarding the need for early education may decide to adopt new values that they have encountered. However, when a surgical procedure is suggested to correct a malformation of the child's hands, the same family members may elect not to have the surgery. It is their belief that the child's hands represent a sign that is spiritually significant to them. In this situation, the family's decision may be at odds with the values of many others in the mainstream society but highly consistent with the values held by the cultural group with which they identify.

Given the diversity of our society, families may be monocultural (identify with one primary group), bicultural (identify with two different groups and move comfortably between these groups), or even multicultural (identify with more than two groups and move from group to group). Further, even families whose values and beliefs are tied strongly to a particular cultural group may, on occasion, adopt the values or practices of another group. Thus, as the previous example demonstrated, belief systems in one area of family life (e.g., early educational experiences) may be consistent with those held by one cultural group, and beliefs and practices in another area of family life (e.g., health care practices) may reflect the values of another group. The degree of exposure to other cultural groups and, in the case of immigrants, the length of time in this country and place of residence may influence the degree of mixing of cultural practices.

The characteristics of a particular situation also may influence the degree to which the person responds according to cultural traditions. The expectations for performance, degree of formality or informality, the size of a group, the potential for embarrassment, and the potential for negative repercussions such as referral to protective services, to name a few factors, all influence the person's behavior. It is simply a matter of human nature that persons respond differently in different situations. This phenomenon is easily observed in young children. Parents often remark how good their child was at school or when visiting someone else's house, yet lament about the child's "bratty" behavior at home with the parents! The situational nature of behavior is as applicable to adult behavior. Parents may agree to give an antibiotic, to feed the child a particular food, or to provide an opportunity for a child with a disability to play with nondisabled peers, yet their actual behavior may differ. When meeting with professionals from the society's service delivery systems, they may agree to recommendations made by these professionals; however, they may practice very different methods of care when at home and within their own cultural enclaves. Because cultural identity can be situational and occur (or not occur) in a variety of transactions that families have with interventionists who come from cultures that differ from their own, it is important to learn about the family's cultural boundaries.

The recognition of the transactional and/or situational nature of cultural identity may be the most important point to consider in working with families from a variety of cultures. This point guides the interventionist away from overgeneralizing about families or stereotyping families based upon their cultural background. The behavior of each individual is dynamic and it is modified by each interaction. Many factors other than cultural identity also influence an individual's behavior. It is this acceptance of the constant dynamic interplay of the individual's beliefs and background with the daily demands of the society that will guide interventionists to greater understanding and sensitivity in their work with families. This focus, in turn, will better support families in their transactions with the human services system.

Mitigating Factors in Cultural Identification

A person's cultural identity exerts a profound influence on his or her lifeways, but it is not the only critical factor. Every individual and every family is defined by more than these characteristics, and the influence of cultural identity may vary from one time to another. As pointed out in Chapter 1, other mitigating factors also shape the ways in which individuals and families live, as well as the way in which they identify themselves and wish to be identified. These mitigating factors include:

- Socioeconomic status
- Educational level
- Time of arrival in the United States
- Premigration and migration experiences
- Proximity to other members of their cultural or ethnic community
- Proximity to other cultural groups
- Age
- Gender
- Language proficiency

These factors not only may strongly define an individual's life practices but they also may interact with cultural factors in influencing the potency of culture and ethnicity in self-identity.

For example, some families who fled their country of origin because of war and came to the United States seeking a safe haven may choose to put the pain of the past behind them. They may work diligently to adapt to a new way of life and identify with the mainstream culture of the United States. Other families who had similar migration experiences may seek to keep their original cultural identity alive and strong in themselves and in their children. They may place considerable emphasis on maintaining the beliefs, customs, and language of their country of origin and plan to return if that should ever become possible.

Socioeconomic status and education also may influence individuals' and families' identification with their native culture. These variables may interact with cultural considerations in influencing individuals' and families' interactions with the larger community and their access to the community's resources. Affluent families whose members are highly educated may have a broad world view and they may move comfortably between two or more cultures and languages. Families with very limited resources, however, may have more difficulty finding educational opportunities, health care, employment, housing, and services for their children and family. Being poor and non–English speaking, for example, can be a considerable disadvantage in many parts of the country. These families may be compromised even in gaining access to services that are designed to assist families in overcoming obstacles. For many of these families, issues of survival such as obtaining adequate food and shelter may dictate their lifeways far more than their cultural perspective does.

Each individual and each family is different, and culture-specific information cannot be assumed to apply in every situation. Its value is that it raises issues that should be considered, poses questions that may need to be answered, and underscores the interventionists' desire to respond sensitively to each family and each family member.

Personal Growth and Change

The importance of self-awareness has been emphasized throughout this book. Until one understands the impact of his or her own culture, language, and ethnicity on attitudes, beliefs, values, and ways of thinking and behaving, it is not possible to appreciate fully the cultures of others (Chan, 1990; Hanson, Lynch, & Wayman, 1990; Wayman, Lynch, & Hanson, 1990). Thus, examining one's own roots is the place to begin any journey toward increased intercultural competence.

This exploration may uncover many unknown facts that lead to insights about attitudes and behaviors that can help to reframe practice. For example, anyone who has grown up hearing, "Where there's a will there's a way," "He pulled himself up by his own bootstraps," "God helps those who help themselves," and "Never say I can't, say I'll try" has a dramatically different view of the world (and of intervention) than someone who has heard, "It's God's will,"

It is not easy to study our own culture because it is so much a part of us. Many of the beliefs and behaviors that are taken for granted are really nothing more than the long-term influence of culture. There is, for example, no inherent reason to drive on the right-hand side of the road, to use knives and forks rather than chopsticks, or to eat cereal rather than beans for breakfast. Yet, when one is confronted with behaviors that are different, the most common first response is that the other person or culture is wrong. As the humorist Douglas Adams said, "Assumptions are the things you don't know you're making . . . the shock is that it had never occurred to you that there was any other way of doing it. In fact, you had never even thought about it at all, and suddenly here it is— different. The ground slips" (Adams & Carwardine, 1990, p. 141). Moving past the little differences allows us to consider the larger differences that can lead to cross-cultural misunderstanding.

Increased self-awareness also helps interventionists discover unknown prejudices that can have subtle but pervasive effects on intercultural interactions. The long-standing tensions between and among various cultural groups sometimes emerge when least expected. This became most evident when one of the authors' close friends, a normally cheerful, adventurous, and open-minded traveling companion, became increasingly grumpy and ill-tempered on a trip through England. After several oblique attempts to determine the cause of this change of affect, the author gently asked, "What in the world is the matter with you?" The answer tumbled out, "I can't stand being in this country because of what they've done to the Irish!" An unknown feeling and deep-seated prejudice had popped out, surprising both people. The Irish roots and childhood memories of hearing what the English had done to the Irish expressed themselves years later in a negative feeling about a country, its people, and its culture.

Learning about one's own culture, weeding out prejudices, and understanding the profound impact of culture on all aspects of life prepares individuals for change. For all interventionists who work with families whose backgrounds are different from their own, some changes in practice are probably necessary.

CREATING A CULTURALLY APPROPRIATE INTERVENTION PROCESS

The intervention process has multiple components. Although the process may be lengthy in some systems such as education or social services and compressed in others such as health care, all systems follow a similar model in planning, implementing, and evaluating intervention services. Regardless of the service system, the process typically begins with a family–professional exchange of information and planning for assessment. Once the relationship with the family is initiated and the family's concerns, priorities, and needs determined, assessment planning begins, followed by the actual data gathering and assessment. This is followed by implementation of the intervention or treatment plan and monitoring and evaluation of the procedures (Hanson & Lynch, 1989; Lynch, Jackson, Mendoza, & English, 1991). Intercultural effectiveness is an important aspect of each step. The paragraphs that follow briefly discuss each of the components in terms of the interventionist's role in making the interaction sensitive to those from a variety of cultural groups.

Establishing Family–Professional Collaboration and Assessment Planning

The importance of family–professional collaboration has received increased attention in recent years (Dunst, Trivette, & Deal, 1988; Johnson, McGonigel, & Kaufmann, 1989; Turnbull & Turnbull, 1990). Although its value has been discussed for children of all ages and in a variety of service delivery systems, it has particular relevance to working with young children with disabilities and their families. Learning culture-specific information about the groups represented in one's community and working with a cultural mediator or guide can help interventionists begin to develop a collaborative relationship with families. It also can provide clues about the extent of participation and involvement that families may choose and help the interventionist separate cultural differences from lack of information or personal preferences. Knowing some words and phrases in the family's language and recognizing patterns of family interaction, religious practices, and views about health, healing, and causation can increase the interventionist's ability to interact sensitively and effectively with the family, thus increasing the likelihood of beginning a successful partnership.

A partnership with the family provides the basis for planning an assessment that addresses their concerns. Although it is still common for assessments to be driven by pre-established protocols based on systems' regulations, a number of changes in this process have been proposed (Johnson et al., 1989; Kjerland, 1986; Lynch, Mendoza, & English, 1990). The changes would tailor assessments to the child's needs and the family's concerns and priorities. Although this reconceptualization of how assessments should be planned is a far more sensitive and effective approach to working with *all* families, it is particularly relevant to families from diverse cultures. Basing assessments on family concerns and priorities helps to ensure that their cultural perspective is honored.

To make this component of the intervention process more culturally appropriate, there are several things that an interventionist can do:

- Learn about the families in the community that you serve. What cultural groups are represented? Where are they from? When did they arrive? How closely knit is the community? What language(s) is spoken? What are the cultural practices associated with childrearing? What are the cultural beliefs surrounding health and healing, disability, and causation?
- Work with cultural mediators or guides from the families' cultures to learn more about the extent of cultural identification within the community at large and the situational aspects of this identification and regional variations.
- Learn and use words and forms of greeting in the families' languages if families are limited– or non–English proficient.
- Allow additional time to work with interpreters to determine families' concerns, priorities, and resources and to determine the next steps in the process. Remember that rapport building may take considerable time, but that it is critical to effective intervention.
- Recognize that some families may be surprised by the extent of parent–professional collaboration that is expected in intervention programs in the United States. Do not expect every family to be comfortable with such a high degree of involvement. However, never assume that they do not want involvement and are not involved from their own perspective. Likewise, do not assume that they will become involved or will feel comfortable doing so.
- For limited– or non–English proficient families, use as few written forms as possible. If forms are used, be sure that they are available in the family's language. Rely on the interpreter, your observations, and your own instincts and knowledge to know when to proceed and when to wait for the family to signal their readiness to move to the next step.

Data Gathering and Assessment

Cultural bias is often most evident in the assessment process. Instruments that have been designed for use with English-speaking children and families who are part of the dominant culture in the United States are not always appropriate for children and families with other life experiences. Instruments must be selected with care because developmental norms and expectations may differ from group to group. This is especially true in situations in which children have not had the opportunity to practice behaviors that are reflected in the test or they have not yet been expected to perform at those levels. For example, in some cultures, children are expected to "behave" and control their impulses from early in the preschool years. In other cultures, few demands are made upon children until they are 6 or 7 years of age.

In some cultures, language is the primary way in which family members communicate with young children and children become language oriented at a very early age. In others, touch is the primary mode of communication and far less emphasis is placed on verbal input and output. As a result, tests with mainstream U.S. norms may not adequately measure the child's performance or potential in these areas. Further, the child's prior experiences may influence his or her responses in the assessment. For example, in the experience of one of the authors, a young child whose family had recently moved to California from Samoa was observed to exhibit clumsiness and delayed motor development during an assessment conducted by an early intervention team. When the child was observed later in his home he was able to move more freely and functionally. The home had none of the furniture or large obstacles found in most American homes, but rather contained mats and low-lying furniture. Thus, the child had never received practice ambulating around the types of objects found in most homes or test situations. Without a greater knowledge of the family's cultural background and practices, the staff members would not have been able to perform an appropriate assessment of this child's developmental status and areas of need.

In other instances, the language of the assessment instrument is a barrier to its use. Tests that are not available in bilingual editions cannot be assumed to be appropriate when they are directly translated. Perhaps the best strategy in information gathering is to interview the family through a trained interpreter to gather information about the child and the family's particular concerns. If formal assessments are used, they should be conducted in the child's/family's primary language.

Even the process of interviewing can be inappropriate for some families. This is true both of the manner in which the interview is conducted and also the content of questions (e.g., questions related to marital relationships). A recent situation in the local community of one of the authors is an example. Families were selected from each of the early intervention programs in the community to respond to a community services needs assessment; information was gathered through structured interviews with families. For interviewees whose primary language was not English, community interpreters conducted the interview in conjunction with the professsional who was performing the needs assessment. At one point, a mother indicated to the interpreter that she was very uncomfortable being singled out for questioning and embarrassed being asked questions about her child's disability and her thoughts about service needs. She indicated that it reflected badly on her to have a child with a disability and that it was inappropriate for parents to be questioned about services because "that was the job of the professionals to decide." In this case, the process of interviewing this mother was not culturally sensitive and had a negative influence on her "face saving" with respect to her child's disability, even though the professional conducting the needs assessment had the best of intentions in gathering input from families in the community. It is the interventionist's job to determine when and how data gathering and assessment can be conducted in a culturally sensitive manner and this determination can be challenging in many situations.

Hanson et al. (1990) proposed a paradigm of ethnic competence in data gathering and assessment that includes values clarification by the interventionist, collection and analysis of ethnographic information regarding each family's cultural community, determination of the degree to which each family operates transculturally, and examination of each family's orientation to specific issues of childrearing. Using this model would help to ensure that the assessment process is both family focused and conducted in a manner desired by families— prerequisites to being culturally sensitive.

In the data-gathering and assessment phase of the intervention process, there are several ways to gather more accurate information and to make the experience more sensitive to and appropriate for families from diverse cultures:

- When selecting commercially available assessment instruments, choose only those that are appropriate for the language and culture of the child and family.
- If the family is limited– or non–English proficient, work with a trained interpreter who can interpret language as well as *cultural cues,* and follow the guidelines suggested for working with interpreters presented in Chapter 3. Remember that what is not said can be as meaningful in some cases as what is said.
- Arrange the assessment at a time that allows the people important to the family to be present. For example, although the father may not have any direct caregiving responsibilities for the child, it may be important for him to be present during an assessment. In fact, it may be the father, or another family member such as the grandmother, who holds the decision-making powers in the family with respect to the child's education or treatment.
- Conduct the assessment where the family can be most comfortable. Although the home is typically the preferred place, if the family is not comfortable with outsiders visiting, use the program site or another neutral place.
- Gather only the data necessary to begin to work with the child and family. Limit the numbers of forms, questionnaires, and other types of paperwork.
- Include as few assessors as possible. Additional observations or information can be obtained at another time.
- Gather information in those areas in which the family has expressed concern. Tending to the families' issues first is a sign of respect for *all* families.
- Explain every step of the assessment and its purpose to the family. Explanations may need to occur several times and be made in several different ways.

Developing the Intervention Plan

Regardless of whether the intervention plan is a medical treatment or an educational program, the intervention will be only as effective as those who implement it. Therefore, it is important that each person who will be involved in implementation "buy in" to the plan. When plans are based on highly valued behaviors and perceived needs, it is much easier to get follow-through and support. As the family and other members of the team formulate goals and objectives for the child or outcomes for the family, it is essential to have the family's point of view represented. Although this representation is assumed to be direct, verbal participation in the planning meeting when mainstream, Anglo-European American families are involved, involvement may be different for families from other cultures. A third party may serve as the family's representative, and the family may or may not elect to participate actively. As Lynch and Stein (1982) pointed out, families from different cultures have very different ways of participating in interventions for their children. What may be considered active participation by one group is viewed as passive by another.

Most families report that planning meetings (e.g., meetings to develop Individualized Education Programs [IEPs]) are intimidating. This may be even more true for families whose cultural background differs from that of the majority of others present at the meeting. The recent emphasis in education and early intervention on parent–professional collaboration, joint decision making, and family-focused plans makes this planning process even more complicated. Interventionists throughout the United States have been working to increase their skills in family-centered practice, yet there will be many families from different cultures who do not expect or prefer not to take such an active role. Without ruling out these families' desire to participate, interventionists may have to rethink some of their new practices. That is, if a family does not wish to participate in joint decision making, this does not mean that the interventionist has failed. To help make planning meetings more culturally sensitive, the interventionist may wish to incorporate some of the following practices:

- Brief the family about the meeting, its purpose, and who will be present well in advance of the meeting.
- Reduce the number of professionals present unless the family has requested that others be present.
- Encourage families to bring those people who are important to them— relatives, clergy, friends, and so forth—and be sure that a skilled interpreter is present if families are non– or limited–English proficient.
- Incorporate practices that are culturally comfortable for the family (e.g., serving tea), taking time to get acquainted before beginning the more formal aspects of the meeting, or, for some families, conducting the meeting in a highly formal manner.

- Be sure that family input is encouraged without creating embarrassment. If it is felt that family members will not interact comfortably in such a public forum, be sure that the interventionist who knows the family best has spoken with them ahead of time and can represent their perspective at the meeting.
- Ensure that the goals, objectives, or outcomes that are being developed are matched to the family's concerns, priorities, and needs.
- As appropriate, use resources that are designed for or are a part of the family's cultural community; for example, child care sponsored by the religious group to which they belong or a referral to a health care provider who shares the same language and culture.
- Allow time for questions, but be prepared to comment on questions that other families often have asked. This allows questions to be answered without having to be asked.

Implementation

Putting the intervention or treatment into action is the component of the intervention process that is most critical. Assessments are conducted to determine what the intervention should be, and monitoring and evaluation are used to ensure that the intervention is working. Yet implementation may be the area in which there is the greatest likelihood for cultural conflicts. If assessment and

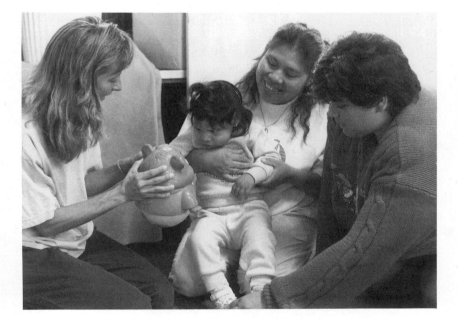

intervention planning are done well, the chance of conflicts arising during implementation is significantly decreased, but it may still occur.

If family members had a different understanding of the goals, if they viewed their roles in implementation differently than did the interventionists, or if they were simply too polite to disagree at the time that the goals were being written, conflicts may arise. The signs of conflict vary dramatically from one person to another as well as from one culture to another, so it may be important for a cultural mediator or guide to work with the interventionist and family to determine what each wants and what each believes is occurring. For example, the intervention plan for a young child may include a goal related to self-feeding. At the time that the goal was written, everyone seemed to agree that it was a desired outcome. However, the family has chosen to continue to feed the child at home and is making no attempt to let the child feed himself, something that he is encouraged to do at the early intervention center. Upon closer examination, the interventionist may discover that such a goal was of no importance to family members. Although they had nothing against it and felt that it was acceptable since it was what the interventionist wanted to do, they also saw no reason for it and simply continued their original feeding practices.

In another instance, the child's weight gain and nutrition were of concern both to the parents and to the health care professionals. The nutritionist working in conjunction with the primary care physician recommended a new diet for the child. A visiting nurse later found that the family was not following the recommended regimen because some of the foods were considered to be "hot" foods or "cold" foods in that culture and, therefore, were not appropriate for the child's condition. Cultures may differ radically in terms of daily life practices such as food selection and preparation. In fact, a practice such as eating bananas may be encouraged in one culture and absolutely forbidden in another. Once again, if the interventionist gathers culture-specific information, works with cultural guides, and attempts to work with, rather than against, other practitioners or care providers who are important to the family—be they healers, shamans, medicine men, or priests—the likelihood of designing and implementing appropriate interventions and treatments will be maximized.

Implementation can be made more effective by incorporating some of the practices that follow into the program:

- Put a lot of time and energy into ensuring that the goals and outcomes proposed are those that are of primary importance to the family.
- Adjust typical goals to match the family's priorities, for example: learning to eat with chopsticks rather than with a spoon and fork, behaving in cooperative rather than competitive ways, learning words in the language of the home, being taken to the potty rather than independently toileting, or sleeping and napping in the parent's bed rather than alone.
- Involve the family to the extent that they choose to be involved in all aspects of the program.

- If families choose to take a less active role, continue to provide information to them about the program and their children's progress through cultural mediators, photos, and/or videotapes, as appropriate.
- Create a program that fits into the cultural communities that it serves. Use the multicultural aspects of the program to strengthen its implementation through creating a community center where people want to be, and partnering with other community services such as child care and health clinics.
- Involve the various cultural communities' leaders in the program and invite their participation and advice through advisory boards.

Monitoring and Evaluating

The final component of the intervention process is monitoring and evaluating the services provided to each child and family. It may mean determining whether or not the child has met the specified objectives and/or whether or not family members are satisfied with the degree to which they have reached the outcomes that they specified.

- Have children met the full range of objectives that are a part of their individual plan or treatment?
- Is their rate of success consistent with their predicted rate of gain or has the rate of gain been accelerated?
- Are adaptations being made to enable each child to participate in activities considered to be normal for the child's chronological age and culture?
- Have families been assisted and psychologically supported to meet any outcomes that they have specified for themselves? For example, if family members felt that they needed more information in order to explain their child's disability to other family members, has that occurred? Or if families felt that they needed additional child care, have they been assisted in finding resources within the community?

In addition to evaluating the effectiveness of individual services, the effectiveness of the program or agency as a whole should be included in the evaluation.

- Is the work of the program/agency still consistent with the mission?
- Is the program/agency effective as determined by client success, staff perceptions, families' satisfaction, and the perceptions of other agencies?
- Are resources allocated in the most effective way?
- Has staff development been effective in keeping interventionists up to date with best practices?
- Do changes in staffing or overall program implementation need to occur?

The suggestions that follow provide specifics related to program monitoring and evaluation at the individual child and family level as well as the programmatic level:

- Ensure that individual child progress or change is systematically monitored and evaluated in order to determine if goals are met within prescribed timelines and conditions.
- Develop an evaluation plan using external evaluators to assist in the design and analysis if possible. External evaluators have no vested interest in the program/agency and may provide a helpful and objective examination of the practices that are effective and those that need revision.
- Develop ways to examine the degree to which families are accomplishing the outcomes that they have specified. Consider practices such as goal attainment scaling, interviews, or other unobtrusive, family-oriented approaches to gathering this information.
- Be sure that families' perceptions of the program/agency are assessed on an annual basis. Find a system for doing this that is most appropriate for the families being served. Consider using a combination of face-to-face interviews and short questionnaires in the families' languages.
- Seek input from other community members (e.g., advocacy groups, human services agencies, university personnel) regarding their perceptions of the program/agency and its effectiveness.
- Maintain logs of staff development activities, new initiatives, and innovative ideas on which the program/agency is working.

The overall goal of all intervention programs is to provide high-quality services that have been demonstrated to be effective and to provide those services in ways that are culturally appropriate, caring, and cost-effective. Regardless of the service system or setting, when this goal is accomplished, children will make progress, families will be satisfied participants and consumers, and the community as a whole will profit from the efforts.

IN CONCLUSION

This book has emphasized the importance of intervention that is culturally sensitive, and it has suggested specific skills that interventionists can learn and incorporate into their practice to increase their cross-cultural competence. It also has provided culture-specific information to help interventionists learn more about the range of attitudes, values, and beliefs that shape individuals' and families' views of the world. It is the authors' hope that this information will be used and shared by staff and parents in programs for young children and their families, especially in those programs that provide services to young children with disabilities and their families. But the book is only the beginning—it is only a vehicle for helping readers consider the value of cultural diversity and its impact on the programs in which we all work.

Skills and information are also only the beginning, a first step in cross-cultural competence—for this is an area in which the head is less important than the heart. After all of the books have been read and the skills learned and practiced, the cross-cultural effectiveness of each of us will vary. And it will vary more by what we bring to the learning than by what we have learned. Enthusiasm, openness, respect, awareness, the valuing of *all* people, and the willingness to take time are underlying characteristics that support everything that can be taught or learned. It is these characteristics that distinguish those who understand the journey from those who will actually take it.

> How do we choose among what we experience, what we are taught, what we run into by chance, or what is forced upon us? What is the principle of selection? . . . It would be terrible if centuries of culture are lost simply because there is not time.
> —Susan Nunes (1990, p. 136)

REFERENCES

Adams, D., & Carwardine, M. (1990). *Last chance to see.* New York: Harmony Books.

Barth, F. (1969). *Ethnic groups and boundaries.* Boston: Little,Brown.

Chan, S.Q. (1990). Early intervention with culturally diverse families of infants and toddlers with disabilities. *Infants and Young Children, 3*(2), 78–87.

Dunst, C.J., Trivette, C.M., & Deal, A.G. (1988). *Enabling and empowering families: Principles and guidelines for practice.* Cambridge, MA: Brookline Books.

Green, J.W. (1982). *Cultural awareness in the human services.* Englewood Cliffs, NJ: Prentice-Hall.

Hanson, M.J., & Lynch, E.W. (1989). *Early intervention: Implementing child and family services for infants and toddlers who are at-risk or disabled.* Austin, TX: PRO-ED.

Hanson, M.J., Lynch, E.W., & Wayman, K.I. (1990). Honoring the cultural diversity of families when gathering data. *Topics in Early Childhood Special Education, 10*(1), 112–131.

Johnson, B.H., McGonigel, M.J., & Kaufmann, R.K. (Eds.). (1989). *Guidelines and recommended practices for the individualized family service plan.* (Available from Association for the Care of Children's Health, 3615 Wisconsin Ave., N.W., Washington, DC 20016)

Kjerland, L. (1986). *Early intervention tailor made.* Eagan, MN: Project Dakota.

Lynch, E.W., Jackson, J.A., Mendoza, J.M., & English, K. (1991). The merging of best practices and state policy in the IFSP process in California. *Topics in Early Childhood Special Education, 11*(3).

Lynch, E.W., Mendoza, J.M., & English, K. (1990). *Implementing individualized family service plans in California: Final report.* (Available from Early Intervention Programs, Department of Developmental Services, 1600 9th Street, Sacramento, CA 95814)

Lynch, E.W., & Stein, R. (1982). Perspectives on parent participation in special education. *Exceptional Education Quarterly, 3*(2), 56–63.

Nunes, S. (1990). A moving day. In S. Walker (Ed.), *The Graywolf annual seven— Stories from the American mosaic* (pp. 130–137). Saint Paul, MN: Graywolf Press.

Storti, C. (1989). *The art of crossing cultures.* Yarmouth, ME: Intercultural Press.

Turnbull, A.P., & Turnbull, H.R. (1990). *Families, professionals, and exceptionality: A special partnership* (2nd ed.). Columbus, OH: Charles E. Merrill.

Wayman, K.I., Lynch, E.W., & Hanson, M.J. (1990). Home-based early childhood services: Cultural sensitivity in a family systems approach. *Topics in Early Childhood Special Education, 10*(4), 56–75.

SUGGESTED READINGS

One does not worship, display, or teach culture; one acknowledges it as a whole way of life grounded in the past, and one necessarily lives a culture.
—Houston Baker, Jr. (1990, p. 1)

Much of what we know about culture is learned from bicultural people—those who walk in two worlds and are able to communicate their life experience across cultural boundaries. Those with whom we share a common culture can also inform us as they explore and discover their own and other cultures through life experience. We are lucky indeed when we have the opportunity to walk in other worlds and participate in other cultures or to be with those who are bicultural. But even if we do not have these opportunities, we can learn from the growing number of books in the popular press that focus on cross-cultural experiences and interactions. Almost daily, a new book of fiction or nonfiction, poetry or prose, enters the market and invites us to accompany the author on a cultural odyssey—an adventure of the spirit that brings us closer to understanding ourselves and others. This brief list of suggested readings is intended to open the door, to provide a sampling of books that can expand the heart and the mind and help us to understand what it is like to live one's culture.

The suggestions for further reading that follow include works of fiction and nonfiction in which culture and cultural differences serve as the focus or the backdrop. No attempt has been made to develop a list that is exhaustive or one in which each group discussed in this book is equally represented. Many of the books listed here describe the life experiences of people of color in America; others chronicle experiences of Anglo-Europeans adjusting to life in unfamiliar cultures. Some detail cultures from a historical perspective; a few highlight cultural values, beliefs, and attitudes through words and pictures. The list is only the beginning, the first step in a long journey . . . but it is a wonderful beginning.

ANGLO-EUROPEAN AMERICAN

Lake Wobegon Days
Garrison Keillor (Viking Penguin, New York, 1985)
An amusing chronicle of the history and traditions of small-town American life.

Thanks to Dawn Thompson, doctoral student in the San Diego State University–Claremont Joint Doctoral Program, for her assistance in assembling this reading list.

On the Road with Charles Kuralt
Charles Kuralt (Putnam, New York, 1985)
>Wonderful descriptions of American life as told by a reporter during his travels around the country. Another book by Kuralt, *A Life on the Road* (1990), continues to chronicle these experiences.

Centennial
James A. Michener (Random House, New York, 1974)
>The epic saga of the origins, founding, and shaping of the United States from prehistoric to contemporary times. Generations of families are followed throughout the course of the nation's history.

Chesapeake
James A. Michener (Random House, New York, 1978)
>The complete history of the Chesapeake Bay region from the days of the original Native American Indians to contemporary times. This book gives a flavor to the arrival of settlers from the British Isles and the clashes and blending of their culture with those of the native population.

Texas
James A. Michener (Random House, New York, 1985)
>The complete history of the state of Texas from the first Spanish explorers and settlers to its separation and independence from Spain, on to its becoming a state.

A Connecticut Yankee in King Arthur's Court
Mark Twain (Samuel L. Clemens, 1889; now available through Bantam, New York, 1981)
>A comic satirical novel that describes a quintessential New Englander who brings the inventions and ingenuity of the American 19th century to King Arthur's Age of Chivalry.

NATIVE AMERICAN

Spider Woman's Granddaughters
Paula Gunn Allen, Ed. (Fawcett Columbine, New York, 1989)
>An anthology of stories by Native American women from long ago to contemporary times. Each reflects the influence of cultural bonds and traditions and the influence of contact with Anglo-Europeans on the culture.

Love Medicine
Louise Erdrich (Holt, Rinehart & Winston, New York, 1984)
>Multigenerational family portraits of two Native American families give a moving account of contemporary Native American life and experience in this country. Other books by Erdrich that describe Native American life include *The Beet Queen* and *Tracks*.

A Thief of Time
Tony Hillerman (Harper & Row, New York, 1988)

One among several of Tony Hillerman's well-crafted mysteries that are centered in the Southwest, portray two Navajo investigators, and provide some insight into the culture of the Navajo Nation. Although not a Native American, Hillerman presents readable and colorful accounts of aspects of contemporary Navajo life. (See also: *Skinwalkers, People of Darkness, Talking God,* and others.)

Alaska
James A. Michener (Random House, New York, 1988)

A journey from prehistoric times to the present day state of Alaska. This novel describes the crossing of the Bering Strait and settlement of what is now Alaska by the original peoples and gives a good account of the history and life experiences of Native Alaskan Indians and Eskimos.

AFRICAN AMERICAN

Coming of Age in Mississippi: An Autobiography
Anne Moody (Dial, New York, 1968)

A powerful autobiographical account of a young girl, which describes the experience of growing up black in Mississippi.

Song of Solomon
Toni Morrison (Alfred A. Knopf, New York, 1977)

A novel about four generations in an African American family, the importance of family bonds, and one man's search for knowledge of his own heritage. *Beloved,* the most recent of Morrison's books, is the story of Sethe, a runaway slave, who is haunted by her past and the ghost of her murdered daughter. A new exploration of some of the less well-known horrors of slavery. Other books written by Morrison that also bring to life the African American experience include: *Tar Baby, Sula,* and *The Bluest Eye.*

Every Good-Bye Ain't Gone
Itabari Njeri (Vintage Books, New York, 1990)

An autobiography of Njeri and her family that describes the diversity of the African American experience with humor, power, and finely drawn characterizations.

The Color Purple
Alice Walker (Harcourt Brace Jovanovich, New York, 1982)

A moving account of the struggles and joys in the life of an African American woman from childhood through adulthood as told through her letters. *The Temple of My Familiar,* another book by Walker, weaves together stories told by central characters to portray the heritage and experiences of several families. Other books by Walker, *Meridian* and *The Third Life of Grange Copeland,* describe African American experiences in a similar vein.

Roots
Alex Haley (Dell Books, New York, 1974)
> An epic story that spans seven generations. This major novel chronicles the African American experience from life in a small village in Africa through slavery and into contemporary life.

Disappearing Acts
Terry McMillan (Washington Square Press, New York, 1989)
> An unromanticized look at an African American couple's efforts to escape their individual pasts.

The Cheneysville Incident
David Bradley (Harper & Row, New York, 1981)
> A young African American historian returns to his hometown to care for his father's old friend, and begins an irresistible search into his family's past.

Can't Quit You, Baby
Ellen Douglas (Atheneum, New York, 1988)
> Cornelia, a rich, southern woman, and Tweet, her storytelling housekeeper, create a unique and supportive relationship through adversity.

Once Upon a Time When We Were Colored
Clifton L. Taulbert (Council Oak Book, Tulsa, OK, 1989)
> Recollections of life in a small Mississippi town before integration, with emphasis on the strength of kinship and friendship bonds.

Talk That Talk: An Anthology of African-American Storytelling
Linda Goss & Marian E. Barnes, Eds. (Simon & Schuster, New York, 1989)
> Stories of history remembered, home and family, and the supernatural, along with fables, anecdotes, sermons, and rhymes. Includes works by Maya Angelou, Langston Hughes, Zora Neale Hurston, Martin Luther King, Jr., and Winnie Mandela. A tour de force of African American storytelling.

LATINO

Woman Hollering Creek
Sandra Cisneros (Random House, New York, 1991)
> An excursion into a wonderful variety of lives in the Hispanic community.

Our House in the Last World
Oscar Hijuelos (Washington Square Press, New York, 1991)
> The tale of the immigration of the Santinios, a rural Cuban couple, to New York City, as told by their American-born son.

Getting Home Alive

Aurora Levins & Rosario Morales (Firebrand Books, Ithaca, NY, 1986)

A collection of poetry, stories, and comments on geography, politics, and culture by a Puerto Rican-American-Jewish mother and daughter.

Hunger of Memory—The Education of Richard Rodriguez

Richard Rodriguez (Bantam Books, New York, 1982)

An autobiography that chronicles the loss of Rodriguez's Mexican American culture as he climbs the ladder of academic success.

Stones for Ibarra

Harriet Doerr (Penguin, New York, 1984)

A tender story of love and culture about an Anglo-European American couple who go to Mexico to reopen an old family mine.

ASIAN

The Woman Warrior

Maxine Hong Kingston (Alfred A.Knopf, New York, 1976)

An enthralling description of Chinese immigrant life in California and the conflicts and paradoxes of the Chinese American experience as told often through the mother "talking story." Another book by Kingston, China Men, also portrays the Chinese American experience, particularly that of the early Chinese who came to America and labored in the development of this country.

Thousand Pieces of Gold

Ruthanne Lum McCunn (Beacon Press, Boston, 1981)

A biographical novel about Lalu Nathoy, a Chinese woman, who was sold by her father into slavery and taken to a mining town in Idaho in 1872. The novel describes her struggles, survival, and growth as a woman, and her experiences as a Chinese woman in the American West.

Iron and Silk

Mark Salzman (Vintage Departures, New York, 1990)

Salzman recounts his experiences as a young English language teacher in the Hunan Medical College. Open to the cultural differences that he experiences, this well-told story is truly a celebration of diversity. Salzman's latest book, The Laughing Sutra, is a humorous adventure novel that uses the clash between Chinese and American culture as a backdrop.

The Joy Luck Club

Amy Tan (G.P. Putnam's Sons, New York, 1989)

Four Chinese women come together in San Francisco and meet regularly over a game of mahjong. Their marvelous stories chronicle relationships between generations and friends, and the interface between experiences from the old world (China) and those of the new life in America. Similar themes are woven in *The Kitchen God's Wife,* another recent work by Tan.

PILIPINO

Video Night in Katmandu
Pico Iyer (Vintage Departures, New York, 1989)
A series of essays on the interplay between Eastern and Western culture. In the essay devoted to the Philippines, Iyer presents a grim picture of the influence of American ways on the lives of Pilipinos.

NATIVE HAWAIIAN AND PACIFIC ISLAND

Hawaii
James A. Michener (Random House, New York, 1959)
A saga of the history of the Hawaiian islands from settlement by the first Polynesians to statehood and contemporary life. The novel chronicles the range and experiences of the many cultural and ethnic groups that make up contemporary Hawaii.

Changes in Latitude—An Uncommon Anthropology
Joana McIntyre Varawa (Harper & Row, New York, 1989)
An Anglo-European American marries a Fijian and chronicles her life with him and his extended family in the village. The cultural clashes that inevitably occur are discussed and inform Varawa and the reader about the power of culture and cross-cultural learning.

Amerika Samoa—An Anthropological Photo Essay
Frederic Koehler Sutter (University of Hawaii Press, Honolulu, 1984)
A beautiful photographic essay captioned with Samoan proverbs.

MIDDLE EASTERN

A History of the Arab Peoples
Albert Hourani (The Belknap Press of Harvard University Press, Cambridge, MA, 1991)
A comprehensive book that chronicles the history of Arab-speaking parts of the Islamic world from the 7th century into the 1980s. For each time period, there is an emphasis on society and culture.

Baghdad Without a Map
Tony Horowitz (Dutton, New York, 1991)
A freelance journalist describes his search for stories throughout the Middle East. As each chapter unfolds, so too do the differences between the West

and the Middle East, as well as the diversity among the Middle Eastern countries that in some ways are linked only by geographical designation.

Motoring with Mohammed
Eric Hansen (Houghton Mifflin, Boston, 1991)
> In search of his travel journals buried after a shipwreck 10 years earlier, Hansen returns to Yemen to find them. The direct and demanding Anglo-European American approach is gradually smoothed by the Yemeni culture, customs, and people.

MISCELLANEOUS

The Graywolf Annual Five: Multicultural Literacy—Opening the American Mind
Rick Simonson & Scott Walker, Eds. (Graywolf Press, St. Paul, MN, 1988)
> An anthology of short stories from writers of color that seeks to ensure that we expand cultural literacy to include multicultural literacy.

The Graywolf Annual Seven: Stories from the American Mosaic
Scott Walker, Ed. (Graywolf Press, Saint Paul, MN, 1990)
> Fifteen fictional stories that focus on diverse cultures' interactions with mainstream United States culture. The various stories highlight misunderstanding, confusion, conflict, and the beginning of mutual respect and understanding.

The Spirited Earth—Dance, Myth, and Ritual from South Asia to the South Pacific
Victoria Ginn (Rizzoli, New York, 1990)
> A beautiful photographic anthology of the rituals of South Asia and the Pacific as enacted through myth and dance.

Working Together—How to Become More Effective in a Multicultural Organization
George Simons (Crisp Publications, Los Altos, CA, 1989)
> A workbook of exercises to help organizations and the people in them examine their own feelings about diversity and develop ways to improve their cross-cultural effectiveness.

REFERENCE

Baker, H.A., Jr. (1990). *Long black song—Essays in black American literature and culture*. Charlottesville: The University Press of Virginia.

AUTHOR INDEX

Page numbers followed by "*n*" indicate footnotes.

Abad, V., 157
Abalos, D.T., 155, 161
Abe, H., 36
Adams, D., 360
Affonso, D., 281
Agbayani, A., 263, 270, 272, 274, 275, 276, 291
Agresta, A.J., 182, 183, 192
Allen, L., 129, 131, 138
Allen, W.R., 128
Allgood-Hill, B.A., 51
Althen, G., 15, 36, 38, 48, 72, 73, 80
Alvirez, D., 163
Andersen, P.A., 44, 45
Anderson, P.P., 3, 5, 238
Arce, C.H., 161
Arias, A.M., 159
Arnold, F., 182, 259, 270
Asante, M.K., 46
Axtell, J., 92

Baker, H., Jr., 371
Ball-Rokeach, S.J., 23
Barnes, M.E., 374
Barth, F., 356
Batmanglij, N., 332
Baumrind, D., 338
Bean, F., 163
Bell, B., 310
Bello, M., 266
Beman, A., 164
Ben, R., 224
Benhamida, L., 55
Bennett, L., Jr., 121, 122, 123, 124, 126, 127, 128
Berkhofer, R.F., Jr., 93
Bernal, G., 161, 162, 163
Betham, M., 301
Billingsley, A., 127, 131, 133, 134, 135, 136
Blackburn, T.C., 197
Blaisdell, K., 302, 310
Bliatout, B.T., 210, 224

Bliatout, H.Y., 224
Boas, F., 49
Boekestijn, D., 159
Bohm, D., 24
Bond, J., 310, 311
Bopp, J., 104, 105
Bopp, M., 104, 105
Bouvier, L.F., 182, 183, 192
Boyce, E., 157
Bozorgmehr, M., 327, 338
Bradley, D., 374
Braganti, N.L., 47, 49, 255, 296, 299
Brannon, E., 55
Bremner, R.H., 125
Brislin, R.W., 23, 24, 31, 36, 211
Brooten, D.A., 228
Brown, L., 104, 105
Brown, L.P., 228
Brown, R., 19
Buck, P., 302
Bulosan, C., 264
Buriel, R., 221
Byrnes, F.C., 23

Cariño, B.V., 183, 259, 265, 266, 270
Carlyle, T., 19
Carwardine, M., 360
Chan, S.Q., 35*n*, 36, 37, 50, 181, 183, 212, 213, 214, 220, 221, 229, 231, 239, 240, 241, 243, 244, 259, 360
Chandler, W.U., 28
Chang, N., 305, 307
Chen, J., 185
Chen, V., 233
Cheng, C-Y., 188
Cheng, L.L., 191, 240
Cherrie, C., 24, 36
Chhim, S-H., 199, 200, 205, 207
Chinn, P.C., 211
Chrisman, N.J., 284
Chu, T.L., 233
Church, A.T., 275, 281, 282

Cisneros, S., 374
Cleveland, J.O., 243
Cohon, D., 210
Coles, R., 103
Cromwell, R., 162
Crystal, D., 233
Cupach, W.R., 36
Cushner, K., 24, 36

Dang, V.V., 225
Davis, A., 46
Davis, L., 172
Deal, A.G., 29, 361
DeAnda, D., 172
DeAngelis, T., 210
Delgado, M., 168
Devine, E., 47, 49, 255, 296, 299
Devore, W., 172
Diab, L.N., 329
Dien, T.T., 208, 225, 239
Dillard, J.L., 128
Do, H.K., 228
Dobyns, H.R., 92
Doerner, W., 185
Doerr, H., 375
Douglas, E., 374
Doutrich, D., 228
Draine, C., 19, 24
Driver, H.E., 97
Drogin, B., 266
DuBray, W.H., 100
Dudley, M., 307
Dung, T.N., 215
Dunn, A., 168
Dunst, C.J., 29, 361

Egawa, J., 224, 243
English, K., 8, 29, 361
Enriquez, V.G., 274, 276
Erdrich, L., 372

Farley, R., 128
Fawcett, J.T., 182, 183, 259, 270
Federico, G., 167
Feliciano, R., 108
Fenichel, E.S., 3, 5
Fiatoa, L., 312
Fisher, S.N., 320, 321
Fitzpatrick, J., 163

Franklin, J.H., 126, 128
Franklyn-Stokes, A., 51
Freedgood, S., 67
Fu, V.R., 221
Fuentes, N., 285

Garcia-Preto, N., 157, 161
Gardner, R.W., 182, 259, 270
Genovese, E.D., 122, 128, 133, 135, 150
Gibbs, J.T., 166
Gibson, C., 93
Giles, H., 51, 233
Gilliam, O.L., 90n
Ginn, V., 377
Gochenour, T., 260, 261, 262, 266, 267,
    268, 269, 271, 272, 273, 274,
    276, 288, 297
Gollnick, D.M., 211
Gomez, E., 157, 164, 166
Gonzalez-Whippier, M., 156
Goodman, M.E., 164
Good Track, J.G., 104
Gordon, L.W., 199, 209
Goss, L., 374
Green, J.W., 9, 15, 16, 17, 28, 41, 49,
    124, 131, 132, 356
Gudykunst, W.B., 233
Gullahorn, J., 23, 25
Gunn, P., 372
Guthrie, G.M., 19, 23, 273, 274, 281

Haertig, E.W., 309, 310
Hagen, E., 55
Haley, A., 374
Hall, B., 19, 24
Hall, E.T., 35, 36, 44, 45, 231, 232
Hammer, M.R., 36
Handlin, O., 324, 325, 327
Handy, E.S., 306
Hannerz, U., 128
Hansen, E., 377
Hanson, M.J., 3, 7, 8, 9, 10, 13, 29, 36,
    41, 43, 65, 78, 238, 355, 360,
    361, 364
Harrison, A.O., 221
Hecht, M.L., 44, 45
Helms, J.E., 51
Hepworth, D., 168
Hernandez, R., 153, 157
Hijuelos, O., 374

Hilger, S.M.I., 99
Hillerman, T., 373
Ho, D.Y.F., 215
Ho, M.K., 101, 163
Hoffman, F., 91
Hoguet, D., 38
Hollingsworth, A.O., 228
Horowitz, T., 376
Hough, R., 161, 162
Hourani, A., 323, 324, 376
Howard, A., 307
Hoxie, F., 90
Hsu, F.L.K., 189, 190
Huang, L.N., 166, 185, 199, 200, 204, 211
Hui, C.H., 211
Hull, F., 23
Hurh, W.M., 194

Inclan, J., 152
Iyer, P., 376

Ja, D.Y., 182
Jackson, J.A., 361
Jacobs, P.J., 281
Jennings, F., 92
Joe, J.R., 89, 91, 116
Johnson, B.H., 29, 361
Johnson, D., 46, 98, 310
Juarez, R., 164

Kagan, J., 333
Kanahele, G., 304, 305
Kaufmann, R.K., 29, 361
Kealey, D.J., 36
Keillor, G., 371
Keiter, J., 183, 199, 204, 209, 239, 244
Kennedy, J.F., 73
Kim, B-L.C., 198
Kim, H-C., 193
Kim, I., 197
Kim, K.C., 194
Kim, L.I.C., 193, 198, 215, 217
Kim, S.C., 216
Kingston, M.H., 375
Kjerland, L., 29, 361
Klineberg, O., 23
Kluckhohn, F.R., 99, 103, 164
Kochman, T.E., 128, 133

Kolody, B., 160
Kourmarn, Y.S., 201
Kuralt, C., 372

Labov, W., 128
LaDue, R., 51
Lane, P., 104, 105
Larsen, J., 168
Lawless, R., 274
Le, D.D., 211
Lee, C., 309, 310
Lee, C.S., 196, 197
Lee, D.T-T., 224
Lee, R.V., 221, 222, 228, 229
Lee, S., 220
Leigh, J.W., 124, 131, 132
Lenneberg, E., 19
Leung, B., 52, 190, 191, 219, 220, 239
Leung, E.K., 186, 188, 213, 214, 239, 243
Leung, P., 182
Levine, E., 161
Levins, A., 375
Lew, L.S., 222, 223
Lewis, J., 11
Lewis, R.B., 11
Lewis, R.G., 101
Li, C., 196, 208, 267, 268
Licuanan, P.B., 275
Lim-Yee, N., 227
Lin, C.C., 221
Lin, K-M., 210, 223
Lin-Fu, J.S., 209, 210
Luangpraseut, K., 201, 205, 206, 207, 215
Lynch, E.W., 7, 8, 9, 10, 11, 13, 19, 29, 35, 36, 41, 43, 78, 238, 355, 360, 361, 364, 365

MacMahon, H., 195
Majidi-Ahi, S., 129, 131, 138
Major, J.S., 184, 187, 188, 189, 190, 191, 211
Malach, R.S., 89, 98, 101, 109, 114
Malraux, A., 3
Mancini, J.K., 128
Mandulo, R., 125
Maquet, J., 127
Markoff, R., 310, 311
Marquez, E., 287

Marsella, A.J., 16
Masterson, L. C-C., 225, 228
Masuda, M., 210, 223
McAdoo, H.P., 129, 130
McAdoo, J.L., 129, 130
McCunn, R.L., 375
McDermott, J., 309, 310
McGonigel, M.J., 29, 361
McKenzie, J.L., 284
McMillan, T., 374
Meinert, D., 265
Mendoza, J.M., 8, 29, 361
Metje, L., 228
Michener, J.A., 372, 373, 376
Miller, D.L., 91, 104, 116
Minocha, U., 182
Mizio, E., 157
Mokuau, N., 301, 305, 307
Montepio, S.N., 283, 284, 285
Montiel, M., 161
Montijo, J., 152, 161
Moody, A., 373
Morales, A., 166
Morales, R., 291
Morales, Rosario, 375
Morales, R.F., 265
Morey, S.M., 90n
Morrison, T., 373
Morrow, R.D., 215
Mostyn, T., 323, 324
Muecke, M.A., 222, 224, 225
Mun, S.H., 195
Murase, K., 243

Neal, A., 51
Nehru, J., 35
Neihardt, J.G., 104
Nguyen, L.H., 225
Nguyen, N., 225
Nguyen, N.T., 211
Nguyen, P.H., 225
Njeri, I., 373
Nordyke, E., 302, 305, 310
Nunes, S., 370

Oberg, K., 23
O'Hagan, P., 310
Okamura, J.Y., 263, 270, 272, 274,
    275, 276, 291
Old Coyote, H., 89, 90n

Olness, K.N., 216
Olson, J.S., 98
Orlov, A., 324, 325, 327
Ortiz, F., 156

Padilla, A., 161
Palafox, N., 312
Park, S.J., 192n
Patterson, W., 193
Peckham, H., 93
Pernia, E.M., 265
Pine, C.J., 221
Plantz, M.C., 99
Porter, J., 184, 186, 188
Posadas, B.M., 263
Powell, G., 166
Price-Williams, D., 163
Proctor, E., 172
Prothro, E.T., 329
Pukui, M.K., 301, 306, 309, 310

Quetone, A., 89, 90n
Quigg, A., 301

Ramirez, M., 163
Ramirez, O., 161
Randall-David, E., 13, 46, 52, 55, 129,
    131, 135, 136, 142
Reyes, V., 266
Reyhner, J., 108
Ribeau, S.A., 44, 45
Robbins, B., 128
Robertiello, R.C., 38
Roberts, R.N., 238
Robey, B., 182
Roces, A., 296
Roces, G., 296
Rodriguez, R., 375
Rogow, S.M., 243
Roland, A., 162, 164
Romero, A., 161, 162, 165, 166
Rothbaum, F.M., 197
Ruben, B.D., 36
Rubinstein, D., 156
Ruiz, R.A., 162
Rumbaut, R.G., 210
Russell, G., 152
Rutledge, P., 201, 202, 203, 204, 206
Ryan, A.S., 243

Sabagh, G., 327, 338
Sakata, R., 182
Salcido, R.M., 160
Salgado de Snyder, N., 158
Salzman, M., 375
Sanchez-Hucles, J.V., 16
Santos, R.A., 264, 268, 270, 271, 272, 276, 279, 282, 287, 288, 299
Sardinas, M., 169
Satir, V., 338
Schilling, B., 55
Schlesinger, E., 172
Schneller, R., 48
Schrag-Fenichel, R., 238
Schreiner, D., 12
Segel, N., 98, 101
Serafica, F.C., 213, 241
Shade, B.J., 143
Sharifzadeh, S., 319
Shon, S.P., 182, 232
Shu, K.E., 243
Siao, G.W-T., 198
Sigel, I.E., 215
Simons, G., 377
Simonson, R., 377
Sluzki, C., 154
Smalley, W., 23
Smith, M.J., 243
Smith, P.C., 182
Smith-DeMateo, R., 155, 168, 169
Snipp, C.M., 98
Soldevilla, E., 285, 287
Solnit, A., 25
Song, K.S., 192n
Spitzberg, B.H., 36
Stark, M., 25
Stein, H.F., 99
Stein, R.C., 29, 365
Stevenson, H.W., 220
Stinson, F.S., 99
Storti, C., 36, 39, 355
Strodtbeck, F.L., 99, 103, 164
Sue, D., 239
Sue, S., 240
Sung, B.L., 184
Sutter, F.K., 376
Suzuki, B.H., 270
Szapocznik, J., 153, 157

Takaki, R., 182, 184, 185, 186, 192, 194, 196, 198, 200, 201, 204, 209,

210, 211, 235, 261, 262, 263, 264, 270
Tan, A., 52, 190, 191, 219, 220, 239, 375
Tashima, N., 224, 243
Tauili'ili, P., 301
Taulbert, C.L., 374
Te, H.D., 188, 199, 201, 202, 203, 205, 206, 207, 208, 212, 225, 231, 234, 235, 239, 255
Thernstrom, S., 324, 325, 327
Thomas, T., 98, 101
Thornton, R., 92, 94
Thuy, V.G., 216
Tiedt, I.M., 37, 50, 51, 128, 150
Tiedt, P.L., 37, 50, 51, 128, 150
Ting-Toomey, S., 233
Tinloy, M.T., 52, 190, 191, 219, 220, 239
Titiev, M., 105
Tom, K.S., 221, 222, 224, 225, 255
Tong, B.R., 51
Torres-Matrullo, C., 164
Tou-Fou, V., 201
Triandis, H.C., 211
Trivette, C.M., 29, 361
Turnbull, A.P., 29, 361
Turnbull, H.R., 29, 361
Twain, M., 372

Valle, R., 160
Varawa, J.M., 57, 376
Vega, W., 160, 161, 162

Walker, A., 373
Walker, C.L., 208
Walker, S., 377
Wang, W.S-Y., 196
Washburn, W., 90, 91
Wayman, K.I., 7, 9, 29, 36, 41, 43, 78, 238, 360, 364
Wegner, E., 310, 313
Wei, T.T.D., 208, 225, 239
Weisz, J.R., 196
Wiemann, J., 233
Williams, D., 163
Willis, W., 121
Wilson, M.N., 221
Wilson, R., 98

Winter, F.H., 260, 261, 262, 263, 265, 266, 269
Wiseman, R.L., 36
Wolfensberger, W., 80
Wong, C., 222

Yamamoto, J., 166
Yao, E.L., 243
Yap, J., 279, 281
Ybarra-Soriano, L., 161, 162
Yeatman, G.W., 225
Ying, Y-W., 185

Yong, M., 24, 36
Young, B., 302, 308
Young, R.F., 330
Young-Kwon, K., 195
Yu, E-Y., 194, 196, 197, 198
Yu, K.H., 193, 198, 215, 217
Yum, J-O., 195, 233

Zane, N., 240
Zangwill, I., 50
Zintz, M., 100
Zuniga, M., 151, 161, 165

SUBJECT INDEX

Page numbers followed by "*n*" indicate footnotes.

Acceptance of events
  Asian Americans and, 213, 214
  Native Americans and, 103–104
Acculturation
  degree of, 16
  of Latinos, 158
  of Native Americans, 99
  see also Assimilation
Achievement
  Asian American view of, 219–220
  mainstream American view of, 74
  Middle Eastern view of, 327–328
  Pilipino view of, 275
Action, mainstream American view of,
    74
Adaptation of immigrants, *see* Ac-
    culturation; Assimilation; Immi-
    grants, adaptation of
Adjustment, culture shock and, 27
Afghans
  immigration of, political events and,
    325
  see also Middle Easterners
African Americans, 121–145
  attitudes of
    toward causation, 142
    toward disability, 142–143
  background of, 121–128
  beliefs of, 137–143
    mainstream beliefs versus, 147
  Black English dialect of, 127–128,
    143, 150
  case examples of, 130, 137, 140
  celebrations and holidays of, 149
  childrearing beliefs of, 137–139
  civil rights and, 70, 125–126
  concept of family and, 131–134
  contemporary life of, 128–131
  courtesies and customs of, 148
  culture of, mainstream culture versus,
    147
  developmental milestones and, 104
  education of, 134–135
  eye contact and, 46
  geographic origins of, 121

heroes of, 125
high-context culture of, 44–45
historical origins of, 122
    18th and 19th centuries, 122–124
    17th century, 122
    20th century, 124–126
humor of, 135–136
language issues with, 143–144, 150
language origins of, 127–128
literature about, 373–374
medical care and, 139–142
recommendations for working with,
    144–145
religion of, 136
religious origins of, 126–127
respect for elders of, 134–135
social distance and, 46
term defining, 51
therapeutic agents and, 13
in U.S. population, 7
values of, 131–136
    mainstream values versus, 147
Age
  at cultural understanding, 19–20
  at developmental milestones, *see* De-
    velopmental milestones
  ease of cultural learning and, 20
  see also Children; Elders; Infants
'Aiga, 307
'Aina, 306
Alaska Natives, *see* Native Americans
Ambiente, 164
American culture, mainstream, *see*
    Anglo-Europeans; Mainstream
    American culture
American Indian Freedom of Religion
    Act of 1978, 96
American Indian Movement (AIM), 96
American Indians, *see* Native Americans
Americans with Disabilities Act, 80
Amor propio, 274, 289, 292
Ancestor worship
  Chinese, 189
  Vietnamese, 206
Anger, culture shock and, 26, 27

Anglo-Europeans, 65–82
  background of, 66–69
  beliefs of, 76–80
  case examples of, 75, 78, 79
  celebrations and holidays of, 86–87
  communication style of, 74, 81
  contemporary life of, 69–70
  courtesies and customs of, 85
  developmental milestones and, 104
  family involvement and, 81–82
  geographic and historical origins of,
      66–68
  intrafamily interactions and, 82
  language origins of, 69
  literature about, 371–372
  low-context culture of, 45
  organization and scheduling with, 82
  recommendations for working with,
      81–82
  religious origins of, 68–69
  self-awareness of, 37, 38
  social distance and, 46
  values of, 71–76
    contrasted with other cultures'
      values, 84
  see also Mainstream American culture
Animism
  Brahmanism and, 205
  shamanism and, 195
Arabic language, 323, 351
Arabs, see Middle Easterners
Asian Americans, 181–244
  alternative service delivery and train-
      ing models for, 243–244
  attitudes of
    toward causation, 225–229
    toward disability, 225–231
  beliefs of, 214–231, 237
    mainstream beliefs versus, 251–252
  birthdays and, 255
  body language and, 48
  case examples of, 226–227, 230–231
  celebrations and holidays of, 255
  childrearing practices of, 214–221
  communication styles of, assertiveness
      and, 241–242
  competition versus cooperation and,
      20
  courtesies and customs of, 253–254
  education of, 213
  eye contact and, 46
  face saving and, 240–241, 242
  facial expressions and, 46
  family values of, 211–212
  gestures and, 48, 49
  harmony and, concept of, 213
  healing techniques of, 12
  health beliefs of, 221–223
  health practices of, 223–225
  high-context culture of, 44–45
  initial expectations and orientations of,
      240
  language issues with, 231–235
    interpreters and, 239
  literature about, 375–376
  medical care and, 221–225
  nonverbal communication and,
      46–49, 232–234, 242, 254
  numbers and, symbolism of, 256
  origins of, 182
  outreach and, 238–239
  physical contact and, 47
  reciprocity and, 242–243
  recommendations for working with,
      238–243
  social distance and, 46
  therapeutic agents and, 13
  values of, 211–214, 236–237
    mainstream values versus, 251–252
  virtues valued by, 213–214
  vocabulary of, 257
  see also specific groups, e.g., Viet-
      namese Americans
Assertiveness
  Asian Americans and, 241–242
  mainstream American culture and, 74,
      85
Assessment
  data gathering and, 362–364
  family–professional partnership and,
      361–362
  of services, 368–369
Assimilation
  Native Americans and, 91, 95–96
  see also Acculturation; specific groups
Assumptions
  culture-specific issues and, 41
  of mainstream American culture, 15,
      38, 71–76, 80
Attitudes
  communication of, through words,
      50–51
  see also specific groups; specific
      topics, e.g., Disabilities
Authority, Pilipinos and, 272–273, 279
Autonomy, Native Americans and, 104

Awareness
  culture-specific
    cautions relating to, 44
    cross-cultural competence and,
      39–44
  self-, cross-cultural competence and,
    36–39, 60–62, 359–360
Azabache, 169

Babies, *see* Infants
Baci ceremony, 205–206
Bahala na, 275–276, 285, 289, 291
Bahrainians, *see* Middle Easterners
Bat gio, 12
Beckoning, gestures used in, 49
Behavior
  culture shock and, 24–25
    see also Culture shock
  factors governing, 3–4, 22, 44
  long-standing patterns of, in expres-
    sion of values, 21
  nonverbal, *see* Nonverbal communi-
    cation
  punished, Asian Americans and, 219
  see also Customs
Beliefs
  African American, 137–143
  Anglo-European, 76–80
  Asian American, 214–231, 237
  culture shock and, 30
  Hawaiian, 308–310
  Latino, 164–169
  Middle Eastern, 330–334, 348
  Native American, 104–108
  Pilipino, 277–287, 295
  Samoan, 310–312
  self-awareness of, 36–39, 359–360
    Cultural Journey for, 21, 60–62
  see also Values; *specific group; spe-
    cific topic*
Bias
  cultural, in data gathering and assess-
    ment, 362–364
  see also Racism
Bicultural individuals, 15–16, 357
  Native Americans, 91
  see also Native Americans
Bilingual teachers
  Native Americans and, 109
  see also Language
Black English, 127–128, 143, 150
Blacks, *see* African Americans

"Boat people," 204
Body language, 47–48
  Asian Americans and, 234
  see also Nonverbal communication
Brahmanism, 205–206
Breastfeeding, *see* Feeding practices
British
  Native Americans and, 93
  see also Anglo-Europeans
Brown v. Board of Education, 125
Brujo(a), 166
Buddhism
  Chinese Americans and, 188–189
  Korean Americans and, 195
  Pilipinos and, 267
  Southeast Asian Americans and, 205

Cambodian Americans
  geographic and historical origins of,
    199–200
  see also Asian Americans; Southeast
    Asian Americans
Cantonese dialect, 190, 257
Cao gio, 12
Carabao, 268
Case examples
  African American, 130, 137, 140
  Anglo-European, 75, 78, 79
  Asian American, 226–227, 230–231
  Hawaiian, 306
  Latino, 159, 167, 170
  Middle Eastern, 326, 341, 344
  Native American, 102, 107
  Pilipino, 278–279, 286
  Samoan, 303
Case management, Native Americans
  and, 113–114
Casualness, 72
Catholicism
  Latinos and, 155–156, 168
  Pilipinos and, 266
  Vietnamese Americans and, 206
  see also Christianity
Causation, views of, 9–10
  African American, 142
  Anglo-European, 79
  Asian American, 225–229
  Latino, 168–169
  Native American, 105–106
  Pilipino, 285–287
Celebrations and holidays
  African American, 149

Celebrations and holidays—*continued*
　Anglo-European, 86–87
　Asian American, 255
　Hawaiian, 317
　Latino, 178
　Middle Eastern, 335, 350
　Native American, 119
　Pilipino, 299
　Samoan, 317
　see also Ceremonies
Central Americans
　background of, 154
　in U.S. population, 152
　see also Latinos
Ceremonies
　Laotian, 205–206
　Native American, 105, 106, 119
　see also Celebrations and holidays
Change
　personal growth and, cross-cultural
　　competence and, 359–360
　view toward, mainstream American
　　culture and, 73
Character traits
　Pilipino, 275–276
　valued, by Asian Americans, 213–214
　see also specific groups
Chicanos, *see* Latinos; Mexican
　Americans
Childbirth, *see* Pregnancy
Childrearing practices
　African American beliefs and,
　　137–139
　Anglo-European beliefs and, 76–77
　Asian American beliefs and, 214–221
　　early childhood and, 218
　　family structure and, 215
　　infancy and, 216–218
　　marital roles and, 215–216
　　parental roles and responsibilities
　　　and, 216
　　school age and, 218
　educational interventions and, 11–12
　Hawaiian beliefs and, 309
　Latino beliefs and, 164–166
　Middle Eastern beliefs and, 332–334
　　discipline and, 338–340
　Native American values and, 101, 102,
　　106–108
　Pilipino beliefs and, 277–282
　　early childhood and, 281–282
　　family structure and, 277–279
　　infancy and, 280–281

　　marital and parental roles and ex-
　　　pectations and, 279–280
　Samoan beliefs and, 310–311
Children
　cultural understanding in, 19–20
　developmental milestones in, *see* De-
　　velopmental milestones
　with disabilities
　　population estimate of, 7
　　see also Disabilities
　ease of cultural learning and, 20
　Hawaiian views of, 308–310
　independence of, 12
　Middle Eastern
　　in context of family, 334–343
　　guests and, 335–336
　　number of, 329–330
　　responsibilities and work of,
　　　336–337
　in U.S. population, 7
Chinatowns, 185, 192
Chinese Americans, 183–192
　contemporary life of, 191–192
　geographic and historical origins of,
　　183–186
　health beliefs of, 221–223
　immigration of, 68, 184–185
　language and linguistic origins of,
　　190–191
　　Korean language and, 196
　religious origins of, 186–190
　in U.S. population, 192
　vocabulary of, 257
　see also Asian Americans
Chinese Exclusion Act of 1882, 184
Christianity, 76
　African Americans and, 126–127
　Korean Americans and, 195–196
　Middle Easterners and, 321–322, 323
　Pacific Island groups and, 303–304
　Pilipinos and, 266
　see also Catholicism; Protestantism
Church, *see* Religion; Religious origins;
　specific religion
Citizenship, Native Americans and,
　94–95
Civil disobedience, Native Americans
　and, 96
Civil Rights Act, 126
Civil rights movement, 70, 125–126
Class status, *see* Socioeconomic status
　(SES)
Collaboration, family–professional, es-

tablishment of, 361–362
Communication
  African Americans and, 133
  Anglo-Europeans and, 81
  in Asian American families, 220
  of attitudes, through words, 50–51
  cross-cultural, 44–56
    acknowledgment of differences and,
      50
    characteristics in effectiveness of,
      51–52
    choice of words and, 50–51
    general principles of, 44–50
    interpreters and translators in, see
      Interpreters
  directness of, in mainstream Ameri-
    can culture, 74
  in high-context and low-context cul-
    tures, 44–45
  indirect
    Asian Americans and, 232–234
    Middle Easterners and, 343
    see also Nonverbal communication
  interpreters and, see Interpreters
  language and
    culture shock and, 26, 28
    Native Americans and, 109–110
    see also Language
  listening to family's perspective in,
    49–50
  Native Americans and, 109–110,
    111–112
  nonverbal, see Nonverbal
    communication
  styles of, 13–14
    Asian Americans and, 241–242
    Pilipinos and, 292
    see also specific groups
  see also Conversation
Community
  participation in, cross-cultural under-
    standing and, 40–41
  tribal
    in health care, 11
    see also African Americans; Native
      Americans
Compadres, 277
Competition, cultural values and, 20
Complementarity, polytheism and, Chinese Americans and, 189–190
Conflicts, between family and interventionists, 4–5
  implementation and, 367

Confucianism
  Chinese Americans and, 186–187
  Korean Americans and, 195
    Korean language and, 197
  Southeast Asian Americans and, 206
Consensus, group, Native Americans
  and, 103
Context, information transmission
  through
  cross-cultural communication and,
    44–45, 232–233
  see also Nonverbal communication
Conversation
  with Asian Americans, 254
  with Pilipinos, 297
  see also Communication
Counseling process
  face saving and
    Asian Americans and, 240–241
    Pilipinos and, 291–292
  see also Intervention; Interventionists
Countertransference, interpreters and,
  54–55
Courtesies
  African Americans and, 148
  Anglo-Europeans and, 85
  Asian Americans and, 253–254
  Hawaiians and, 316
  Latinos and, 177
  Middle Eastern, 349
  Native Americans and, 117–118
  Pilipino, 296–298
  Samoans and, 316
Cradle boards, 117
Cross-cultural communication, 44–56
  acknowledgment of differences and,
    50
  choice of words and, 50–51
  effective
    characteristics of users of, 51–52
    general principles of, 44–50
  interpreters and translators in, 52–56
Cross-cultural competence
  defined, 356
  development of, 35–57
    communication in, 44–56
    culture-specific awareness and un-
      derstanding in, 39–44
    elements in, 36
    self-awareness in, 36–39
  importance of, 5–9
  recommendations for, see Interven-
    tionists, recommendations for

Cross-cultural interactions
among children, 20
for culture-specific awareness, 40–41
Cubans
background of, 153–154
religious origins of, 156
therapeutic agents and, 13
in U.S. population, 152
see also Latinos
Cues, nonverbal, see Nonverbal communication
Cultural bias
in data gathering and assessment,
362–364
see also Racism
"Cultural clashes," see Conflicts
Cultural differences
acknowledgment of, respect for and,
50
poverty-related differences versus,
131, 145, 161
Cultural diversity, see Diversity
Cultural enclaves, 16
Cultural events, see Celebrations and
holidays; Ceremonies
Cultural groups
names for, 50–51
overgeneralizing about, 5
see also Generalizations
see also specific groups
Cultural identification
continuum of, 15–17
mitigating factors in, 14–15, 44,
358–359
Cultural identity, 14–17
influence of, factors mitigating,
14–15, 44, 358–359
transactional and situational nature of,
356–358
Cultural integration
categories of, 15–16
see also Acculturation; Assimilation
Cultural Journey, 21, 60–62
Cultural learning
age and, 20
from culture shock to, 19–33
methods of, 39–41
Cultural mediators, 40
Cultural patterns, new, children's relative
ease in learning and, 20
Cultural programming, 21
Cultural self-awareness, 21, 36–39,
60–62

Cultural understanding
community participation and, 40–41
in first culture
age at, 19–20
errors in interpretation of second
culture and, 20–21
Cultural values, see Values
Culturally different individuals, 16
Culturally marginal individuals, 16
Culture
defined, 3
interpretation of, understanding of
first culture and, 20–21
Culture shock
amelioration of, 27–31
for long-term residents, 31
for new immigrants, 28–30
concept of, 22–27
cultural learning from, 19–33
defined, 23–25
family's viewpoint and, 25–26
impact of, sensitization to, 31–33
interventionist's viewpoint and, 27
reasons for, 19–22
reverse, 25
stages of, navigation of, 25–27
Culture-specific awareness
cautions relating to, 44
cross-cultural competence and, 39–44
reading for, 40, 371–377
Culture-specific issues, intervention and,
41–43
Curandero(a), 166, 167
Customs
African American, 148
Anglo-European, 85
Asian American, 253–254
Hawaiian, 316
Latino, 177
Middle Eastern, 349
Native American, 117–118
Pilipino, 296–298
Samoan, 316

Data gathering, assessment and,
362–364
Deities, see Religion; Religious origins
Demographics
changing, 7–8
see also Population statistics
Dermabrasion, Asian Americans and,
225

Development, intellectual, Middle Easterners and, 340
Developmental milestones
African Americans and, 104
Anglo-Europeans and, 104
Native Americans and, 101, 102, 104
Dialects
Black English, 127–128, 143, 150
Chinese and, 190
Koreans and, 196
Latinos and, 170–171
Pilipino, 267–268, 300
see also Language
Diet
African Americans and, 138
in pregnancy, Pilipino beliefs about causation and, 285
Differences, see Cultural differences; Diversity; Individual differences
Directness, mainstream American culture and, 74, 85
Disabilities
African American beliefs about, 142–143
Anglo-European beliefs about, 79–80
Asian American beliefs about, 225–231
causation of
views of, 9–10
see also Causation
children with, population estimate of, 7
fatalistic view of, 9
Hawaiian beliefs about, 309–310
Latino beliefs about, 168–169
Middle Eastern beliefs about, 340–343
Native American beliefs about, 105–106
Pilipino beliefs about, 285–287
Samoan beliefs about, 311–312
Disability rights movements, 80
Discipline
Asian Americans and, 219
Middle Easterners and, 338–340
see also Childrearing practices
Distance, social, see Social distance
Diversity
acknowledgment of, respect for and, 50
among Asian Americans, 235
in intervention settings, 3–17
cultural considerations for intervention-

tionist and, 4–5
cultural identity and, 14–17
importance of cross-cultural effectiveness and, 5–9
nature of early intervention and, 9–14
among Native Americans, 90–91, 98
understanding of, self-awareness and, 37
see also Cultural differences; specific cultural groups
Down syndrome, see Disabilities

Early intervention
agents of, 13
culture shock and, 30
family focus in, 8–9
methods of, 10–13
nature of, 9–14
see also Intervention
Education
African Americans and, 135
Anglo-European views of, 77
Asian Americans and, 213
childrearing and, see Childrearing practices
childrearing practices and, 11–12
Korean Americans and, 197
Latinos and, 162
Native Americans and
language and, 108–109
in 19th century, 93–94
parent, for Asian Americans, 244
of Pilipinos, 270
status and, 276
segregated, 125
see also Learning
Education for All Handicapped Children Act of 1975 (PL 94-142), 80
Education of the Handicapped Act Amendments of 1986 (PL 99-457), 6
communication and, 14
importance of cross-cultural effectiveness and, 6, 8–9
parent involvement and, Anglo-Europeans and, 82
Emotion
facial expressions and, 46
illness and, Asian American beliefs about, 222–223
see also specific emotions

Employment, *see* Self-employment; Socioeconomic status (SES)
Enclaves, cultural, 16
England, *see* Anglo-Europeans
English language, 69
  Black English dialect of, 127–128, 143, 150
  Pilipinos and, 267–268
  see also Language
Equal rights, 70
Equality, principle of, 72, 85
Eskimos, *see* Native Americans
Ethnic competence, *see* Cross-cultural competence
Ethnic diversity, *see* Diversity
Ethnic groups
  names for, 50–51
  overgeneralizing about, 5
  see also Generalizations
  see also specific groups
Europeans, *see* Anglo-Europeans; Southern Europeans
Evaluation
  monitoring and, in intervention process, 368–369
  see also Assessment
Extended family
  African Americans and, 133
  Asian Americans and, 215
  Hawaiians and, 309
  Middle Easterners, 327, 331, 345–346
  Native Americans and, 101, 102, 111
  childrearing and, 106, 107
  Pilipinos and, 277–279
Eye contact, 46
  Anglo-Europeans and, 85
  Asian Americans and, 234
  see also Nonverbal communication

Face saving
  Asian Americans and, 240–241, 242
  interviewing process and, 363–364
  Pilipinos and, 274, 288, 291–292
Facial expressions, 46
  Asian Americans and, 234
  see also Nonverbal communication
Faith healers, 284–285
Family
  African American concept of, 131–134

Asian American values and, 211–212
childrearing practices of, *see* Childrearing practices
communication style of, 14
  see also Communication
"cultural clashes" with, 4–5
culture shock and, 25–26
  see also Culture shock
extended, *see* Extended family
IFSP for, *see* Individualized Family Service Plan (IFSP)
interpreters from, 53–54
involvement of
  Anglo-European view of, 81–82
  culture shock and, 29
Korean American, conflicts within, 198
Latino, organization of, 161–162
mainstream American culture and, 74–75
Middle Eastern
  role of, 327–328
  size of, 329–330
Native American
  inclusion of members of, 111
  roles and relationships in, 101, 102
patterns of, 70
  see also Family structure
perspective of, listening to, 49–50
Pilipino values and, 271–272
working with
  establishment of collaboration and assessment planning in, 361–362
  importance of cross-cultural effectiveness in, 8–9
  see also Filial piety; Home visits; Parents; Siblings
Family structure
  Asian American, childrearing and, 215
  Latino, 161–162
  Pilipino, childrearing and, 277–279
  see also Family, patterns of
Farsi, 323, 324, 351
Fatalistic view, 9
  Anglo-European view versus, 79
  Asian Americans and, 214
Father
  Middle Eastern, role of, 337–338, 345, 346
  see also Family; Parents
Feeding practices, 12

Middle Eastern, 331–332
see also Diet
Filial piety, Confucianism and, 187
Asian Americans and, 212, 240
Filipinos, *see* Pilipinos
Fofo, 312
Folk beliefs
about disabilities, Latinos and, 169
medical
Asian Americans and, 221–223
Mexican Americans and, 166–167
Pilipinos and, 283–284
see also Beliefs
Freedom of Religion Act, Native Americans and, 96

Gender roles, *see* Marital roles; Sex roles
Generalizations
assumptions and, 15
danger of, 44
see also Overgeneralizing
Geographic origins
of African Americans, 121
of Anglo-Europeans, 66–68
of Asian Americans, 182
of Chinese Americans, 183–186
of Korean Americans, 192–194
of Latinos, 152–155
of Middle Easterners, 320
of Pacific Island groups, 302
of Pilipinos, 260–266
of Southeast Asian Americans, 198–205
Gestures, 48–49
Asian Americans and, 234
see also Nonverbal communication
Ghettoes, *see* Inner-city areas
Gift giving
Asian Americans and, 254
Pilipinos and, 298
God, *see* Religion; Religious origins
Grandparents, *see* Extended family
Great Atlantic Migration, 65–66
Greetings, 47
Anglo-Europeans and, 85
Asian Americans and, 253
Middle Easterners and, 344–345
Pilipinos and, 296
Grief, immigration process and, 154–155

Group orientation, of Native Americans, 103
Growth, personal, cross-cultural competence and, 359–360
Guests, young children and, Middle Easterners and, 335–336
"Guidelines for the Home Visitor," 41, 42–43
Guilt, Middle Easterners and, 340

Haitians, therapeutic agents and, 13
Handshaking, *see* Greetings
Hangul script, Korean and, 196
Harmony
as Asian American value, 213
see also Yin and yang
with nature, Native Americans and, 100–101
as Pilipino value, 273–274
Hawaiians
beliefs of, 308–310
mainstream beliefs versus, 315
case example of, 306
courtesies and customs of, 316
values of, 305–307
mainstream values versus, 315
vocabulary of, 318
see also Pacific Island groups
Head
nodding of, 48
patting of, 47
Healing techniques, *see* Medical practices
Health beliefs
Asian American, 221–223
Pilipino, 283
see also Illness; Medical practices
Hebrew, 324
Herbal medications, Asian Americans and, 224
Hiapo, 309
High-context cultures
low-context cultures versus, communication in, 44–45, 232–233
see also specific cultures
Hinduism, Southeast Asian Americans and, 205
Hispanics
in U.S. population, 152
see also Latinos

Historical origins
of African Americans, 122–126
of Anglo-Europeans, 66–68
of Chinese Americans, 183–186
of Korean Americans, 192–194
of Latinos, 152–155
of Middle Easterners, 320–321
of Native Americans, 90–97
of Pacific Island groups, 302–303
of Pilipinos, 260–266
of Southeast Asian Americans,
198–205
Hiya, 273–274, 289, 291
Hmong tribe, 201
see also Southeast Asian Americans
Holidays, *see* Celebrations and holidays
Holistic approaches to health care, African Americans and, 139–140
Home visits
Asian Americans and, 254
guidelines for, 41, 42–43
Native Americans and, 113, 117–118
Pilipinos and, 297
Hong Kong immigrants, 191
see also Chinese Americans
Humanity, goodness of, mainstream
American belief in, 73
Humor
African Americans and, 135–136
Pilipinos and, 275
see also Laughter
Hungarians, *see* Anglo-Europeans
Hwa-Byung, 223

IDEA, *see* Individuals with Disabilities
Education Act
Identity, cultural, *see* Cultural identity
IEPs, *see* Individualized education programs (IEPs)
IFSP, *see* Individualized Family Service
Plan
Illegal immigrants, 160
Illness
Asian American beliefs about,
222–223
causation of, *see* Causation
Native American beliefs about,
105–106
Pilipino beliefs about, 283
in Southeast Asian refugees, 210
see also Medical practices

Immigrants
adaptation of
assistance with, 12, 28–30
social supports and, 158–160
see also Acculturation; Assimilation
Anglo-European, 65
Native Americans and, 65–66,
91–93
waves of, 67–68
Chinese, 68, 184–185
illegal, 160
Korean, 193–194, 197
Middle Eastern, 324
political events and, 325–326
new, culture shock amelioration for,
28–30
Pilipino, waves of, 263–266
quotas for, 68
Southeast Asian, waves of, 203–205
stages of migration and, 154–155
see also specific groups
Immigration, patterns of, 70
Immigration Act of 1924, 68
Immigration Act of 1965, 68
Immigration Act of 1990, 265
Immigration and Nationality Act
Amendments, 185
Immigration and Nationality Amendments Act of 1965, 185, 194
Immigration and Naturalization Services,
160
Implementation, effectiveness of,
366–368
Income, *see* Poverty; Socioeconomic status (SES)
Independence
of children, 12, 39
Asian American beliefs and, 218
Middle Eastern beliefs and,
333–334
interdependence versus, 39
culture shock and, 12, 30
Indian Child Welfare Act of 1978 (PL
95-608), 96
Indian Citizenship Act, 95
Indian Health Care Improvement Act of
1976, 96
Indian Health Service, 95
Indian Self-Determination and Education
Assistance Act of 1975 (PL
93-638), 96

Indians
  American, *see* Native Americans
  gestures and, 48, 49
Individual differences, respect for, An-
    glo-Europeans and, 82
Individualism, mainstream American
    culture and, 71–72
Individualized Education Programs
    (IEPs), planning meetings for,
    365–366
Individualized Family Service Plan
    (IFSP), 8
  Anglo-Europeans and, 82
Individuals with Disabilities Education
    Act (IDEA, PL 101-476), 8, 80
Indochina, 198–199
  see also Southeast Asian Americans
Infant mortality, African American
    versus white, 129–131
Infants
  Asian American view of, 216–218
  feeding of, *see* Feeding practices
  Middle Eastern, physical contact with,
    332–333
  Pilipino view of, 280–281
Informality, mainstream American cul-
    ture and, 72
Information
  culture-specific
    cautions relating to, 44
    gathering of, 39–41, 371–377
    transmission of, through context,
      44–45
Integration, cultural
  categories of, 15–16
  see also Acculturation; Assimilation
Interaction
  Anglo-Europeans and, 85
  cross-cultural
    among children, 20
    for culture-specific awareness,
      40–41
    harmony of, Pilipinos and, 273–274
    Native Americans and, 111–112
    styles of, 13–14
Interdependence, independence versus,
    39
  culture shock and, 30
  Middle Easterners and, 333–334
Interpreters, 28, 52–56
  Asian Americans and, 239

effective, characteristics of, 52–53
family members as, 53–54
interviewing process and, 363–364
Middle Easterners and, 345
Native Americans and, 109–110, 112
non–family members as, 54
preparation of, 55
stress and, 54–55
working with, guidelines for, 55–56
Intervention
  attitudes about, 9–10
  communication and interaction styles
    in, 13–14
  culture-specific issues and, 41–43
  early, *see* Early intervention
  family participation in, culture shock
    and, 29
  methods of, 10–13
  reasons for, 9–10
Intervention plan, development of,
    365–366
Intervention procedures, recommenda-
    tions regarding, Native Ameri-
    cans and, 113
Intervention process, culturally appropri-
    ate, 361–369
  data gathering and assessment in,
    362–364
  family–professional collaboration and
    assessment planning in, 361–362
  implementation in, 366–368
  intervention plan development in,
    365–366
  monitoring and evaluation in,
    368–369
Intervention settings, diversity in, 3–17
  see also Diversity, in intervention
    settings
Interventionists
  communication style of, 13–14
  cross-cultural competence of, *see*
    Cross-cultural competence
  cultural considerations for, 4–5
  culture shock and, 27
    sensitization to impact of, 31–33
    see also Culture shock
  interpreter and, guidelines for working
    with, 55–56
  recommendations for, 355–370
    African Americans and, 144–145
    Anglo-Europeans and, 81–82

Interventionists—*continued*
   Asian Americans and, 238–243
   cross-cultural competence definition
      and, 356
   cultural identity mitigation and,
      358–359
   intervention process and, 361–369
   Latinos and, 172–173
   Middle Easterners and, 346–347
   Native Americans and, 111–114
   nature of cultural identity and,
      356–358
   Pacific Island groups and, 313
   personal growth and change,
      359–360
   Pilipinos and, 290–292
   role of, in helping to bridge cultures,
      12
Interviewing, appropriateness of,
   363–364
Iranians
   case example of, 326
   immigration of, political events and,
      325
   religion of, 323
   see also Middle Easterners
Iraqis, *see* Middle Easterners
Irish, *see* Anglo-Europeans
Islam
   African Americans and, 126
   origins of, 322
   Pilipinos and, 266–267
   see also Muslims
Israelis
   Middle East conflicts involving, immi-
      gration and, 325
   see also Middle Easterners
Italians, *see* Anglo-Europeans

Japanese Americans
   language and linguistic origins of, 196
   see also Asian Americans
"Jim Crow" laws, 124–125
Jordanians, *see* Middle Easterners
Judeo-Christian belief system, 76

Kahuna lapaʻau, 310
Kampuchea, 199–200
Kapwa, 274, 289
Karma, Buddhism and, 188

Khmer language, 207
Khmer people, 199
   see also Southeast Asian Americans
Khmer Republic, 200
Kinship bonds
   African Americans and, 131–132
   Pilipinos and, 277–279
   see also Family
Korean Americans, 192–198
   contemporary life of, 197–198
   geographic and historical origins of,
      192–194
   immigration of, 193–194, 197
   language and linguistic origins of,
      196–197
   religious origins of, 195–196
   vocabulary of, 257
   see also Asian Americans
Kurdish emigration, political events and,
   325
Kurdish language, 323, 324, 351
Kuwaitis, *see* Middle Easterners

Land
   Hawaiian attitudes toward, 306–307
   Native American attitudes toward,
      100–101
Language
   African Americans and, 143–144, 150
   Anglo-Europeans and, 81
   Asian Americans and, 231–235
   of assessment instruments, 363
   cross-cultural competence and, 41
   culture shock and, 26, 28
   Latinos and, 169–171
      see also Spanish-speaking persons
   Middle Easterners and, 343–345
   Native Americans and, 108–110, 112
   origins of, *see* Language origins
   Pacific Island groups and, 312
   Pilipinos and, 287–288
   translators of, *see* Interpreters
   see also Communication; Vocabulary
Language diversity, *see* Diversity
Language origins
   of African Americans, 127–128
   of Anglo-Europeans, 68–69
   of Chinese Americans, 190–191
   of Japanese Americans, 196
   of Korean Americans, 196–197
   of Latinos, 156–157

of Middle Easterners, 323–324
of Native Americans, 97–98
of Pacific Island groups, 304
of Pilipinos, 267–269
of Southeast Asian Americans, 207–208
Lao language, 207
Laotian Americans
 geographic and historical origins of, 200–201
 see also Asian Americans; Southeast Asian Americans
Latinos, 151–173
 acculturation process and, 158
 attitudes of
  toward causation, 168–169
  toward disability, 168–169
 background of, 151–157
 beliefs of, 164–169
  mainstream beliefs versus, 176
 case examples of, 159, 167, 170
 celebrations and holidays of, 178
 childrearing practices of, 164–166
 competition versus cooperation and, 20
 contemporary life of, 157–160
 courtesies and customs of, 177
 eye contact and, 46
 geographic origins of, 152–155
 gestures and, 48, 49
 group identity of, 51
 high-context culture of, 44–45
 historical origins of, 152–155
 language and linguistic origins of, 156–157
 language issues with, 169–171
  see also Spanish-speaking persons
 literature about, 374–375
 medical care and, 166–168
 recommendations for working with, 172–173
 religious origins of, 155–156
 social distance and, 46
 social supports for, 158–160
 therapeutic agents and, 13
 in U.S. population, 7, 151–152
 values of, 161–164
  mainstream values versus, 176
Learning
 cultural
  age and, 20
  from culture shock to, 19–33

  methods of, 39–41
language, cross-cultural competence and, 41
 see also Education
Least restrictive environment, 80
Lebanese, see Middle Easterners
Libyans, see Middle Easterners
Life expectancy, African American versus white, 129
Linguistic diversity, see Diversity; Language
Literature, for culture-specific awareness, 40, 371–377
Long-term residents, culture shock amelioration for, 31
Low-context cultures
 high-context cultures versus, communication in, 44–45, 232–233
 see also specific cultures

Machismo, 161
Mainstream American culture
 African American culture versus, 147
 Asian American culture versus, 251–252
 assertiveness in, 74
 attitudes of
  toward achievement, 74
  toward causation, 79
  toward disability, 79–80
 belief in goodness of humanity in, 73
 belief systems in, 76–80
 childrearing in, 76–77
 competition versus cooperation in, 20
 concept of time in, 21, 74
 directness in, 74
 equality and, 72
 family life in, 74–75
 health care in, 78
 individualism and, 71–72
 informality in, 72
 Latino culture versus, 176
 materialism of, 74
 Native American culture versus, 116
 predominant values and assumptions in, 15, 38, 71–76, 80
 privacy and, 71–72
 religion in, 75–76
 therapeutic agents and, 13
 touching in, 20–21
 views toward future in, 73

Mainstream American culture—*continued*
  work in, 74
  see also Anglo-Europeans
Mal ojo, 166, 167
Mal puesto, 166
Mandarin language, 190, 257
Mandas, in Latino religion, 155, 156
Marital roles
  Asian American, childrearing and,
    215–216
  Muslim, 331
  Pilipino, childrearing and, 279–280
  see also Sex roles
Matai, 307
Materialism, mainstream American cul-
    ture and, 74
Mediators, cultural, 40
Medical practices, 10–11
  African American beliefs and,
    139–142
  Anglo-European beliefs and, 78
  Asian beliefs and, 12, 223–225
  Hawaiian beliefs and, 310
  Latino beliefs and, 166–168
  Middle Eastern beliefs and, 331–332
  Pilipino beliefs and, 282–285
  Samoan beliefs and, 312
  see also Illness; Wellness
Medicine man, 11
Medicine Wheel, four principles of,
    104–105
Mediterranean roots, *see* Anglo-
    Europeans
Melting pot, 66
  emphasis on diversity versus, 50
Mental disabilities, *see* Disabilities
Mental health problems, in Southeast
    Asian refugees, 210
Mexican Americans
  background of, 152
  language of, 157
  medical folk beliefs of, 166–167
  religious origins of, 155
  therapeutic agents and, 13
  in U.S. population, 151
  see also Latinos
Middle Easterners, 319–347
  attachment versus individuation in,
    333–334
  attitudes toward disability of,
    340–343
  background of, 320–324

beliefs of, 330–334
  Anglo-European beliefs versus, 348
  case examples of, 326, 341, 344
  celebrations and holidays of, 335, 350
  children's responsibilities and work
    and, 336–337
  contemporary life of, 324–326
  courtesies and customs of, 349
  discipline among, 338–340
  family of
    child in context of, 334–343
    role of, 327–328
    size of, 329–330
  father's role and, 337–338
  feeding and health care and, 331–332
  forms of family entertainment for, 335
  geographic origins of, 320
  gestures and, 48, 49
  guests of, young children and,
    335–336
  high-context culture of, 44–45
  historical origins of, 320–321
  immigration of, 324
    political events and, 325–326
  intellectual development and, 340
  language issues with, 343–345
  language origins of, 323–324
  literature about, 376–377
  physical contact and, 47
  pregnancy and childbirth and,
    330–331
  proximity and physical contact with,
    332–333
  recommendations for working with,
    346–347
  religious origins of, 321–323
  social distance and, 46
  values of, 326–330
  vocabulary of, 351
  see also Muslims
Mien tribe, 201
  see also Southeast Asian Americans
Migration
  stages of, 154–155
  see also Immigrants; Immigration
Monocultural individuals, 357
Moroccans, *see* Middle Easterners
Moslems, *see* Muslims
Moxibustion, 225
Multicultural individuals, 357
Muslims
  body language and, 48

celebrations and holidays of, 350
family size and, 329
marital roles of, 331
physical contact and, 47
see also Islam; Middle Easterners
Myu-po-jung, 234

Names
Asian American, 253
for groups, attitudes and, 50–51
National Association for the Advancement of Colored People
(NAACP), 125
National Council of Negro Women, 125
National Tribal Chairmen's Association
(NTCA), 96
Native Americans, 89–114
acceptance of events by, 103–104
Anglo-European immigrants and,
65–66, 68, 91–93
attitudes of, toward health and causation, 105–106
autonomy of, 104
background of, 90–98
beliefs of, 104–108
Anglo-European beliefs versus, 116
recommendations regarding,
112–113
case examples of, 102, 107
childrearing practices of, 106–108
competition versus cooperation and,
20
contemporary life of, 98–99
courtesies and customs of, 117–118
cultural events of, 119
developmental milestones and, 101,
102, 104
facial expressions and, 46
family roles and relationships of, 101,
102
gestures and, 48
group orientation of, 103
harmony with nature and, 100–101
historical origins of, 90–91
period from 1492 to 1800, 91–93
period from 1800 to 1900, 93–94
period from 1900 to present, 94–97
language issues with, 108–110, 112
language origins of, 97–98
literature about, 372–373

recommendations for working with,
111–114
religious origins of, 97
relocation of
to cities, 95
to reservations, 94, 95
self-reliance of, 104
therapeutic agents and, 11, 13
time orientation of, 101, 102
tribal terminations and, 95–96
U.S. population of, 92, 94, 99
values of, 99–104
Anglo-European values versus, 116
contrasted with other cultures'
values, 100, 116
Native Hawaiians, see Hawaiians
Natural healers, Latinos and, 166
Nature, harmony with, Native Americans and, 100–101
Networks
ethnic, 159–160
social, 158–160
Nodding, 48
Nonverbal communication, 45–49
African Americans and, 143–144
Asian Americans and, 232–234, 242,
254
in high-context versus low-context cul-
tures, 44–45
Native Americans and, 110
Pacific Island groups and, 312
Pilipinos and, 288, 296
see also Communication, indirect;
specific type, e.g., Eye contact
Normalization, 80
North American Indians, see Native
Americans
NTCA, see National Tribal Chairmen's
Association
Nun-chi, 233
Nutrition, see Diet; Feeding practices

'Ohana, 306
Outreach
Asian Americans and, 238–239
Pilipinos and, 291

Pacific Island groups, 301–313
background of, 302–304
beliefs of, 308–312

Pacific Island groups—*continued*
case examples of, 303, 306
celebrations and holidays of, 317
contemporary life of, 304–305
geographic origins of, 302
gestures and, 48
historical origins of, 302–303
language issues with, 312
language origins of, 304
literature about, 376
recommendations for working with, 313
religious origins of, 303–304
in U.S. population, 304–305
values of, 305–308
see also Hawaiians; Samoans
Pakikipagkapwa-tao, 275
Pakkisama, 273, 289, 292
Pakistanis, *see* Middle Easterners
Palestinians, *see* Middle Easterners
Parents
Asian American, education of, 244
blaming of, for disability, 9
Pilipino, roles and expectations of, 279–280
roles and responsibilities of, Asian Americans and, 216
see also Childrearing practices; Family
Patriarchy
Middle Eastern, 337
see also Marital roles
Persian (Farsi), 323, 324, 351
Personal growth, cross-cultural competence and, 359–360
Personalismo, 163–164
Personality characteristics, *see* Character traits; *specific groups*
Philippines, *see* Pilipinos
Physical proximity, 46–47
see also Social distance; Touching
Pilipinos, 259–292
attitudes of
toward causation, 285–287
toward disability, 285–287
authority among, 272–273
background of, 260–269
beliefs of, 277–287, 295
case examples of, 278–279, 286
celebrations and holidays of, 299
childrearing practices of, 277–282

communication styles of, 292
concept of family and, 271–272
contemporary life of, 269–271
courtesies and customs of, 296–298
education of, 270
status and, 276
face saving and, 274, 288, 291–292
family structure of, 277–279
geographic and historical origins of, 260–266
harmony concept of, 273–274
immigration of, waves of, 263–266
initial expectations and orientations of, 291
language and linguistic origins of, 267–269
language issues with, 287–288
literature about, 376
marital and parental roles and expectations of, 279–280
medical care and, 282–285
outreach and, 291
recommendations for working with, 290–292
religious origins of, 266–267
character traits and, 275–276
in U.S. population, 269
values of, 271–277
vocabulary of, 300
PL 93-638 (Indian Self-Determination and Education Assistance Act of 1975), 96
PL 94-142 (Education for All Handicapped Children Act of 1975), 80
PL 95-608 (Indian Child Welfare Act of 1978), 96
PL 99-457, *see* Education of the Handicapped Act Amendments of 1986
PL 101-476 (Individuals with Disabilities Education Act), 8, 80
Platicando, 164
Plessy v. Ferguson, 123
Pluralistic view, 16, 17
Pochismos, 156
Political events, Middle Eastern immigration patterns and, 325–326
Political movements, Native Americans and, 96
Polynesians, *see* Pacific Island groups
Polytheism
complementarity and, Chinese Ameri-

cans and, 189–190
Pilipinos and, 267
Population statistics, 7
  African American, 128
  Chinese American, 192
  Latino, 151–152
  Native American, 92, 94, 99
  Pacific Island group, 304–305
  Pilipino, 269
  Southeast Asian American, 209
Postures, *see* Body language
Poverty
  African American
    diet and, 138
    medical care and, 140–141
  differences attributable to, cultural
    differences versus, 131, 145, 161
  Latino, 158, 161
  Native American, 99
    tribal termination program and,
    95–96
  Southeast Asian American, 210
  see also Socioeconomic status (SES)
Pregnancy
  Asian American beliefs and, 227–228
  Middle Eastern beliefs and, 330–331,
    340
  Pilipino beliefs and, 285
Prejudice, *see* Racism
Privacy
  for children, 12
  mainstream American culture and,
    71–72
  Middle Easterners and, 334
  see also Independence
Professionals, *see* Interventionists
Progress, view toward, mainstream
    American culture and, 73
Protestantism
  Reformed, 68–69
  see also Christianity
Proximity, *see* Social distance
Psychological stress, *see* Stress
Puerto Ricans
  background of, 152–153
  religious origins of, 156
  spiritism and, 168
  therapeutic agents and, 13
  in U.S. population, 151–152
  see also Latinos
Punctuality, 21

Anglo-Europeans and, 85
  see also Time
Puritanism, 68–69
Putonghua language, 190

Quotas, immigration, 68

Racial segregation, 123–124, 125
Racism
  African Americans and, 123, 125, 131
    sensitivity of, 134
    see also African Americans
  Asian Americans and, 182
    Chinese Americans, 184–185
  Pilipinos and, 263–264
Reading, for culture-specific awareness,
    40, 371–377
Reciprocity, Asian Americans and,
    242–243
Refugee Act of 1980, 208
Refugees, Southeast Asian, 198–211
  waves of, 203–205
  see also Southeast Asian Americans
Relatives, *see* Extended family
Religion
  African Americans and, 136
    causation beliefs and, 142
  Asian American views of causation
    and, 228–229
  mainstream American culture and,
    75–76
  Pilipinos and, 275–276
    beliefs about causation of, 285
  Samoans and, 307–308
  U.S. statistics on, 69
  see also specific religions
Religious origins
  of African Americans, 126–127
  of Anglo-Europeans, 68–69
  of Chinese Americans, 186–190
  of Korean Americans, 195–196
  of Latinos, 155–156
  of Middle Easterners, 321–323
  of Native Americans, 97
  of Pacific Island groups, 303–304
  of Pilipinos, 266–267
  of Southeast Asian Americans,
    205–206

Reservations, 94, 95
  population of, 99
  see also Native Americans
Residents, long-term, culture shock ame-
      lioration for, 31
Respect, see specific group
Reverse culture shock, 25
Rights
  disability, 80
  equal, 70
  see also specific group; specific type,
      e.g., Voting rights
Roman Catholicism, see Catholicism

Samoans
  beliefs of, 310–312
    mainstream beliefs versus, 315
  body language and, 48
  case example of, 303
  courtesies and customs of, 316
  values of, 305, 307–308
    mainstream values versus, 315
  vocabulary of, 318
  see also Pacific Island groups
San Yi Man, 185, 186
Santeria, 156
Saudi Arabians, see Middle Easterners
Saving face
  Asian Americans and, 240–241, 242
  Pilipinos and, 274
Schooling, see Education
Segregation, racial, 123–124, 125
Self-awareness, cross-cultural compe-
      tence and, 36–39, 60–62,
      359–360
Self-Determination Act, Native Ameri-
      cans and, 96
Sensitivity
  to face-saving needs, Asian Ameri-
      cans and, 241
  to impact of culture shock, 31–33
  importance of, 5–9
  to racial prejudice, among African
      Americans, 134
"Separate but equal" doctrine, 123–124,
      125
Separation/individuation
  Middle Easterners and, 333–334
  see also Independence
Sephardis, 323
Service providers, see Interventionists

Services
  acceptance of, difficulty with, 28–29
  alternative, Asian Americans and,
      243–244
  Anglo-European view of, 80
  location of, 10–13
  see also Intervention
SES, see Socioeconomic status
Sex roles
  Latino, 161–162
  Middle Eastern, interpreters and, 345
  see also Marital roles; Women
Shamanism, 11
  Korean Americans and, 195
Shame, Middle Easterners and, 340
Shi'a'ism, 322
Siblings
  relationships of, Asian Americans
      and, 218
  see also Family
Silence
  Asian Americans and, 233–234
  Middle Easterners and, 344
Simpson-Mazzolli Immigration Act of
      1985, 152
Situational nature of cultural identity, 16,
      358
Slang, Black English versus, 128
Slavery, African Americans and, 122,
      123
  family and, 131–132
  religion and, 127
  see also African Americans
Smiling, 46
  Asian Americans and, 234
  see also Nonverbal communication
Sobador, 167–168
Social distance, 46–47
  Anglo-Europeans and, 85
  Asian Americans and, 234–235
  Middle Easterners and, 332–333, 344
  see also Touching
Social supports, Latinos and, 158–160
Socialization, African American family
      and, 134
Socioeconomic status (SES)
  African American, 129–131
    Black English and, 128
  Latino, 161
  in mitigation of cultural identification,
      359
  of Pilipinos, 269–270

Puerto Rican, 153
see also Poverty
South Americans
in U.S. population, 152
see also Latinos
Southeast Asian Americans, 198–211
contemporary life of, 208–211
fatalistic view of, 9
geographic and historical origins of, 199–205
language and linguistic origins of, 207–208
religious origins of, 205–206
in U.S. population, 209
waves of refugees and, 203–205
see also Asian Americans; Pilipinos
Southern Europeans
gestures and, 48
social distance and, 46
Spanish-speaking persons, 156–157
Pilipino, 269
support groups for, 160
vocabulary of, 179
see also Latinos
Spiritism, healing and, Puerto Ricans and, 168
Spiritual beliefs, see Religion; Religious origins
Stereotyping, see Generalizations
Stress
African American families and, environment of, 131
illness and, Asian American beliefs about, 223
interpreters and, 54–55
Suffering, acceptance of, Asian Americans and, 214
Suspicion, trust versus, see Outreach
Susto, 166
Syrians, see Middle Easterners

Tagalogs, 260, 267
vocabulary of, 300
see also Pilipinos
T'anh can cu, 214
Taoism
Chinese Americans and, 187–188
health beliefs of, 221–223
Korean Americans and, 195
Southeast Asian Americans and, 206

Terminology
for defining groups, 51
Pilipino, 259n
see also Vocabulary
Thai Americans, see Southeast Asian Americans
Therapeutic practices, see Medical practices
Time
concept of, 21
mainstream American culture and, 21, 74
Time orientation, of Native Americans, 101, 102
Toilet training
Asian Americans and, 217
culture shock and, 29–30
timing of, 13
Touching, 20–21, 46–47
Asian Americans and, 253
Middle Easterners and, 332–333, 344–345
see also Social distance
Training, Asian Americans and, 243–244
Transactional nature of cultural identity, 16, 356–358
Transference, interpreters and, 54–55
Translations
difficulty with, 28
see also Interpreters
Tribal communities
in health care, 11
see also African Americans; Native Americans; Southeast Asian Americans
Trust, suspicion versus, see Outreach
Tunisians, see Middle Easterners
Turkish language, 323, 324, 351
Turks, see Middle Easterners
Tuyaw, 283
Tydings-McDuffie Act of 1934, 262, 264

Unhae, 242–243
United States
changing demographics of, 7–8
see also Population statistics
immigration into, see Immigrants; Immigration
mainstream culture of, see Mainstream American culture

United States—*continued*
  as melting pot, *see* Melting pot
  religious groups in, 69
United States citizenship, Native Americans and, 94–95
Usog, 283
Utang na loob, 272, 274, 276, 289, 291

Values
  African American, 131–136
    mainstream versus, 147
  Anglo-European, 15, 38, 71–76, 80
    contrasted with other cultures' values, 84, 116, 348
  Asian American, 211–214, 236–237
    dominant culture versus, 251–252
  cultural determination of, 20
  culture shock and, 24
    see also Culture shock
  expression of, long-standing behavior patterns in, 21
  factors influencing, 22, 44
  Hawaiian, 305–307, 315
  Latino, 161–164
  Middle Eastern, 326–330
    Anglo-European versus, 348
  Native American, 99–104
    Anglo-European versus, 116
  Pilipino, 271–277, 295
  predominant, in mainstream American culture, 15, 38, 71–76, 80
  Samoan, 305, 307–308, 315
  self-awareness of, 36–39, 359–360
    Cultural Journey for, 21, 60–62
Ventosa technique, 283–284
Verb-final languages, 196–197
Verb-initial languages, 268
Verbal communication
  African Americans and, 133
  nonverbal versus, 44–45
    see also Nonverbal communication
  words used in, attitudes and, 50–51
  see also Communication; Language
Vietnamese Americans
  fatalistic view of, 9
  geographic and historical origins of, 201–203
  see also Asian Americans; Southeast Asian Americans
Vietnamese language, 207–208, 257

Vocabulary
  Asian, 257
  Hawaiian, 318
  Middle Eastern, 351
  Pilipino, 300
  Samoan, 318
  Spanish, 179
  see also Terminology
Voting rights, 85
  Native Americans and, 95
Voting Rights Act of 1965, 126

Wai greeting, 47
War Brides Act of 1946, 264
WASPs, *see* White Anglo-Saxon Protestants
Wellness
  Native American beliefs about, 105–106
  see also Illness; Medical practices
Western Europeans, *see* Anglo-Europeans
White Americans, mainstream, *see* Mainstream American culture
White Anglo-Saxon Protestants (WASPs)
  cultural values of, 38
  see also Anglo-Europeans
Women, roles and rights of, 70
  culture shock and, 32
  Latinos and, 161–162, 163
  Muslims and, 330–331
  see also Marital roles
Words
  attitudes and, communication of, 50–51
  see also Vocabulary
Work
  children's, Middle Easterners and, 336–337
  mainstream American view of, 74
  see also Achievement
Wu-wei, 234

Yemenites, *see* Middle Easterners
Yin and yang
  Taoism and, 187
    health beliefs and, 221
  see also Harmony

Zen Buddhism, 188